An Introduction to Carbonate Sediments and Rocks

Scott W. Starratt
Dept. of Paleontology
U. C. Berkeley
Berkeley, Ca. 94720

To the expedition

An Introduction to Carbonate Sediments and Rocks

TERENCE P. SCOFFIN
Reader in Geology
University of Edinburgh

Blackie

Glasgow and London

Published in the USA by
Chapman and Hall
New York

Blackie & Son Limited,
Bishopbriggs, Glasgow G64 2NZ
7 Leicester Place, London WC2H 7BP

Published in the USA by
Chapman and Hall
in association with Methuen, Inc.
29 West 35th Street, New York, NY 10001

British Library Cataloguing in Publication Data

Scoffin, Terence P.
 An introduction to carbonate sediments
 and rocks.
 1. Rocks, Carbonate
 I. Title
 552'.5 QE471.15C3

 ISBN 0-216-91789-1

Library of Congress Cataloging-in-Publication Data

Scoffin, Terence P.
 An introduction to carbonate sediments and rocks.

 Includes bibliographies and index.
 1. Rocks, Carbonate.   2. Sediments (Geology)
 3. Carbonates.   I. Title.
 QE471.15.C3S38 1986   552'.5   86-18827
 ISBN 0-412-00891-2 (pbk.)

Photosetting by Thomson Press (India) Limited, New Delhi
Printed in Great Britain by Bell & Bain (Glasgow) Ltd.

Preface

The subject of carbonate sediments and sedimentary rocks has expanded to a point where it is a significant part of many undergraduate earth science curricula. There is now a need for an intermediate- to advanced-level textbook which has a broad approach, starting from basic fundamentals leading to a platform from which research studies may follow. My aim has been to prepare a book for the advanced undergraduate geologist, which may also have appeal to scientists working, for example, in the marine environment or on basin stratigraphy, who periodically seek guidance on some aspects of the elements of carbonate sedimentology. I intend the book to be an appropriate introduction to research-level books on carbonates, for example, on chemistry and mineralogy, *Carbonate Minerals* edited by R.J. Reeder (Mineralogical Society of America, 1984); on carbonate grains and environments of deposition, *Marine Carbonates* by J.D. Milliman (Springer Verlag, 1974), *Carbonate Sediments and their Diagenesis* by R.G.C. Bathurst (Elsevier, 1974), *Carbonate Depositional Environments*, edited by P.A. Scholle, D.G. Bebout and C.H. Moore (American Association of Petroleum Geologists, 1983); on limestone facies, *Carbonate Facies in Geologic History* by J.L. Wilson (Springer Verlag, 1975); on petrography of carbonates, *Carbonate Rock Constituents, Textures, Cements and Porosities* by P.A. Scholle (American Association of Petroleum Geologists, 1978), *Recognition of Invertebrate Fossil Fragments in Rocks and Thin Sections* by O.P. Majewski (E.J. Brill, 1969), *Introductory Petrography of Fossils* by A.S. Horowitz and P.E. Potter (Springer Verlag, 1971), *Microfacies Analysis of Limestones* by E. Flügel (Springer Verlag, 1982).

In the interests of brevity and readability I have tried not to clutter the text with too many references. Instead, I have included recommended reading lists at the ends of chapters, and have presented more of a state-of-the-art approach than a comprehensive historical background to all concepts. Though necessarily a large portion of such an introductory book is definition and documentation, I have tried to emphasize processes, illustrating them with examples where possible.

I am indebted to several colleagues who read the first draft of my manuscript and made many useful suggestions for its improvement. In particular I wish to thank Colin Braithwaite and Sandy Tudhope who read the entire book, Michael Talbot and Julian Andrews who criticized the section on diagenesis, and Charles Eccles and Euan Clarkson who criticized the section on skeletal grains. Most of the diagrams were drawn by Ray Harris of the Department of Geography, University of Edinburgh. The secretaries of the Department of Geology, University of Edinburgh, typed the manuscript with enthusiasm and charm and I am especially grateful to Heather Hooker for her unstinting willingness and cheerful help throughout. Several geologists supplied photographs I have used, and my thanks go to Julian Andrews, David Cooper, Graham Davies, Simon Eaton, Douglas Gillies, Bill Martindale, Roy McGregor, Conrad Neumann, Bob Parks, Andrew Racey, Colin Scrutton, Graham Shimmield, David Stoddart, Sandy Tudhope and Gordon Walkden.

Much of my field work has been spent on research vessels and on remote coral islands. I am indebted to several funding agencies (especially NERC) who made this possible, to numerous ships' captains (notably Jim Waddell, John Futcher, Gerry Lawley and George Selby) and their crews, who safely, pleasurably, and occasionally excitingly, delivered me to my field areas, and to three shipmates Long John, The Leader and Sandy, who were always close friends during times that were often difficult and hazardous but always memorable.

TPS

Contents

Introduction

Carbonate sediments and rocks by definition contain more than 50% carbonate minerals, and these minerals are composed of CO_3^{2-} and one or more cations. The most common carbonate mineral is calcite, $CaCO_3$, which is the principal component of limestones.

Carbonate sediments are found today in many marine and some terrestrial settings but the site of their greatest abundance is on the floor of shallow tropical seas, the environment to which most attention will be given in this book. Carbonate minerals precipitate from carbonate-saturated water by biochemical or chemical processes and accumulate in a variety of ways, for example as skeletal remains, inorganic growths that nucleate on fine mobile debris in shallow seas, as crusts within arid soils, and laminated precipitates on the walls of limestone caves or on the ground around hot springs.

Of the rock-forming carbonates, *calcite* ($CaCO_3$) and *dolomite* ($CaMg(CO_3)_2$) are the most abundant, accounting for more than 90% of natural carbonates as limestones and dolomites. These minerals can occur with impurities of terrigenous quartz and clay minerals and locally with minor amounts of common non-calcareous authigenic minerals such as chert, gypsum, anhydrite and pyrite. Limestones and dolomites represent about 1/6 of the global sedimentary mass and are found throughout the sedimentary rock record, though, as it is energetically easier for limestones to be altered to dolomites than vice versa, we find in general that the ratio of dolomites to limestones increases with age. Precambrian carbonates are now mainly dolomitic, and we believe most originated as inorganic precipitates of $CaCO_3$, or by the biochemical agency of very simple organisms, such as bacteria. As would be expected, the nature of the organically precipitated carbonates

has changed through geological time. There were two main bursts in the abundance of skeletal benthonic organisms, one at the start of the Palaeozoic and another in the Ordovician, and there has been one main burst in the abundance of skeletal planktonic organisms in the Mesozoic.

We can learn more about past Earth surface conditions from limestones than from any other group of sedimentary rocks. Firstly, the sedimentary particles may have a texture and structural arrangement which indicates the conditions of erosion, transportation and deposition, in a way similar to that of many siliciclastic rocks; secondly, many limestones contain abundant fossils which when living had their own particular environmental needs; thirdly, the chemical composition of carbonates reflects both the compositions of the aqueous solutions from which they originated and the physico-chemical conditions that prevailed at the time of precipitation. So studies of carbonate rocks are of great value to the stratigrapher in the interpretation of such issues as former climates, depth of water, wave or current strength, temperature, salinity, proximity to shore and depth of burial.

Of more immediate practical significance is the fact that limestones and dolomites are common aquifers (carriers of water), and reservoirs of hydrocarbons, oil and gas. Further, several valuable metals, most notably lead, zinc, silver and mercury are concentrated as ores in certain types of carbonate rocks. Limestones have numerous other industrial uses, principally as a source of CaO in the chemical industry, but also as a flux for smelting, as a base in agriculture, as a primary ingredient in cement manufacture, and as road stone and building stone.

When the sedimentologist studies limestones he is often confronted with a two-dimensional section of rock such as on a quarry wall, or cliff face, or drill core, from which he is trying to reconstruct the environments of deposition and perhaps the post-depositional (diagenetic) history. If he can accurately interpret the origin of that particular piece of rock he can make meaningful predictions about neighbouring rocks which are inaccessible to him. In order to do this he has to apply models based on modern analogues, he may have to see through an overprint of diagenetic textural and compositional alterations, and finally he will have to note how the rock types he sees are associated one with another, i.e. what areal or vertical patterns or sequences are apparent. This line of reasoning very broadly moulds the course of this book which adopts a present through to past approach.

After a brief introduction to carbonate minerals and their chemistry, carbonate grains, the building blocks of limestones, are described in sufficient detail to help in their recognition and to understand their origins. Various processes affect these grains before they are ultimately preserved in rocks. Firstly, they are subjected to physical and biological processes on the sea-bed which influence the style of their accumulations, then, during and after deposition, diagenetic processes, in salt and fresh water, transform the unconsolidated, commonly chemically unstable, sediment into the stable limestones and dolomites of the stratigraphic record. Armed with an understanding of depositional and diagenetic processes we are now able to examine the major carbonate depositional environments, for example, shallow reef, tidal flat, deep-sea bed, to record the typical suites of grains, sedimentary and biogenic structures, biotas and diagenetic overprints by which each setting is characterized. Examples of sequences of carbonate rocks which illustrate the major structural and petrographic characteristics of the commonly occurring facies in carbonate provinces are then presented from various periods of geological history.

The economic aspects of carbonate rocks are briefly outlined in the final section of the book.

Part 1 Carbonate minerals and grains

1. Carbonate minerals

1.1 Crystallography

The CO_3 group is the fundamental chemical unit from which the carbonate minerals derive their identity. There are a number of minerals in which the CO_3 group is one of several anions in the structure—hydroxyl is perhaps the most common other anion, e.g. malachite $(Cu_2(OH)_2CO_3)$. These mixed anion carbonates are rare rock-forming minerals and will not be discussed further here. The CO_3 group has a configuration resembling an equilateral triangle with oxygen atoms at the corners and a carbon atom at the centre. The common rock-forming carbonate minerals are either *rhombohedral* or *orthorhombic* in crystal habit. Table 1.1 lists some of the common cations incorporated in carbonates.

We note generally that those cations with small ionic radii are incorporated into carbonates having a trigonal (rhombohedral) unit cell in which the cations are energetically favoured in a 6-fold coordination (2 cations for every oxygen), while the larger cations form orthorhombic carbonates having 9-fold coordination (3 cations for every oxygen). Calcium has an ionic radius intermediate between the small and large cations and is near the limit for 6-fold coordination; thus $CaCO_3$ is dimorphous, forming either rhombohedral (*calcite*) or orthorhombic (*aragonite*) structures. In calcite, layers of Ca atoms alternate with carbonate layers, the layers being equidistant along the z-axis. The triangular CO_3 groups have identical orientations within each layer but reversed orientations in successive layers; each oxygen has two Ca as nearest neighbours. Modern descriptions of rhombohedral carbonates are usually given in terms of the so-called triple hexagonal cell. Figure 1.1 shows the relationship between the true rhombohedral unit cell, the morphologic (or cleavage) cell in calcite and hexagonal unit cell. In aragonite, the CO_3 groups do not lie midway between Ca layers and are rotated 30° to right or left so that each oxygen atom has three neighbouring Ca atoms.

There are two synthetic forms of $CaCO_3$ known only at high temperatures. There is also a

Table 1.1 Cation ionic radii and common carbonate minerals. After Speer, in Reeder (ed.) 1983

Cation	Ionic radius (nm)	Mineral	Crystal habit
Ni	0.069	Gaspeite $NiCO_3$	
Mg	0.072	Magnesite $MgCO_3$	
Zn	0.074	Smithsonite $ZnCO_3$	
Co	0.075	Sphaerocobaltite $CoCO_3$	Rhombohedral
Fe	0.078	Siderite $FeCO_3$	(trigonal system)
Mn	0.083	Rhodochrosite $MnCO_3$	
Ca	0.100	Calcite $CaCO_3$	
Ca	0.118	Aragonite $CaCO_3$	
Sr	0.131	Strontianite $SrCO_3$	Orthorhombic
Pb	0.135	Cerussite $PbCO_3$	
Ba	0.147	Witherite $BaCO_3$	

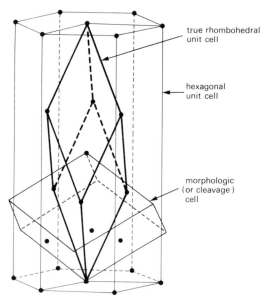

true rhombohedral
unit cell

hexagonal
unit cell

morphologic
(or cleavage)
cell

Figure 1.1 The relationship between the true rhombohedral unit cell, the morphologic (or cleavage) cell and the hexagonal unit cell. After Reeder (1983)

metastable hexagonal form which crystallizes at lower temperatures and pressures, called *vaterite* (μ-CaCO$_3$), but it is very rare in nature.

Dolomite, CaMg(CO$_3$)$_2$, a highly ordered double carbonate, is a common rock-forming mineral, often occurring as the alteration product of a limestone. Dolomite belongs to the rhombohedral group, with alternating layers of cations and CO$_3$ groups, in which the cation layers are alternately Ca^{2+} and Mg^{2+}.

We shall focus our attention on the three most common carbonate minerals in sedimentary rocks: calcite, aragonite and dolomite, whose crystal properties are summarized in Table 1.2.

1.2 Substitutions

Solid solution between the various end-member carbonates exists to varying degrees. The closeness of cation size is the dominant factor governing the completeness of miscibility, with small differences generally giving complete miscibility, and large differences, limited miscibility. It is therefore rather surprising that one of the most important carbonate solid solutions in nature, magnesian calcite, has up to 30 mol % MgCO$_3$ in naturally occurring low-temperature calcite when the ionic radii of Ca^{2+} and Mg^{2+} are so different in size. However, as it is easier for a small cation (Mg^{2+}) to occupy a large site (Ca^{2+}) than vice versa, we rarely find Ca^{2+} substituting for Mg^{2+} in magnesite (MgCO$_3$). The calcite structure shrinks at higher Mg concentrations over the

Table 1.2 Properties of aragonite, calcite and dolomite

	Aragonite	Calcite	Dolomite
Formula	CaCO$_3$	CaCO$_3$	CaMg(CO$_3$)$_2$
Crystal system	Orthorhombic	Trigonal	Trigonal
Indicatrix	Biaxial negative $2V = 18°$	Uniaxial negative	Uniaxial negative
Cleavage	{010} fair	{10$\bar{1}$1} perfect	{10$\bar{1}$1} perfect
Colour	Colourless or white	Colourless or white	Colourless or white often tinged with yellow or brown
Refractive index	n_x 1.530 n_y 1.681 n_z 1.685	n_o 1.658 n_e 1.486	n_o 1.679 n_e 1.500
Birefringence	0.155	0.172	0.179
Specific gravity	2.94	2.72	2.86
Common trace elements	Sr, Ba, Pb	Mg, Fe, Mn, Zn, Cu	Fe, Mn, Zn, Cu
Effect of cold dilute HCl	Readily soluble with effervescence	Readily soluble with brisk effervescence	Poorly soluble

range 0–18 mol % $MgCO_3$. The term *magnesian calcite* or Mg calcite, (sometimes referred to as high-magnesium calcite or high-Mg calcite) is normally reserved for those metastable (or unstable) calcites with greater than 5 mol % $MgCO_3$. Calcite with less than 5 mol % $MgCO_3$ is simply called calcite or in some texts low-magnesium calcite (low-Mg calcite). In natural magnesian calcites with greater than 12 mol % $MgCO_3$ there is more Mg^{2+} and Ca^{2+} than the contained CO_3^{2-} balance. It is likely that $Mg(OH)_2$ is contained in these structures. With time, Mg calcite loses its Mg and is converted into calcite.

Small amounts of Fe^{2+} (several thousand ppm) may also substitute for Ca^{2+} in calcite or for Mg^{2+} in magnesian calcite giving *ferroan calcite* (Fe calcite). Manganese may also substitute in trace amounts in calcite.

Inorganically precipitated aragonite does not incorporate Mg^{2+} into the lattice, though some aragonitic organisms can contain 10ppm Mg^{2+}. A large part of the Mg^{2+} present in some aragonitic skeletons is most probably adsorbed, or present in organic compounds. The larger divalent cations are more readily incorporated in the orthorhombic structure; for example strontium is taken up to maximum concentrations of about 10000 ppm in aragonite. Sodium is present in amounts up to 1% Na in naturally occurring $CaCO_3$ but it is not preferentially incorporated in either calcite or aragonite.

Ferrous iron may substitute for Mg^{2+} in the limited solid solution series dolomite–ankerite, with up to 70 mol % $CaFe(CO_3)_2$ in dolomite. The compound $CaFe(CO_3)_2$ does not occur naturally. The term *ankerite* Ca(Mg, Fe, Mn) $(CO_3)_2$, is normally preferred for the more Fe-rich phases, and the name *ferroan dolomite* is used for those with low Fe.

There has been much research, particularly on modern carbonates, into the factors that govern substitutions in carbonate minerals, for they have significant value. For example, as the contents of trace elements in calcites and arag-onites vary systematically with the physical and chemical nature of the environments in which organisms grow, calcareous fossil remains are potential palaeoindicators. Further, where the pattern of incorporation of substituted trace elements into inorganic $CaCO_3$ can be revealed visibly by experiments (e.g. by staining or cathodoluminescence) the unravelling of crystal growth histories is considerably facilitated. A summary of the main factors governing trace element substitutions in calcite and aragonite is given below and the subject is discussed further in the later section on diagenesis.

Magnesium: The amount of magnesium present in naturally occurring magnesian calcite decreases with decreasing temperature (i.e. with increasing latitude and increasing ocean depth) for both organically and inorganically precipitated varieties.

Experiments to precipitate Mg calcites show that the Mg/Ca ratio of the precipitate depends on the ratio of Mg^{2+}/Ca^{2+} in the solution, and at one Mg^{2+}/Ca^{2+} value for the solution, the Mg/Ca in the solid decreases with decreasing temperature. So we find that in normal sea water, with a fairly constant Mg^{2+}/Ca^{2+} ratio, temperature is the critical factor in governing the precipitated Mg content of calcite. But with extreme values of Mg^{2+}/Ca^{2+} (e.g. within micropores of skeletal materials or hypersaline environments) the absolute value of the ratio can play a role in determining the final Mg content. The CO_3^{2-} concentration of surface sea water varies latitudinally and may affect the Mg content of skeletal magnesian calcite, with lower CO_3 concentrations (at high latitudes and upwellings) favouring lower Mg content in magnesian calcite.

Organisms with high calcification rates have high Mg content in their skeletons but the overriding control could again be temperature.

Strontium: The relations between variations in Sr in aragonite skeletons and compositions of the water have been examined in natural and experimental systems. There is a linear relationship between the solution Sr^{2+}/Ca^{2+} ratio and the Sr/Ca ratio in aragonitic skeletons. Because present ocean water has a fairly uniform Sr^{2+}/Ca^{2+} ratio, the Sr/Ca ratios of certain skeletal aragonites show a correlation with temperature, the higher the temperature the lower the Sr content. Theoretical considerations predict a similar trend of decreasing Sr/Ca with increase in temperature for inorganically precipitated aragonite. Though much smaller amounts of strontium substitute in calcite the same trend (decrease in Sr with increase in temperature) is noted in magnesian calcites while calcite organisms show the reverse trend (increase in Sr with increase in temperature).

There is a strong phylogenetic affect on the Sr content of skeletal $CaCO_3$; some genera, families, orders and phyla are characterized by a certain range of Sr/Ca ratio values.

Carbon and oxygen isotopes: The distributions of the stable carbon (^{12}C, ^{13}C) and oxygen (^{16}O, ^{17}O, ^{18}O) isotopes are described by fractionation factors, characteristic of the isotope, organism and prevalent physico-chemical conditions. Some organisms appear to secrete carbonate at or near oxygen isotopic equilibrium with ambient water, while others do not. Carbon isotopic equilibrium is seldom recorded in biogenic carbonate precipitation. Examples of marine calcareous organisms with deviations from the predicted equilibrium are shown in Figure 1.2. Concentrations of isotopes are reported in delta units (δ), in which $\delta^{13}C$ and $\delta^{18}O$ are defined relative to an international standard. In carbonate rocks and minerals the PDB standard is normally used for both carbon and oxygen. This standard was prepared from the marine Cretaceous Peedee belemnite so that its isotopic composition is $\delta^{13}C = 0$ and $\delta^{18}O = 0$ by definition. The delta values are determined by the relationship (e.g. for oxygen)

$$\frac{^{18}O/^{16}O \text{ (sample)} - {}^{18}O/^{16}O \text{ (standard)}}{^{18}O/^{16}O \text{ (standard)}} \times 1000$$

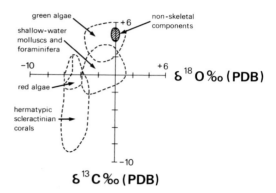

Figure 1.2 Range in $\delta^{13}C$ and $\delta^{18}O$ values for different groups of shallow water organisms. After Anderson and Arthur (1983)

A positive delta value indicates enrichment in the heavy isotope, vice versa for a negative delta value. 1% enrichment of ^{13}C is equivalent to a $\delta^{13}C$ of $+10‰$.

The mineralogical structure can influence the isotope composition of the calcium carbonate precipitated. Co-precipitated calcite is enriched by 1.8‰ in $\delta^{13}C$ and depleted by 0.6‰ in $\delta^{18}O$ relative to aragonite, and magnesian calcite is isotopically heavier than calcite.

Certain organisms, including bivalves, corals and planktonic foraminiferans, show a temperature-dependent fractionation in their skeletons of oxygen isotopes. This has allowed the reconstruction of past climates by the oxygen isotope analysis of certain fossil skeletons. Isotope values for fossil skeletons are not straightforward to interpret, however, since the $\delta^{18}O$ values for modern sea water vary according to depth, temperature, salinity and latitude. Further, there is a trend of decreasing $\delta^{18}O$ in carbonate rocks of increasing age which may represent a progressive change in $\delta^{18}O$ of the oceans. The carbon isotope is only weakly positively temperature-dependent. The effects of environmental perturbations on stable isotopes (^{13}C, ^{18}O) are shown in Table 1.3.

Biochemical fractionation processes, including photosynthesis, play the dominant role in controlling carbon isotope ratios and the diver-

Table: 1.3 Effects of environmental perturbations on stable isotopes with emphasis on the coral reef environment. After Aharon and Chappell (1983).

Perturbation type	$^{18}O/^{16}O$ in $CaCO_3$	$^{13}C/^{12}C$ in $CaCO_3$	Range in coral reef
Sea-surface warming	falls	(rises)	Up to 1/‰ in $\delta^{18}O$
Freshwater run-off dilutes ocean	falls	falls	Up to 0.5‰
Evaporation	(rises)	–	–
Ocean upwelling	–	falls	Up to $-0.7‰$
Major glaciation	rises	–	Up to 1.2‰ in Pleistocene
Biomass productivity increase	–	rises	Up to 2‰ in a lagoon
Organic matter oxidation	–	falls	Up to 2‰ in a lagoon
Fossil fuel burning (brackets mean small effect)	–	(falls)	?

gence of $\delta^{13}C$ values from the zero value of the PDB marine calcium carbonate standard. The $^{13}C/^{12}C$ ratio in plants is 2% lower than in the atmosphere (where $\delta^{13}C = -7$). Thus organic carbon is isotopically light, averaging about $\delta^{13}C = -24$ for land plants. This 'light' carbon persists into organically derived acids which on reaction with marine carbonates, for example, produce light calcium carbonate precipitates as in soil limestones and limestones undergoing freshwater diagenesis. These processes and their effects will be discussed at greater length in the section on diagenesis (Part 4).

Selected reading

Aharon, P. and Chappell, J. (1983) Carbon and oxygen isotope probes of reef environment histories. In D.J. Barnes (ed.), *Perspectives on Coral Reefs*, Australian Institute of Marine Science publication by Brian Clouston, Manuka, ACT, 1–15.

Arthur, M.A., Anderson, T.F., Kaplan, I.R., Veizer, J. and Land, L.S. (1983) *Stable Isotopes in Sedimentary Geology*. SEPM Short Course Notes, No. 10.

Bathurst, R.G.C. (1975) *Carbonate Sediments and their Diagenesis*. Elsevier, Amsterdam.

Berner, R.A. (1971) *Principles of Chemical Sedimentology*. McGraw-Hill, New York.

Chave, K.E. (1954) Aspects of the biochemistry of magnesium 1. Calcareous marine organisms. *J. Geol.* **62**, 266–283.

Goldsmith, J.R. (1959) Some aspects of the geochemistry of carbonates. In Abelson P.H. (ed.), *Research in Geochemistry*, John Wiley & Sons, New York, 336–358.

Graf, D.L. (1960) Geochemistry of carbonate sediments and sedimentary carbonate rocks. Part 1, carbonate mineralogy—carbonate sediments. *Illinois Geol. Surv. Circ.* **297**.

Kinsman, D.J.J. (1969) Interpretation of Sr^{2+} concentrations in carbonate minerals and rocks. *J. Sed Petrol.* **39**, 486–508.

Leeder, M.R. (1982) *Sedimentology: Process and Product*. George Allen & Unwin, London.

Lippman, F. (1973) *Sedimentary Carbonate Minerals*. Springer Verlag, Berlin.

Milliman, J.D. (1974) *Marine Carbonates*. Springer Verlag, Berlin.

Reeder, R.J. (1983) *Reviews in Mineralogy, Vol. II, Carbonates: Mineralogy and Chemistry*. Min. Soc. Am., Washington DC.

Swart, P.K. (1983) Carbon and oxygen isotope fractionation in scleractinian corals: a review. *Earth Sci. Rev.* **19**, 51–80.

Wilkinson, B. (1979) Biomineralization, paleo-oceanography and the evolution of calcareous marine organisms. *Geology* **7**, 524–527.

Wolf, K.H., Chilingar, G.V. and Beales, F.W. (1976) Elemental composition of carbonate skeletons, minerals and sediments. In Chilingar, G.V., Bissell, H.J. and Fairbridge, R.W. (eds.), *Carbonate Rocks: Physical and Chemical Aspects*, Elsevier, Amsterdam, 23–149.

2. Limestone classification

Early petrologists subdivided limestones according to the sizes of the dominant mechanically deposited grains: *calcilutite* (grains < 63 μm), *calcarenite* (grains > 63 μm < 2 mm), *calcirudite* (grains > 2 mm). These terms are still frequently encountered today. Since the 1950s several methods of classification of limestones have been proposed. Most are based on criteria recognizable in thin section with the aid of a microscope, leading either to a descriptive or a genetic subdivision. When we examine limestones under the microscope we find that they consist of bundles and masses of crystals of $CaCO_3$. These bundles of crystals normally represent three fundamental components: (1) the framework, which is made of discrete grains or clasts (normally sand-sized, but may be gravel or silt) or *in-situ* organic structures; (2) a fine-grained detrital matrix (*micro-crystalline calcite* or *micrite*); and (3) cement which was chemically precipitated after deposition of grains in interstices and commonly appears as *sparry calcite* (Figure 2.1). Incompletely filled spaces remain as pores which

may store and transmit fluids through the rock.

Two classifications have been equally adopted fairly universally, that of Folk (1959), and that of Dunham (1962). Both of these classifications subdivide limestones according to a blend of descriptive and genetic parameters, that is, knowing the name of a particular limestone transmits some idea of how it was formed.

2.1 Folk classification

Folk's classification is based upon the idea that, in principle, the sedimentation of carbonates is comparable to that of sandstones. Most carbonates (except for growth structures such as coral reefs) are made of three end-members (Figure 2.1):

 I Grains (Folk uses the term 'allochemical constituents', sometimes abbreviated to allochems)
 II Microcrystalline matrix (micrite), equivalent here to clays in sandstones
III Sparry calcite cement which precipitates from solution after deposition in intergranular pores.

Four grain categories are dominant in limestones: *fossils* (which have the prefix 'bio-' in the classification), *ooids* (oo-), *pellets* (pel-) and *intraclasts* (intra-). These grain types are described in Chapters 4 and 5.

One or other of these prefixes for grain type combines with the appropriate suffix for matrix type, -micrite for microcrystalline matrices, e.g. *biomicrite*. (Figure 2.3*A*) or -sparite for sparry calcite matrices, (e.g. *oosparite* (Figure 2.3*B*; *intrasparite*, Figure 2.3*C*, and *pelsparite*, Figure 2.3*D*), according to the grain and matrix compositions of the limestone. Terms can be modified to give an indication of coarse grain size, e.g. *biospar-rudite*. Folk coined the word *biolithite* for autochthonous reef rocks which had grown *in situ* (Figure 2.3*E*). Folk went on (1962) to devise a spectral subdivision of limestone

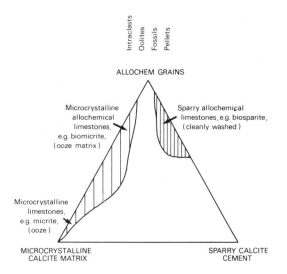

Figure 2.1 Three end members of mechanically deposited limestones and common limestone types. After Folk (1959)

Percent Allochems	OVER 2/3 LIME MUD MATRIX				SUBEQUAL SPAR & LIME MUD	OVER 2/3 SPAR CEMENT		
	0–1%	1–10%	10–50%	OVER 50%		SORTING POOR	SORTING GOOD	ROUNDED & ABRADED
Representative Rock Terms	MICRITE & DISMICRITE	FOSSILI-FEROUS MICRITE	SPARSE BIOMICRITE	PACKED BIOMICRITE	POORLY WASHED BIOSPARITE	UNSORTED BIOSPARITE	SORTED BIOSPARITE	ROUNDED BIOSPARITE
	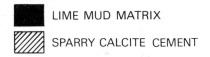							
Terrigenous Analogues	Claystone		Sandy Claystone	Clayey or Immature Sandstone		Submature Sandstone	Mature Sandstone	Supermature Sandstone

■ LIME MUD MATRIX

▨ SPARRY CALCITE CEMENT

Figure 2.2 Folk's spectral subdivision of limestone types indicating an increase in textural maturity to the right. After Folk (1962).

types which set these essentially descriptive terms in a genetic framework.

Folk's main premise in his spectral subdivision is that the various degrees of hydraulic energy during deposition are reflected in the ratio of micrite to sparry calcite; the percentage of allochemical grains in micrites relates to the water turbulence in low-energy environments and the textural maturity (sorting, roundness) of the allochems in a sparite relates to the turbulence in high-energy environments of deposition (Figure 2.2).

2.2 Dunham classification

Dunham's classification (Table 2.1) is also based on the depositional texture of the limestone, but now the fundamental criterion of subdivision is not the composition of the matrix but rather the nature of the framework of the sediment, i.e. whether it is *mud-supported* or *grain-supported*. The former implies low hydraulic energy of deposition, the latter high energy. Limestones with very few grains (< 10%) in a mud matrix

are *mudstones*, and those mudstones with greater than 10% grains, but insufficient to be in mutual contact, are *wackestones* (Figure 2.3A). Limestones in which the grains touch are *packstones* or *grainstones*; the former usually have a mud matrix and owe their grain-support to compaction (Figure 2.3F), the latter were grain-supported at deposition and normally have cement crystals in intergranular pores (Figures 2.3B, C, D). Dunham uses the term *boundstone* for limestones whose fabric indicates the original components were bound together during deposition, as in a reef (Figure 2.3E). It is equivalent to the term 'biolithite' of Folk.

Embry and Klovan later (1971) further subdivided this boundstone category into autochthonous (in-place) and allochthonous (derived) reef limestones. Autochthonous reef deposits are termed *bafflestones*, *bindstones* and *framestones* according to whether the principal in-place organic components of the reef acted as a baffle in which sediment could be trapped, encrusted or organically bound the sediment, or provided a

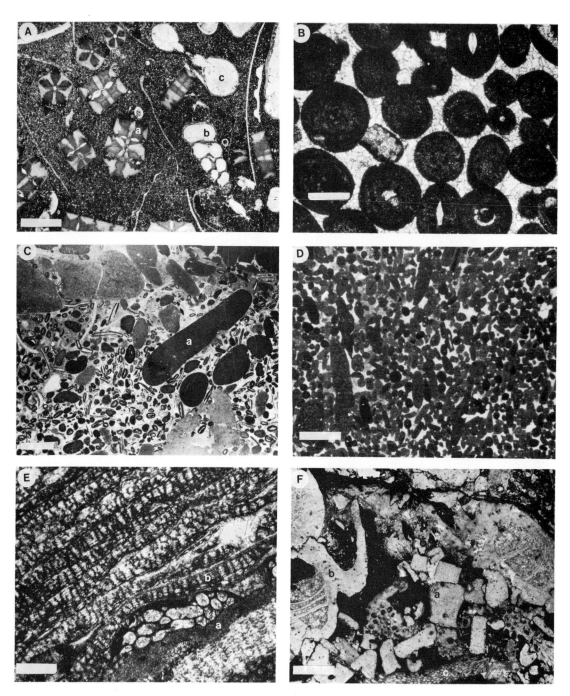

Figure 2.3 Thin sections of limestones illustrating Folk and Dunham subdivisions. (*A*). Biomicrite/wackestone: *a*, crinoid; *b*, gastropod; *c*, ammonite. Ppl. Scale 5 mm. Middle Jurassic, Dorset, England. (*B*). Oosparite/grainstone. Ppl. Scale 0.3 mm. Lower Carboniferous, South Wales. (*C*). Intrasparite/grainstone (some micrite present): *a*, intraclast. Ppl. Scale 0.5 mm. Middle Jurassic, Skye, Scotland. (*D*). Pelsparite/grainstone. Ppl. Scale 0.5 mm. Upper Jurassic, Dorset, England. (*E*). Biolithite/boundstone. Encrusting layers of red algae (*a*) and forminiferans (*b*). Ppl. Scale 0.5 mm. Miocene, Mangaia, Cook Islands. (*F*). Biomicrite/packstone. *a*, crinoid; *b*, tabulate coral (*Halysites*); *c*, bryozoan. Ppl. Scale 2 mm. Silurian, Much Wenlock, England.

Table 2.1 Dunham's 1962 classification of limestones.

Depositional texture recognizable				Depositional texture not recognizable
Original components not bound together during deposition			Original components were bound together during deposition	Crystalline carbonate
Contains mud (particles of clay and fine silt size)		Lacks mud and is grain-supported	as shown by intergrown skeletal matter or lamination contrary to gravity	
Mud-supported		Grain-supported		
Less than 10 percent grains	More than 10 percent grains			
Mudstone	Wackestone	Packstone	Grainstone	Boundstone

rigid contiguous framework. Allochthonous reef sediments include *floatstones* in which more than 10% of the particles in the rock are larger than 2 mm and are matrix-supported, and *rudstones* which are clast-supported.

Dunham's classification is in essence closely similar to Folk's, but the bipartite division is now based on the distinction between mud-support and grain-support as opposed to mud matrix *v.* cement matrix.

Both Folk's and Dunham's classifications have their advantages and disadvantages. The combination terms (prefix for grains, suffix for matrix) of Folk's classification are succinct and easy to use and interpret, which has accounted for their widespread adoption. But, as we will see later in the section on processes of carbonate sediment deposition (Chapter 6), though it may be reasonable to relate micrites to lower energies of deposition than most sparites, thus providing a useful binary division of limestones, there are many instances where the finer subdivisions of Folk's textural spectrum do not hold, so that, on the whole, it is perhaps unreasonable to equate the deposition of a limestone with that of a sandstone. Regarding Dunham's classification, though the mud- or grain-supported framework may well more precisely equate with low and high depositional energy, these fabrics are not always simply discerned in the two-dimensional perspective of a thin section. (Dunham himself

goes to some pains to point this out, by, for example, sectioning a pile of cornflakes to reveal the limited number of touching points of sedimented platy grains when seen in vertical section.)

Whatever the shortcomings, we do need classifications to help to communicate our ideas, and students should be familiar with the two briefly outlined here, as they will be encountered throughout the limestone literature. The other classifications that are assembled in the volume on limestone classifications edited by Ham and Pray (1962) should also be inspected, for though some classifications and their introduced terms may not be widely preferred, an understanding of the criteria used in their construction gives a good insight into the characteristics of limestones.

Selected reading

Dunham, R.J. (1962) Classification of carbonate rocks according to depositional texture. In W. E. Ham (ed.), *Classification of Carbonate Rocks*, Am. Ass. Petrol. Geol. Mem. 1, 108–121.

Embry, A.F. and Klovan, J.E. (1971) A late Devonian reef tract on northeastern Banks Island Northwest Territories. *Bull. Can. Petrol. Geol.* **19**, 730–781.

Folk, R.L. (1959) Practical petrographic classification of limestones. *Am. Ass. Petrol. Geol. Bull.* **43**, 1–38.

Folk, R.L. (1962) Spectral subdivision of limestone types. In W.E. Ham (ed.), *Classification of Carbonate Rocks*, Am. Ass. Petrol. Geol. Mem. 1, 62–84.

Ham, W.E. and Pray, L.C. (1962) Modern concepts and classifications of carbonate rocks. In W.E. Ham (ed.) *Classification of Carbonate Rocks*, Am. Ass. Petrol. Geol. Mem. 1, 2–19.

3. Definitions of some common marine environmental and ecological terms

Before proceeding with the origins of carbonate sediments it is necessary to introduce some terms describing the marine setting and modes of life of marine organisms.

3.1 Marine environmental terms

We normally subdivide the marine environment into depth-related zones as shown in Figure 3.1. The broad term *platform* is used here to encompass the shallow settings of *epeiric seas, shelf seas* and *mid-ocean banks.*

Epeiric (epicontinental) seas lie semi-enclosed upon stable continental areas, and *shelf* (pericontinental) seas occupy marginal areas around the continent. Epeiric seas may spread for thousands of square of kilometres over the craton. They have relatively shallow depths, giving very low bottom slopes of 0.005°. Shelves, on the other hand, have steeper slopes of about

0.1°, as they are narrower (100–400 kilometres in width) and reach depths of about 200 m at the break in slope at the edge of the continental shelf. *Banks* are shallowly submerged platforms (of continental or oceanic origin) surrounded by margins that descend into deep ocean water. Tropical shelves and banks commonly have elevated rims. Platforms with gradual gradients into deeper water without a marked break in slope or an obvious rim are sometimes referred to as *ramps.* The differences in shape, bottom slope and position have profound effects on water circulation, environment and ultimately nature of sedimentation of the various settings. It is apparent that in a dynamic world these sedimentary foundations may grade into one another, split into two forms, or with time develop a new character. For example, an epeiric sea may split by faulting to form two shelves and an interven-

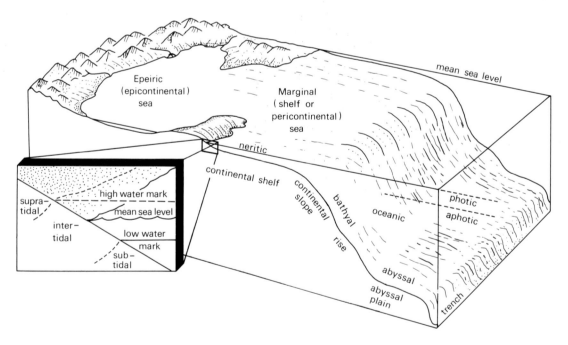

Figure 3.1 Marine environments

ing basin; a shelf may become a ramp through differential subsidence along a hinge line; a ramp may develop into a shelf with active sediment progradation or reef growth.

Epeiric seas are relatively rare today compared with the geological past, on account of the lower-than-average present sea-level. Typical modern epeiric seas are Hudson's Bay, the North Sea and the Persian Gulf; typical shelf seas include the shallow areas around NE Australia and the eastern margin of North America; examples of banks are the Bahama Banks, Chagos Bank and Rockall Bank.

The approximate latitudinal limits of the bio-geographical realms are:

Tropics	0–25°
Temperate	25–50°
Boreal (N. Hemisphere)	50–70°
Polar	70–90°.

3.2 Marine ecological terms

Marine organisms can be simply classified according to where they live, whether they are capable of self-propulsion, and how they feed.

The ecological terms defined below are illustrated in Figure 3.2.

The total organic assemblage is the *biota*; the animal component is the *fauna*, and the plant component the *flora*.

Organisms that live in waters overlying continental masses are called *neritic*, those living in the sea beyond the continents are called *oceanic* Organisms living above the bottom are *pelagic*; if they move mainly by swimming they are *nektonic* but if they float and move mainly by currents they are *planktonic*. Animal and plant plankton are called *zooplankton* and *phytoplankton* respectively. Organisms living at the bottom are *benthonic* (or benthic). *Epifaunal* (or *epifloral*) relates to organisms living on the substratum and *infaunal* (*infloral*) relates to organisms living in the substratum. If the organisms grow on a hard substratum they are termed *epilithic*, but if they live within a hard substratum, either in cracks or excavations, they are known as *endolithic*. Burrows are produced by animals digging into soft sediment (bioturbation), and borings result from organic excavation by mechanical or chemical processes into solid substrates. *Epibionts* are

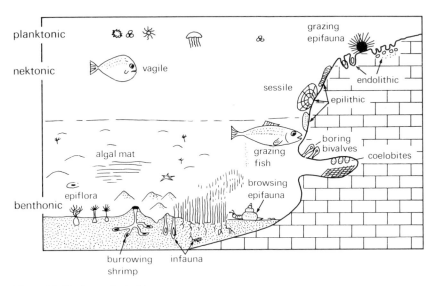

Figure 3.2 Marine ecological terms

organisms that attach to other organisms; *epiphytes* being plants with this habit, and *epizoans*, animals. *Vagile* means capable of loco-motion, whereas *sessile* means immobile.

Organisms that prefer to live in the light are *photophilic*; those that prefer to live in the dark are *sciaphilic*. We call those organisms that inhabit underwater caverns *coelobites*.

Carnivores (predators and scavengers) feed mainly on other animals. *Suspension feeders* feed upon suspended micro-organisms and de-tritus, and *deposit feeders* feed upon the detritus deposited on the bottom together with its as-sociated micro-organisms. *Herbivores* include *grazers* that feed on plants attached to firm substrates and *browsers* that feed on soft sub-strate plants.

Organisms that can tolerate a wide range of conditions of salinity are said to be *euryhaline*, those with narrow tolerances are called *stenohaline*.

Selected reading

Emery, K.O. (1969) The continental shelves. *Sci. Am.* **221**, 106–122.
Hallam, A. (1981) *Facies Interpretation and the Stratigraphic Record.* W.H. Freeman, Oxford.
Hedgpeth, J.W. (ed.) (1957) *Treatise on Marine Ecology and Paleoecology.* Vol. 1: *Ecology.* Mem. Geol. Soc. Amer. 67/1, New York.
Reading, H.G. (ed.) (1986) *Sedimentary Environments and Facies.* Blackwell, Oxford.
Rigby, J.K. and Hamblin, W.K. (eds.) (1972) *Recognition of Ancient Sedimentary Environments.* SEPM Sp. Pub. **16**.
Selley, R.C. (1985) *Ancient Sedimentary Environments.* Chapman and Hall, London.
Wilson, J.L. (1975) *Carbonate Facies in Geologic History.* Springer Verlag, New York.

Part 2 Carbonate grains

The framework grains of limestone owe their origin to organic processes, inorganic processes or both. For example, skeletal remains result from the biochemical precipitation of $CaCO_3$; ooids, small round grains with a radial or concentric internal structure, are thought to result from direct physico-chemical precipitation from saturated water without organic intervention; pellets and aggregate lumps may owe their cohesion to both organic and inorganic processes of $CaCO_3$ precipitation. Framework grains are usually split into two groups: skeletal and non-skeletal.

4 Skeletal carbonates

The skeletal components of a limestone relate to the distribution of carbonate-secreting organisms through time and space. The age range and taxonomic diversity of the major groups of skeletal organisms are shown in Figure 4.1. At any one time, environmental factors such as

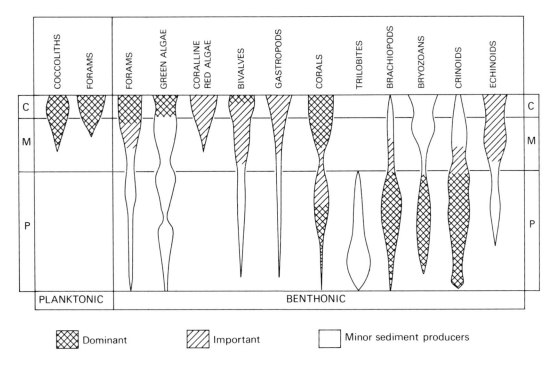

Figure 4.1 Diversity, abundance and relative importance of various calcareous marine organisms as sediment producers. After Wilkinson (1979).

depth, light, temperature, salinity and turbulence control the spatial distribution of organisms and their preservable remains.

Organisms secrete a skeleton to support and protect soft tissue. The poorly organized skeletons of some calcareous plants are probably produced purely as an efficient method of removing $CaCO_3$ from the system. We do not fully understand the controls organisms exert on the mineralogy of their skeletons. It appears that normally some sort of organic template acts as a precursor for skeletal precipitation. Skeletal

Table 4.1 The mineralogy of the major groups of carbonate-secreting organisms. After Scholle (1978).

Skeletal compositions

Taxon	Aragonite	Calcite Mol% $MgCO_3$ 0 10 20 30	Both aragonite and calcite
Calcareous algae			
Red		× —— ×	
Green	×		
Coccoliths		×	
Foraminiferans			
Benthonic	0	× —— ×	
Planktonic		× — ×	
Sponges	0	× —— ×	
Coelenterates			
Stromatoporoids*	×	× ?	
Milleporoids	×		
Rugose*		×	
Tabulate*		×	
Scleractinian	×		
Alcyonarian	0	× —— ×	
Bryozoans	0	× —— ×	0
Brachiopods		× ×	
Molluscs			
Chitons	×		
Pelecypods	×	× — ×	×
Gastropods	×	× — ×	×
Pteropods	×		
Cephalopods (most)	×		
Belemnoids*		×	
Annelids (serpulids)	×	× —— ×	×
Arthropods			
Decapods		× —— ×	
Ostracods		× — ×	
Barnacles		× — ×	
Trilobites*		×	
Echinoderms		× —— ×	

× Common   0 Rare   *Not based on modern forms

mineralogy varies with taxonomic level of the organism and is also influenced by environmental conditions, notably temperature.

Table 4.1 indicates the mineralogy of the major groups of skeletal organisms.

The identification of skeletal grains in thin section is normally based on the following criteria: size and shape, internal microarchitecture, and original mineralogy (as revealed by fabric or chemical evidence).

The particle configuration has to be ascertained from the two-dimensional view seen in thin section. The internal structure is produced by the arrangement of crystal aggregates within the skeleton. The principal types of skeletal microarchitecture are illustrated in Table 4.2. The skeletal mineralogy may have changed during diagenesis, but fabric and chemical evidence can be used to suggest the original composition, as we shall see later (section 9.3).

The purpose of this section is to present a brief description of the morphology, crystal structure and composition of the skeletons of the major groups of calcium-carbonate-secreting organisms, to aid in their identification (usually in thin section) in sediments and rocks. The organisms are chiefly grouped in phyla, and included in each group is a general introduction to the mode of life, occurrence, history and preservation of the more important members of the phylum and their geological ranges.

4.1 Foraminiferida

Skeletal structure. Foraminiferans are animals belonging to the phylum Protozoa. They are unicellular, or acellular, and most secrete or agglutinate a mineralized covering. Most of the chambered skeletons are between 1 mm and 10 mm in maximum size.

Agglutinating foraminiferans (textulariids) attach particles (such as fine sand grains or tests of other micro-organisms) with a calcitic or ferruginous cement on to a layer of tectin, an organic compound composed of protein and polysaccharides. This is the geologically oldest method

Table 4.2 The common types of skeletal microstructure in thin section seen in plane polarized light and crossed nicols under the microscope.

Microstructure Common minerals (rare minerals in parenthesis)	Appearance of thin section in ordinary transmitted light	Appearance of thin section under crossed polars	Examples
Homogeneous prismatic Calcite (Aragonite)	No visible structure	Extinction in one direction. Optic axes parallel and usually normal to the surface of skeleton	Trilobites, Ostracods
Granular Calcite Aragonite	Irregular grains (if fine and uniform in size sometimes referred to as sugary or sucrosic)	Random orientation of optic axes	Foraminiferans
Normal prismatic Calcite (Aragonite)	Polygonal prisms normal to outer surface _transverse_ long.	Each prism extinguishes as a unit long. _transverse_	Punctate brachiopods *Inoceramus*
Foliated Calcite	Thin parallel leaves of calcite commonly having a wavy banded appearance	Variable orientation of optic axes of leaves	Bryozoans, pseudopunctate brachiopods, worm tubes, oysters
Nacreous Aragonite	Regular thin parallel leaves of aragonite (separated by organic films)	Parallel extinction	Molluscs
Single crystal Calcite	Coarse single calcite grain showing cleavage	Grain extinguishes as a unit	Echinoderms sponge spicules

Contd.

Table 4.2 (*Contd.*)

Microstructure Common minerals (rare minerals in parenthesis)	Appearance of thin section in ordinary transmitted light	Appearance of thin section under crossed polars	Examples
Crossed lamellar Aragonite (Calcite)	Layer of large lamellae, each lamella composed of small flat crystals, uniformly inclined in plane of larger lamella giving herringbone pattern	Uniform orientation of optic axes in small crystals sometimes causes large lamellae to extinguish as a unit	Molluscs
Spherulitic fascicle Aragonite (Calcite)	Fibres radiating fan-like outwards from a point centre which is dark due to the concentration of very fine crystals	Each fibre extinguishes as a unit	Coelenterates

These arrangements of crystals in skeletons may lose their characteristic fabric during diagenesis by neomorphic processes. The common end-products of neomorphism are:

1. Microcrystalline calcite (aragonite) crystals 1–10 μm

2. Sparry calcite (aragonite) crystals 10–500 μm

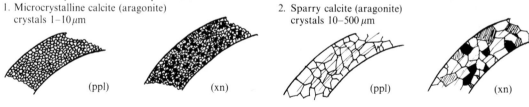

(ppl)   (xn)   (ppl)   (xn)

of foraminiferal test construction. Microgranular walls evolved during the Palaeozoic and may link the agglutinated and precipitated tests in foraminiferans. Microgranular walls have grains packed together (without obvious cements), giving this wall type its characteristic sugary appearance. There is usually more than one layer with the grains arranged in radial rows, giving a pseudofibrous effect with no crystallographic orientation. In thin section the wall is so dense as to appear almost opaque. Calcareous walls may be composed of either calcite or magnesian calcite (aragonite tests are confined to only two families) and they adopt either a *hyaline* texture (rotaliids), which has minute perforations in the wall, or a *porcellaneous* texture (miliolids), which has a smooth shiny appearance (Figures 4.2, 4.3). The hyaline types may be composed of a single Mg calcite crystal (spirilliniids), aragonite crystals (robertiniids) or many Mg calcite crystals (nodosariids). In nodasiriid tests, the calcite crystals may be oriented with their *c*-axes normal

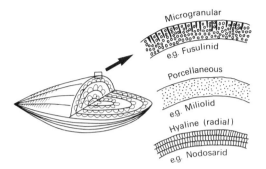

Figure 4.2 Varieties of wall structure of skeletal foraminiferans

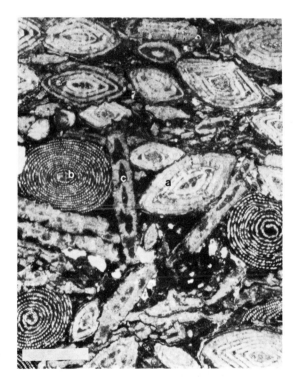

Figure 4.3 Thin section of hyaline (*a*, *Nummulites*; *c*, *Assilina*) and porcellaneous (*b*, *Alveolina*) foraminiferan skeletons. Ppl. Scale 5 mm. Eocene, Oman. Specimen courtesy of Andrew Racey

to the test surface (radial hyaline) or crystallites are randomly oriented (granular hyaline). In cross-section the hyaline wall shows organic layering and calcareous laminations. Lamellar tests are recognized by the thicker early chambers, thinner later chambers and single-thickness final chamber. In thin section, under polarized light, the radial types exhibit a diagnostic radial fibrous extinction. Porcellaneous tests have an outer surface which is smooth, shiny and white but, in thin section under plane polarized light they have a honey-brown tinge, and in cross-polars have low birefringence (Figure 4.3). The wall is made up of randomly oriented small crystallites orientated like parquet flooring in the outer layer, which give the shiny appearance. The aragonite forms (robertiniids) appear radial under crossed polars in thin section whereas the spirilliniids extinguish all as one crystal.

Foraminiferal tests may possess one or more chambers. Chambers may be arranged in a single row (uniserially); if it forms a curved row it is arcuate, if a straight series it is rectilinear. The spiral arrangement of chambers around an axis of coiling may be in a single plane (planispiral), may progress up to the axis of coiling (trochospiral), or may be in several planes of coiling (streptospiral). When a series of chambers is coiled, one complete revolution is termed a whorl. If two or three chambers, instead of one, are added in each whorl to a serial arrangement then the series is biserial or triserial.

Overall test shape is very plastic and uncoiling of coiled forms is a common feature within populations of the same species. Hyaline foraminiferans may be ornamented with ribs, ridges, furrows and spines whereas porcellaneous foraminiferans are usually ornamented with striae or ridges. Ornamentation can vary within a species with environment.

Occurrence. Modern benthonic and planktonic foraminiferans are found in surface sediments in many parts of the world's oceans. Benthonic forms are especially abundant in lagoonal, back-

Figure 4.4 Benthonic foraminiferans (*a, Alveolinella; b, Marginopora*). Scale 2 mm. Recent, 53 m depth, central region of the Great Barrier Reef, Australia

reef and shallow neritic settings (Figure 4.4), where their principal mode of life is loose on the sea-bed. Some forms attach to sea-grasses and algae and a few varieties (notably the red *Homotrema rubrum*) encrust rocky surfaces and are particularly common in cavities in reefs (Figure 4.5). Miliolids are the dominant forms in modern shallow carbonate environments. Life

span of an average individual is about one year, and living benthonic forms generally range in abundance from 1 to 100 individuals per m².

Temperature is the most important variable affecting the distribution of benthonic foraminiferans. Water depth is important both in governing the hydrostatic pressure on the animal and in limiting the amount of light that reaches the symbiotic algae (zooxanthellae) known to be associated with many foraminiferal species. The availability of food also naturally influences the distribution of benthonic and planktonic species.

In bottom sediments there is a transition between 200 and 400 m from dominantly benthonic to dominantly pelagic forms (Figure 4.6), i.e. at about the platform edge to upper slope position. Planktonic forms live in surface waters down to about 1000 m depth, though they are less abundant in coastal waters. They show greater diversity in lower latitudes. On death, planktonic foraminiferan tests rain down to the sea-bed, where they accumulate on the abyssal plain and may constitute 75 to 95% of the microfaunal remains. However, as the depth increases to the carbonate compensation depth (CCD, the depth at which all calcium carbonate is dissolved, e.g. approximately 4 500 m in the Eastern Pacific, see Chapter 8) dead foraminiferal tests are dissolved and the deep abyssal areas are covered by non-calcareous sediment.

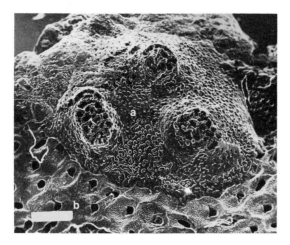

Figure 4.5 Foraminiferan *Homotrema rubrum* (*a*) (with three truncated projections on the test) encrusting bryozoan *Labioporella* (*b*). SEM scale 0.2 mm. Recent, 10 m depth, Barbados, W.I. Photo courtesy Bill Martindale

Figure 4.6 Globigerinid planktonic foraminiferans (*a*). SEM scale 100 μm. Recent 350 m depth, Rockall Bank, N. Atlantic

History. Lower Palaeozoic foraminiferal faunas consist mainly of agglutinated types and single-chambered genera. Devonian times saw the development of multi-chambered tests and new wall types. It was not till the Jurassic that foraminiferal evolution adapted to a planktonic mode of life. Many foraminiferal species have a great biostratigraphic significance; they are common in marine sediments and small enough for many to be found in a narrow core or one thin section, they have short geological ranges and a widespread distribution. The planktonic forms have great value in palaeoceanography: their distributions and susceptibility to cold water solution allow an interpretation of palaeodepth and their oxygen isotope ratios have been used to great effect to reconstruct palaeotemperatures.

Preservation. Although foraminiferal tests are chambered, the wall structure of most benthonic forms is compact and relatively resistant to breakage, so skeletons are commonly preserved whole (Figure 4.7). Under extreme hydraulic conditions the coiled structures often fracture or wear in such a way as to result in the loss of the outer chambers or whorl only. Planktonic foraminiferans generally have a much lower ratio of test wall thickness to chamber size than do benthonic forms, thus the planktonic structures fracture more readily under compressive stress. However, planktonic tests are normally deposited in deep-sea areas of low hydraulic energy where preservation potential is high, so they too are often found whole in sediments and rocks.

Most genera of both benthonic and planktonic skeletons consist of calcite. The former contain magnesium carbonate in the range 0–15 mol% $MgCO_3$, the latter 0–5 mol% $MgCO_3$. Thus the skeletal microarchitecture of both forms is normally preserved during freshwater diagenesis. The composition and structure of calcitic foraminiferal tests make this skeletal group one of the most resistant to neomorphic alteration. The aragonitic forms (robertiniids), however, are easily dissolved during diagenesis and are commonly represented in limestones only by moulds.

4.2 Calpionellida

Calpionellids are extinct pelagic protozoans having an axially symmetrical calcareous test that is bell- or vase-shaped, 5–20 μm in diameter (Figure 4.8). In thin section they appear U- or V-shaped, having a wall consisting of spirally arranged calcite prisms normal to the test surface. They have unknown affinities but have a similar morphology to the organic test of living tintinnids (to which some workers relate them). They occur in fine-grained, basinal, pelagic limestones of Jurassic and Cretaceous age, commonly rich in micro-planktonic tests such as those of radiolarians and coccoliths.

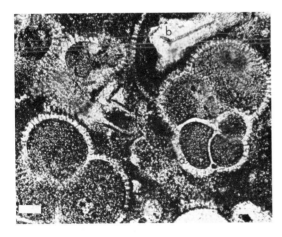

Figure 4.7 Thin section of pelagic limestone containing tests of globigerinid foraminiferans (*a*) and fragments of sponge spicules (*b*). Ppl. Scale 100 μm. Eocene, Cyprus

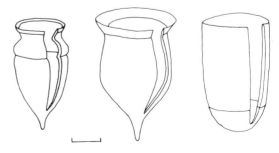

Figure 4.8 Calpionellid skeletal structure. Scale 10 μm

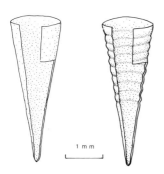

Figure 4.9 Cricoconarid skeletal structure

4.3 Cricoconarida

Cricoconarids (e.g. tentaculitids, nowakiids, styliolinids) are small, narrow, straight, ringed, gradually tapering cones found only in Palaeozoic sedimentary rocks. Cones are between 1 mm and 80 mm in length with a maximum diameter of about 6 mm (Figure 4.9). Rings occur and longitudinal ridges may be present. The shell wall is prismatic calcite and consists of concentric laminae which may be undulating. The juvenile portions of some members of the group are septate.

These shells are usually found lying parallel to the bedding in basinal limestones. Most are thought to have been pelagic, principally planktonic, though the thicker-shelled Tentaculitidae were probably nektobenthonic scavengers capable of living in agitated waters.

4.4 Mollusca

All classes of molluscs contain calcium-carbonate-secreting species. The geologically important classes are bivalves (pelecypods), gastropods, scaphopods, chitons and cephalopods.

Typical molluscan shells contain three or more layers. The outermost layer is usually chitinous periostracum, the inner layers are calcareous with 2–3% organic matrix. Seven types of microstructure have been recognized in molluscs (see examples in Table 4.2).

 (i) Nacreous (built of small aragonitic tablets)
(ii) Prismatic (simple striated prisms of calcite

or aragonite, and composite prisms of aragonite)
(iii) Homogeneous (very finely crystalline aragonite)
(iv) Foliated (fine sheets of regularly arranged calcite tablets grouped into larger lenticular units which are sub-parallel to the shell surface)
 (v) Crossed-lamellar (threefold structural hierarchy of aragonitic plates forming first-, second- and third-order lamels)
(vi) Complex crossed-lamellar (complicated arrangement of units of second-order lamels of aragonite)
(vii) Myostracal layers (aragonitic deposits beneath the muscle attachment area).

4.4.1 Bivalvia

The bivalved molluscs are one of the major benthonic carbonate producers in modern shallow marine sediments. The common size of shells is between 10 and 100 mm diameter.

Skeletal structure. The valves are hinged along a dentate margin and growth proceeds by secre-

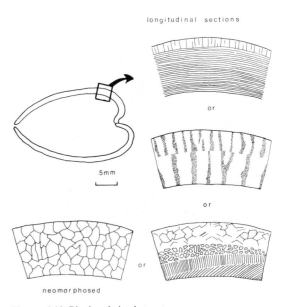

Figure. 4.10 Bivalve skeletal structure

tion of calcium carbonate at the outer interface of the mantle. Typical skeletal structures are shown in Figure 4.10. Most bivalve shells are aragonite (e.g. *Tridacna* and *Arca*) with nacreous and crossed-lamellar (Figure 4.11) internal structures being particularly common. Oysters (e.g. *Ostrea* and *Crassostrea*) are the only common group of calcitic (0–5 mol% MgCO$_3$) bivalves which have a foliated structure (Figure 4.12). In those shells with mixed mineralogies (e.g. *Mytilus* and *Pinna*), the outer layers (generally prismatic or foliated) are calcitic, the inner layers (generally nacreous or laminated) are aragonitic. Shells may show a periodicity in growth pattern.

Occurrence. Most bivalves are marine. They may be sessile on sediment (epifaunal), e.g. *Tridacna*; active-crawling e.g. *Venus*; buried deeply, e.g. *Ensis*, or shallowly, e.g. *Tellina*, within the sediment (infaunal); attached to rock (epilithic) by byssal threads e.g. *Mytilus*, or calcium carbonate cement e.g. *Spondylus*; entombed in limestone into which they have bored (endolithic) e.g. *Lithophaga*; or free-swimming, e.g. *Pecten*. They are found in abundance in all latitudes. Generally thicker-shelled varieties live in areas of higher water turbulence. Juveniles of several groups are planktonic and have thin shells which may accumulate in pelagic sediments.

History. Bivalves appeared in the middle Cambrian and, though subordinate to brachiopods in the Palaeozoic, they have become a significant contributor to limestones from the Jurassic onwards. The evolution of the unusual reef-building rudist bivalves reached a climax in the Cretaceous, but the group became extinct shortly afterwards. The number of species of bivalves is still increasing today.

Preservation. The dense structure of bivalves makes then relatively resistant to fragmentation, though the skeletons of some species with a high amount of organic matrix decay on death, by a process known as maceration, to discrete crystallites. Under turbulent conditions, shells may wear so that outer layers split off. Calcitic portions of shells are normally well preserved, retaining the microarchitecture of the skeleton on freshwater diagenesis, but aragonitic shells are altered. There are two common styles to this alteration: (1) the entire shell dissolves leaving a void which may later be filled with calcite spar precipitated from solution; (2) the conversion to calcite takes place by a poorly understood process in which the skeletal texture is retained, either with little visible change or with consider-

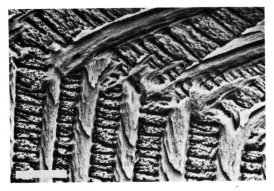

Figure 4.11 Molluscan cross-lamellar structure. SEM scale 20 μm.

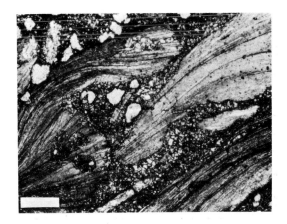

Figure 4.12 Foliated calcite structure of oyster shell fragments. Thin section. Ppl. Scale 500 μm. Middle Jurassic, Skye, Scotland. Photo courtesy of Julian Andrews

able change so that only a ghost of the original structure is seen. It is thought that this latter process takes place as an advancing front of dissolution–precipitation on a micro-scale. (Aragonite alteration to calcite is further discussed in section 9.3).

4.4.2 Gastropoda

Skeleton structure. Gastropods are univalves and their skeletons have an unpartitioned helical spiral structure (Figures 4.13, 4.14), at least in the young stages. The majority of gastropods are aragonitic; only a few genera are mixed aragonite and calcite, with calcite being the uppermost layer. Aragonite layers most commonly occur with nacreous and crossed-lamellar structures (Figure 4.13).

Occurrence. Gastropods are widespread in fresh and salt waters. On account of their salinity tolerance, monotypic gastropod skeletal are common in the record (e.g. *Viviparus*, *Paludina*). Like bivalves, marine gastropods tend to be smaller and thin-shelled in colder, deeper waters. Most gastropods are herbivores, and in their grazing of plant-covered sediment or limestone they may ingest large quantities of calcium carbonate which they excrete as faecal pellets. Some species burrow into loose sediment and others can bore into limestone. Some coiled forms (vermetid gastropods) are commonly encrusted in association with calcareous red algae on reefs and rocky coasts.

Pteropods belong to a subclass of gastropods. They are planktonic and have small thin homogeneous shells of aragonite. Shell shapes are normally conical (Figures 4.15, 4.16). These organisms are restricted to surface waters of tropical and subtropical deep seas. They are not

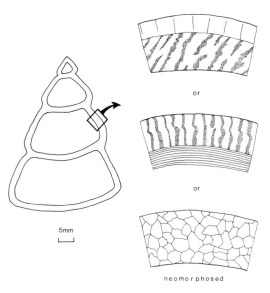

Figure 4.13 Gastropod skeletal structure

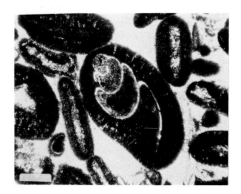

Figure 4.14 Thin section showing gastropod shell replaced by sparry calcite encased in an oolitic coat with radial fabric. Ppl. Scale 100 μm. Jurassic, Raasay, Scotland

Figure 4.15 Pteropod skeletons: *a, Cavolina*; *b, Creseis.* Scale 1 mm. Recent 240 m depth, central region of the Great Barrier Reef, Australia

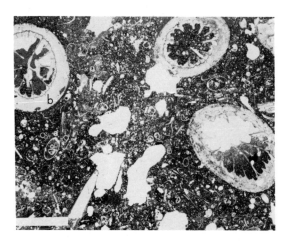

Figure 4.16 Thin section of pteropod tests (*a*) and *Lophelia* coral skeletons (*b*) in a micrite matrix. Large clear patches are holes in the limestone produced by boring sponges. Ppl. Scale 3 mm. Recent 700 m depth, Florida Straits

preserved in very deep waters on account of their relatively soluble aragonitic skeleton.

History. Gastropods evolved in the Ordovician and reached a peak in diversity in the Tertiary. Though recognized in many shallow marine limestones, they are rarely more than a minor constituent.

Preservation. The dense skeletal structure inhibits fragmentation, though excessive wear may leave only the thicker centre of the spiral (columella). The aragonitic skeletal structure is not normally preserved on freshwater diagenesis but is replaced by sparry calcite; they are recognized in thin section by their characteristic unchambered coiled shape.

4.4.3 Scaphopoda

Scaphopods have a tapered curved tubular shell, open at both ends, which is normally a few centimetres long and a few millimetres wide. The shell is aragonitic, built of crossed-lamellar structure with thin layers of myostracal prisms. They are found within sandy and muddy marine sediments from Silurian to Recent. Though they are quite abundant in some Mesozoic and Cenozoic clays, they do not form a significant component of limestones and are of little stratigraphic value.

4.4.4 Polyplacophora (*chitons*)

Chitons are primitive molluscs, usually having a segmented shell made of eight overlapping articulated plates, which may become reduced to a number of spicules situated in a leathery mantle. They possess a flat creeping foot and a mouth armed with a chitinous radula with which they scrape algae from mainly intertidal, rocky surfaces. Their shell is aragonitic, typically in four layers. Their range is from Ordovician to Recent. Their main geological significance is in their role as bioeroders of limestone coasts.

4.4.5 Cephalopoda

These marine molluscs have a foot modified to a ring of tentacles around the mouth. The univalve shell, where present, may be either internal or external and is normally aragonite. The shell is wholly chambered where external, and partially chambered where internal. Chambers are bounded by septal walls through which a siphuncle passes. The animals can float by filling chambers with gas, and their skeletons, which mainly range from 20–200 mm in maximum diameter are significant components of some Mesozoic pelagic limestones.

Nautiloid shells may be coiled, curved or straight, and have a three-layered structure. The siphuncle is in a central position for most members of the group and they all share a simple suturing pattern. They are nektonic, living in open seas from Cambrian to Recent, but are not numerically important in limestones after the Palaeozoic.

Ammonoids evolved from Palaeozoic cephalopods in the Silurian and died out in late Cretaceous times. They show an increase in complexity of the suture line and the siphuncle migrates to the outer margin of the shell. The shell is aragonite and has an outer, finely prismatic porcellaneous layer and an inner nacreous layer. The operculum (aptychus), which is the plate closing the aperture of the outer chamber, is calcitic.

Belemnoids have an internal skeleton consisting of a solid guard and a chambered phragmacone. They lived from late Carboniferous to early Tertiary, but are not common in limestones older than Triassic. The shells are preserved as calcite today, but it is thought that only the rostrum was originally calcite; the remainder may all originally have been aragonite.

4.5 Brachiopoda

Brachiopods are bivalved marine animals with a calcareous or chitinous shell usually less than 100 mm in diameter. Some forms have internal calcareous structures for the support of some internal organs. Primitive forms have no hinge structure (inarticulate) and their shell is normally calcium phosphate (a few are calcareous). Articulate forms have a hinge structure and normally possess a calcite (0–7 mol% $MgCO_3$) shell. Recent brachiopod shells have three layers—an outer chitinous layer (the periostracum), beneath

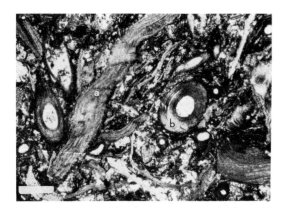

Figure 4.18 Thin section of brachiopod valve (*a*) and spine (*b*) fragments. Ppl. Scale 0.5 mm. Carboniferous, Edinburgh, Scotland

which is the primary layer made of fine fibres of calcite elongated perpendicularly to the shell surface and, under the primary layer, the secondary layer in which the long fibres lie at the low oblique angles to the inner surface of the primary layer. Internal calcareous extensions are constructed of the secondary layer. Some forms (endopunctate) have canals up to 100 μm wide which traverse the shell wall, other forms (impuncate) lack such structures, and a third group have pseudo-punctae which result from a rod-like pattern of foliation of the fibres in the secondary layer (Figure 4.17). Brachiopod spines are sometimes seen in thin sections of limestone; they are hollow and have long axes of the calcite fibres arranged concentrically (Figure 4.18).

Occurrence. Modern brachiopods live in seas of high and low latitudes at water depths down to about 400 m. They are fairly common cavity dwellers (coelobites) in shallow-water reefs. During the Palaeozoic they occupied a wide range of benthic environments, but most of these niches have subsequently been filled by bivalves. All brachiopods are attached to the sea-bed, some by a muscular stalk (pedicle) which passes through an aperture in the larger valve; others are

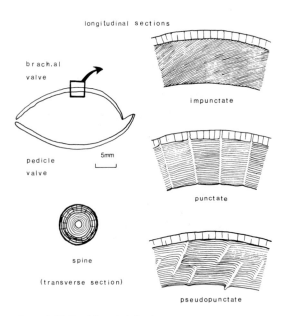

Figure 4.17 Brachiopod skeletal structure

cemented to the substratum or anchored by spines.

History. Articulate and inarticulate brachiopods range from lower Cambrian to Recent, though they decreased in numbers after the Mesozoic. Their diversity became severely restricted after the Permian, only Terebratulids and Rhynchonellids surviving in significant numbers.

Preservation. Brachiopod shells are normally well preserved. Valves are normally found articulated in rocks. Unlike bivalves, the valves have no ligament and rely on muscle movement for opening; thus they remain firmly closed on death, whereas the bivalves (unless buried in sediment) normally spring open. The low magnesian calcite skeleton undergoes relatively little observable structural change during freshwater diagenesis.

4.6 Echinodermata

Skeletal structure. There are five major living groups: echinoids (sea urchins), asteroids (starfish), ophiuroids (brittle stars), crinoids (sea lilies) and holothurians (sea cucumbers), and one extinct group, which includes the blastoids and cystoids, in the phylum Echinodermata. Echinoderms are exclusively marine and a common element of the benthonic fauna in tropical and temperate seas. The phylum is sometimes divided into two groups: one group, the Pelmatozoa, consists mainly of those forms fixed to the seabed, the other group, the Eleutherozoa, are free-living forms. Their calcareous remains (plates, spines and sclerites) are found in modern sediments from the intertidal zone to the deep sea but rarely constitute more than 10% of the carbonate fraction of modern sediments. Echinoderms had much greater quantitative significance in the past, especially the Palaeozoic era.

The skeleton is mesodermal and has two elements, the calcareous stereom and the organic stroma. In modern echinoderms the stereom is exceedingly porous (*c.* 50%, with pore diameter

c. 25 μm) with a reticulate structure composed of Mg calcite (5–15 mol% $MgCO_3$). Each plate, spine or sclerite behaves as a single crystal of calcite when viewed under the light microscope, giving unit extinction under crossed polars (Table 4.2). The optically uniform crystals are really masses of submicroscopic crystals with their *c*-axes almost perfectly aligned and the *a*-axes aligned to within only a few degrees.

Occurrence and history. The pelmatozoans (fixed forms), cystoids and blastoids are primitive echinoderms which have a calyx of irregular arranged plates and variable number of arms on a stem (columnal). They range from Cambrian to Carboniferous. The blastoids probably evolved from the cystoids and have a similar skeleton with a more regular arrangement of calyx plates, and commonly show pentameral symmetry. They range from Ordovician to Permian. The crinoids (feather stars and sea lilies), have a root-like structure, a stem (in fixed forms only) and a calyx

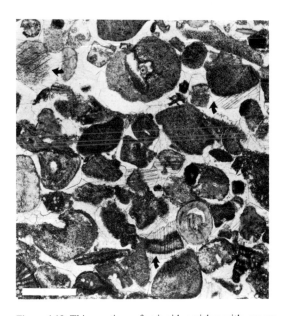

Figure 4.19 Thin section of crinoid ossicles with sparry cement overgrowths in optical continuity with the single calcite crystals. Note cleavage extends through grain and cement overgrowth. Ppl. Scale 2 mm. Silurian, Much Wenlock, England

bearing five pinnate arms. The whole skeleton is made of separate plates and ossicles. Stem plates form the columnal, which has an axial canal (lumen) and a peripheral radial pattern. Sessile crinoids were very common in shallow seas of the Palaeozoic era, and their plates are the dominant skeletal particles of many reefal limestones formed at that time (Figure 4.19). Some pelagic limestones of the Mesozoic contain specimens of planktonic crinoids. Modern crinoids are benthonic and most stalked forms are found in the deep sea; cirri-attached (cumatulid) varieties are found on rocky substrates in deep (see Figure 6.11) and shallow (coral reefs) seas.

Eleutherozoans are free-living forms. *Echinoids* (sea urchins) have a globular or disc-shaped test up to about 100 mm in diameter, covered with various kinds of spines. Modern echinoids live on and in sand, and on rock. Many ingest $CaCO_3$ while feeding on endolithic plants, and some are important limestone bioeroders. Some species excavate hollows in limestone in which they spend their entire lives. They are common (i) in exposed locations such as on rocky coasts and reefs, and (ii) in more sheltered settings such as in lagoons, and on shallow platforms, and present in variable numbers down to about 1000 m water depth. They are equally common in warm and cold seas and range from Ordovician to Recent. *Asteroids* (starfish) and *ophiuroids* (brittle stars) are star-shaped with a central (commonly disc-like) body surrounded by arms in multiples of five. Their skeletons have more prominent stroma and less $CaCO_3$ in their structure than other skeletal echinoderms. Asteroids are more abundant on sandy substrates, whereas ophiuroids prefer gravels and rocky substrates. Both may be found in densities up to several hundred per m². They range from lower Ordovician to Recent but are not major components of limestones.

The plates of *holothurians*, or sea cucumbers, are reduced to small ornamental sclerites, normally 0.25 to 0.5 mm in size, situated in a leathery integument. The sclerites are single crystals of

Figure 4.20 Holothurian sclerites. Scale 250 µm

calcite and may be hook-, needle-, anchor-, star-, or wheel-shaped (Figure 4.20). These structures may constitute a minor component of the fine fraction of carbonate sediments. Modern holothurians live chiefly on sandy substrates, where they gather food, either by filtering sea water or by ingesting large quantities of sediment from which they glean their food (see section 6.4.1).

Preservation. On death the organic matrix of echinoderms decays and individual plates, ossicles and spines disarticulate. These plates (normally 1–10 mm in size), though exceedingly porous, are fairly sturdy and are often found whole in limestones. The magnesian calcite alters to stable calcite on freshwater diagenesis without noticeable structural change (see section 9.3.2). During burial, calcite cement precipitates as syntaxial rims in optical continuity with the single calcite crystals of echinoderm plates such that twin lamellae and cleavage planes transgress skeletal plates and cement overgrowth (Figure 4.19). Under the petrological microscope the medium-grey reticulate structure of the single calcite crystals of echinoderm particles enables easy identification to phylum level, but prohibits the distinction between plates of different echinoderm groups.

4.7 Bryozoa

Skeletal structure. The phylum Bryozoa (Ectoprocta or Polyzoa) is a group of sessile colonial animals, almost all of which are attached to a substratum and live in the sea, although one class and a few other species occur in fresh water. The colonies (zoaria) vary from 1 mm to 1 m in diameter, but are most commonly a few centimetres across, and occur as encrusting sheets, plant-like tufts, fleshy lobes or erect branching calcareous structures. The individual members of a colony (zooids) have body walls (zooecia) which are horny, calcareous or gelatinous. The zooids are generally less than 0.5 mm in diameter and there may be just a few or up to millions in a colony. Colonies usually have a characteristic cellular arrangement of zooecia, and the thin calcareous walls have a granular, laminar, or foliated texture (Figure 4.21). In thin section, bryozoans can be distinguished by their cellular colonial structure with tubes and pores of various widths and parallel arrangements. The lamellar calcite crystals of the zooecia often have a foliated appearance. The diameter of their chambers is normally intermediate between those of corals (5–10 mm) and red calcareous algae (0.01 to 0.1 mm). Bryozoan skeletons in different orders demonstrate characteristic patterns of calcite crystal orientation and structure.

There are three classes: Stenolaemata and Gymnolaemata are exclusively marine, and Phylactolaemata are freshwater. Stenolaemata includes the orders Cyclostomata (Ordovician to Holocene), Trepostomata (Ordovician to Triassic) Cystoporata (Ordovician to Permian) and Cryptostomata (Ordovician to Permian). The Gymnolaemata comprise the orders Cteno-stomata (Ordovician to Holocene) and Cheilosto-mata (Upper Jurassic to Holocene). The Class Phyloctolaemata and the order Ctenostomata of the Gymnolaemata are poorly mineralized, containing more than 50% organic matter; the rest are calcareous. In the Stenolaemata the skeleton is composed of calcite only (less than 8 mol% $MgCO_3$). The crystals may appear as a granular layer without texture or laminar layers with lath-like crystals. Among the Gymnolaemata, the primitive members possess a skeleton of calcite only, whereas the more specialized cheilostomes may have a secondary thickening of aragonite.

The Cyclostomata consist of bundles of distally open calcareous tubes which may be unpart-itioned or have dividing calcareous diaphragms. The Trepostomata have more massive zooecia (Figure 4.22). Between larger zooecia, smaller modified zooecia occur. In branched colonies the zooecia in the axial zone are thin-walled and subparallel to the branch axis; they become thicker and bend normal to the axis where they meet the zoarium surface.

The Cystoporata have many pores with cysts between the larger zooecia.

Cryptostomata are commonly reticulate fronds with the zooecia opening on one side of the zoarium only (fenestellids) or may be cylindrical or ribbon-shaped. The zooecial tubes are short and thicken distally.

Cheilostomata usually form unilaminar encrustations, uni- or bilaminar foliose expansions

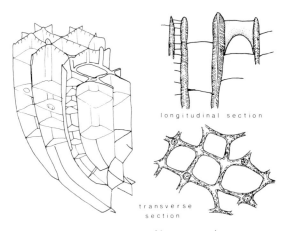

Figure 4.21 Skeletal structure of bryozoan colony

longitudinal section

transverse section

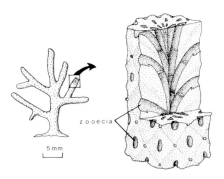

Figure 4.22 Trepostomata bryozoan skeletal structure

zooecia

5 mm

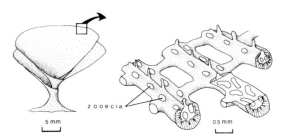

Figure 4.23 Cheilostomata bryozoan skeletal structure

(Figure 4.23) or branched stems. The zooecia are boxlike.

Occurrence. Bryozoans are sessile and their distributions are controlled by such factors as the nature of the substrate, water turbulence, rate of sedimentation, salinity and temperature. They are normally attached to a solid stable substrate; rock, pebbles, shells, or algal or sea-grass fronds. Their shapes reflect the local hydrodynamic energy—encrusting and massive colonies can cope with a high degree of turbulence, whereas the erect, foliose and branching forms usually live in quiet-water zones. Shapes may vary even within species to suit the local environment. Modern bryozoans are found in tropical and temperate seas on continental shelves. Their remains often constitute a few percent of reefal debris. In some temperate areas especially in the

Figure 4.24 Bryozoan-rich gravel (*a*, *Domopora*; *b*, *Porella*; *c*, *Sertella*). Scale 5 mm. Recent, 90 m depth, Rockall Bank, N. Atlantic

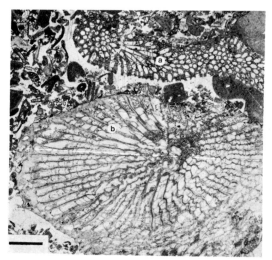

Figure 4.25 Trepostome bryozoan (*a*) and rugose coral (*b*) in thin section. Ppl. Scale 5 mm. Silurian, Much Wenlock, England

depth range 30–100 m they are the major component of the skeletal assemblage of the sediment (Figure 4.24).

History. Trepostomata were common in Ordovician and Silurian shallow-water and reefal deposits (Figure 4.25), and the Cryptostomata were abundant in some Carboniferous and Permian deposits, in places forming the framework of reefs.

Preservation. As is to be expected the massive calcareous forms resist breakage far better than the delicate lacy branching varieties with high organic content. Those forms that line the cavities of reefs may well be the first organic structures in the reef to suffer the effects of circulating porewaters during later diagenesis. Thus these particular encrusting skeletons may show evidence of corrosion. The calcite skeleton preserved retains the original microarchitecture, which commonly appears dark in transmitted light (perhaps due to fine crystal size or high organic content).

4.8 Cnidaria

Representatives of this group, which includes the hydroids, jellyfish, sea anemones and corals, are found on the sea-bed from the shore to abyssal depths, and also floating in the plankton. There are two forms in the phylum, a cylindrical polyp form which is usually attached to a solid substratum, and a medusa form, which is usually free-swimming. The subphylum Anthozoa occurs only as the polyp form, whereas the subphylum Medusozoa occurs as the medusa form or as both medusa and polyp form in the life cycle. The polyp form often has a skeleton secreted by its external surface or lying within the body wall. Polyps reproduce sexually producing a larva, which is often planktonic, and also reproduce asexually by budding from the parent polyp. Polyps are usually a few millimetres in diameter, but colonies may grow to a metre or more in size.

In many shallow-water corals, small single-celled plants (dinoflagellate algae—zooxanthellae) live in the body tissues. In this symbiotic relationship the zooxanthellae appear to help dispose of coral waste products and the corals use the carbohydrates and oxygen produced by the zooxanthellae to aid their own metabolism and promote calcification. Corals build skeletons quicker when aided by the symbiotic zooxanthellae; consequently we find that most reef-building corals are zooxanthellate.

Three classes of the cnidaria produce sufficient skeletal calcium carbonate to concern us here: the Hydrozoa (Medusozoa), the Alcyonaria and the Zoantharia (Anthozoa).

Hydrozoa. In two families, Milleporidae and Stylasteridae, the polyps are in pits in the surface of a large calcareous skeleton. Milleporid corals are zooxanthellate and live in the shallow tropical waters where they are particularly common on reefs. Their aragonitic colonies have a variety of growth forms, from sprawling encrusting masses to erect platy or boxwork branches, usually oriented at right angles to the waves and currents. The stylasterinids are azooxanthellate and live over a relatively great range of water depths and latitude. They occur in caves and under ledges on reefs, often oriented at right angles to currents. They have a delicate arborescent skeleton which is aragonitic in waters warmer than 3 °C and partially or totally calcitic (*c.* 4 mol % MgCO$_3$) in colder waters.

Alcyonaria (= *Octocorallia*). Six orders of Alcyonaria have skeletal elements which may contribute to calcareous sediments: Coenothecalia, Stolonifera, Telestacea, Pennatalacea, Alcyonacea and Gorgonacea. *Heliopora*, the sole living member of the order Coenothecalia (Cretaceous to Holocene) is the only octocoral to produce a stony skeleton. Other octocorals contain numerous loose calcitic spicules or 'sclerites' which help support the soft mass. However, in the order Stolonifera (Cretaceous to Holocene) the calcareous species, e.g. *Tubipora* (the common red 'organ-pipe' Indo-Pacific coral), have sclerites, which are fused into a hard skeleton. The Telestacea (Holocene) have numerous sclerites which may be free, partially or completely fused to form rigid tubes. Pennatulaceans (sea pens) (Cretaceous to Holocene) are the only octocorals commonly growing on soft sediment. They produce sclerites shaped like smooth rods or bars, or plates and discs.

The Alcyonacea (soft corals) (Lower Jurassic to Holocene) have calcitic sclerites supporting their fleshy masses. Deep-water forms are more erect having a greater density of sclerites. The base of the colony is commonly richer in sclerites as they sink through the soft tissue with time. The Gorgonacea (horny corals) (Cretaceous to Holocene) includes the sea fans and sea whips which have a plant-like growth form with a main stem firmly attached to a hard substrate. The stem is strengthened by horny material (gorgonin) and may contain calcitic sclerites. Alcyonacean and gorgonian sclerites have monaxial shapes with protruding warts and spines (Figure 4.26). They are commonly 100 to 500 microns in length and tens of microns in diameter, and can be white, colourless, pink or purple. Octocoral sclerites are magnesian calcite with about eight

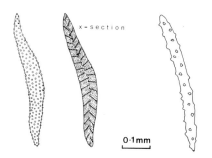

Figure 4.26 Alcyonarian sclerites

mol % MgCO$_3$, though deep-water octocorals contain less magnesium than do shallow-water species. The calcium carbonate at the base of colonies can contain varying proportions of aragonite.

Zoantharia (= *Hexacorallia*). This class includes four calcareous orders, the Scleractinia (Triassic to Holocene), the Heterocorallia (only two genera, Devonian to Carboniferous), the Rugosa (Ordovician to Permian) and Tabulata (Ordovician to Permian).

The Scleractinia (stony hexacorals), our only modern representatives of this class, are solitary or colonial forms possessing hard aragonitic skeletons which lie outside the polyp body. It is this group which predominates on modern coral reefs. The Scleractinia have five skeletal elements, the basal plate (attachment), the septa (vertical radial plates), the epitheca (corallite outer wall), tabulae (horizontal partitions) and the dissepiments (curved plates).

The skeleton is continually formed by the bases of the polyp. Each polyp is housed in a corallite which has six, or a multiple of six, septa radiating inwards from the wall. In several shallow-water species the density of the skeletal structure varies in bands, clearly revealed in x-radiographs (Figure 4.27). These bands have been shown to be seasonal (similar to tree-rings) and may owe their origin to seasonal changes in light, temperature, siltation, nutrients or sexual activity. The aragonitic fibres of the skeleton are

Figure 4.27 X-radiograph of a slice of the coral *Montastrea annularis* revealing seasonal density banding. Fourteen annual bands are apparent. Clear patches at the margins are holes made by boring sponges (1, *Siphonodictyon*; 2, *Cliona*). Scale 10 mm. Recent, 3 m depth, Barbados, W.I

united as radiating sclerites (called fascicles or sclerodermites), in linear series into trabeculae (Figure 4.28), or into laminar sheets of needles. In transmitted light the sclerodermites have dark centres of calcification (Figure 4.29).

The Rugosa were, we believe, calcitic (Figure 4.25). They show a range of forms from simple solitary to complex colonial. Each corallite has septa inserted during development in sets or multiples of four. The calcitic fibres in the septae are in trabeculae (Figure 4.28) but in

Rugose coral

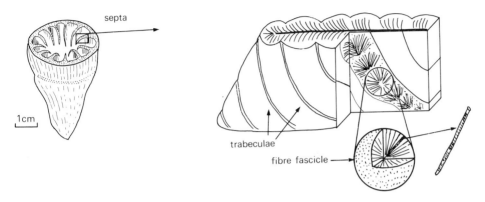

Figure 4.28 Coral skeletal structure showing the arrangement of fibres into trabeculae. After Majewske (1969)

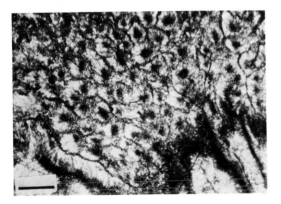

Figure 4.29 Thin section showing fibre fascicles in *Oculina* coral. Ppl. Scale 100 μm. Recent, 20 m depth, Bermuda

Figure 4.30 Luxuriant growth of *Acropora* corals. Scale 10 cm. 3 m depth, Lizard Island, Great Barrier Reef, Australia

the tabulae and dissepiments they lie parallel to each other and normal to the surface.

The Tabulata are believed to be simple colonial corals which have calcareous transverse plates (tabulae) within individual corallites. The corallites may be separate from one another or united in various ways to give the characteristic morphologies of the different genera. The Tabulata have a calcitic fibrous microarchitecture which is similar to that of the Rugosa.

Occurrence. We associate modern corals (Scleractinia) with shallow tropical seas, where they grow together with other organisms into reefs which may build up into the surf (Figure 4.30). Most reef-building corals are colonial and show a variety of growth forms—massive, encrusting, domes, platy branches, shingle-like branches, rod-like branches, according to phylogeny and physical setting. Deep-water scleractinian corals do occur down to 1000 m water depth and at very

Figure 4.31 Thicket of *Lophelia* (azooxanthellate) corals. Scale 10 cm. 260 m depth, Rockall Bank, N. Atlantic

high latitudes. These corals include solitary and colonial types and do not possess zooxanthellae. They are often spindly branched and grow in thickets tens of metres in diameter having one or two metres relief on the sea bed (Figure 4.31).

Scleractinians built reefs in Mesozoic and Cainozoic times. Rugose and tabulate corals were important reef-builders mainly during the Ordovician and Silurian periods.

Alcyonaceans live in abundance today in tropical waters (particularly in back-reef environments in the Indo-Pacific), but a few species also occur in temperate and polar regions. Gorgonaceans are cosmopolitan, but are most abundant in warm shallow seas, particularly on rocky substrates below wave base.

Preservation. Sclerites of soft corals are often preserved whole in the finer fractions of carbonate sediments. When subjected to physical wear their protuberances become smooth. Stony corals break according to the nature of the skeletal structure (e.g. branches) and the style of erosion (see section 6.4). Cobble and boulder-sized coral rubble is common in fore-reef and back-reef talus. Individual branches may break down further into subrounded sand-sized pieces

whose shape and size is governed by the sclero-dermite form. Aragonitic coral skeletons are normally dissolved during freshwater diagenesis. The mould of the corallite is often later filled by sparry calcite (see section 9.3.1). Rugose and tabulate corals usually retain the general fibrous texture of their calcitic structure.

4.9 Porifera

Porifera (sponges) are simple, many-celled, colonial animals which live attached to the substrate in marine and (rarely) freshwater environments. The body is a perforated structure supported by siliceous or calcareous spicules or horny fibres, and consists of a single cavity with a major exhalent opening (osculum) and many small inhalent openings. Sponges reproduce sexually, giving free-swimming larvae, and are capable of regenerating themselves from broken fragments.

The phylum Porifera is usually split into two groups, i.e. those with siliceous spicules (including the Demospongia and the Hexactinellida) and those with calcareous spicules or skeletons (the Calcarea and the Sclerospongia). Siliceous sponges are the more common variety in modern seas and though siliceous skeletons do not build limestones, siliceous sponge spicules are perhaps the most common non-carbonate components of limestones, and further, the siliceous sponges are an important group of limestone-eroding organisms, so some mention will be give to them here.

Spicules, or sclerites, occur in two sizes (Figure 4.32). Megascleres, 3 to 30 μm in diame-

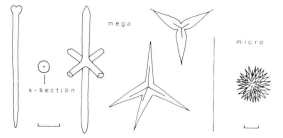

Figure 4.32 Sponge spicules. Scale (left) 100 μm; (right) 25 μm

ter and 100 to 500 μm in length, occur isolated or fused together to form a loose skeletal framework; microscleres, 1 μm in diameter and 10 to 100 μm in length, are exclusively embedded in soft tissue. Megascleres are commonly smooth, monaxial, triradial and quadriradial with a central canal. Microscleres may have similar shapes, but more complex hook, anchor and stellate forms are common.

The remains of siliceous sponges, Demospongia and Hexactinellida, are present in rocks from Cambrian to Holocene. They have occupied a range of niches throughout their histories but are most common in quiet-water pelagic deposits that accumulated in basins, on lower reef slopes or deep shelves. They are also commonly associated with mud mounds in the Carboniferous and Jurassic.

Modern Demospongia live on hard bottoms in areas of moderate currents. An important family is the Clionidae, which bore into limestones by chemical dissolution, producing characteristically shaped calcareous chips 20 to 100 μm in diameter (see Figure 6.5). These sponges play a major role in the destruction of limestone coasts, reefs, corals and shells (see section 6.4.1). The Hexactinellida (glass sponges) abound today on the deep ocean floor (500–1000 m) and are particularly common in the Antarctic.

Those sponges containing calcareous spicules

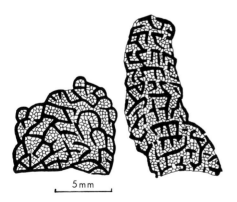

└─ 5 mm ─┘

Figure 4.33 Segmented calcareous chambers of sphinctozoan sponges

(class Calcarea) have chiefly megascleres (monaxons, triradials and quadriradials), composed of Mg calcite.

Fossil calcisponges do not appear to have had a spicular skeleton. The Inozoa and Sphinctozoa, calcisponges, were important calcareous sponges of the past. The non-segmented Inozoan calcisponges are cylindrical, branched, spherical or irregular and commonly occur in limestones from Permian to Cretaceous. The Sphinctozoan calcisponges are segmented with chambers arranged serially, with or without a central cavity or in irregular clusters (Figure 4.33). The Sphinctozoans commonly built and encrusted the framework of reefs from Permian to Jurassic times.

The Sclerospongia (coralline sponges) have massive aragonitic skeletons with siliceous spicules and organic fibres. In the Ceratoporellida, the aragonite crystals are arranged in a radiating column-like microstructure in which the rod-shaped spiny siliceous spicules are embedded. The order Tabulospongida has a skeleton of calcite crystals arranged in a layered microstructure. The rod- or star-shaped spicules of this group are not embedded in the calcareous skeleton.

Sclerosponges have recently been found in abundance on living Caribbean and Pacific reefs. In the shallow zone they are cryptic, occurring deeper within crevices beneath the reef surface in shallower water, but below about 80 m water depth they can occur in sufficient size and numbers on the reef face to contribute significantly to the basal portions of the primary framework.

There is good evidence that the sclerosponges are the living representatives of the extinct group, the stromatoporoids. Some workers also believe that the fossil tabulate corals were related to sponges.

Preservation. Sponge spicules are commonly preserved whole in pelagic deposits. The siliceous forms are originally opaline ($SiO_2 n H_2O$) but on diagenesis readily change to crystalline silica and are commonly replaced by calcite in limestones. Dissolved siliceous spicules may be an important source of silica in the early diagenetic formation of nodular chert.

Calcisponges are often well preserved in reef frameworks; little is known of their rates of growth or contribution to sediments.

Stromatoporoidea. The taxonomic position of this group was uncertain for some time but they are now regularly placed in the Sclerospongia class of the Porifera. The stromatoporoids have no spicules, however. The colonies, which are usually tens of centimetres in size, have an irregular layered form, usually forming thin flat sheets, discs or domes, but can also be cylindrical and branching (Figure 4.34). They could modify their shape according to the environment in which they lived, so that some forms can be used as palaeocurrent indicators. The surface may have small swellings (mamelous) and characteristic stellate grooves (astrorhizae). Internally they consist of horizontal plates (laminae) separated by vertical rod-like elements (pillars) (Figure 4.35), though commonly the differentiated structure is lost and only a reticulate pattern of anastomosing elements remains. Some forms have upwardly, convexly curved overlapping plates called cysts. There may also be tabulae making partitions between chambers. The skeletal microstructure of the Lower Palaeozoic stromatoporoids was apparently highly porous and displayed a variety of textures including compact, fibrous, flocculent, striated, cellular, microreticulate. The original composition was probably aragonitic and many of the microstructures we see today relate to neomorphic fabrics.

Mesozoic stromatoporoids have a two-layered structure: a central fine, dark, granular layer and a fibrous layer.

Palaeozoic stromatoporoids were important reef-building colonies in the Ordovician, Silurian and Devonian and lived in agitated shallow warm seas. But the Jurassic and Cretaceous

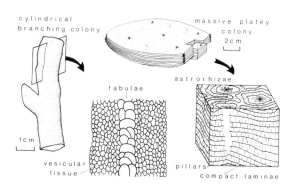

Figure 4.34 Stromatoporoid skeletal structure

Figure 4.35 Thin section of *Labechia* stromatoporoid. Ppl. Scale 1 mm. Silurian, Much Wenlock, England

forms were more adapted to life in muddy environments

4.10 Archaeocyathida

Animals of this phylum lived only during the Lower and Middle Cambrian. They have a biological affinity with the Porifera and lived attached to the sea bottom, filter-feeding water pumped through their skeletons. They can be solitary or colonial and their skeleton has a cup- or vase-like shape 10 to 100 mm in maximum dimensions. The skeleton has porous inner and outer walls joined by vertical septae (parieties). The walls consist of a very fine granular mosaic of calcite crystals 0.02 mm diameter. Some archaeocyathids have accessory structures: radial rods, perforate flat plates (tabulae) and imperforate arched plates (dissepiments).

These organisms are often found in growth position attached to one another and commonly associated with algae. They are thought to have been the earliest reef-building organism, living in shallow, warm agitated sea water.

4.11 Ascidiacea

Some families within the primitive chordate group of Ascidians (tunicates) contain carbonate spicules which give structural support to the otherwise fleshy body. Some spicules are simple rods, others are stellate (see Figure 6.5) and disc-shaped. They are aragonitic in composition and range in diameter from 20 to 300 microns. Ascidians are solitary or colonial benthic organisms that are common in shelf seas. Their spicules can be a common component of the finer fractions of low-energy carbonate deposits.

4.12 Crustacea

The Crustacea are arthropods which have bilaterally symmetrical segmented bodies with hard outer skeletons (exoskeleton), made of chitin (a complex organic compound allied to cellulose or cuticle), calcium phosphate and calcite, and jointed appendages for movement and for feeding. The group includes the Decapoda (crabs, shrimps, lobster), Cirripedia (barnacles) and Ostracoda. The extinct trilobites (Cambrian to Permian) are related, and may represent a subphylum. The bulk of the crustaceans are marine. The mobile bottom dwellers are mainly scavengers, feeding on all kinds of vegetable and animal matter; sessile forms (e.g. barnacles) filter feed; tiny pelagic forms are the main link in the food chain between diatoms, on which they feed, and larger animals. Crustaceans periodically moult their hard outer skeletons to allow the soft parts to increase in size.

Decapoda. The carapaces and appendages of some crabs, shrimps and lobsters can supply carbonate to the sediment, though decapod fragments are rare in limestones. The outer shell is chitinous, and the inner shell is a calcified layer (magnesian calcite) sandwiched between chitin layers. The decapods occur over a wide range of depths and latitude, living in the water column and on and in sediments and rocks. Some play an important role in the breakdown of large shells and in the bioturbation and biological sorting of the sediment (see Chapter 6).

Cirripedia. Barnacles are an entirely marine group, most of which attach to solid substrates by a cement-like secretion. They have many curved appendages, which are borne by body segments, used to convey food to the mouth. Barnacles range in size from a few millimetres to a few centimetres. The carapace which encloses the body and limbs is usually strengthened with calcareous plates (Figures 4.36, 4.37). An outer circle of compartmental plates (usually 6 to 8) surround a series of inner opercular plates. The plates are composed of calcite, though the basal disc may be aragonitic. Internally, the plates normally have prominent parallel longitudinal canals (Figure 4.36). The microstructure may be granular or laminated.

Barnacles are cosmopolitan, but are especially abundant in shallow temperature seas on rocky, high-energy coasts. As they may densely populate intertidal and subtidal rocks and undergo

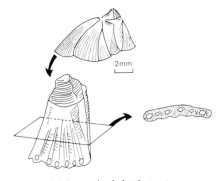

Figure 4.36 Barnacle skeletal structure

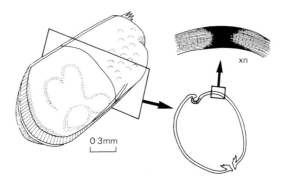

Figure 4.38 Ostracod skeletal structure

Figure 4.37 Worn barnacle plates. Scale 2 mm. Recent, 25 m depth, Malin Shelf, Scotland

moulting of their calcareous plates during a relatively short lifespan (of about one year), they can produce significant quantities of carbonate (locally more than 50% of the skeletal fraction) of inshore sediments.

Some tropical barnacles are endolithic: they either bore into carbonate substrates or else attach to a living calcareous colony (e.g. coral) and grow at the same pace as the host around them.

Though fossil cirripedes are found in rocks from Ordovician onwards, they are a major component only in Cainozoic (cold-water) limestones.

Ostracoda. Ostracods are minute bivalved crustaceans which live in both fresh and marine waters. The hinged valves overlap along the free margin and completely enclose the body and appendages. The shell (0.5 mm to 4 mm in length) is commonly ovate or reniform and is usually ornamented with a variety of punctae, reticulations, nodes, ridges, grooves, spines and swellings (Figure 4.38). Each valve has two parts, an outer calcareous wall (outer lamella) and an inwardly projecting calcareous and chitinous wall around the free margin (inner lamella or duplicature). This recurved edge of the shells (and valve overlap) plus the absence of growth lines help to distinguish ostracods from other

small bivalves in thin section. Most ostracod shells are composed of two or more layers, which may be penetrated by numerous canals. The prismatic microstructure consists of fine crystals of Mg calcite ($1-5 \, mol \% \, MgCO_3$) which show undulose extinction under crossed polars in the microscope. In plane polarized light, thin sections of ostracods (Figure 4.39) have a honey-coloured sheen due to the chitin admixture.

Modern forms live chiefly in the uppermost few centimetres of fine-grained sediments on shallow sea-beds, though some forms are pelagic.

Ostracods have existed since the Ordovician period, and their valves are normally found in fine-grained limestones (and shales) which may be pelagic, lagoonal or freshwater in origin.

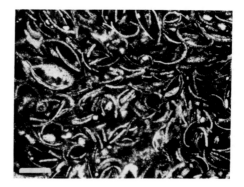

Figure 4.39 Thin section of ostracod valves in micrite. Ppl. Scale 0.3 μm. Upper Jurassic, Dorset, England

Trilobita. Trilobites are extinct marine arthropods characterized by a segmented skeleton that has three longitudinal lobes: an axial and two lateral portions. It is differentiated (Figure 4.40) into a head shield (cephalon), a series of up to about forty body segments (thorax) and a tail shield (pygidium). The shield and segments are commonly recurved inwards at their margins which gives fragments a characteristic hook shape when seen in cross-section (Figure 4.41). The skeleton was composed of chitin, calcium phosphate and calcite (probably low in magnesium). The cuticle, normally less than 1 mm thick, consists of poorly defined layers or laminae roughly parallel to the cuticle margin.

The layers are made of fine calcite prisms perpendicular to the surface. Straight or coiled tubular canals may traverse the skeleton. Trilobite fragments usually appear bright in thin section, have a smooth outline, and display an undulose extinction (Figure 4.41).

Trilobites lived from early Cambrian to Permian times, chiefly on the floor of shallow seas, where they probably scavenged food.

4.13 Annelida

Annelida are segmented worms including earthworms, leeches and many types of marine worms. The class Polychaeta are marine worms which contain the only calcified forms of worms—the families Serpulidae and Spirorbidae. These two families are benthic and most adopt an encrusting habit. Their exoskeleton consists of a calcareous tube which is planispiral in the genus *Spirorbis* and normally straight or sinuous in serpulids (Figure 4.42). In transverse section the tubes show concentric, sub-parallel, laminations. Serpulid skeletons can be composed of calcite (normally 6–16 mol% $MgCO_3$), aragonite or mixtures of both minerals.

Serpulids live in a range of marine environ-

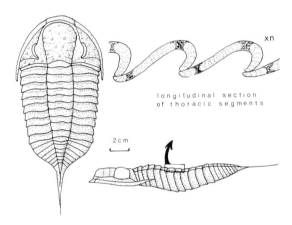

Figure 4.40 Trilobite skeletal structure

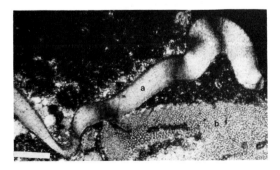

Figure 4.41 Thin section of trilobite fragment (*a*) and crinoid ossicle (*b*) in micrite. Xn. Scale 0.5 mm. Silurian, Much Wenlock, England

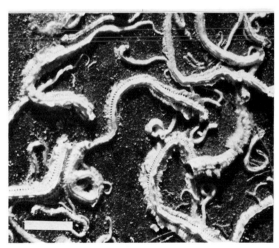

Figure 4.42 Encrusting serpulid worm tubes. Scale 10 mm. Recent, 25 m, Jamaica

ments from coastal waters to shelf edge, though they invariably are associated with firm substrates—rocky outcrops, boulders or shells. Their presence attached to grains commonly indicates a break in sedimentation. They normally form a minor component of the secondary framework of modern coral reefs, but in certain restricted environments (normally extreme salinities) they can be the primary frame-builders of small reefs.

Other polychaete worms include the sabellarians that can agglutinate sand grains into rigid or flexible tubes. Masses of these tubes may bind the sediment into small mounds.

Some types of polychaetes, notably members of the order Eunicida, secrete a parchment-like tube in which to live. Where these worms live in close association with corals (e.g. *Eunice florida* and coral *Lophelia pertusa*) the coral precipitates aragonite around the tube and thus the worm and coral together build a rigid framework.

Though worms do not provide significant quantities of skeletal calcium carbonate to the sediments, they do have other important sedimentological roles; some bring about a mixing of the sediments by their burrowing activities and others facilitate the disintegration of limestones by their boring into calcareous substrates.

4.14 Calcareous algae

Algae are aquatic plants that manufacture their own food using photosynthetic energy, and lack the vascular tissues characteristic of the higher plants. The plant body or entire algal colony is known as the thallus. Only about 10% of the thousands of species of marine benthonic algae are calcified. Most non-marine calcareous algae belong to one group, the Charophyta.

Calcium carbonate in the forms of aragonite or calcite (not both together) is precipitated either intracellularly by metabolic processes or at the cell surface during CO_2 extraction from water during photosynthesis.

Calcareous algae are separated by sedimentologists into two groups: those that can precipi-

Table 4.3 Subdivision of the major groups of calcareous algae. After Wray, in Haq and Boersma (1978).

Phylum Cyanophyta (= Cyanobacteria) blue-green algae
    (Precambrian to Holocene)
Phylum Rhodophyta—red algae
  Family Corallinaceae
    Subfamily Melobesioideae (crustose corallines) (Mid-Jurassic to Holocene)
    Subfamily Corallinoideae (articulated corallines) (Late Cretaceous to Holocene)
    Subfamily uncertain (ancestral corallines) (Carboniferous to Permian)
  Family Squamariaceae (?Carboniferous to Holocene)
  Family Solenoporaceae (Cambrian to Miocene)
  Family Gymnocodiaceae (Permian to Cretaceous)
Phylum Chlorophyta—green algae
  Family Codiaceae (Ordovician to Holocene)
  Family Dasycladaceae (Cambrian to Holocene)
Phylum Charophyta
  Family Characeae (Silurian to Holocene)
Phylum Chrysophyta
  Class Coccolithophyceae (Jurassic to Holocene)
Groups of uncertain affinities—phylloid algae, calcispheres, Tubiphytes.

tate calcium carbonate within, between and upon their tissues, the skeletal variety, and those sticky filamentous or coccoid algae (which may or may not promote extracellular $CaCO_3$ precipitation) that trap and bind fine sediment into laminated calcareous structures called *stromatolites*. Modern algae have characteristic pigmentation that provided a guide to primary classification. The groups of important limestone-building algae are shown in Table 4.3.

4.14.1 Cyanophyta

These plants (considered to be bacteria by an increasing number of authors) are microscopic

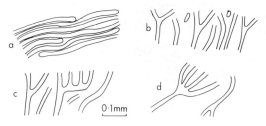

Figure 4.43 Tubiform structure of calcareous filamentous Cyanophyta. *a, Girvanella; b, Ortonella; c, Garwoodia; d, Hedstroemia*

and consist of filaments or unicells (coccoids) that live within a sticky mucilaginous sheath. Only a few forms produce a biochemically precipitated skeleton, and this is usually tubiform— e.g. *Girvanella, Ortonella, Cayeuxia, Hedströemia* (Figures 4.43, 4.44). The true affinities of these types are not well established, some may be blue-green algae, others green algae. However, here they are all placed in one group of the Cyanophyta, the *Porostromata*.

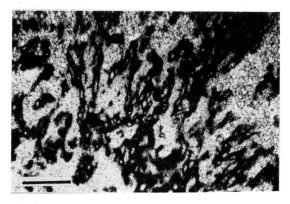

Figure 4.44 Thin section of *Cayeuxia*, calcareous filamentous cyanophyta. Ppl. Scale 0.5 mm. Jurassic, Skye, Scotland

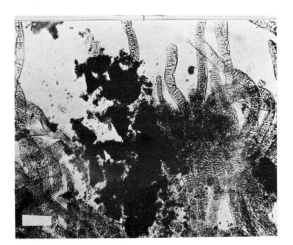

Figure 4.45 Filaments of *Lyngbya* (blue-green alga) binding carbonate grains (opaque). Scale 20 μm. Recent, Abaco, Bahamas

Those microscopic filamentous algae that do not grow a normal skeleton but generate organic films on the sediment surface which can mechanically agglutinate fine sediment grains (Figure 4.45) are placed in the group *Spongiostromata*. This surface film of filaments is known as an algal mat (see Section 6.6.3). Rhythmic variations in algal filament growth, with relation to sedimentation, produces a laminated structure (laminites) of alternate light sediment-rich laminae and dark organic-rich laminae. If the laminae are flat-lying they are referred to as *algal laminated sediments*, but if these laminated biosedimentary structures have vertical relief they are called *stromotolites*. Algal bound sediments with a homogeneous clotted or digitate fabric are termed *thrombolites*. The carbonate grains in stromatolites may originate by the mechanical trapping and binding of detrital sedimentary particles or by the blue-green algal precipitation of carbonate or by both processes. Modern stromatolites appear to precipitate calcium carbonate in only freshwater environments, though some pre-Cainozoic stromatolites precipitated lime in marine waters also. Oncolites (or oncoids) are defined as unattached stromatolites and usually have a spheroidal structure of concentric laminations around a nucleus (Figure 4.46). Oncolites and stromato-

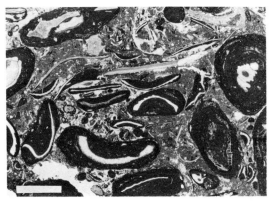

Figure 4.46 Thin section of oncolites in a micrite matrix. Ppl. Scale 5 mm. Jurassic, Gloucester, England

lites can incorporate identifiable skeletal calcareous algae as well as encrusting foraminiferans,
serpulids, and bryozoans.

Stromatolites are common today in supratidal
and intertidal tropical carbonate environments;
they are only rarely found in shallow subtidal
settings.

Modern subtidal algal mats tend to be dynamic structures. They trap, and grow over,
sediment, but are broken down by a vast range of
micro-infauna which depends on the mat for
sustenance and habitation. Laminated structures
develop best where sediment supply is incre-
mental, lithification is rapid, and infauna is
sparse.

Though modern stromatolites are all found in
very shallow water, sedimentological evidence
from the enclosing rocks indicates that they
occupied a far wider spectrum of ecological
niches in the geological past, particularly in
Precambrian times. It may be that the early
marine forms built more by calcification than by
sediment trapping on soft filaments, so they had
a greater preservation potential than modern
marine forms; or, the change in abundance of
marine stromatolites from the Precambrian to
the Phanerozoic could relate to predation pressure. Modern filamentous algae are an important
source of food for bottom-feeding invertebrates
and vertebrates such as gastropods and fish;
consequently stromatolites are best developed
today in those inter- and supratidal environments hostile to such predators. However, in the
Precambrian no such predators existed, so the
stromatolitic algae could colonize the full range
of marine environments within the photic zone.
Some authors conjecture that growth of some
stromatolitic fabrics was independent of bathy-
metry and light, since such structures have been
found *in situ* in limestones of deep-water settings.

The detailed microstructure of stromatolites
depends upon the assemblage of algal species
present (e.g. *Schizothrix calcicola*, *Scytonema
crustaceus*, although there may be many species
in one algal mat). The gross morphology appears

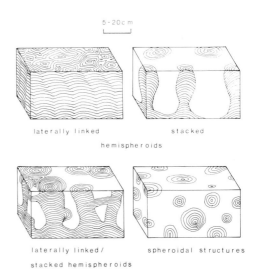

5-20cm

laterally linked   stacked
hemispheroids

laterally linked/   spheroidal structures
stacked hemispheroids

Figure 4.47 Growth forms of stromatolites

to relate to environmental factors such as sediment supply, water depth, current speed and
frequency of exposure. The geometry of the
forms is the common way of subdividing these
non-skeletal calcareous algae. They may be
domical, columnar, polygonal, branching or
digitate. Three main growth forms are recognized (Figure 4.47):

1. Laterally linked hemispheroids which con-
    tain horizontally continuous layers, most
    common in supratidal and intertidal
    environments
2. Vertically stacked hemispheroids in which
    laminae between domes are not connected,
    restricted to protected arid areas with high
    tidal range
3. Spheroidal structures (= oncolites), found
    in agitated waters.

Most stromatolites have vertical dimensions of
some centimetres (though some Precambrian
forms are metres in size) with a single lamina
about 0.5 to 1 mm thick.

4.14.2 Rhodophyta

The calcareous red algae (rhodophyta) usually precipitate calcium carbonate within and between cell wells so that the details of the tissue and reproductive organs are preserved. Four families are recognized in the fossil record.

Family Corallinaceae. The cellular tissue of this family can usually be divided into (i) the *hyperthallus*, the basal or central part of the thallus with cells which are arranged parallel to the substrate and which are larger than in peripheral areas; (ii) the *perithallus*, the cell layers over and around the hyperthallus, generally consisting of

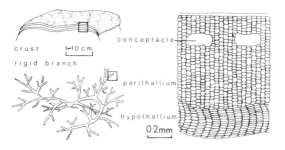

Figure 4.48 Skeletal structure of crustose coralline (melobesioid) algae. After Wray, in Haq and Boersma (1978)

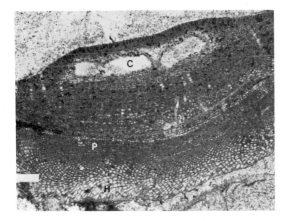

Figure 4.49 Thin section of encrusting red alga *Neogoniolithon*. The radial section shows coaxial hypothallus (*H*) overlain by dense perithallus (*P*) which has large oval conceptacles (*C*) near the surface. Ppl. Scale 0.2 mm. Recent, 2 m depth, Barbados. Photo courtesy Bill Martindale

tiny cells oriented perpendicularly to the substrate (Figures 4.48, 4.49). *Spores* (specialized cells which are released from the parent plant and are capable of producing a new adult individual) are contained in the perithallus in isolated *sporangia* or in cavities called *conceptacles* (Figures 4.48, 4.49).

The cell walls are built of two layers in which minute fibres (tenths of microns in length) of magnesian calcite crystals ($8–30 \, mol\% \, MgCO_3$) are arranged at right angles to each other. The corallines are clearly recognized in thin section (Figure 4.49) by their rectangular cellular structure, with individual cells about $5 \, \mu m$ in diameter, and their moderately dense brownish colour in plane light (and lack of notable birefringence due to the small size of the component crystals). The skeletons are prone to early diagenesis. The cellular framework and conceptacles readily fill with cement crystals precipitated from sea water. The whole skeleton can lose its cellular structure on neomorphism and be transformed into a uniform dark cryptocrystalline (micrite) mass.

The subdivision of the corallinaceae is still debated, since many of the subgroups distinguished in living forms cannot be recognized in fossil material. A practical subdivision separates two groups on gross morphology: the crustose corallines (subfamily, Melobesioideae), and the articulated corallines (subfamily Corallinoideae).

The crustose corallines show a variety of growth forms: laminated crusts, bulbous irregular masses, rigid branching habits and nodules. The crusts, which may be several millimetres in thickness and several centimetres in diameter, are firmly attached to rock substrates but some rigid branching forms and nodules are free-living on the sea-bed. Crustose coralline algae are important binding and cementing agents on reefs, where they are commonly a significant component of the framework (see section 7.2.2). Some forms (especially *Porolithon, Goniolithon* and *Lithothamnium*) are the major components of various geomorphological

Figure 4.50 Algal ridge, low water, windward margin of Suwarrow Atoll, Cook Islands, Pacific

Figure 4.51 Intertidal red algal terrace (arrowed). Scale 1 m. North coast, Jamaica

constructions in the intertidal zone of tropical and subtropical seas, where they may grow in an intimate association with other encrusting organisms, especially vermetid gastropods. They form the *algal ridges* (Figure 4.50) in the surf zone on the windward margins of modern coral reefs, the intertidal terraces ('Trottoir' zone) on rock headlands (Figure 4.51) and the cup or boiler reefs (Figure 4.52) on the exposed margins of some subtropical carbonate platforms.

Free-living crustose corallines may be branched in two or three dimensions, generally living in monospecific assemblages, termed *maerl* (Figures 4.53, 4.54), for example *Phymatolithon calcareum* or *Lithothamnium corallioides*, or may be nodular termed *rhodoliths* (Figures 4.55, 4.56), e.g. *Lithophyllum* and *Goniolithon* living associated with other corallines or encrusting foraminiferans and ver-

Figure 4.52 Algal cup reefs. Scale 300 mm. South coast, Bermuda

Figure 4.53 Megaripple of free-living branching calcareous red algae, *Phymatolithon calcareum* (Maerl). See Figure 4.54 for close-up. 5 m depth, Iona, west coast, Scotland

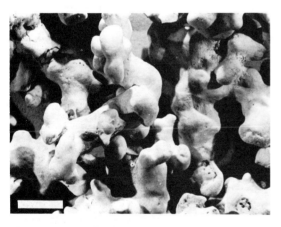

Figure 4.54 Branching calcareous red algae, *Phymatolithon calcareum*. Scale 2 mm. Recent, 5 m depth, Iona Sound, west coast, Scotland

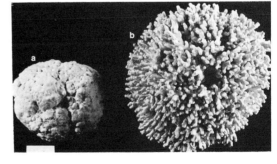

Figure 4.55 Branching rhodoliths, *Lithophyllum* exposed at low water. Scale 10 cm. Muri Lagoon, Rarotonga, Cook Islands, Pacific

metid gastropods. The radial internal structure of these unattached forms indicates an all-round peripheral growth for which periodic movement is essential. Rhodoliths may be compact laminar, columnar, globular or open branching (Figure 4.56). The growth form seems to depend both on specific composition and environmental factors. Different species are found in shallow and deep, warm and cold waters, usually in areas of strong currents but low wave action, where terrigenous input is low.

Figure 4.56 Massive, *Porolithon* (*a*) and branching *Lithophyllum* (*b*) rhodoliths. Scale 10 mm. Recent, intertidal, Muri Lagoon, Rarotonga, Cook Islands, Pacific

Encrusting algal sediments and algal limestones are common on the outer edge and upper
slope of some continental shelves; they are also
found on the crests of several deep-water sea-
mounts. Most of these are not living today, but
are relicts of earlier Quaternary times when sea-
level was lower.

The articulated corallines, represented in modern seas by three common genera *Amphiroa*,
Corallina and *Jania*, consist of articulate branches with calcareous portions separated by un-
calcified joints or nodes (Figure 4.57). These
forms are more delicate than the crustose
varieties; they live in sheltered settings and
readily disintegrate into sand-sized rod-shaped
sedimentary particles (Figure 4.58).

The true systematic position of the 'ancestral

corallines' is not yet established. These late
Palaeozoic red algae are divisible into cellular
(e.g. *Archaeolithophyllum*) and fibrous forms
(e.g. *Ungolarella*).

Family Squamariaceae. Living representatives of
this family are found in shallow, warm tropical
seas, usually on rocky substrates. The important
genus is *Peyssonelia*, which has a polygonal
cellular structure in which aragonite is laid down
in concentric layers of radially arranged acicular
crystals. Calcification may also be extracellular,
below the thallus as a hypobasal layer of small
aragonite botryoids. The squamariaceans may
be relatives of an important fossil group of
calcareous algae with leaflike or platy external
morphology, the '*phylloid algae*' (Figure 4.59).

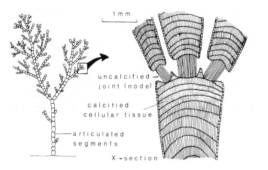

Figure 4.57 Skeletal structure of articulated coralline algae.
After Wray, in Haq and Boersma (1978)

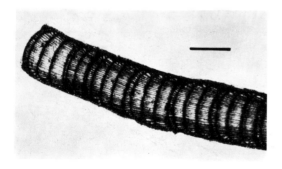

Figure 4.58 Thin section of branch of articulated coralline
alga, *Corallina*. Ppl. Scale 1 mm. Recent, 3 m depth,
Barbados

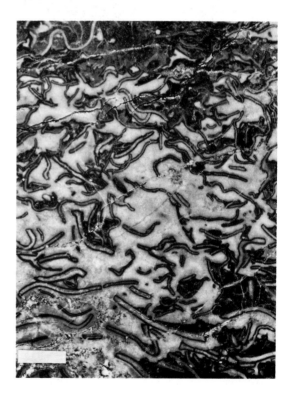

Figure 4.59 Polished slab of limestone composed of phylloid
algal plates in a sparry calcite matrix. Scale 20 mm. Permian,
N. Canada. Specimen courtesy of Graham Davies

Figure 4.60 *Solenopora* algae (*a*) encrusting oysters and bryozoans. Coin 25 mm diam. Upper Jurassic, Dorset, England

Family Solenoporaceae. The Solenoporaceae are extinct and differ from the Corallinaceae in having larger cells which are commonly polygonal rather than rectangular in transverse section. Also, the differentiation into hyperthallus and perithallus is not apparent. They show a development of horizontal layers or cross-partitions within vertical threads of cells, and though the internal structure is grossly different in scale, it can resemble that of some tabulate corals. The Solenoporaceae occur as encrusting, rounded nodular masses a few millimetres to a few centimetres in size (Figure 4.60). Discrete sediment particles and reef framework constructions of Solenoporaceae are found in Palaeozoic and Mesozoic limestones.

Family Gymnocodiaceae. Members of this extinct family have hollow segmented thalli with thin perforated walls. The segments may be cylindrical, oval, conical, spherical, barrel- or rod-shaped.

4.14.3 Chlorophyta
There are two carbonate-secreting families of marine green algae, the Codiaceae and the Dasycladaceae; both have aragonitic skeletons.

Family Codiaceae. Most forms in the Codiaceae are erect plants (a few centimetres high) generally

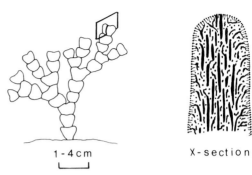

1-4cm   X-section

Figure 4.61 Codiacean algal skeletal structure. After Wray, in Haq and Boersma (1978)

segmented and branching, with an internal structure of a network of tubular filaments (Figure 4.61). The calcification begins at the surface of the thallus and progresses inwards, so young portions of plants are less calcified than older portions. When a living segment is broken open, the calcified portion appears like a rind enclosing a stringy organic-rich interior.

Modern members of the Codiaceae include *Halimeda*, *Penicillus*, *Rhipocephalus* and *Udotea*, which are all common lime-secreting algae in the tropics (see Figure 5.3). They form minute needles of aragonite (5 μm long, 0.3 μm diam) in the thalli (Figure 4.62), which, on death and disintegration of the skeleton, may disperse in the sediment and be unrecognizable as algal in

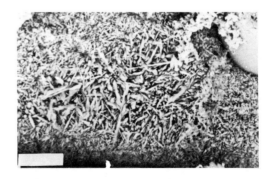

Figure 4.62 Loosely bound aragonite needles within a *Halimeda* segment. SEM scale 20 μm. Recent. 3 m depth, Davies Reef, Great Barrier Reef, Australia. Photograph courtesy of Sandy Tudhope

origin. These algal aragonite needles are a potential source of lime mud (see Section 5.2). *Halimeda* consists of disjunct calcified segments of fused aragonite needles (smaller than other codiacean needles). Whole segments have a characteristic morphology which can be lobed, disc-shaped, or cylindrical, and an external surface covered with minute pits, the utricles. They have a distinctive internal structure which is usually brown and dense in thin section (Figure 4.63): the segments consist of a central core of medullary filaments and surrounding cortex of lateral branches. On death *Halimeda* segments separate from one another, but though they may break into fragments they do not disintegrate down to the primary building units (the needles of aragonite) as readily as do other modern members of the Codiaceae, but remain as distinct sedimentary fragments.

The Codiaceae are abundant in lagoonal, back-reef environments, where they attach with a holdfast of root-like filaments to the sediment. Several species of *Halimeda* prefer to attach to rock substrates. They are common on reefs and fore-reefs and may live down to 100 m depth. Their segments are a major component of the talus of many Cainozoic reefs, though, being aragonitic, their internal structure is normally quickly lost on diagenesis.

The nodular or encrusting forms with internal branching tubular filaments e.g. *Ortonella* and *Hedstroemia*, here placed in the Cyanophyta, are placed in the Codiaceae by some authors.

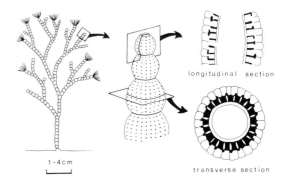

Figure 4.64 Dasycladacean algal skeletal structure. After Wray, in Haq and Boersma (1978)

Family Dasycladaceae. The calcareous Dasycladaceae are erect, segmented branching plants usually several centimetres high. Most forms have a large central stem surrounded by tufts of radiating branches. The primary branches bear tufts of secondary branches which in turn bear tertiary branches (Figure 4.64). On preservation they appear as hollow perforated cylinders, spheres or discs (Figure 4.64). Sporangia are developed adjacent to the stem. The cell walls are enclosed in precipitated aragonite, so on decay of the soft tissue a mould of the original plant remains.

4.14.4 Charophyta

This group lives in freshwater. The plant has tufts of branches from a central stem and may be

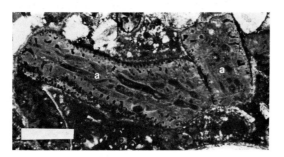

Figure 4.63 Thin section of *Halimeda* plates (*a*). Ppl. Scale 1 mm. Miocene, Mangaia, Cook Islands, Pacific

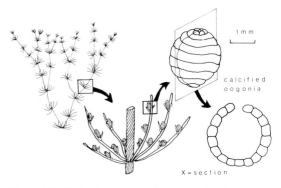

Figure 4.65 Skeletal structure of charophytic algae. After Wray, in Haq and Boersma (1978)

several centimetres tall. Only the reproductive organs (*gyrogonites* or *oogonia*) are calcified. These calcareous structures are spherical or elliptical, about 1 mm in diameter, and are composed of spirally arranged tubes which appear as ridges on the exterior (Figure 4.65). Their walls are made of radial-fibrous calcite.

4.14.5 *Chrysophyta*

Family Coccolithophyceae. These algae are minute, single-celled forms that live in the surface waters of the oceans. They have a skeleton that consists of crudely circular shields (2–20 μm diameter) of calcite crystals packed around their single cell. Post-mortem disintegration of the whole coccosphere usually dislodges and scatters the constituent shields on to the sea-bed. Each shield or *coccolith* is made of tiny platy crystals between 0.25 μm and 1 μm in diameter and composed of calcite with less than 1 mol% $MgCO_3$. These crystals commonly have flattened rhomb form, and are stacked in an imbricate fashion which gives a spiral pattern to the coccolith (Figures 4.66, 4.70).

Coccoliths are placed in the broad group *calcareous nanoplankton*. There are other members of this group which are probably unrelated to the Coccolithophyceae, the most common of which are the discoasterids. These have disc- or star-shaped microskeletons in which each ray is a single calcite crystal, and flourished in the Tertiary period.

Coccolithophorids are abundant (commonly as many as half a million individuals per litre of water) in the photic zone (0–150 m) of modern oceans. Populations are denser in the cold waters of high latitudes, or at the sites of upwelling of deep nutrient-rich water, but coccolith-rich sediments are generally restricted to low latitudes. The very small calcite particles of the skeletons dissolve as they sink below the carbonate compensation depth. Coccoliths are seen (usually only with the aid of an electron microscope) in fine-grained basinal limestones. They are the main constituents (see Figure 14.64) of the Cretaceous chalk in Western Europe, which is thought to have been deposited at depths of 100 to 300 m.

4.14.6 *'Phylloid' algae*

The name phylloid refers to the leaf-like shapes of the members of this Late Palaeozoic group (Figure 4.59) which, according to some authors, are related to the Squamariaceae, according to others to the Corallinaceae or Codiaceae. An extinct genus common in Upper Carboniferous and Permian limestones is *Archeolithophyllum*, whose internal structure of hypothallus, perithallus and conceptacles is similar to that of the modern crustose coralline *Lithophyllum*. Some phylloid algae, e.g. *Ivanovia*, are especially poorly preserved in limestones, which could indicate an original aragonitic composition like the modern Squamariaceae.

4.14.7 *Calcispheres*

Hollow spheres with thin, rarely layered, calcitic walls with radial pores are common components of many fine-grained limestones of the Palaeozoic

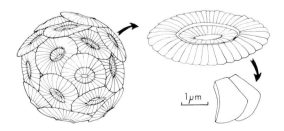

Figure 4.66 Skeletal structure of coccolithophorids

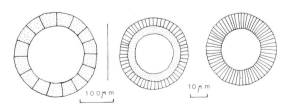

Figure 4.67 Sections of calcispheres

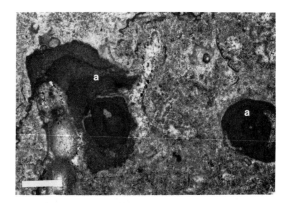

Figure 4.68 Thin section of *Tubiphytes* (*a*). Ppl. Scale 2 mm. Permian, W. Texas, USA

and Mesozoic eras (Figure 4.67). Their true affinities are not established, but they are probably derived from planktonic algae, though they are much larger than coccolithophorids, being from 30 μm to 300 μm in diameter. It has been suggested that they are reproductive bodies of green algae.

4.14.8 Tubiphytes

These skeletons, present from Lower Carboniferous to Upper Jurassic, are particularly common in Permian and Triassic reefs. They have an encrusting habit and a lobed or rounded outline. In thin section they have a fine dense tubular meshlike structure which occurs in encrusting lobes having dark micritic boundaries (Figure 4.68). They are probably algal, although the absence of filamentous tubes suggest they may not be members of the phylum Cyanophyta. Some workers consider them to be hydrozoans.

4.15 Non-calcareous skeletal groups

It is appropriate to give a brief mention of the non-calcareous skeletal organisms. Their remains may be present in carbonate sediments and limestones, or the deposits in which they are the major skeletal component may occur closely associated with limestones.

4.15.1 Porifera

As described earlier, the Demospongia and Hexactinellida classes of sponges have siliceous spicules. In Demospongia the spicules, which are fundamentally four-rayed, are scattered throughout the body. In the Hexactinellida the spicules are six-rayed and commonly fused into a framework.

4.15.2 Radiolaria

Radiolaria are marine planktonic protozoa in which a central capsule and surrounding spicules consist of opaline silica. In well-preserved material the silica substance is clear, transparent and isotropic with a glassy appearance in transmitted light. The skeleton typically consists of a network of siliceous bars and spines which form an inner medullary shell and an outer cortical shell (Figures 4.69, 4.70). They range from 100 μm to 300 μm in diameter. Radiolaria are only rarely preserved in pelagic limestones, since the chemical environment is too alkaline. Where present in significant numbers in limestone environments, they may contribute silica to the formation of chert nodules. Tests usually accumulate in siliceous oozes (particularly in low latitudes) which lithify to a chert called radiolarite. Where

Figure 4.69 Actinommid radiolarian skeleton. SEM. Scale 30 μm. Recent, 280 m depth, Rockall Bank, N. Atlantic

Figure 4.70 Coccoliths filling the chambers of radiolarian test of Figure 4.69. SEM scale 3 μm. Recent, 280 m depth, Rockall Bank, N. Atlantic

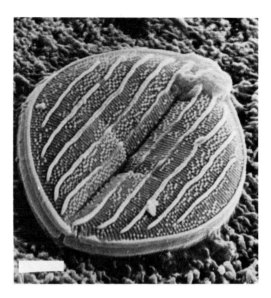

Figure 4.71 Diatom test resting on *Penicillus* (codiacean alga) skeleton. SEM, scale 5μm. Recent, 3 m depth, Bimini, Bahamas

radiolarian cherts overlie pelagic limestones, it is indicative of a lowering of the sea-bed relative to sea-level (for example near a mid-ocean ridge), below the carbonate compensation depth.

4.15.3 Diatoms

Diatoms are aquatic, microscopic, single-celled algae. Some are planktonic, others benthonic and some live in freshwater environments. They secrete an external shell made of opaline silica. The shell has two valves; one (the hypotheca) fits into the other (the epitheca) rather like a cylindrical box (Figure 4.71). The cell wall (which may have pores or striations) can be either a single layer of silica, or a more complex double silica wall separated by vertical silica slats.

The distribution of diatoms in the sea relates to the nature and supply of nutrients, particularly phosphorus, nitrate and silica. An area of upwelling in the ocean will bring a constant supply of these nutrients to the surface and cause productivity blooms. Coastal regions which receive high concentrations of nutrients from the nearby land will also support large diatom populations.

Diatoms are an important basic link in the food chain both for open ocean organisms and for benthonic organisms feeding on organic matter in the surface sediments. There are some types of benthonic diatoms that secrete thick mucilaginous sheaths. Dense populations of such types create a sticky organic film or mat on the sea-bed, to which sediment grains adhere, throughout even turbulent water conditions.

Diatomaceous oozes are prevalent in high latitudes. These deposits form *diatomites* which, when unlithified, form white, earthy, friable, fissile, porous layers, but on lithification become dense, hard cherts.

4.15.4 Conodonts

Conodonts are minute blade- or tooth-shaped fossils from 0.2 to 6 mm in size and of uncertain affinities, though recent studies suggest that they may have been part of the jaw mechanism of primitive fish. Though not volumetrically important, they are widespread in limestones from Cambrian to Triassic in age. They are normally brown or opaque and consist of lamellae containing very small crystals of calcium phosphate set in an organic matrix.

4.15.5 Vertebrata

Vertebrate remains such as bone fragments, teeth and fish scales are rare in marine sediments, but may be locally concentrated, commonly along with molluscan fragments, in nearshore carbonates. Coral reef islands may have a veneer of phosphatized carbonate (see Figure 11.8) brought about by the chemical action of rain water draining through guano (accumulations of bird droppings), and these deposits may contain recognizable skeletal remains of fish. Vertebrate remains are composed of calcium phosphate in the form of collophane which is colourless, amber or brown in thin section under plane light, and bluish-black with undulose extinction under crossed nicols. Fragments of bone have irregular shapes and a vesicular internal structure formed by dense, fibrous or structureless calcium phosphate enclosing irregular hollow cavities.

Otoliths, small disc-shaped pieces of aragonite formed in fish ears, are the only form of skeletal calcium carbonate precipitated by vertebrates. They are a very rare component of deep-sea carbonate sediments.

Selected reading

Carbonate grains and their identification

Adams, A.E., Mackenzie, W.S. and Guilford, C. (1984) *Atlas of Sedimentary Rocks Under the Microscope*. Longman, Harlow.

Bathurst, R.G.C. (1975) *Carbonate Sediments and their Diagenesis*. Elsevier, Amsterdam.

Fisher, A.G., Honjo, S. and Garrison, R.E. (1967) Electron micrographs of limestones and their nanofossils. *Monogr. Geol. Paleont. 1.*

Flügel, E. (1982) *Microfacies Analysis of Limestones.* Springer Verlag, Berlin.

Haq, B.U. and Boersma, A. (eds.) (1978) *Introduction to Marine Micropalaeontology*. Elsevier North-Holland Inc., New York.

Horowitz, A.S. and Potter, P.E. (1971) *Introductory Petrography of Fossils*. Springer Verlag, Berlin.

Majewske, O.P. (1969) *Recognition of Invertebrate Fossil Fragments in Rocks and Thin Sections*. E.J. Brill, Leiden.

Milliman, J.D. (1974) *Marine Carbonates*. Springer Verlag, Berlin.

Scholle, P.A. (1978) *A colour illustrated guide to carbonate rock constituents, textures, cements and porosities*. Am. Ass. Petrol. Geol. Mem. 27.

Wilkinson, B. (1979) See p. 7.

Calcareous animals and their identification

Boardman, R.S., Cheetham, A.H. and Oliver, W.A. (eds.) (1973) *Animal Colonies:Development and Function Through Time*. Dowden, Hutchinson and Ross, Stroudsburg.

George, D. and George, J. (1979) *Marine Life: an Illustrated Encyclopedia of Invertebrates in the Sea*. Douglas & McIntyre, Vancouver.

Calcareous plants and stromatolites

Adey, W.H. and Macintyre, I.G. (1973) Crustose coralline algae: a re-evaluation in the geological sciences. *Geol. Soc. Am. Bull.* **84**, 883–904.

Flügel, E. (ed.) (1977) *Fossil Algae. Recent Results and developments*. Springer Verlag, Berlin.

Ginsburg, R.N., Rezak, R. and Wray, J.C. (1972) Geology of calcareous algae (Notes for a short course). *Sedimenta* **1**. (Univ. Miami).

Hofmann, H.J. (1973) Stromatolites: characteristics and utility. *Earth Sci. Rev.* **9**, 339–373.

Johnson, I.H. (1961) *Limestone Building Algae and Algal Limestones*. Quart. Colorado School of Mines.

Logan, B.W., Rezak, R. and Ginsburg, R.N. (1964) Classification and environmental significance of stromatolites. *J. Geol.* **72**, 68–83.

Monty, C. (ed.) (1981) *Phanerozoic Stromatolites: Case Studies*. Springer Verlag, Berlin.

Walter, M.R. (ed.) (1976) *Stromatolites*. Elsevier, Amsterdam.

Wray, J.C. (1977) *Calcareous Algae*. Elsevier, Amsterdam.

5. Non-skeletal grains

5.1 Carbonate lithoclasts

Carbonate lithoclasts may be fragments of limestone eroded from a nearby cliff and deposited with the contemporary sediments; these are called *extraclasts*. They are derived from outside the basin of deposition. They may contain anachronistic skeletal remains and also diagenetic fabrics that are not commensurate with those of the host rock. Other carbonate lithoclasts may be derived from within the basin of deposition;

these are *intraclasts*. They may be well-cemented, as would be pieces of beachrock or hardground, or they may be only semi-consolidated, as may be expected of pieces of an algal stromatolite. Intraclasts contain grains that are contemporary with those of the host rock, and any diagenetic fabrics present in the intraclast that are not present in the host rock should only be those likely to form in the depositional environment.

Extraclasts are not common in limestones. Rivers do not normally carry limestone fragments from land to sea as they do with other terrigenous rock fragments; they carry the carbonates in solution. Carbonate boulders in fluvial deposits are found only in arid regions where flash floods have rapidly eroded and dumped the clasts. Fragments broken off exposed limestone cliffs are normally not transported far.

Intraclasts, in contrast, are quite common in limestones (Figure 2.3*C*). Marine lithification (or merely the agglutination) of carbonate sediments is a widespread phenomenon, and where forces of erosion are also prevalent, e.g. reef front, tidal channel, or beach, then intraclasts can be generated.

Intraclasts are not always easy to recognize in thin section, since once the whole rock is cemented they may blend in with the surrounding grains. One would expect to find evidence of truncation of grains within the aggregates, or of sedimentary structures such as laminations. Intraclasts of microcrystalline carbonate are often well-rounded and show signs of peripheral cracking, though rounded homogeneous fine-grained carbonate grains may have a variety of origins.

Some aggregates of grains, or lumps, may not show signs of truncation at their borders. These aggregates were presumably only weakly lithified at the time of erosion, when they must have broken from the parent substrate by a sort of crumbly fracture. *Grapestones* presumably formed this way. Grapestones (Figure 5.1) are aggregates of grains (skeletal fragments, ooids or pellets, etc.) that resemble in external shape microscopic bunches of grapes. The grains are

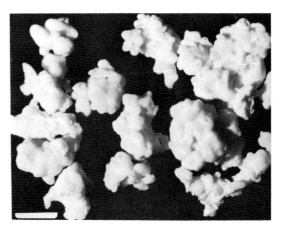

Figure 5.1 Grapestones. Scale 1 mm. Recent, Cockroach Cay, Bahamas

commonly highly micritized (see section 8.3.5) and are incipiently cemented together by fine-grained aragonite. These types of grains are abundant today in the sheltered shallow-water zones of the Bahama Banks and Persian Gulf. They are not common in other carbonate provinces of the world and are not very common in limestones. The origin of grapestone is not well understood. The accepted view is that they form when the constituent grains are stabilized for a period of time, perhaps within an algal mat on the sea-bed, so that thin, laterally impersistent and incipiently cemented crusts develop, which may periodically break by bioturbation or storms to produce grapestone aggregates. Grapestone constituent grains may be relict and have formed at an earlier level of the sea to that prevailing during aggregation.

5.2 Carbonate mud

Carbonate muds (grain size $< 63\,\mu m$ (4ϕ)) are very common in many sheltered shallow-water tropical settings such as lagoons in the lee of islands or reefs. They also occur in some deep-sea oozes. The grains are usually too small to identify with the light microscope. Using the better resolution of an electron microscope, it may be possible to recognize the characteristic morphologies or internal structure of very small whole skeletons, e.g. coccoliths and sclerites, or the fine eroded fragments of grains, e.g. sponge chips and comminuted skeletons. If we simulate mechanical erosion by agitating skeletal grains in a tumble mill we note that after some time the grains wear and break down to mud-sized particles whose sizes and shapes vary according to the micro-architecture of the parent grains.

It is much harder to understand the origin of the single crystal aragonite needles, 1–10 μm in length, 0.5 μm in width, that form the bulk of the clay-size fraction over thousands of square kilometres on the shallow central parts of the Bahama Banks, e.g. to the west (lee) of Andros Island on Great Bahama Bank (see Figure 14.28) and in the Bight of Abaco on Little Bahama Bank, and in the back reef and bay environments of the Florida shelf (see Figure 14.20), and in the sheltered inshore waters of the Trucial Coast of the Persian Gulf (see Figure 8.14). In terms of size and shape alone, these needles are similar both to those produced in the laboratory by inorganic experiments, and to those that result from the natural disintegration on death of calcareous green algae, *Penicillus*, *Halimeda*, *Udotea* and *Rhipocephalus* (Figures 4.62, 5.3). However, similarity of size

Figure 5.3 *Halimeda* (*a*), *Penicillus* (*b*) and *Udotea* (*c*). Scale 10 mm. Recent, 4 m depth, Bermuda

and shape may be insufficient to prove a causal relationship. We have to use mineralogical, chemical and CaCO$_3$ budget studies of each specific area to elucidate the origin of these needles. For example, codiacean algae produce only 25–40% needles, the rest being subrounded nanograins, whereas many lime-mud deposits are 90% needles. Also, aragonite in codiacean algae has a Sr/Mg ratio of 2, whereas lime muds commonly have a ratio of 4.

Lime mud accumulation has been studied extensively in several tropical areas.

Bahama Banks (see Figure 14.28). To the west (lee) of Andros Island, the broad central portion of the Great Bahama bank is shallow, 1–5 m, and the ocean water has a long residence time (normally 100 to 200 days, though a major storm may replenish the bank water in one day). A salinity gradient develops with high values (42‰) in the bank centre where residence time is longest, and relatively low values (37‰) at the bank margins where mixing with normal oceanic waters occurs. Seawater analyses reveal CaCO$_3$ supersaturation everywhere, but from bank margin to centre the ion activity product $a\mathrm{Ca}^{2+} \cdot a\mathrm{CO}_3^{2-}$ first increases and then falls steadily. These measurements represent CaCO$_3$ precipitation at bank margin at rates estimated at 0.8 kg/m^2/year and at the bank centre of

Figure 5.2 Aragonite needles. SEM. Scale 1 μm. Intertidal, Andros, Bahamas. Photograph courtesy Julian Andrews

0.3kg/m²/year. The rate of $CaCO_3$ precipitation is proportional to the degree of supersaturation which is the result expected if the precipitation is inorganic; if it were physiological this relationship need not hold. We know insufficient about water movements across the bank to determine if purely inorganic precipitation could produce sufficient aragonite needles to account for the 3 m thickness of mud (of which about three-quarters is skeletal debris) that has accumulated here over the last 4000 years, though it is clear that a precipitation rate of 0.3 kg $CaCO_3/m^2$/year would not produce a 3 m pile of even very loosely packed needles over 4000 years. However, it is hard to accept that many of the needles are of algal origin, since algae are relatively uncommon in this area.

It is thought that it may be possible to determine the origin of the needles by comparing the various oxygen isotope values for mud and calcareous green algae. As described earlier, the $^{18}O/^{16}O$ ratio in marine precipitated calcium carbonate depends on three factors: it follows the ratio in the water, decreases with rising temperature, and varies according to the fractionating ability of the organism. Initial isotope studies on the Bahama Bank deposits gave the following calculated temperatures for the precipitating solution: aragonite muds, 27.6°–31.7 °C; algae, 22.8°–39.8 °C. Knowing that the prevailing water temperatures of the area are 22°–29 °C, it would seem from the values obtained for the aragonite mud that it could not all have been precipitated inorganically in equilibrium with sea water. The precipitating temperatures of the aragonite mud do however fall well within the algal range. For a while an algal origin was favoured. But later work suggested that salinity corrections should be incorporated in determinations. This brings down the calculated temperatures, so that now the values for precipitation temperatures of mud fall within the range of prevailing water temperatures. Thus the isotope data do not appear to have solved the problem one way or the other.

In the Bight of Abaco on Little Bahama Bank to the north, there is a dense population of calcareous green algae, particularly *Halimeda* and *Penicillus*. These plants have six to nine crops each year and, assuming their abundance and rate of growth have been steady over the last 4000 years, they would have been responsible for more aragonite needles than are presently preserved in the column of sediment in the Bight.

South Florida Shelf. Similar budget studies on the rate of production of aragonite needles by codiacean algae in the South Florida shelf showed that a large proportion of the aragonite mud in the sediment pile could be accounted for by an algal origin.

The small quantity of calcite mud which is present may be derived from the small colonies of crustose coralline algae (*Melobesia* sp.) which grow profusely on sea-grass (*Thalassia testudinum*) blades. (Budget estimates for the rates of calcium carbonate (high-Mg calcite) production by *Melobesia* on *Thalassia* blades in shallow-water grass beds of Jamaica and Barbados are 0.2 kg $CaCO_3/m^2$/yr and 2.8 kg $CaCO_3/m^2$/yr respectively).

SE Persian Gulf. The inshore zones of the SE coast of the Persian Gulf contain aragonitic muds but no codiacean algae. In fact there are few suitable aragonite-producing organisms here. When one compares the strontium content of the muds (9390 ppm Sr^{2+}) and that of the common aragonitic skeletons present (e.g. corals 7740 ppm Sr^{2+}, molluscs 1500–2000 ppm Sr^{2+}) there is no obvious organic candidate as chief supplier of this fine sediment. The Sr^{2+} value in the muds is close, however, to the expected value for aragonite precipitation in equilibrium with these waters at the prevailing temperatures. Much aragonite precipitates inorganically in this coastal zone as crusts of fine crystals directly on to sand grains, but the exact mechanism of aragonite mud formation in the lagoons is unknown. Some workers have suggested that precipitation from sea water is spontaneous, being brought about by the sharp CO_2 uptake during the photosynthetic activity of diatoms at the times of blooms. These speculations are supported by the occurrences of *whitings*—large white patches, up to 10 km across, of mud-laden water which may suddenly appear in open water. Whitings are associated with spontaneous precipitation of aragonite mud in the Dead Sea during the hot summer months. The surface waters double their concentration of suspended aragonite, and the concentration of HCO_3^- in the water then falls. But it is not known whether all the whitings of the Persian Gulf and the Bahamas are due to this sudden precipitation, or whether they may merely represent resuspended bottom sediment stirred up by large shoals of bottom-feeding fish. Several patches of cloudy water have been sampled and found to contain not just aragonite but high- and low-Mg calcite, all in the same proportions as found in the bottom sediments, suggesting resuspension. It could be, of course, that waters concentrated in $CaCO_3$ by evaporation require suitable nuclei in suspension on which aragonite needles could grow.

In conclusion, we note a strong correlation of abundant inorganically precipitated aragonite mud, long residence time and high salinities. Such circumstances are most often encountered on wide tropical banks and in shallow epeiric seas with warm arid climates. Open coral reefs, such as atolls, where water, even in lagoons, is regularly replenished, do not have large amounts of aragonite mud; and none is found in temperate seas. Codiacean algae are a major supplier of aragonite needles in those areas where they thrive in dense populations.

It is this lime mud material which on diagenesis lithifies and recrystallizes to become micrite (see section 9.11) which may build, with or without admixtures of coarser grains, thick units of limestone in the geological record. Abundant micrite in a limestone is normally correlated with low-energy conditions of deposition.

5.3 Pellets and peloids

Several groups of marine organisms, vertebrates and invertebrates, ingest calcareous grains during grazing on organic-rich sediment or algal-infested limestones, and excrete calcium carbonate with their waste products. This calcium carbonate is commonly excreted as a faecal pellet which may be soft and rich in organic matter when fresh, but in highly supersaturated waters may soon harden with interstitial precipitation. The pellets stay dull and pitted in low-energy environments, but in agitated waters become smooth and polished. Not all calcareous faeces lithify; some, perhaps on account of the organic substances present, do not harden but steadily disintegrate.

Faecal pellets are generally round, elliptical, oval or rod-like in shape (Figure 2.3D). The most abundant producers are gastropods, worms and shrimps which ingest muddy sediments and produce pellets from 0.1 mm to 3 mm long and 0.05 mm to 1 mm broad. In thin section these grains are dark, mottled to homogeneous and consist of organic-rich microcrystalline calcite and/or aragonite. Some crustaceans produce faecal pellets that have an internal structure of several cylindrical holes parallel to the length of the pellet (Figure 5.4). These rod-like holes may later be filled with cement, and the pellets have a striated texture in longitudinal section and a speckled appearance in transverse section.

Faecal pellets are produced primarily in quiet saline waters with muddy substrates. It is often found that one species of pellet-producer dominates a pellet-rich area. In such cases the uniformity of size of the pellet grains is biologically controlled and has little relation to the prevailing hydraulic regime.

Rounded, dark microcrystalline grains may not all be faecal in origin. Some may be small rounded mud intraclasts, others may be skeletal or oolitic with an internal structure transformed to a microcrystalline texture by a process termed *micritization* (section 8.3.5). Unless a faecal origin for the structureless, ovoid, microcry-

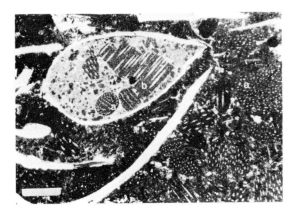

Figure 5.4 Thin section showing transverse (*a*) and longitudinal (*b*) sections of *Favreina* faecal pellets. The pellets merge into one another where they are not protected from compaction by articulated shells. Ppl. Scale 1 mm. Jurassic, Eigg, Scotland

Figure 5.5 Ooids. Scale 0.5 mm. Recent, intertidal, Joulters Cay, Bahamas

stalline particles is unequivocal, it is more appropriate to use the term *peloid* for such grains.

Pelleted and peloidal micrites and sparites are fairly common in the rock record. Many rocks initially identified as pure micrites on closer inspection may be seen to represent compacted homogeneous pellets (see Figure 5.4). The presence of pellets in limestones usually indicates low-energy, warm supersaturated seas of restricted circulation.

The individual laminae range from 3 to 15μm in thickness and the component aragonite rods or needles average $1-4\,\mu$m in length. There may be 20 to 200 lamellae in one cortex. In thin section, modern unaltered marine ooids with tangentially arranged aragonite crystals are easily recognized by the positive pseudo-uniaxial figure under crossed polars. The concentrically arranged laminae of the cortex may be partially or wholly lost in some ooids with a micritic texture (Figure 5.6). Relict ooids tend to have a high proportion of micrite cortices.

5.4 Ooids

An ooid is a grain that has one or more regular lamellae formed as successive coatings around a nucleus. The nucleus may be a fragment of a skeleton, a peloid or another ooid, or it may be a lithoclast such as a quartz grain. Ooids are spherical to ovoid, 0.2 mm to 1.0 mm in diameter (Figure 5.5), white to cream in colour and may have a dull (quiet water) or pearly (agitated water) lustre, according to the degree of mechanical abrasion and polishing.

5.4.1 Marine ooids
The outer coat, or *cortex* is concentrically lamellar, microcrystalline aragonite for the vast majority of occurrences of modern marine ooids.

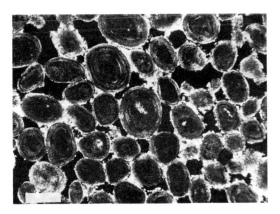

Figure 5.6 Aragonitic ooids with concentric laminae and micritic cortices partially lithified by a meniscus sparry calcite cement. Thin section Xn. Scale 0.5 mm. Pleistocene, Andros, Bahamas

The limited data we have suggests that growth of individual ooids may be very slow, though modern Bahamian oolite shoals are accumulating at rates of almost 1 m per 1000 years.

Substantial accumulations of ooids are best developed on tropical and subtropical shallow platforms. The sites of active ooid formation are shallow agitated waters, commonly of slightly higher temperature and salinity than normal open ocean water. Well-described areas of modern marine ooid formation include the Bahama Banks (see Figure 14.28), the Persian Gulf (see Figure 8.14) and Shark Bay, West Australia. We do not find ooid shoals today on mid-ocean atolls. The common characteristics of the environments of ooid formation are as follows:

   (i) Warm shallow water, normally 0 to 4 m deep, commonly close to a supply of deep cold water rich in dissolved $CaCO_3$.
   (ii) Agitation of grains by tidal currents, wind-driven currents and waves. This turbulence removes fines, and rolls sand grains to and fro without sweeping the bottom clean. The agitation drives off CO_2 from the warmed sea water and promotes the precipitation of $CaCO_3$.

The cortices of modern ooids have a high organic content, some of which may derive from endolithic micro-organisms. However the general consensus is that ooids grow by physico-chemical precipitation of $CaCO_3$ without the intervention of organisms.

It is thought that the initial aragonite components grow on the nucleus with a haphazard or radial orientation, creating a loose fabric, and that this fabric is modified to a secondary tangential orientation in high-energy environments where crystals are physically compacted to create a dense fabric. In the SE coastal area of the Persian Gulf, quiet-water ooids tends to retain their primary radial structure.

There are only a few reported occurrences of marine calcitic ooids, and it is possible that some of these are relict. At one locality near the shelf edge on the Great Barrier Reef of Australia, radial fibrous Mg calcite ooids have been found. In Baffin Bay, Texas, Mg calcitic ooids have a radial structure, whereas aragonitic ooids have a tangential or micritic structure. Here, ooids of one or other mineral plus bimineralic forms show distinctive patterns of distribution. Grains of identical diameter increasingly consist of aragonite in higher-energy areas; Mg calcite cortices (or high-percentage Mg calcite within mixed cortices) are more abundant in low-energy areas. When size fractions of these mixed mineral ooids are inspected we note that with decreasing size the proportion of cortical Mg calcite relative to aragonite increases. The outer cortical layers (coarser) are usually aragonite. The indication is that, as water composition and temperature are the same in the two settings of Mg calcite or aragonite-dominated ooids, it must be the hydraulic energy that in some way controls the mineralogy. High energy results in greater expulsion of CO_2 from the water; this produces faster growth, which favours aragonite over Mg calcite. The environments of deposition of marine ooids are discussed further in section 14.4.1.

5.4.2 Non-marine ooids and pisoids

Ooids are found growing today in a limited number of non-marine environments. They may

Figure 5.7 Thin section of pisoids with a fitted fabric. Ppl. Scale 2 mm. Permian, West Texas, USA

grow larger than 2 mm, the upper limit for ooids, and are then termed *pisoids*. Ooids and pisoids of this origin are quantitatively insignificant in the rock record when compared to marine ooids.

Ooids and pisoids grow as calcite concretions in arid calcareous soils, caliche or calcrete (see section 12.1.2.). They grow with a concentric and radial fabric replacing pre-existing sediment and commonly show a fitted polygonal structure (Figure 5.7). Cave ooids form in splash pools in caves among speleothem precipitations. They are generally constructed of radial fibrous calcite. Lake ooids occur in lakes of high $CaCO_3$ supersaturation, such as the Great Salt Lake of Utah. These ooids may show tangential and radial aragonite fabrics and cross-cutting radial calcite fabrics. Tangentially coated aragonitic ooids are also found in hot springs.

Limestones consisting principally of ooids are known as oolites, and those containing pisoids, pisolites. Except in a few Quaternary limestones which are not yet diagenetically mature, the ooids in ancient oolitic limestones are of calcite, not aragonite. Either the original grains were calcite or the aragonite has transformed to calcite (see section 9.5).

5.5 Relict grains

In describing the types of skeletal and non-skeletal carbonate grains, the existence of relict grains has been mentioned. These are grains which did not form under the prevailing physical and chemical conditions but are of an older origin—they are anachronistic. A common situation is where grains of shallow-water origin (e.g. algal skeletons, ooids), which formed during a low level of the sea in the Pleistocene, have subsequently been drowned during the Holocene transgression when sea rose to its present levels over the last 10 000–15 000 years. This rapid rise has been too quick for sediment of deeper-water origin to form and bury the relict grains. Burrowing organisms may mix relict and contemporary grains, prolonging their exposure at the sea bed. Radiometric (^{14}C) dating of individual grains in

one surface sample of temperate carbonates on the shelf west of Britain has shown age differences of up to 5000 years. This study also revealed that the skeletons of certain taxonomic groups had high average ages because they persisted longer than others. Skeletal durability relates to composition and microarchitecture.

These observations compel us to draw up criteria to recognize relict grains, so we can more accurately interpret the conditions of deposition of ancient limestones; this, unfortunately is easier said than done. Grains that have been on the sea-bed for a prolonged time, on the one hand may show infestation by endoliths and encrustation by micro-organisms, on the other hand they may be well worn, rounded, and polished. The recognition of relict grains is hardest in present high-energy environments. The abrasion of grains is a great leveller. In low-energy environments sea-bed exposure is represented by corrosion of grains, commonly with a chalky or micritic exterior; infestation by endoliths such as algae and fungi; encrustation by small epilithic organisms such as bryozoans, serpulids, forminiferans and calcareous red algae; and oxidized interstitial Fe and Mn salts with a buff, rust, or brown coloration. Glauconite and phosphate can precipitate from sea water within skeletal chambers. Pyrite formation, usually in the form of spherical framboids, is the result of anoxic post-depositional environments. There may be a connection between black (and brown) stained grains and occurrence of some terrigenous sediment which was the initial source of the iron. This iron may enter the system originally as insoluble haematitic coats on grains or as adsorbed particles on clay-sized material. Once the sediment is buried and reducing conditions set in, the oxidized iron in the presence of sulphate-reducing bacteria will reprecipitate as iron sulphide. This precipitation is most likely to take place within the chambers of organisms that contain putrefying tissue where sulphate-reducing bacteria will promote iron sulphide generation. On re-exposure at the sediment/water interface during bioturbation, any blackened pyrite-rich grains may be oxidized to brown ferric hydroxides such a limonite, giving these relict grains their rust colour.

Selected reading

Davies, P.J., Bubela, B. and Ferguson, J. (1978) The formation of ooids. *Sedimentology* **25**, 703–730.

Fabricius, F.H. (1977) Origin of marine ooids and grapestone. *Contrib. Sed.* 7.

Halley, R.B. (1977) Ooid fabric and fracture in the Great Salt Lake and the geologic record. *J. Sed. Petrol.* **47**, 1099–1120.

Land, L.S., Behrens, E.W. and Frishman, S.A. (1979) The ooids of Baffin Bay, Texas. *J. Sed. Petrol.* **49**, 1269–1278.

Loreau, J.P. and Purser, B.H. (1973) Distribution and ultrastructure of Holocene ooids in the Persian Gulf. In Purser, B.H. (ed.), *The Persian Gulf*, Springer Verlag, Berlin, 279–328.

Newell, N.D., Purdy, E.G. and Imbrie, J. (1960) Bahamian oolitic sand. *J. Geol.* **68**, 481–497.

Peryt, T.M. (1984) *Coated Grains*. Springer Verlag, Berlin.

Simone, L. (1980) Ooids: a review. *Earth Sci. Rev.* **16**, 319–355.

Part 3 Depositional processes

Carbonates differ from terrigenous sediments in their origin, structure and composition. The patterns of both carbonate grain breakdown and hydraulic behaviour are complex, and the modes of accumulation are markedly influenced by organisms.

6 Sedimentation of carbonate grains

The two overriding controls on carbonate sedimentation are the tectonic and climatic settings. The tectonic setting and climate both influence, among other things, the supply of terrigenous sediment to the sea. Areas of maximum terrigenous sedimentation (generally nearshore) are not sites of significant carbonate accumulation for several reasons:

(i) Rapid deposition of terrigenous sediment dilutes indigenous carbonate
(ii) Fine terrigenous sediments form unfavourable substrates for most skeletal benthos
(iii) Excessive rain of fine-grained detritus reduces light penetration and can suffocate sessile organisms
(iv) Terrigenous sediments are associated with large volumes of fresh water that reduce salinity.

The tectonic setting, along with global climate, also governs the variations in relative sea-level, and since the important ecological controls of hydraulic energy, light, degree of atmospheric exposure, pressure and temperature vary with water depth, it is clear that carbonate sediment type is strongly related to sea-level. The regional tectonics control the orientation of shorelines and platform margins as well as the width and slope of platforms. These physiographic configurations, in conjunction with climate, determine seawater circulation patterns and the energy level and direction of waves and currents. The main agencies that erode, transport and deposit carbonate sediments are storms, wind, waves, tides, gravity on slopes and biogenic activity. It is assumed that the student is familiar with the principal physical processes of clastic sedimentation and these will not be dealt with here, though reference to these processes will be made in later sections of the book. Attention is focused here on those attributes and processes of deposition of carbonates which set them apart from the terrigenous sediments.

6.1 Intrabasinal origin

Marine carbonate sediments are formed in the sea by physico-chemical precipitation and organic secretion; they are not derived by the erosion of pre-existing rocks in the manner of terrigenous sediments. Consequently, carbonate grains are local or *intrabasinal* in origin. Thus, though a phase of transportation by currents is normally necessary during the history of terrigenous deposits, it is not essential for carbonate sediments. Accumulations of carbonate sediments tend to 'grow' in place rather than to be spread over wide areas. There are several important consequences of this:

(i) Traction current structures are less common in limestones than sandstones
(ii) Currents of removal may be more important in calcareous sedimentation than currents of delivery.
(iii) Grain-size and grain-size distributions of limestones do not necessarily relate to the

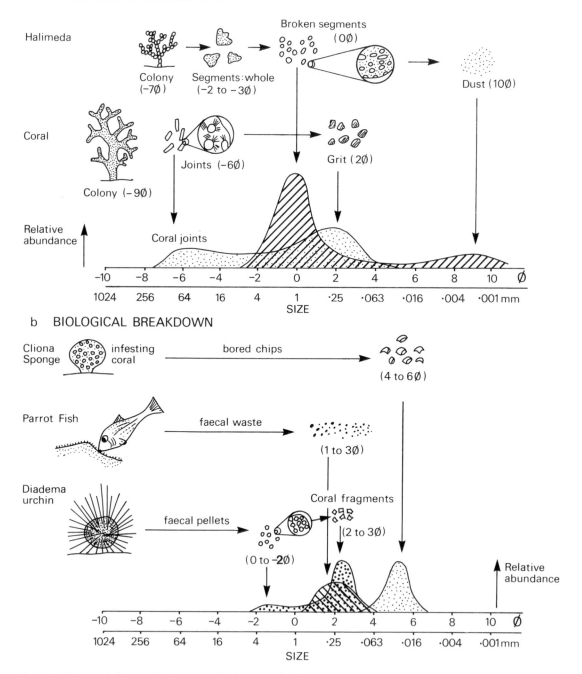

Figure 6.1 Diagram indicating the dominant size fractions of grains produced by the mechanical breakdown (*a*) of *Halimeda* and *Acropora* coral skeletons (after Folk and Robles, 1964) and the biological breakdown (*b*) of massive corals by sponges, fish and urchins

hydraulic regime. For example, an accumulation of large oyster shells does not necessarily mean that they were deposited in a zone of high hydraulic energy. Likewise, an accumulation consisting entirely of similar-sized tests of one species of benthonic foraminiferans does not necessarily imply persistent currents of uniform strength prevailed, giving good hydraulic sorting.

6.2 Organic influence on sedimentation

Organisms play a crucial role in the sedimentation of carbonate grains. Not only are they the principal producers of grains but they can influence the mode of disintegration, erosion, transport, deposition, burial and preservation of grains. The grain size of skeletal sediments generally reflects the original size of calcified hard parts, and further, the size and shape of disintegrated grains may relate more closely to the internal architecture of the skeletons, or the style of biological erosion, than to the hydraulic regime (Figure 6.1). Organic stabilization of sediment (e.g. the trapping and binding of grains by algal mats), and the bioturbation of sediment by infauna, may produce accumulations whose grain-size distributions do not reflect the overall hydraulic setting. These organic controls make the textural maturity of carbonate sediments (a major parameter in the subdivision and classification of terrigenous sediments) of limited value in carbonate sediment subdivision.

6.3 Component composition of carbonates

The component composition of carbonate sediments and limestones is influenced by the following factors:

(i) The areal distribution of skeletal organisms and non-skeletal grains
(ii) Their rates of $CaCO_3$ production
(iii) Their relative rates of breakdown to transportable sediment
(iv) Any physical, chemical or biological effects selectively sorting the sediment.

(i) The *areal distribution* of marine organisms, which may produce skeletal debris or calcareous faecal pellets, naturally varies with numerous environmental factors such as light, temperature, depth, hydraulic energy, exposure, salinity, substrate, turbidity, food supply and predator–prey relationships. A change in the prevailing marine conditions produces changes in the organic assemblage. For example, during a transgression, not only does the water deepen and the hydraulic energy decrease, but hard substrates supporting mainly epilithic organisms (such as corals, bryozoans, calcareous red algae) are gradually covered and replaced by soft sediment substrates which support epibenthos and infaunal assemblages (such as molluscs, calcareous green algae and benthonic foraminiferans).

(ii) *Rates of production* vary according to setting. The greatest production of $CaCO_3$ occurs at the margins of shallow platforms where deep cold nutrient-rich waters well up and are consequently heated and agitated by wave action, which drives off dissolved CO_2, promoting $CaCO_3$ precipitation. Organic and inorganic $CaCO_3$ production (in reefs and ooid shoals respectively) is favoured at topographic highs or breaks in slope; thus the rapid generation of $CaCO_3$ at local sites can have a positive feedback response, maintaining the sites as ideal production areas. Reef crests have an estimated net $CaCO_3$ productivity of 4–5 kg $CaCO_3/m^2$/year, whereas back-reef lagoons have a net $CaCO_3$ productivity of less than 3 kg $CaCO_3/m^2$/year. A hierarchy was established by Enos and Perkins (1977) for the productivity of South Florida shelf margin habitat communities, which had the following sequence: outer reef > patch-reef > shoal fringe ≫ grass-covered mud ≫ grass on sand > dead reef, open marine > dead reef, restricted > fore-reef ≫ bare mud > bare sand > rubble.

Though the sites of high $CaCO_3$ productivity (*factories*) may not be the sites of high $CaCO_3$ accumulation (*sinks*), nonetheless, for carbonates, the factories and sinks are usually close together.

(iii) The *rate of breakdown* of grains and rock

to transportable sediment varies with (a) density and structure of grains, e.g. an oyster is stronger than a bryozoan; (b) amount of organics within the grain e.g. a foraminiferan (organic-poor) is stronger than a *Halimeda* (organic-rich); and (c) susceptibility to bioerosion, e.g. an encrusting coral is more resistant to erosion than a branched coral with much exposed dead skeleton.

The sequence of resistance to breakdown for skeletal grains on the south Florida Shelf (Ginsburg *et al.*, 1963; Enos and Perkins, 1977) is as follows:

	Spicules	Sponges, alcyonarians, holothurians, ascidians
	Sheaths	*Penicillus, Udotea, Rhipocephalus*
increasing resistance	Segments	*Halimeda*, echinoid spines, articulated red algae
to breakdown	Branches	Red algae, corals, bryozoans
	Chambers	Gastropods, bivalves, foraminiferans, echinoid tests, serpulid worms
	Crusts	Crustose red algae, corals, foraminiferans, *Millepora*
	Massive	Corals, molluscs

On the South Florida shelf, fine sediment is mainly from the sheath type and from abrasion of the others, the sand-sized grains are segments and chambers, and the coarse sediment is from branches, chambers and massive groups.

(iv) *Sorting*, or dispersion, of the sediment is primarily governed by the prevailing hydraulic conditions and any overriding biological control.

To understand more about the distribution of carbonate sediments we should now examine how carbonate grains break down to transportable sediment and behave when subjected to currents and waves.

6.4 Breakdown of grains

The original morphology and microarchitecture of grains governs the style of their mechanical disintegration and the size distribution of their breakdown products. (This is sometimes called the *Sorby principle*, after Henry Clifton Sorby who first made this observation in 1879.) A few examples follow.

Platy and branching corals initially break down into tabular and rod-like fragments respectively (Figure 6.1); further abrasion creates equant gritty fragments related to the trabecular structure of the corals, and still further erosion produces fragments consisting of individual crystallites of coral a fraction of a micron in size (Figure 6.1). *Halimeda* plants first disarticulate into segments of 2 mm–8 mm. The more platy segments commonly snap in half. As the segments have a somewhat pithy interior, they are easily crushed, and skeletons disintegrate to individual needle-shaped crystallites once segments have lost their integral margins. Spheroidal, ovoid or disc-shaped structures with a strongly concentric internal structure, such as some foraminiferan tests or ooids, tend to break down by the loss of complete layers of the structure into smaller versions of the same general shape (like layers of an onion). If their internal structure has a strong radial element, then breakage is commonly into halves through the centre, after which segments may split off (like segments of an orange). Mechanical wear of organic binding in mollusc shells causes breakdown into three prevalent groups: layers (0.25–0.5 mm), sublayers (0.004–0.03 mm) and unit crystals (0.1–0.5 μm).

The surface area to weight relationship influences skeletal breakdown. We find that in any given abrasive environment, shells with a small surface area per unit weight are generally more durable than those with a large surface area per unit weight.

6.4.1. Bioerosion

Erosion of calcium carbonate by the direct activity of organisms is a critical process in the breakdown of grains, coral reefs and limestone coasts. There are several styles of bioerosion:

(i) Destruction of loose carbonate grains

(a) by mechanical or chemical disintegration during the mastication and digestion of grains by deposit feeders (e.g. worms)

(b) by fragmentation of exoskeletons in order to gain access to soft tissue for food (e.g. crabs)

(c) by repeated infestation by microborers (e.g. algae and fungi)

(ii) destruction of rocky substrates such as reef framework and limestones by grazing organisms

(iii) Destruction of rocky substrates by boring organisms.

(i) *Destruction of loose carbonate grains.* Vast quantities of sediment pass through the intestines of deposit feeders and browsers in their search for food. The principal ingesters of loose carbonate grains are worms, holothurians, gastropods, crustaceans and fish. Although there have been several studies to quantify the rates of carbonate ingestion and defaecation by these organisms (dense concentrations of worms and holothurians have been found to ingest as much as 650 and 120 kg/m^2/year respectively) there are no universally accepted estimates for the quantities of sediments destroyed by this action. Several authors have indicated that the digestive fluids of deposit feeders have a low pH (5-7) which could dissolve $CaCO_3$, and some have noted a decrease in sediment particle size after digestion, but an equal number maintain that there is no change in the grain size of ingested carbonate, with the structure of the most delicate grains being preserved. Little is known about the biochemical alteration of the organic matrix of grains as they pass through digestive tracts, though it is hard to envisage that there is no change whatsoever in the organic (and inorganic) constitution of particles after prolonged reworking.

Fragmentation of exoskeletons takes place during predation and scavenging. For example, crabs use their pincers to fracture bivalve shells,

sea-birds drop shellfish on rocks, and fish use their teeth to break into molluscs and urchin tests.

Perhaps the most significant mode of organic disintegration of loose carbonate particles is by the infestation by microborers such as algae and fungi. These organisms secrete acids which dissolve tubular boreholes in which the filaments reside (Figure 6.2). Boring algae (greens, blue-greens and reds) require light for growth, and thus occur mainly in shallow-water sediments and colonize only the well-lit perimeter of grains. They excavate tubes up to 1 mm in length and 15 μm in diameter. Fungi can live without light, and occur in sediments above and below the photic zone. Their borings, which are usually narrower than algal borings (1-4 μm diameter), may penetrate to the centre of grains. These microborer excavations result directly in the solution of calcium carbonate (of the order of 0.4 kg/m^2/year for lagoonal sediments) and also in the structural weakening of grains, making them more prone to mechanical fragmentation.

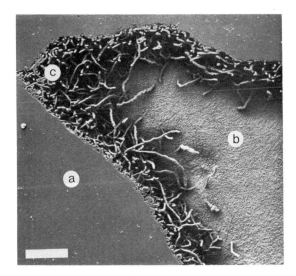

Figure 6.2 SEM of resin cast of microborings into a shell fragment: *a*, resin; *b*, etched portion of grain; *c*, cast of microborings (algal). Scale 100 μm. Recent, 5 m depth, Davies Reef, Great Barrier Reef, Australia. From Tudhope and Risk (1985)

The vacated holes of microborers may be sites of accumulation or precipitation of fine CaCO₃ crystals. Repeated organic infestation and deposition of microcrystalline $CaCO_3$ fill may bring about the structural and mineralogical alteration of the perimeter (and interiors) of grains to produce *micrite envelopes* and *micritized grains*.

(ii) *Destruction of rocky substrates by grazing organisms*. The important grazers that attack calcareous substrates in search of epilithic and endolithic plants for food include gastropods, chitons, echinoids and fish. Several groups have special hard rasping devices to facilitate the scraping of the rock; for example, limpets have goethite- and silicate-reinforced radulae, chitons have magnetite denticle cappings, some echinoids have dolomitic teeth, and scarid fish have hardened beaks for scraping plus pharangeal teeth for grinding. These organisms can produce characteristic scrape markings: meandering lines of parallel shallow pits are produced by limpets, echinoids gouge stellate patterns with their five teeth, and parrot-fish usually make two pairs of short parallel grooves with their beaks. The consumed calcium carbonate passes through the gut and is excreted as pellets in the case of gastropods, chitons and echinoids, but fish defaecate loose grains. The pellets may or may not

retain their integral character during transportation and burial. Each grazer species normally produces one dominant size of rock fragment in its faeces. For *Diadema antillarum* this dominant size is 0.1 to 0.2 mm (Figures 6.1, 6.3), and on reefs where these urchins abound, this same size is commonly a mode in the grain-size distribution of reefal sediments. Grazing organisms, especially fish, are major transporters of sediment as well as eroders of limestones. Further, though principally seeking algal food, they can, by their scraping activities, influence the distribution pattern of settling larvae of sessile animals.

There is now a considerable literature on the rates of $CaCO_3$ removal from rocky substrates by grazing organisms. Only a few examples are quoted here (Table 6.1). They are given in kg/m²/year to conform with rates of growth and

Table 6.1 Rates of $CaCO_3$ erosion by grazing organisms

Intertidal gastropods (*Littorina, Nerita, Cittarums*)	—	0.2–1.5 kg/m²/year
Limpets (*Acmaea*)	—	1.6–4.5 kg/m²/year
Chitons (*Acanthozostera*)	—	0.3 kg/m²/year
Echinoids (*Diadema antillarum*)	—	16 kg/m²/year
(*Echinometra lucunter*)	—	0.5 kg/m²/year
Parrot-fish	—	0.4–0.6 kg/m²/year

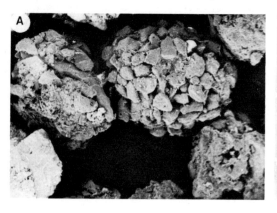 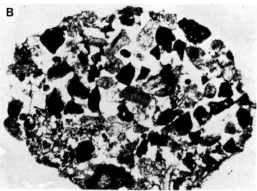

Figure 6.3 Diadema faecal pellets. (*a*) SEM. Scale 0.5 mm, (*b*) Thin section ppl. Scale 0.2 mm. Recent, 2 m depth, Barbados, WI

destruction presented elsewhere. They are based on average individual rates, but high population densities.

(iii) *Destruction of rocky substrates by boring organisms.* As well as the microborers, which have already been described, there are several important groups of rock- boring organisms: sponges, molluscs, worms, and crustaceans. These organisms play a dual role in carbonate breakdown. First, they weaken the rock by their undermining excavations creating, with mechanical erosion, cobble- and boulder-sized clasts, and second, they produce fine fragments of characteristic shape and size in the process of excavating a borehole.

Several genera of *sponges*, notably *Cliona* and *Siphonodictyon*, infest calcareous substrates to secure a sheltered site to inhabit. The surface of a dead coral may reveal just a scattering of red, yellow or black sponge papillae (inhalent and exhalent openings) but underneath the surface the coral skeleton may be riddled with sponge tissue occupying ramifying cavities (Figure 6.4). Sponges excavate the substrate by secreting a corrosive substance along the thin edge of each penetrating cell which encases a scoop-shaped chip of calcium carbonate. The chips have a very

distinctive shape and are normally 20–80 μm in diameter (Figure 6.5). They are ejected by the sponge and a faceted borehole is produced. Most sponge borings penetrate 10–50 mm, depending upon species and thickness of substrate.

Experiments with planted substrates show that initial infestation rates are very high (up to 7 kg/m^2/year), but that sponge boring rate slows down once a dwelling site has been excavated. The rate may not speed up again until there is a disturbance, such as mechanical or grazing erosion of the sponge-infested substrate.

Boring sponges are common in limestone substrates from the intertidal zone down to hundreds of metres. They play an especially vital role in intertidal notch formation, reef framework destruction, the moulding of coral growth form at depth and the production of silt-sized carbonate particles. Sponge boring chips have been demonstrated to constitute 30% of the total lagoonal sediment on the Pacific atoll of Fanning Island.

Boring *molluscs* include bivalves such as *Lithophaga, Gastrochaena* and *Tridacna*, which are

Figure 6.5 Chips (*a*) produced by boring sponges. Star-shaped fragments (*b*) are ascidian spicules. SEM. Scale 20 μm. Recent, 5 m depth, Davies Reef, Great Barrier Reef, Australia. Photograph courtesy of Sandy Tudhope

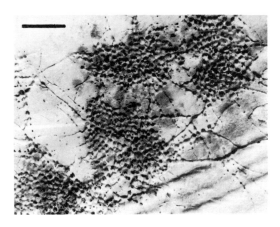

Figure 6.4 Borings made by *Cliona* sponge into *Triton* shell. Scale 10 mm Recent, intertidal, Howick Island, Great Barrier Reef, Australia.

commonly seen in intertidal limestones such as beach rock and also in reef frameworks (Figure 6.6). It is thought that they bore by mechanical abrasion, moving the retractor and adductor muscles, but some may also use this action in combination with chemical corrosion. Little is known of the nature of sediment that is excavated, though the amount may be considerable (up to $0.2\,kg/m^2/year$ for intertidal reef clams *Tridacna crocea*). Some bivalves secrete a calcareous lining to their boring which has an unusual laminated botryoidal fabric. Boring gastropods are not as common as boring bivalves. The mechanism they use is a combination of chemical corrosion of the organic matrix and carbonate components of the substrate, followed by scraping and ingestion of the loose carbonate crystals. Molluscs can achieve boring rates of $0.5\,kg/m^3/year$.

Polychaetes and sipunculids are the *worms* commonly found in small holes and crevices in shallow-water limestones, but not all of those found inhabiting the substrate have necessarily excavated the hole themselves. Again, the substrate is attacked by a combination of chemical and mechanical erosion; chemical secretion by the epidermal glands weakens the substrate and fine particles are removed by the setae. Worm borings are smooth-walled sinuous or U-shaped

Figure 6.6 Boring into *Tridacna* shell; *a, Lithophaga* bivalve; *b, Cliona* sponge. Scale 10 mm. Recent, intertidal, Meguera reef, Great Barrier Reef, Australia

tubes from 0.3 mm to 3 mm in diameter, depending on species. Few figures are available on worm boring rates, but based on their abundance compared to that of borers whose rates are known, it would appear that they are capable of excavating $0.1\,kg/m^2/year$.

Amongst *crustaceans*, boring crabs and isopods are rare, but the boring shrimp *Upogebia* and *Alpheus* are significant eroders of some modern coral reefs. The shrimp borings are intricately branching cylindrical passageways, 5–10 mm in diameter, lined with fine sediment. Boring barnacles such as *Lithotrya* are the other major group of boring crustaceans. The larvae penetrate the substrate by chemical erosion and the adult enlarges the hole, using its chitinous teeth, to a diameter of a few millimetres. Some barnacle cavities are in living corals, so the borings extend upwards as the coral grows.

Other boring organisms which do not produce significant quantities of sediment, but may noticeably weaken the rock substrate, include bryozoans and brachiopods.

6.5 Hydraulic behaviour of grains

The main controls exerted by the fluid on the erosion, transportation and deposition of grains are the threshold velocity and the settling velocity. The threshold velocity is the point at which movement of particles begins, and settling velocity is the velocity at which the frictional drag of the fluid approaches the value of the impelling force, i.e. the difference between the force due to gravity and the buoyancy force.

For spherical quartz grains in water at 20 °C, the relationship between these velocities and grain size is shown in Figure 6.7. If particles of higher density than quartz were used, then the velocities increase for the same grain sizes; if densities were lower then the velocities would decrease. As quartz has a specific gravity of 2.65 and those of calcite and aragonite are both greater, 2.71 and 2.94 respectively, we may expect carbonate grains of any size to have higher threshold and setting velocities than

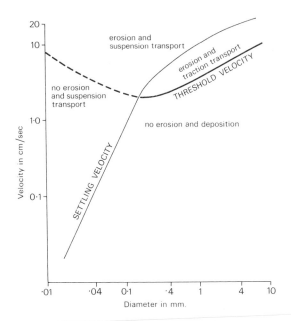

Figure 6.7 The relationship between threshold and settling velocities for quartz grains. After Orme (1977)

Figure 6.8 Large reef boulder on the reef flat of Waterwitch Pass Reef, Great Barrier Reef, Australia

quartz grains of the same size. However, most carbonate particles have *bulk densities* much lower than those of the pure minerals, on account of the highly porous nature of most grains. For example, coral fragments have bulk densities ranging from about 1.2 for porous forms such as *Porites* to 2.0 for compact structures such as *Agaricia*. Chambered-foraminiferan tests have similarly low bulk densities, as do *Halimeda* segments. The more compact skeletal structures, such as mollusc shells, have higher bulk densities, generally greater than 2.0. Consequently grains of similar size and shape will behave differently in a fluid due to their different bulk densities. Conversely, grains of different shapes and sizes (e.g. a *Halimeda* flake 3 mm in diameter and an ooid grain 0.5 mm in diameter) may be hydraulically equivalent.

Though, no doubt, it took great storms to lift and transport the huge coral boulders deposited on the ocean margins of some modern reef flats (Figure 6.8) the blocks may actually have been more buoyant than they appear. There are even reports of coral blocks floating in the sea, supported by trapped gases produced by the decay of tissue in pores.

Besides bulk density, the shape, size, and surface texture of grains affect particle buoyancy. Equidimensional shapes may take straight paths as they fall through water, but plates and rods may oscillate and spin. The settling velocities for common bioclastic particle shapes and sizes are shown in Figure 6.9. The departures in settling behaviour between different grain types become most pronounced in the coarser sand grades. We find certain skeletal grains tend to stay in suspension longer than others. This will affect their final distribution pattern. It will also influence the degree and style of mechanical breakdown. For example, when certain buoyant skeletal types, like *Halimeda* segments, stay in suspension, they are selectively cushioned from fragmentation; those less buoyant types, such as bivalves, which are more commonly transported by bottom traction, suffer prolonged abrasion and become more spherical. So the dense, less buoyant, skeletal types show the least disparity between 'sieving size' and 'hydraulic size'. Further, experimentation shows that coarser grains erode faster than finer grains.

The common polymodality of skeletal carbo-

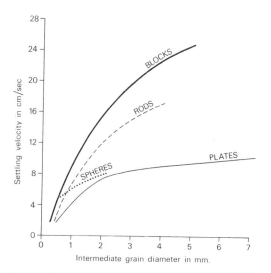

Figure 6.9 Settling velocities for common bioclastic shapes. After Maiklem (1968)

Figure 6.10 Partially lithified crust on ooid sands. 2 m depth, Little Bahama Bank. Photograph courtesy of Conrad Neumann

nate sediments is in part due to the mixing of distinct skeletal populations and in part due to the different modes of transportation, i.e. suspension, saltation and surface creep, and also carriage by organisms such as fish. We must conclude that a texturally mature carbonate sediment with a hydraulically well-balanced mixture of all components results only after prolonged steady agitation.

6.6 Mechanical stabilization of grains
The binding together of sedimentary particles necessarily makes them more difficult to erode and transport. There are various mechanisms of binding carbonate grains together, including the inorganic and organic precipitation of calcareous cement and the sticking together of grains by mucilaginous organic matter.

6.6.1 Precipitation of interstitial cements
Physico-chemical and organically-induced precipitations of fine aragonite and Mg calcite crystals around grains on the sea-bed produce crusts or hardgrounds (Figures 6.10, 6.11), and also create aggregates and lumps such as grapestones. The mechanical stability of the sea-bed is

Figure 6.11 Lithified crust (hardground) supporting soft corals and cumatulid crinoids. Scale 100 mm. 700 m depth, Florida Straits, off Little Bahama bank (see Figure 4.16 for thin section of crust)

markedly enhanced by this marine lithification, so that erosion is inhibited and steeper-than-normal sediment slopes may be maintained. A cemented substrate influences the nature of water flow over the sea-bed and may also provide suitable sites for colonization by rock-encrusting biota.

The mechanisms of sea-bed lithification will be discussed in Chapter 8, on marine diagenesis.

6.6.2 Pelletization

The formation of faecal pellets from fine-grained constituents helps to stabilize the sediment by increasing effective grain size and thus raising the settling and threshold velocities. Even where the faecal waste of deposit feeders is not pelletized, the individual mineral particles may remain in an organic slime which affects their resuspension.

6.6.3 Algal mats

Subtidal films or mats of filamentous and coccoid algae and diatoms are exceedingly common on shallow tropical sea-beds (Figures 6.12, 6.13). Mineral particles physically adhere to the mucilaginous algal sheaths, then growth of algal filaments entwines grains in a sticky network (Figures 4.45, 6.14). Many different microscopic algae may be responsible for the mat, though in one area a particular species normally dominates. Common varieties include blue-green (*Ly-*

Figure 6.13 Mat of entwined *Lyngbya* filament peeled from the sea-bed. 0.5 m depth, Abaco, Bahamas. From Neumann, Gebelein and Scoffin (1970)

ngbya, Schizothrix) green (*Enteromorpha*) and red algae (*Polysiphonia, Laurencia*). Though these subtidal mats trap grains and then grow over them, they do not develop subsurface laminations because the mats are dynamic features which disaggregate about 2 cm below the surface. Many small invertebrates, such as ostracods, copepods, cumaceans, tanaidaceans and worms, dwell in and on the mats. The organic slime around grains is gleaned for food by this microscopic infauna.

Mats can withstand normal prevailing tidal currents that are seen to transport nearby unbound sediments. Sea-bed experiments with an underwater flume, which generates unidirectional currents of variable speeds on the sea-bed, revealed that intact algal mats can resist erosion by currents three times stronger than those required to mobilize the same sediment with its organic coat removed by bleach treatment. Resistance to erosion depends upon the type of algal

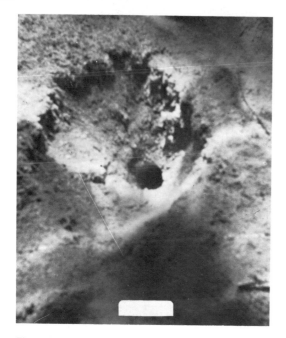

Figure 6.12 Crustacean (*Callianassa*) burrow hole through filamentous algal surface mat, (*Schizothrix*, blue-green alga). Scale 50 mm. 1 m depth, Abaco, Bahamas. From Neumann, Gebelein and Scoffin (1970)

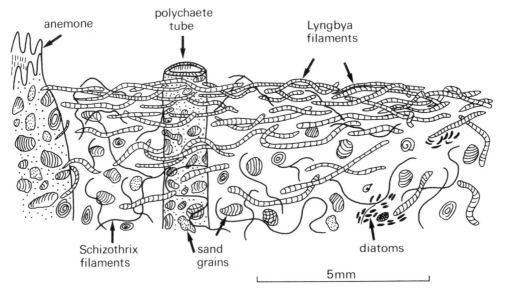

anemone   polychaete   Lyngbya
tube   filaments

Schizothrix   sand   diatoms
filaments   grains

5mm

Figure 6.14 Schematic diagram of *Lyngbya* algal mat. After Neumann, Gebelein and Scoffin (1970)

population, the mat smoothness and continuity of cover. When subjected to increasing current speeds, mats begin to rupture at inhomogeneities (bumps and hollows) in the surface. The film then starts to peel back and flake off, and the exposed unbound sediment transforms into migrating ripples.

6.6.4 Sea-grass beds and other binding vegetation

Sea-grasses (e.g. *Thalassia, Halophila, Posidonia, Cymodocea, Syringodium, Zostera*) have blades 100–500 mm long above the sea-bed (Figure 6.15) and dense tufted rhizome root systems that extend down to 500 mm below the sea-bed. The blades have a baffle effect, and reduce current speeds at the sea-bed so that grains that might otherwise saltate or stay in suspension settle out. Waves and tidal currents are ineffective in winnowing sediment because kinetic energy is absorbed in the movement of the grass blades. The greater the density of the grass, the greater the abundance of fine sediment that accumulates. The rhizome roots are particularly strong, and have been known to hold down the sediment even throughout the full force of a

Figure 6.15 Seagrasses, *Thalassia* and *Syringodium*, growing on burrowed sea-bed. Scale 200 mm. 2 m depth, Abaco

hurricane. Grass blades provide a substrate for calcareous encrusting organisms such as *Melobesia* (a red alga), encrusting foraminiferans and bryozoans, which ultimately contribute, along with those skeletal organisms such as gastropods that seek shelter here, to the sediment pile. Sea-grasses can tolerate a wide range of salinities, but are found mainly in water from 32‰ to 55‰. Though individual species have different depth requirements, sea-grass beds are most prolific in water 2–15 m deep. Once well established, modern sea-grass meadows may localize muddy sediment accumulation to build lensoid banks having up to 10 m topographic relief, e.g. Shark Bay, West Australia.

There are numerous erect plants, such as the green algae *Caulerpa*, *Batophora*, *Halimeda*, *Penicillus*, and *Udotea*, that live 'rooted' in loose sediment. Though they may not all be responsible for the building of significant banks of sediment, nonetheless their holdfasts all play a part in agglutinating sedimentary particles and consequently stabilizing the sea-bed.

The most effective sediment stabilizers near to coasts are mangrove trees. These plants range in occurrence from scattered shrubs 1 m tall to dense forests of trees 20 m tall. They are capable of living in waters of a wide salinity range from brackish to metahaline. There appears to be a natural progression in the population of mangroves, as the sediment and peat accumulations build from the subtidal (e.g. *Rhizophora*) through the intertidal (e.g. *Avicennia*) into the supratidal (e.g. *Ceriops*) settings. The prop roots and breathing shoots (pneumatophores) of mangroves form effective baffles (Figure 6.16) reducing even quite strong tidal currents of

Figure 6.16 Aerial roots of the red mangrove *Rhizophora mangle*. Scale 300 mm. Intertidal, Pipon Reef, Great Barrier Reef, Australia

0.5 m/second to zero within a metre. The suspended mud particles eventually settle among the roots and may build, with the mangrove peat, extensive coastal flats and islands.

6.6.5 Agglutinating invertebrates

A variety of invertebrates agglutinate sand grains to build a protective tube or network which enhances the overall cohesion of the upper few centimetres of the substrate (Figure 6.14). Examples include sabellid worms, harpacticoid copepods, tanaiids and anemones. Mussels use their byssal threads to bind the surface sediment and thus stabilize the sea-bed in the area of their colonization.

6.6.6 Encrusting calcareous organisms

Some skeletal organisms by their encrustations stabilize the sediment. An example is the group of encrusting calcareous red algae, such as *Neogoniolithon*, which envelope the surface of rubble deposits. The coarse fragments are organically cemented together, forming a boundstone which resists erosion. Those sessile skeletal invertebrates which colonize rocky substrates making a skeletal framework may ultimately build a reef. Though their ramifying structures trap grains, they do not strictly stabilize the loose sediment of the sea-bed in the sense meant here. Reefs are described in Chapter 7 and in section 14.4.2.

6.7 Bioturbation

Bioturbation, the mixing of sediments by organisms, can take place on the sea-bed by surface feeders such as holothurians, and within the sediment to a depth of more than a meter in the case of certain shrimps. Organisms may mix sediment in the process of feeding and in the process of excavating a home. The deposit feeders such as worms and holothurians that ingest large quantities of sediment (as much as 250 g/day per individual holothurian) tend to excrete a homogenized mixture of grains, whereas the burrowers, such as crustaceans, though capable of extensive mixing may also biologically sort the sediment, stacking in deep chambers those grains too coarse to lift, and ejecting fine grains into the water column, building moderately sorted fine-grained mounds on the sea-bed (Figure 6.17). In this way the shrimps generate a fine-grained surface layer which is a dynamic feature, always at the surface during active sedimentation, and which will not be preserved under steady conditions. Crustaceans can excavate complex branching burrow systems (Figure 6.18). Some crustaceans line their burrows with sediment of characteristic grain sizes and may also collect faecal pellets in special chambers (perhaps later to harvest the microorganisms developing there).

Figure 6.17 *Callianassa* mounds. Scale, knife 300 mm. 20 m depth, Davies Reef, Great Barrier Reef, Australia. From Tudhope and Scoffin (1984)

The organic reworking of sediment performs several significant functions, including:

(i) Aerating subsurface sediment
(ii) Obliterating primary sedimentary structures
(iii) Obscuring the primary sedimentary texture by mixing grains of different origins (sizes, shapes, etc.)
(iv) Creating biogenic structures which may modify the porosity/permeability character of the sediment—vertical burrows especially may reduce the anisotropically permeable character of layered sediments
(v) Homogenization of the sediment in certain cases, and in others biological sorting of the sediment
(vi) Ejecting sediment into the path of currents, which may effectively winnow fine grains from the area
(vii) Exposing buried sediments to surface processes such as endolithic algal infestation—where the burrower ejects sediment finer than a certain size, this may lead to selective preservation of the large infaunal skeletons and continuous attrition of the finer, mainly allochthonous, sediment
(viii) Creating sediment turnover rates, in the

case of larger burrowers, which may be sufficiently high to prohibit colonization by certain other members of the infauna, by the sessile epifauna and the epiflora
(ix) Creating inhomogeneities in surface organic mats and thus aiding the erosion of the sea-bed
(x) Disruption of surface crusts, perhaps to create aggregates, nodules or breccias
(xi) Enriching the sediment by their own skeletal and faecal remains.

A diagrammatic summary of the principal effects of the burrowing shrimp *Callianassa* is shown in Figure 6.18.

6.8 Summary of the texture of carbonate sediments

The texture (size, shape and arrangement of grains) of carbonate sediments can be seen to be affected by the interplay of five factors:

(i) Hydraulic energy of the environment
(ii) Grain density, shape and surface texture
(iii) Microarchitecture of the grains
(iv) Style of bioerosion
(v) Stabilization (e.g. by algal mats) or bioturbation of the deposit.

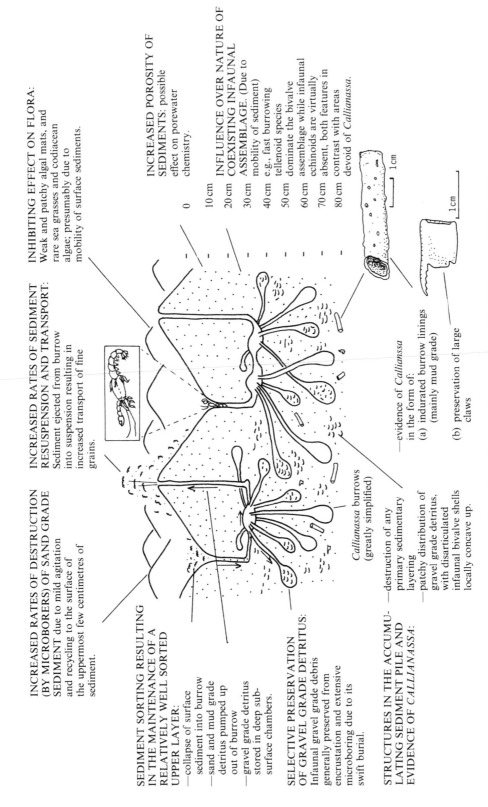

INHIBITING EFFECT ON FLORA:
Weak and patchy algal mats, and rare sea grasses and codiacean algae; presumably due to mobility of surface sediments.

INCREASED POROSITY OF SEDIMENTS: possible effect on porewater chemistry.

INFLUENCE OVER NATURE OF COEXISTING INFAUNAL ASSEMBLAGE. (Due to mobility of sediment) e.g., fast burrowing tellenoid species dominate the bivalve assemblage while infaunal echinoids are virtually absent, both features in contrast with areas devoid of *Callianassa*.

0
10 cm
20 cm
30 cm
40 cm
50 cm
60 cm
70 cm
80 cm

1 cm

1 cm

INCREASED RATES OF DESTRUCTION (BY MICROBORERS) OF SAND GRADE SEDIMENT due to mild agitation and recycling to the surface of the uppermost few centimetres of sediment.

INCREASED RATES OF SEDIMENT RESUSPENSION AND TRANSPORT: Sediment ejected from burrow into suspension resulting in increased transport of fine grains.

SEDIMENT SORTING RESULTING IN THE MAINTENANCE OF A RELATIVELY WELL SORTED UPPER LAYER:
—collapse of surface sediment into burrow
—sand and mud grade detritus pumped up out of burrow
—gravel grade detritus stored in deep sub-surface chambers.

SELECTIVE PRESERVATION OF GRAVEL GRADE DETRITUS: Infaunal gravel grade debris generally preserved from encrustation and extensive microboring due to its swift burial.

STRUCTURES IN THE ACCUMU-LATING SEDIMENT PILE AND EVIDENCE OF *CALLIANASSA*:
—destruction of any primary sedimentary layering
—patchy distribution of gravel grade detritus, with disarticulated infaunal bivalve shells locally concave up.

Callianassa burrows (greatly simplified)

—evidence of *Callianssa* in the form of:
(a) indurated burrow linings (mainly mud grade)
(b) preservation of large claws

Figure 6.18 The effects of burrowing by *Callianassa* shrimps. After Tudhope and Scoffin (1984)

Selected reading

Aller, R.C. and Dodge, R.E. (1974) Animal–sediment relations in a tropical lagoon, Discovery Bay, Jamaica. *J. Mar. Res.* **32**, 209–232.

Braithwaite, C.J.R. (1973) Settling behaviour related to sieve analysis of skeletal sands. *Sedimentology* **20**, 251–262.

Carricker, M.R., Smith, E.H. and Wilce, R.T. (eds.) (1969) Penetration of calcium carbonate substrates by lower plants and invertebrates. *Amer. Zoologist* **9**, No. 3.

Chave, K.E. (1962) Skeletal durability and preservation. In Imbrie, J. and Newell, N.D. (eds.), *Approaches to Paleoecology*, John Wiley & Sons, New York, 377–387.

Crimes, T.P. and Harper, J.C. (eds.) (1970) *Trace Fossils. Geol. J.*, Spec. Issue, **3**, Seel House Press, Liverpool.

Crimes, T.P. and Harper, J.C. (eds.) (1977) *Trace Fossils. 2. Geol. J.* Spec. Issue, **9**, Seel House Press, Liverpool.

Davies, G.R. (1970) Carbonate bank sedimentation, eastern Shark Bay, Western Australia. *Am. Ass. Pet. Geol. Mem.* **13**, 85–168.

Enos, P. and Perkins, R.D. (1977) *Quaternary Sedimentation in South Florida.* Geol. Soc. Am. Mem. 14.

Farrow, G.F. 1971. Back reef and lagoonal environments of Aldabra Atoll distinguished by their crustacean burrows. In Stoddart, D.R. and Yonge, C.M. (eds.), *Regional Variation in Indian Ocean Coral Reefs*, Symp. Zool. Soc. London, **28**, 455–500.

Folk, R.L. and Robles, R. (1964) Carbonate sands of Isla Perez Alacran Reef complex, Yucatan. *J. Geol.* **72**, 255–292.

Force, L.M. (1969) Calcium carbonate size distribution on the west Florida shelf and experimental studies on the microarchitectural control of skeletal breakdown. *J. Sed. Petrol.* **39**, 902–934.

Frey, R.W. (ed.) (1975) *The Study of Trace Fossils.* Springer Verlag, Berlin.

Fütterer, D.K. (1974) Significance of the boring sponge *Cliona* for the origin of fine-grained material of carbonate sediments. *J. Sed. Petrol.* **44**, 79–84.

Ginsburg, R.N. (1956) Environmental relationships of grain size and constituent particles in some south Florida carbonate sediments. *Bull. Am. Ass. Petrol. Geol.* **40**, 2384–2427.

Ginsburg, R.N. and Lowenstam, H.A. (1958) The influence of marine bottom communities on the depositional environment of sediments. *J. Geol.* **66**, 310–318.

Ginsburg, R.N., Lloyd, R.M., Stockman, K.W. and McCallum, J.S. (1963) Shallow-water carbonate sediments. In Hill, M.N. (ed.), *The Seas*, **3**, 554–582.

Golubic, S., Perkins, R.D. and Lukas, K.J. (1975) Boring microorganisms and microborings in carbonate substrates. In Frey, R.W. (ed.), *The Study of Trace Fossils,* Springer Verlag, Berlin, 229–259.

Goreau, T.F. (1963) Calcium carbonate deposition by coralline algae and corals in relation to their roles as reef-builders. *Am. N.Y. Acad. Sci.* **109**, 127–167.

Maiklem, W.R. (1968) Some hydraulic properties of bioclastic carbonate grains. *Sedimentology* **10**, 101–109.

Neumann, A.C. (1968) Biological erosion of limestone coasts. In Fairbridge, R.W. (ed.), *Encyclopaedia of Geomorphology*, Van Nostrand-Reinhold, Princeton, 75–81.

Neumann, A.C., Gebelein, C.D. and Scoffin, T.P. (1970) The composition structure and erodability of subtidal mats, Abaco, Bahamas, *J. Sed. Petrol.* **40**, 274–297.

Ogden, J.C. (1977) Carbonate sediment production by parrot fish and sea urchins on Caribbean reefs. In Frost, S.H., Weiss, M.P. and Saunders, J.B. (ed.), *Reefs and Related Carbonates—Ecology and Sedimentology*, Am. Ass. Petrol. Geol. Studies in Geol. **4**, 281–288.

Orme, G.R. (1977) Aspects of sedimentation in the coral reef environment. In Jones. O.A. and Endean, R. (eds.), *Biology and Geology of Coral Reefs IV, Geology II*, 129–182.

Otter, G.W. (1931) Rock-destroying organisms in relation to coral reefs. *Sci. Rep. Great Barrier Reef Exped.* **1**, 323–352.

Purdy, E.G. (1964) Sediments as substrates. In Imbrie, J. and Newell, N.D. (eds.), *Approaches to Paleoecology*, John Wiley & Sons, New York, 238–269.

Risk, M.J. and McGeachy, J.K. (1978) Aspects of bioerosion of modern Caribbean reefs. *Rev. Biol. Trop.* **26** (Suppl.), 85–105.

Scoffin, T.P. (1970) The trapping and binding of subtidal carbonate sediments by marine vegetation in Bimini Lagoon, Bahamas. *J. Sed. Petrol.* **40**, 248–273.

Scoffin, T.P., Stearn, C.W., Boucher, D. Frydl, P. Hawkins, C.M. Hunter, I.G. and McGeachy, J.K. (1980) Calcium carbonate budget of a fringing reef on the west coast of Barbados. Pt. II Erosion, sediments and internal structure. *Bull. Mar. Sci.* **302**, 457–508.

Seilacher, A. (1964) Biogenic sedimentary structures. In Imbrie, J. and Newell, N.D. (eds.), *Approaches to Paleoecology*, John Wiley & Sons, New York, 296–316.

Shinn, E.A. (1968) Burrowing in recent lime sediments of Florida and the Bahamas. *J. Paleontol.* **42**, 879–894.

Sognnaes, R.F. (ed.) (1963) Mechanisms of hard tissue destruction. Am. Ass. Adv. Sci. Pub. **75**.

Swinchatt, J.P. (1965) Significance of constituent composition, texture, and skeletal breakdown in some Recent carbonate sediments. *J. Sed. Petrol.* **35**, 633–648.

Tudhope, A.W. and Scoffin, T.P. (1984) The effects of *Callianassa* bioturbation on the preservation of carbonate grains in Davies Reef Lagoon, Great Barrier Reef, Australia, *J. Sed. Petrol.* **54**, 1091–1096.

Tudhope, A.W. and Risk, M.J. (1985) Rate of dissolution of carbonate sediments by microboring organisms, Davies Reef, Australia, *J. Sed. Petrol.* **55**, 440–447.

Warme, J.E. (1977) Carbonate borers—their role in reef ecology and preservation. In Frost, S.H., Weiss, M.P. and Saunders, J.B. (eds.), *Reefs and Related Carbonates—Ecology and Sedimentology.* Am. Ass. Petrol. Geol. Studies in Geol. **4**, 261–280.

7 Reef growth

7.1 Reef definition

Reefs have proved notoriously difficult to define, because the term means different things to different people. To mariners, a reef is any rock structure at or just below the sea surface, on which their ships could run aground. Biologists consider reefs as rich assemblages of dominantly sessile and colonial organisms, mainly corals and algae, that grow as rigid wave-resistant masses in shallow seas in the tropics. Geologists are faced with a succession of rocks (normally unbedded carbonates, Figure 7.1) with a certain geometry and petrographic character, and they may have a problem in ascertaining the precise depth of water at the time of formation and the wave-resistant character of the structure. The geologists' reef may or may not contain corals (e.g. Devonian stromatoporoid reefs), may or may not have grown in the surf (e.g. 400 m-deep *Lophelia* banks), and may or may not have been wave-resistant (e.g. delicately branched coral frameworks). Some geologists find the genetic constraints of the biologists' reef too strict, and prefer to use the word *bioherm* for lens-shaped mounds built of organic remains, and *biostrome* for beds built of organic remains. Another term in common usage, describing thick carbonate deposits of limited lateral extent built essentially of organisms but not always with an apparent

rigid framework, is *build-up*. I wish to retain the term 'reef' here as a broad term of use to scientists working in present seas and on ancient limestones. Some of the genetic attributes deemed by some to be significant for modern reef description, e.g. depth of formation, cannot be universally applied, but I maintain that there are sedimentological attributes unique to reefs of all ages and in all settings that can be adopted. The principal attribute is the bound nature of the components.

For the sedimentologist a reef is a laterally restricted mass of carbonate rock whose composition and relationship with the surrounding sediments suggest that the bulk of its components (normally skeletons) were bound together into a framework during deposition, maintaining and developing a structure of positive topographic relief on the sea-bed.

We can satisfactorily explain most stratified accumulations of particulate sediment by a model of mechanical deposition, under gravity, of grains in a fluid medium with variations in either the source of sediment or conditions of deposition responsible for the stratification. However, where the lateral margins of an unbedded pile of sediment either abut directly against beds or are flanked by intertonguing strata, it can reasonably be concluded that the components of

Figure 7.1 Massive reef limestone, approximately 60 m thick, Devonian, Canadian Rockies.

this pile did not behave normally, spreading out while settling under gravity, but rather were bound together into a localized structure. In addition, it may be deduced that this structure was necessarily isolated, most probably by positive topographic relief, from the loose flanking sediments, thereby avoiding being swamped by them. It is this *binding* element, this initial cohesion of particles at deposition, that is the essence of a reef for the sedimentologist.

The evidence for the binding is provided not only by the unbedded nature of the sediment in otherwise normal strata, but by the usual existence of a skeletal framework and common association with reef talus, which consists of fragments of consolidated reef sediment. The existence of positive topographic relief of the reef structure during deposition is confirmed with evidence from geopetals (fossil planes indicating the horizontal at the time of deposition—see Figure 7.2) in flanking sediment, the down dip relationship of the time-equivalent facies, and the occurrence of talus blocks whose mere existence indicates erosion from a face of positive relief and whose structural elevation below the reef suggests a slope.

The binding element essential to reefs is usually of organic origin, though it may be a combin-

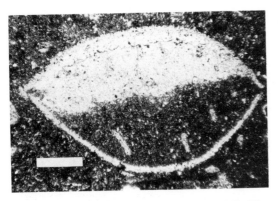

Figure 7.2 A geopetal structure. The micrite partially filling the articulated shell forms a flat floor that was horizontal at the time of deposition. Thin section, ppl. Scale 0.5 mm. Silurian, Much Wenlock, England

ation of organic and inorganic (submarine cement) processes. All marine organisms that firmly attach to an immobile substrate require water movement to carry nutrients to them but, at the same time, their growth is hindered by abundant settling or moving sediment. Consequently, the ideal location for attachment is an elevated solid substrate. This is not to say that some reef builders cannot grow on loose sand, but that the chances of such organisms reaching maturity are greater when attached to an elevated rock. Naturally, different forms have different levels of tolerance to soft sediment—one particular species may instigate reef growth on loose sediment and form the base for later colonization by reef builders. However, if all reef builders could start and continue growth quite adequately on loose sediment, we would imagine that they would cover the soft sea-bed with an even veneer of skeletons in preference to building localized elevated structures where competition for food is greater. From this it can be seen that all epilithic organisms with a rigid skeleton are potential reef builders, because organisms that prefer to start growth on the type of substrate which they themselves can produce (elevated solid substrate) will always tend to build a localized mound structure of one skeleton on another. Sessile filter feeders with rigid skeletons, such as stony corals, give a good example; being immobile they require currents to carry food to them, but they must live elevated above accumulating sand to prevent suffocation.

So, all other environmental factors being favourable and equal, the location of initial reef growth will be governed by substrate. Observations of Recent reefs support this theory. The example of coral growth on the southern margin of Bermuda atoll shown in Figure 7.3 illustrates a linear rocky shore supporting a linear fringing reef except at sandy embayments where there are gaps in the reef; and in the lagoon a patchy distribution of suitable substrates results in the development of patch reefs.

Many modern reefs contain trapped sediment

Figure 7.3 Reefs growing on the south shore of Bermuda islands. In the background waves break on a line of algal cup reefs. Coral reefs fringe the lagoon side of the Pleistocene islands (made of calcareous aeolianites) except where there is excess loose sediment (arrow). Small patch reefs occur in the lagoon. Oblique air photo, 200 m elevation, Bermuda

which has been cemented while in contact with sea water. Reefs, especially those at the edge of platforms, are more prone to this marine lithification than the surrounding sediments of the sea bed. This is partly because the structure of the reef and its trapped interstitial sediment are immobile and partly because they are elevated in the water column and suffer a high water flux from wave and tidal action. Cements interpreted (on chemical, mineralogical and textural grounds, see Chapter 8) as marine are also quite common in ancient reefs. Thus the organic secretion of an anchorage which binds the new skeletal addition to the old substrate is aided in its encrustation of rigid and loose sediment by an inorganic marine cement. The processes may work hand in hand, since the inorganic cement can create a solid substrate suitable for colonization by reef-builders. However, the marine cementation cannot build a reef without some

initial rigid structure; a cemented beach is a beach rock, a cemented ooid shoal is a consolidated bank of ooids, not a reef, since the constituent grains of such deposits started out as discrete unattached entities, susceptible to traction currents and capable of being spread into bedded features, and were not coherent as a reef framework right from inception.

7.2 Structure of reef framework

During their development on the sea-bed the structures of modern reef frameworks are controlled by the interplay of five processes of growth and destruction (Figure 7.4):

(i) Primary framework growth
(ii) Secondary framework encrustation
(iii) Erosion by physical and biological processes
(iv) Internal sedimentation
(v) Marine cementation.

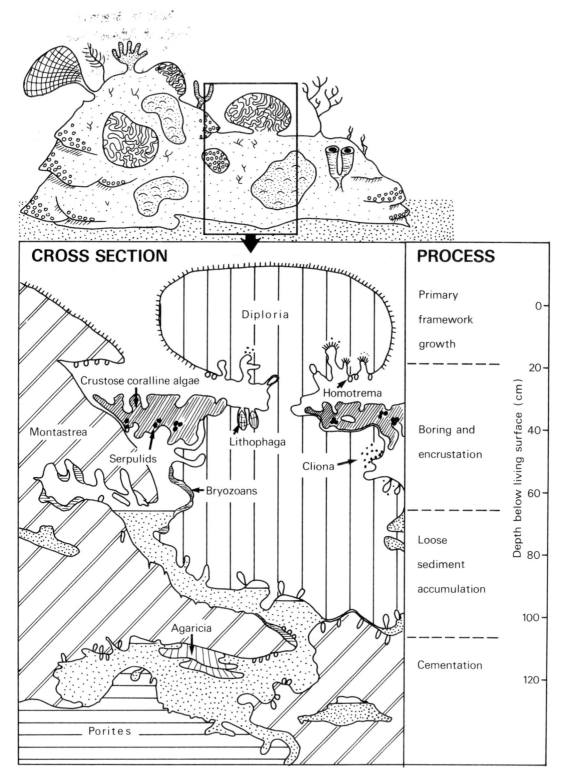

Figure 7.4 The development of the internal structure of a lagoonal patch reef of Bermuda indicating examples of encrusting and bioeroding organisms and the depth below the reef surface of the major internal processes. After Scoffin (1972)

Scott W. Starratt
Dept. of Paleontology
U. C. Berkeley
Berkeley, Ca. 94720

These processes, along with those of post-burial diagenesis, are responsible for the preserved structure of fossil reefs we see in ancient limestones.

7.2.1 Primary framework growth

On modern reefs the primary framework is built by zooxanthellate scleractinian corals. Scleractinian corals have only been building reefs since about the Jurassic. At different times in the geological past other organisms have been the predominant primary frame-builders (Figure 7.5), as we will see later. For the moment we will examine the characteristics of modern reef frameworks and point out where differences may have occurred in the past. Reef-building corals have the marked advantages of being colonial and being able to adopt two methods of reproduction, sexual and asexual. Sexual reproduction puts minute larvae in the water column which may survive several days before they settle on a suitable substrate, secrete a basal attachment, and develop from a single polyp into a colony. Asexual reproduction takes place by budding or splitting of the original polyps in the colony. These two methods of propagation have distinct advantages for sessile reef builders; firstly, if one part of the colony is restricted in its growth, for example by sediment or a neighbouring sessile organism, then new skeletal growth can develop preferentially in a different part of the colony by budding; secondly, should a major disaster strike the colony, killing off all polyps, there is always a chance that sexually reproduced larvae are in the water column and will be able to settle on new substrates to perpetuate the species.

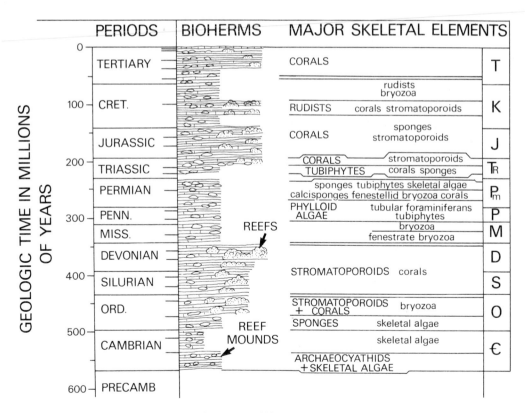

Figure 7.5 Reef builders through time. After James (1983)

Thus, though reef-builders are sessile, they have flexibility in their growth and propagation.

Among the corals (and other groups) the growth form varies according to taxonomy and environment. The specific controls on coral shape are exceedingly complex; only a few empirical generalities will be given here.

The corals that can best withstand high wave energy are the massive and encrusting forms, with broad areas of attachment and low centres of buoyancy (e.g. *Diploria strigosa* and *Montastrea annularis*). Branching varieties such as the elkhorn coral *Acropora palmata* and the staghorn *Acropora cervicornis* live in and just below the surf zone, but are regularly broken during heavy storms into coarse debris of plates and rods, while the massive forms survive unda-

maged (Figure 7.6). Delicately open branched forms (e.g. *Oculina diffusa*) are more common below the levels of heavy wave action. Those corals that live at lower levels may be threatened more presistently by sediment falling off the reef. Branched forms may cope better than broad massive forms with raining sediment, though sediment removal from the colony is closely related to the geometry of the calyx and the polyp's distensional capacity. Massive forms develop a domed morphology with shingle-like platy sides to cope with the shedding of loose sediment. An increase in depth is accompanied by a sharp fall in light intensity. At 20 m depth light levels are only 25% of those at the surface and coral growth decreases due to the restricted photosynthetic activity of the symbiotic zooxan-

Figure 7.6 The effects of a hurricane on a coral reef. The massive corals (mainly *Montastrea*) remain intact and upright but the branching corals (*Acropora cervicornis*) are broken. Scale 300 mm. 3 years after Hurricane Allen, 8 m depth, Discovery Bay Reef, Jamaica

thellae. The corals maximize the low light levels by developing platy shapes at depth. These absorb more radiant energy per unit mass of coral than do domed forms.

The distribution of the primary frame-builders is controlled not only by their own ecological requirements, but also by the distribution of those organisms that compete for space on the reef surface, such as soft corals, algae, and sponges, by predators, and by grazing organisms which inhibit larval attachment.

The growth form of the dominant primary frame-builders imposes an underlying impression on the internal structure of the reef. For example, massive mushroom-shaped corals will develop a pillow structure with cavernous porosity in which reefal sediments accumulate, platy branching forms develop a tabulate network structure which may shelter interstices by an umbrella effect, sprawling encrusting masses will develop a dense layered structure with limited opening for interstitial sediments, and so on.

7.2.2 Secondary framework growth

The secondary framework consists of those calcareous organisms, normally of encrusting habit, that attach themselves to the walls of cavities within the primary frame (Figure 7.7). Some secondary frame-builders attach near the reef surface, others, the coelobites, colonize the darker recesses of the framework. The major secondary frame-builders on modern reefs are:

(i) Crustose coralline algae (e.g. *Neogoniolithon*, *Porolithon*, *Lithophyllum*, *Lithothamnium*, *Mesophyllum*)

(ii) *Corals* (e.g. *Agaricia*, a zooxanthellate colonial scleractinian; *Dendrophyllia*, an azooxanthellate solitary scleractinian; *Millepora* and *Stylaster*, hydrozoans)

(iii) Bryozoans (e.g. *Bugula*, *Callopora*, *Cribrilaria*)

(iv) Bivalves (e.g. *Spondylus*, *Chama*, *Lopha*, *Ostrea*)

(v) Gastropods (e.g. *Dendropona*, *Vermicularia*)

Figure 7.7 *Acropora palmata* coral (*a*) encrusted by layers of coralline algae (*b*) capped by coral rubble (*c*). Scale 50 mm. Pleistocene, Barbados

(vi) Serpulid worms (e.g. *Filograna*, *Serpula*)

(vii) Foraminiferans (e.g. *Homotrema*, *Gypsina*, *Carpentaria*)

(viii) Brachiopods (e.g. *Thecideidae*)

(ix) Sclerosponges (e.g. *Ceratoporella*).

The algal and zooxanthellate coral encrusters require light for growth, and thus dominate the well-lit cavities near the reef surface. However, as the species of encrusting red algae have different compositions of pigments which allow them to utilize different intensities and wavelengths of light, we find each species has its own particular preference for setting, e.g., *Porolithon* on the upper surface and *Mesophyllum* on the undersides of coral branches. Most of the animal encrusters are found in dark cavities within the reef frame down to the sediment–water interface. Some types (e.g. certain bryozoans) have difficulty coping with falling sediment and preferentially colonize the downward-facing undersides of cave walls. The red encrusting foraminiferan *Homotrema rubrum* is common (along with serpulids and rare brachiopods) deep inside reef frames. The encrusters found in the deepest, most cryptic settings of very low light, food and water-circulation levels are scleros-ponges which can be found more than two metres below the reef surface.

As the reef grows, the once well-lit near-surface cavities that supported the *photophilic* (light-loving) encrusters become darker, sup-porting the *sciaphilic* (dark-loving organisms). So a fossil reef cavity that changed from a near-surface to a deep cavernous setting would consist of a crust on the primary frame of sequential (light to dark) secondary frame-builders reflect-ing the gradual construction of the reef (Figure 7.8). If a thick accumulation of coral branches was rapidly dumped, for example by a

storm, then we may expect no such progressional sequence; instead, sciaphilic organisms will be found attached directly to those coral branches that were in the lower part of the storm deposit. A close examination of the type and sequence of secondary frame-building organisms can tell us a lot about the depositional history of the framework.

7.2.3. Erosion by physical and biological processes

Mechanical destruction by waves mainly affects the protruding portions of the primary frame-work. Reef fragments of various sizes may fall down the fore-reef slope or be transported up on to the reef flat. More commonly, they will fall into gaps and crevices in the reef framework, and be fairly rapidly encrusted by secondary and primary framebuilders and incorporated into the structure. This mechanical destruction is aided by the boring and grazing action of organisms whose methods and products of erosion were described earlier.

Grazing organisms feed primarily on endo-lithic algae and thus reduce chiefly external dead coral surfaces of the primary framework. Boring organisms also preferentially attack dead coral surfaces, but many, for example sponges, bivalves, worms, penetrate surfaces deep within the reef framework. There are two important consequences of this. Firstly, boring action may penetrate and dislodge secondary framework as well as primary framework, providing a major source of sediment. The newly exposed internal substrate may be ideal for renewed colonization by secondary frame-builders, but is normally not suitable for primary frame-builder growth, which only expands the outer, well-lit and flushed surfaces. Thus, the interaction of boring and cavity encrustation causes a progressive replacement of primary by secondary frame-work. Secondly, the reef frame may be attacked from all angles by borers operating on several surfaces lying between the uppermost surface of the reef and the level of the interstitial sediment.

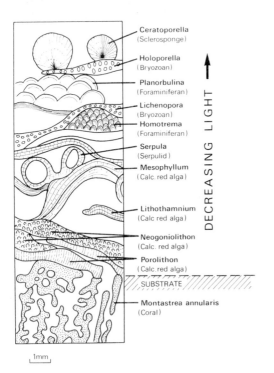

Figure 7.8 Schematic illustration of a sequence of encrusting organisms on a surface that becomes darker as burial proceeds

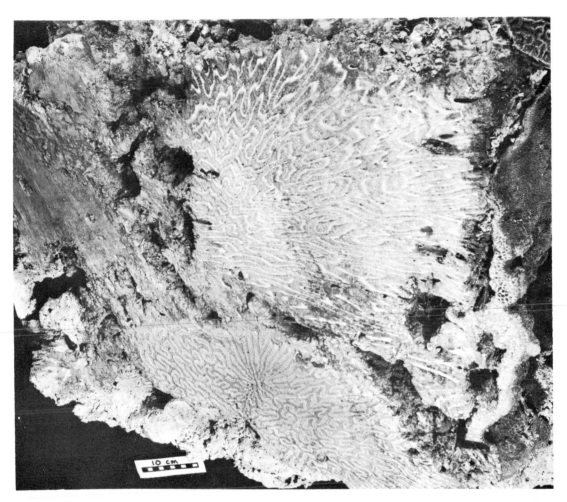

Figure 7.9 Internal structure of patch reef built principally of massive corals. The internal bioerosion results in the loss of anchorages and growth surfaces. Recent, 10 m depth, Bermuda. From Scoffin (1972)

Composite bioerosion features (e.g. *Cliona* sponge borings excavating an earlier bivalve borehole) are common, and each subsequent stage of erosion wipes out the evidence of the earlier events. Advancing fronts of bioerosion diminish the framework, destroying coral anchorages and growth surfaces alike, and appear as minor disconformities within the reef. The contiguous nature of the original framework may be lost (Figure 7.9).

The rates of boring are comparable with the rates of coral growth (*c.* 10 mm/year), so where there are several surfaces of bioerosion within the framework, their combined action may be removing $CaCO_3$ from the frame faster than the single growth surface of the primary framebuilders can add it. In such cases the level of the reef surface will fall, even though it may support a flourishing cover of healthy corals. The effects of bioerosion may be much more significant on those reefs at high latitudes where coral growth is more limited.

7.2.4 Internal sedimentation

Sediment is supplied on the reefs by the break-down of rigid frameworks by mechanical and biological erosion and by the disintegration of reef dwellers—for example the sclerites of soft corals, the segments of *Halimeda* plants, and the skeletal remains of ophiuroids. This sediment is washed into interstices, settles on ledges, and floors the lowermost cavities. Internal sediment is commonly graded, for as the reef grows and encrustation progressively occludes pores, only finer and finer sediment can penetrate the in-nermost recesses. Some cavities are incompletely filled with sediment, and the flat floor may be capped with $CaCO_3$ cement precipitated from later percolating fluids to preserve a geopetal structure (Figure 7.10). Sediment may totally fill cavities, which may give the impression, when seen in cross-section, that the reef organisms grew directly on this sediment. Confirmation of the earlier existence of an open framework through which water flushed is obtained by close examination of the growth attitudes of the pendant encrusting organisms now abutting in-ternal sediment.

Burial by fine sediment terminates primary and secondary framework growth and bioero-sion. It freezes the framework, preserving it in the state the various interacting processes of growth and destruction have reached. The timing of

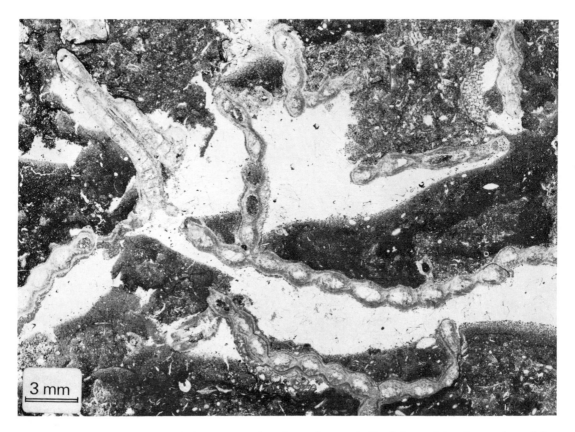

3 mm

Figure 7.10 Internal structure of a reef with a platy coral (*Halysites*) framework. The skeletons shelter the areas beneath from complete mud fill, and the overlying fluid-filled void is eventually filled with sparry cement. Stained peel, scale 3 mm. Silurian, Much Wenlock, England.

burial, which may be considered to be inversely related to the thickness of the reef frame through which water can percolate, governs the degree of alteration of the primary frame. If a fossil coral's growth surface is preserved intact, then it was most likely killed by the sediment that covers it, since bioerosion and encrustation attack unprotected exposed surfaces so rapidly. Those reef-building organisms that can tolerate the greatest sediment flux and therefore live close to sediment, on or in the framework, are the forms most likely to be best preserved on fossilization.

Fine waterladen internal sediments may suffer differential compaction during early burial due to uneven overburden, or tensional forces, within the reef framework. Water escapes upwards and fluid-filled cavities are formed which have irregular roofs and flat floors. In fossil reefs these cavities in mudstones are called *stromatactis*. The roofs are supported by framework organisms, partially consolidated fine internal sediments, or arched-over coarse sediments, whereas the flat floors represent the surface of re-sedimented fine

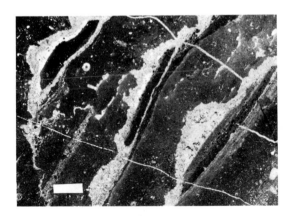

Figure 7.11 Thin section in plane polarized light showing stromatactis cavities in calcareous mudstones. The sparry calcite masses represent former voids which had flat floors (of internal sediment) and irregular roofs. There are clearly several generations of internal sediments, some of which post-date cavity cementation. Scale 5 mm. Carboniferous, Clitheroe, England

internal sediments. There may be several generations of internal sedimentation within reef cavities, and some generations follow periods of cavity cementation (Figure 7.11).

7.2.5 Cementation

Crystals of aragonite and Mg calcite that grow into small pore spaces within reefs appear to be the result of precipitation from sea water with or without organic influences. The cements will be described in more detail later in the section on submarine diagenesis. The type of cement found (its mineralogy and morphology) appears to be controlled by the microenvironment, and a nearby organism (e.g. alga, bacterium, bivalve) may exert some control. Adjacent pores, of say a coral skeleton, may be filled by different cement types; also, sequences of changing cements are common in single pores.

We note that the most exposed seaward reefs are usually the most thoroughly cemented with cement crystals present in pores right at the framework surface, whereas on more sheltered lagoonal reefs, cements are less developed and may only be pervasive some centimetres below the framework surface (Figure 7.4). This marine cementation appears to be a near-surface phenomenon, because beneath about one metre of (Holocene) framework the amount of interstitial cement does not increase significantly.

The cementation of reef framework not only occludes skeletal cavities but also lithifies loose sediment trapped there. Thus interstitial sediment may be hardened and interlaminated with layers of cements, and also the sediment contents of vacated organic boreholes may become solidified and suitable for renewed infestation by borers. The new generation of boreholes once vacated may fill with sediment, then cement, and again be prone to more boring. Repetition of these processes progressively replaces the primary (or secondary) framework with the cemented sediment fills of boreholes, but only the last generation of bores will be clearly preserved on fossilization.

Selected reading

Barnes, D.J. (ed.) (1983) *Perspective on Coral Reefs.* Brian Clouston, Canberra.

Chave, K.E., Smith, S.V. and Roy, K.I. (1972) Carbonate production by coral reefs. *Marine Geol.* **12**, 123–140.

Cuffey, R.J. (1977) Bryozoan contribution to reefs and bioherms through geologic time. In Frost, S.H., Weiss, M.P. and Saunders, J.B., *Reefs and Related Carbonates, Ecology and Sedimentology*, Am. Ass. Petrol. Geol. Studies in Geology **4**, 181–194.

Dunham, R.J. (1970) Stratigraphic reefs versus ecologic reefs. *Am. Ass. Petrol. Geol.* **54**, 1931–1932.

Hopley, D. (1982) *The Geomorphology of the Great Barrier Reef.* John Wiley & Sons, New York.

Heckel, P.H. (1974) Carbonate build ups in the geologic record : a review. SEPM Spec. Pub. No. 18, 90–154.

James, N.P. (1983) See p. 218.

Ladd, H.S., Tracey, Jr. J.I., Well, J.W. and Emery, K.O. (1950) Organic growth and sedimentation on an atoll. *J. Geol.* **58**, 410–425.

Rützler, K. and Macintyre, I.G. (eds.) (1982) *The Atlantic Barrier Reef Ecosystem at Carrie Bow Cay, Belize: I, structure and communities.* Smithsonian Contr, to the Marine Sciences No. 12, Smithsonian Institution, Washington DC.

Schroeder, J.H. and Zankl, H. (1974) Dynamic reef formation : a sedimentological concept based on studies of recent Bermuda and Bahama Reefs. *Proc. 2nd Int. Symp. Coral Reefs, Brisbane,* **2**, 413–428.

Scoffin, T.P. (1972) The fossilization of Bermuda patch reefs. *Science* **178**, 1280–1282.

Scoffin, T.P. and Garrett, P. (1974) Processes in the formation and preservation of internal structure in Bermuda patch reefs. *Proc. 2nd Int. Symp. Coral Reefs, Brisbane,* **2**, 429–448.

Stearn, C.W., Scoffin, T.P. and Martindale, W. (1977) Calcium carbonate budget of a fringing reef on the west coast of Barbados. Pt. 1. Zonation and productivity. *Bull. Mar. Sci.* **27**, 479–510.

Zankl, H. and Schroeder, J.H. (1972) Interaction of genetic processes in Holocene reefs off North Eleuthera Island, Bahamas. *Geol. Rdsch.* **61**, 520–541.

Part 4 Diagenesis

Diagenesis encompasses those natural changes which occur in sediments and sedimentary rocks between the time of initial deposition and the time when the changes caused by elevated temperatures and pressures can be considered metamorphic. The early post-depositional changes to the structure of the sediment deposit, such as bioturbation, dewatering, etc., are normally excluded from the definition. For carbonate sediments, diagenesis is essentially the transformation into stable limestones or dolomites. It includes the dissolution, neomorphism and replacement of unstable minerals, the compaction of grains, and lithification by the precipitation of void-filling cements.

Various factors determine the nature of the end product of diagenesis:

(i) The composition of the original sediments
(ii) The nature of the interstitial fluids and their movements
(iii) The physical and chemical processes involved and the time subjected to them.

So a calcite-dominated sediment will undergo different diagenesis from sediment consisting mainly of aragonite, dissolution and lithification histories will differ in marine or freshwater settings, and grain and cement textures will vary according to the pressures and temperatures experienced.

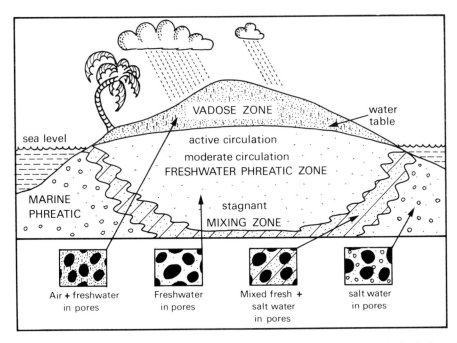

Figure 8.1 Cross-section shows the distribution and relationships of major diagenetic environments in the shallow subsurface in an ideal permeable carbonate sand island. After Longman (1982)

The environment of diagenesis leaves its characteristic imprint (or signature) on carbonate rocks. Because of their marked susceptibility to chemical and textural change, carbonate sediments may commence diagenesis while still in the environment of deposition. So accumulations of even recent carbonate sediments can have a distinctive diagenetic overprint. It is for this reason that the processes and product of diagenesis are dealt with now, before a synthesis of the characteristics of carbonate sediments of particular environments, which will be treated in Part 5.

Experimental work on carbonate diagenesis suggests that most of the critical reactions take place in the presence of fluids; true solid-state transformations are rare in limestones.

Fundamental differences in the properties of interstitial water are found in three main settings, the marine, the meteoric (Figure 8.1) and the deep burial zones (see Figure 9.17):

(i) *Marine setting*: the water ranges from undersaturated with respect to $CaCO_3$ in deep and cold seas through to supersaturated in shallow warm seas.

(ii). *Meteoric setting*: fresh water permeates the rock. Near the surface is the aerated *vadose* zone where pore spaces are occupied by water and air. The base of this zone fluctuates according to rainfall as the water-table changes elevation. Below the water-table is the zone of permanent water saturation, the *phreatic* zone. This has a higher water flux towards the top and is more stagnant near the base. In rocks close to the sea the less dense fresh interstitial waters float on the denser saline interstitial waters beneath, and there is a zone of mixing, the *mixing or schizohaline* zone, at the contact.

(iii) *Deep burial*. Pressures and temperatures increase at depth. The interstitial fluid may be similar to that trapped between grains at the time of deposition i.e. *connate* water, or it may be derived from a different source, for example, waters squeezed from nearby water-saturated clays, or brines associated with hydrocarbon accumulation.

8 Marine diagenesis

8.1 $CaCO_3$ saturation in sea water

Compared to average river water, average sea water contains 300 times more dissolved solids. The measure of the quantity of total dissolved solids in water is salinity; it is the mass in grams of all salts obtained from 1 kg brine dried to constant weight at 480 °C. Normal sea water has a salinity of 36‰. In polar regions and near to land in bays and estuaries the water may become brackish and salinities fall to 20‰, whereas in hot arid regions salinity may rise to 45‰, or even higher in areas of sluggish circulation. Sea water contains the following ions in decreasing order of abundance: $Na^+, Mg^{2+}, Ca^{2+}, K^+, Cl^-,$ SO_4^{2-}, HCO_3^-. The order of ion abundance in river water is $Ca^{2+}, Na^+, HCO_3^-, SO_4^{2-}, Cl^-$. The relatively low concentration of Ca^{2+} in sea water relates to the ease with which it is removed by biological and (to a lesser extent) direct chemical precipitation in the sea.

Terrestrial erosion contributes most of the major cations found in ocean water and also transfers CO_2 from the atmosphere to the oceans as HCO_3^-. In the weathering of a granite, potassium feldspar will break down as follows:

$$4KAlSi_3O_8 + 22H_2O + 4CO_2 \rightarrow$$

potassium feldspar

$$4K^+ + Al_4Si_4O_{10}(OH)_8 + 4HCO_3^- + 8H_4SiO_4$$

kaolinite   silicic acid

The weathering of a limestone can be expressed as:

$$CaCO_3 + H^+ + HCO_3^- \rightarrow Ca^{2+} + 2HCO_3^-.$$

There is a lag between the introduction of dissolved solids in rivers and their precipitation in the sea. Silica, calcium and bicarbonate have relatively short residence times (10^4–10^6 years) whereas chlorine and sodium have extremely long residence times (10^7–10^8 years) in the oceans.

Considering now the degree of saturation of sea water with respect to a given mineral, we find that the product of the concentrations of the ions formed during a mineral's solution reach a limit at which the solution has become saturated with the given mineral. This limit varies with temperature and pressure (depth) of the sea water. The degree of saturation, D, is written

$$D = \frac{([Ca^{2+}][CO_3^{2-}])\, \text{sea water}}{([Ca^{2+}][CO_3^{2-}])\, \text{sea water saturated with calcite}}$$

where the square brackets indicate the concentration of the enclosed ion. Values for the numerator are determined using collected samples of ocean water; values for the denominator are determined in the laboratory by adding $CaCO_3$ to sterile sea water at different temperatures and pressures.

If $D = 1$, the sea water is exactly saturated.

If $D > 1$, the water is supersaturated.

If $D < 1$, the water is undersaturated.

As the calcium content of sea water is fairly constant and variations in CO_3^{2-} are far larger by comparison, we can express D as

$$\frac{([CO_3^{2-}])\, \text{sea water}}{([CO_3^{2-}])\, \text{saturated sea water}}$$

Aragonite is more soluble than calcite at earth surface temperatures, and pressures, and the saturation carbonate ion content for aragonite is higher under corresponding conditions of temperature and pressure than that for calcite (Table 8.1).

Table 8.1 shows that the difference in surface water (1 atm) saturation concentration of CO_3^{2-} ions between the tropics (24 °C) and the polar regions (2 °C), is about 25%. Calcium carbonate is more soluble in colder water or, conversely,

Table 8.1 Saturation carbonate ion content, for calcite and aragonite with varying temperature and pressure. After Broecker (1974)

Temperature (°C)	Pressure (atm) (10 m sea water = 1 atm)	Saturation carbonate ion content (10^{-6} moles/l)	
		Calcite	Aragonite
24	1	53	90
2	1	72	110
2	250	97	144
2	500	130	190

more readily precipitates in the tropics. The solubility of $CaCO_3$ also increases with pressure or water depth. Table 8.1 shows that calcite and aragonite are almost twice as soluble at 500 atm (2 °C) as they are at 1 atmosphere (2 °C). Carbonate sediments are rarely found below depths of about 4500 m in the oceans. The calcareous skeletons of dead plankton are slowly dissolved as the grains sink from surface waters to abyssal depths. The dissolution is somewhat retarded where there is a protective organic film around the grains. Also, the incorporation of fine grains into faecal pellets by zooplankton can cause an increase in the rate of fall of particles, taking fine grains deeper than might be expected on theoretical grounds. We note that at a uniform temperature aragonite will dissolve at a shallower depth than calcite. So the maximum depths of occurrence of pteropod (aragonite) oozes are generally shallower than those for planktonic foraminiferal and coccolith oozes (calcite).

In shallow polar regions the cold undersaturated waters visibly etch the surface of carbonate grains. Even in those shallow temperate seas where calcareous skeletal deposits are locally abundant, there is a general absence of clay-sized carbonate particles, suggesting complete dissolution of the very fine grains with high surface area to volume ratios.

In shallow tropical seas, dissolution of calcium carbonate without the influence of organic activity (such as that of microborers) is unusual. It has been proposed, however, that the increase in the relative abundance of calcitic constituents with decreasing grain size in some shallow water sediments of Campeche Bank (Mexico) and Bermuda atoll (N. Atlantic) reflects the dissolution of fine-grained aragonite.

8.2 Marine cements

In the shallow marine setting, nuclei and impurities abound, supersaturation is high and precipitation of $CaCO_3$ is rapid. As a consequence, cement crystals are fine-grained. Only in the deep sea are coarse-grained cements found and here very rarely. Two minerals are quantitatively important as marine cements (Figure 8.2); arag-

onite and Mg calcite (normally with 12–20 mol% $MgCO_3$). Aragonite generally grows in the form of needles, which may be flat-ended. They are a few microns to several tens of microns long (Figure 8.3A). These can occur individually on substrates or in aggregates as splays, botryoids (Figure 8.3B, C) or fibrous crusts (Figure 8.3D) with needles arranged radially from the substrate. Mg calcite precipitates in the sea as fine-grained needles or blades, commonly with curved three-sided pyramidal terminations, or as small rhombs a few microns in diameter (Figure 8.3E). These Mg calcite crystals form fibrous crusts, spherulitic clusters or very fine equant mosaics (micrites). The micrites com-

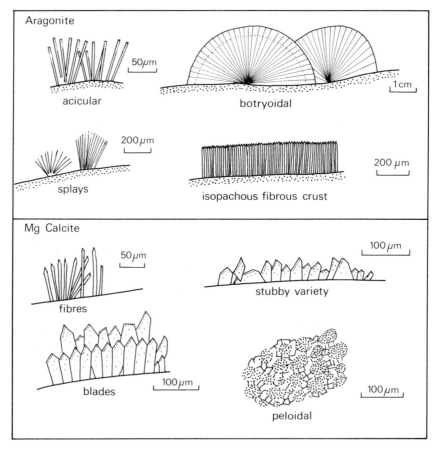

Figure 8.2 Sketches of the varieties of marine cements

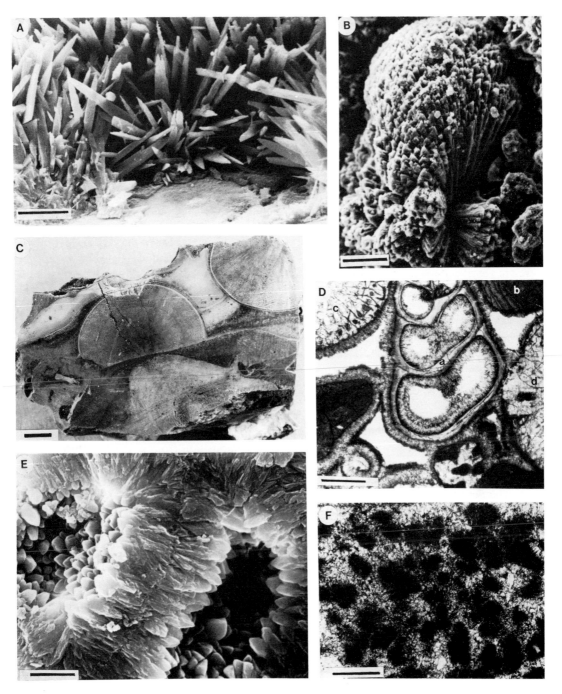

Figure 8.3 Examples of marine cements. (*A*) Aragonite needles on foraminiferan skeleton in beachrock. SEM. Scale 20 μm. Recent, intertidal, Bewick Reef. Great Barrier Reef, Australia. (*B*) Acicular aragonite in spherule form SEM. Scale 10 μm. Recent, 3 m depth, Barbados. From Scoffin *et al.* (1980). (*C*) Botryoidal aragonite in Pliocene reef blocks (this cement has isotopic value $\delta^{13}C_{PDB} = +4.8 \; \delta^{18}O_{PDB} = +3.3$). Scale 10 mm. Politiko, Cyprus. *(D)* Thin section of isopachous fringes of acicular aragonite cement on gastropod (*a*), red algal (*b*), foraminiferan (*c*) and coral (*d*) grains. Ppl. Scale 1 mm. Recent, Beachrock, Mangaia, Cook Islands, Pacific. (*E*) Bladed calcite cement lining the chambers of a coralline alga. SEM. Scale 4 μm. Recent, 0.5 m depth, Rarotonga, Cook Islands, Pacific. (*F*) Peloidal, micritic, calcitic cement. Thin section. Ppl. Scale 0.2 mm. Miocene, Mangaia, Cook Islands, Pacific

monly have a peloidal texture consisting of subspherical bodies 20–60 μm in diameter composed of a mosaic of roughly 1 μm diameter equant Mg calcite crystals, separated by coarser Mg calcite crystals 5–10 μm in diameter (Figure 8.3F).

There is a general trend of decreasing mol% $MgCO_3$ content in calcites precipitated as the water cools with either increasing latitude or increasing depth. In surface waters, calcite generally has 12–25 mol% $MgCO_3$, from 100–1000 m 10–12 mol% is common, and at 1000–3000 m 3–5 mol% $MgCO_3$ is more usual.

There are varying views on what fundamentally controls the mineralogy of marine cements, why Mg calcite and aragonite occur together, and why calcite (low in Mg) is so rarely developed inorganically in the shallow sea. The experimentally determined sequence of decreasing solubilities of calcites and aragonite is: Mg calcite (> 12 mol% $MgCO_3$) > aragonite > Mg calcite (< 12 mol% $MgCO_3$) > calcite (0–5 mol% $MgCO_3$), yet strangely it is the two most soluble varieties that are most commonly found as marine cements. Surface sea water is supersaturated with respect to all the chief carbonate minerals, calcite, aragonite and dolomite. Theoretically, dolomite ought to precipitate most readily, calcite next and finally aragonite. The reason for the gross oversaturation of sea water with respect to dolomite lies in the kinetic problem of nucleating and growing the ordered dolomite crystal with regularly alternating Ca, Mg layers, coupled with the inhibiting effect of sulphate ions (see section 10.2).

It has been suggested (Folk, 1974) that calcite does not precipitate on account of the inhibiting effect of Mg^{2+} ions, which are abundant in sea water and which give a surface formation of high-Mg calcite on any calcites that nucleate. Thus they become more unstable than aragonite, which precipitates first. Any calcite that does manage to crystallize is loaded with Mg-ion impurities (18–20 mol% $MgCO_3$). Further, the difficulty of dehydrating the Mg^{2+} ion during

Mg calcite precipitation could result in water molecules being incorporated in the structure of the solid solution, which must affect its solubility. More recent work (Given and Wilkinson, 1985) argues that the rate of crystal growth is a crucial factor in controlling the mineralogy of inorganically precipitated $CaCO_3$ (see section 9.13).

Other substances, particularly organic compounds, may also directly or indirectly influence the mineralogy of precipitating calcium carbonate. The hydrogen ion of the carboxyl groups of certain organic compounds is easily given up and exchanged for a Ca cation, and this provides a template for $CaCO_3$.

Typical stable isotopic values for marine cements are in the region of + 1‰ to + 4‰ for $\delta^{13}C$, and − 0.5‰ to + 2‰ for $\delta^{18}O$. The higher values suggest enrichment in $\delta^{13}C$ and $\delta^{18}O$ over what might be expected to precipitate at ambient temperatures. Thus some process, probably organic or related to the kinetics of precipitation, must be involved to cause fractionation during precipitation, or produce water of different isotopic composition from normal sea water.

8.3 Place of marine lithification

Precipitation of void-filling carbonate cements occurs in only a limited number of marine settings. As may be expected, it is most frequently encountered in the shallow, warm, $CaCO_3$-supersaturated seas of the tropics. Empirical observations indicate that intergranular cementation necessary to lithify a layer of sediment into rock takes place, to begin with, a few centimetres below the sea floor and requires the following conditions:

(i) Warm supersaturated water
(ii) A high water flux at the sediment–water interface. This might be brought about by strong currents, tidal or wave action. As sea water contains only about 0.05 g $CaCO_3$/litre, tens or hundreds of thousands of pore volumes of sea water must pass through a pore to fill it with cement

(iii) Good permeability in the surface sediments

(iv) A stable substrate combined with a slow sedimentation rate, so that the grains are exposed to flushing water for a prolonged period, yet newly formed delicate crystals are not abraded.

At sites of sea bed lithification we also commonly note:

(v) Photosynthesis and respiration of organisms play a role in increasing pH to greater than 9.

(vi) Turbulence and heating of water brings about CO_2 degassing

(vii) Certain bacteria abound.

In areas of sluggish seawater circulation, or active circulation but unstable substrate, cement crystals form more readily in small pores within grains than on their exterior surfaces, for example, within the cells of calcareous red algae, the chambers of foraminiferans, the interstices of faecal pellets or the vacated borings of microscopic algae in shells. This cementation can be very rapid, as it is found within the vacant skeletal chambers of living colonial organisms. The mineralogical nature of the cement normally reflects that of the host; under more extreme conditions of rapid cementation this host control may be lost. Within the micro-voids of sediment grains, a control on the nature of the cement by organic material may be exceedingly important.

Areas of active precipitation of intergranular calcium carbonate cement from sea water include:

(i) Reefs, particularly their windward edge

(ii) Certain deep-sea settings, including seamount tops and submarine cliffs or steep stable slopes at tropical platform margins

(iii) Stationary lobes of oolite shoals at platform margins, and saline lagoons

(iv) Tropical beaches, intertidal shingle ridges and sand flats.

8.3.1 Reef cements

Submarine excavation into modern coral reefs, using explosives or coring devices, has revealed that most reefs throughout the tropical seas of the world are undergoing contemporaneous lithification. The contemporary age for the cements is indicated by ^{14}C analysis, the common observation within the framework of internal sediment interlayered with cements, and the repeated truncation of cemented reef by contemporary organic boreholes. The most extensive (and near-surface) cementation occurs in those reefs exposed to highest water flux, on the crests and steep slopes of the windward margins. Leeward and lagoonal patch reefs are generally less well indurated. Cementation appears to continue down to about 1 m below the reef's living surface. Cemented reef framework is reported from the surface down to water depths of tens and hundreds of metres. It is only recently, since the advent of deep diving and research submersible techniques, that we have been able to examine directly these deeper marine environments. The bases of fore-reef slopes (hundreds of metres deep) are commonly strewn with large blocks broken off the reef front by a combination of storm and biological action. Lithification of the reef front is responsible for the angular shapes of talus blocks and their composite structure of cemented internal sediments and reef framework. The cemented sediment floors of partially filled reef cavities (geopetals) retain a record of the horizontal during deposition of the internal sediment, which permits the recognition of synsedimentary tilting or movement of reef blocks in many fossil reefs.

The cements found in modern reefs are aragonite and Mg calcite (12–20 mol% $MgCO_3$). The aragonite occurs as crusts, fans and, rarely, botryoids, of acicular crystals. Botryoidal aragonite occurs as masses of coalescing and interpenetrating cones and hemispheroids 10–250 mm in radius (Figure 8.3C). The aragonitic fibres radiate from widely spaced point-sources (few nucleation sites) and terminate along the smooth arcuate surfaces of the botryoids. Significant growths of the botryoidal aragonite cements have been found only in deep internal cavities on the fore-reef slopes. The marine origin is confirmed by $\delta^{13}C$ and $\delta^{18}O$ values of $c. +5‰$ and $+1‰$ respectively.

Mg calcite crystals occur with acicular crusts, blades, equant micrite or peloidal textures. Peloidal cements occur in reefs more than other environments. It appears that these micritic lumps grow in interstitial water by chemical precipitation, but they also can contain small quantities of incorporated extraneous material such as clay minerals and coccoliths. They settle on cavity floors and may develop a crude layering, having size grading (which is commonly inverse), though some adhere to cavity walls, perhaps aided by the suction created within the reef framework by waves. The peloids are not compacted into a homogeneous dense micrite, since the reef framework shelters the interstices from such pressure. The rapid cementation (which may be by Mg calcite or aragonite) of the peloids one to another, inhibits homogenization by compaction from overlying internal sediment. Post-burial neomorphism may bring about some crystal enlargement, obscuring the peloidal and banded texture and producing a clotted texture, sometimes referred to as *structure grumeleuse* when seen in ancient limestones.

8.3.2 Deep-sea lithification

Contemporary limestones have been found in various deep sea areas receiving little sediment accumulation and with relatively high water flux, such as on the tops of many sea-mounts and on the steep slopes of oceanic islands and platform margins. Mg calcite ($c. 12 \, mol\%$ $MgCO_3$) is the dominant carbonate cementing mineral (at depths of $100–1000 \, m$) and it may have an acicular crust or micritic peloidal texture. Deepsea manganese nodules have been collected that were cemented by aragonite. Below about $1000 \, m$ depth, the prevalent carbonate cement is calcite with $3–5 \, mol\%$ $MgCO_3$.

Calcite cemented limestones are occasionally found associated with deep-sea basaltic rocks, and it is assumed that the submarine vulcanism produced the necessary physico-chemical conditions to bring about carbonate precipitation.

Deep-sea lithification takes place a few centimetres below the sediment–water interface and extends down for about $100–200 \, mm$, producing a thin crust of cemented, mainly pelagic, grains. When any overlying loose sediment is removed a *hardground* is exposed (see Figure 6.11). This sediment surface typically has a smooth top and an irregular base, with an uneven gradational contact with the loose underlying sediment. Prolonged contact with sea water may bring about the impregnation of the upper surface of the hardground with Fe^{2+}, Mn^{2+} or phosphatic salts. The hardground surface may support a range of epilithic organisms, capable of living without light, such as sponges, crinoids, alcyonarians, bryozoans and deep-sea corals. It may also provide a suitable substrate for many endoliths, for example molluscs, sponges and fungi. The hardgrounds commonly have a mottled texture resulting from repeated alternations of sedimentation burrowing, cementation, boring, infilling and cementation, and are often rust-coloured due to the impregnation by Fe^{2+} and Mn^{2+} salts.

On platform margins that receive relatively little sediment, lithification of the sea bed may help to stabilize the steep slopes. Any disturbance of a weakly cemented crust, however, by sedimentological, tectonic or biological action, may result in the fragmentation of the layer. The broken lumps or nodules may later be cemented into a breccia during a period of renewed stability.

There is often seen a persistent downslope decrease in the degree of submarine cementation from widespread hardgrounds to multigeneration nodular oozes to unlithified peri-platform oozes. On the north slopes of the Great Bahama Bank, the transition in the degree of cementation correlates well with a downslope decrease in the speed of bottom currents. The degree of current winnowing may control the interstitial porosity of sediment and thus the degree of submarine cementation. However, lateral changes in the relative abundance of mineralogically unstable bank-derived sediments may also play a part in controlling the distribution of cements.

Steep cliffs of oozes, exposed for long periods (400 000 years) in erosional gullies below 1000 m depth on platform margins, can develop superficial crusts giving vertical hardgrounds by the precipitation of 2–4 μm calcite crystal (< 5 mol% $MgCO_3$) during the stabilization of aragonite and Mg calcite in the cold deep waters. The crusts overlie soft unaltered mud consisting of mixtures of aragonite, calcite and Mg calcite, partly pelagic and partly platform-derived.

In semi-enclosed basins, special conditions of high salinity and high temperatures are likely to prevail which can facilitate sea-bed lithification. In parts of the Red Sea, for example, where the bottom waters have 40‰ salinity and temperatures of 20 °C, fibrous aragonite crusts cement pteropod oozes, and Mg calcite crystals cement planktonic foraminiferal oozes.

Cemented crusts (Figure 8.4) lying within local depressions (pockmarks) in the sea bed are found in association with escaping methane gas at various water depths and latitudes. The

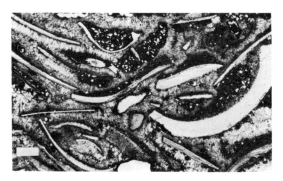

Figure 8.5 Thin section of aragonite-cemented mollusc fragments forming hardground of Figure 8.4. (This cement has isotopic value of $\delta^{13}C_{PDB} = -47$‰ and probably formed in the presence of biogenic methane.) Scale 1 mm, 80 m depth. Passage of Tiree, W. Scotland

cement crystals of aragonite and Mg calcite (Figure 8.5) have oxygen isotopic values that are normal for marine carbonates, but the carbon isotopic compositions are extremely depleted in $\delta^{13}C$ (values of -35 to -65‰) and indicate an origin from the oxidation of biogenic methane.

Platform margin shoals and saline lagoons. At the shallow-water margins of platforms such as the Bahama Banks, the dissolved CO_2 in sea water is driven off by heating and turbulence, and the area is one of active inorganic precipitation. Where the turbulence falls sufficiently for the grains to remain immobile through the tidal cycle, then lithification of the sea-bed may ensue. Abandoned lobes of oolitic shoals are commonly cemented, forming hardgrounds (Figure 6.10). The cement is normally fibrous aragonite of precisely the same composition as the aragonite of the ooids, but instead of the crystals being arranged tangentially as they are in ooids, they are arranged radially as isopachous (even-thickness) fringes around grains. The lithified crusts are a few centimetres thick and may support a population of sponges, oysters, corals and, locally, submarine stromatolites. Endolithic molluscs, worms, sponges and algae are also abundant.

Crusts of similar appearance and having fi-

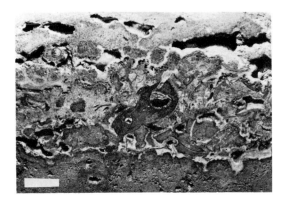

Figure 8.4 Recent hardground. Cemented fragments of molluscs, barnacles and bryozoans in sea bed crust. Scale 10 mm. 80 m depth, Passage of Tiree, W. Scotland

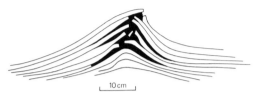

Figure 8.6 Tepee structure

brous aragonite and peloidal Mg calcite cements occur in shallow saline lagoons in the SE Persian Gulf where there is a high water flux, stable substrate and low sedimentation rate. These hardgrounds locally develop a polygonal bed-form due to cracking. Anticlines, and then fractures and thrusts, develop by expansion of the crust induced by the force of crystallization during lithification. Sequential development of overthrust hardground layers produces stacked overlapping concave slabs known, because of their profile shape, as tepees (Figure 8.6).

The sea-beds of some lagoons show incipient lithification with only patchy crusts or aggregate grains developed. In such lagoons, the substrate is usually stabilized by the binding action of algal mats, and precipitation of interstitial aragonite occurs mainly at grain contacts, perhaps itself promoted by the algae and associated micro-organisms in the surface sediments. The aggregates, commonly grapestones, may owe their origin to the disturbance of a superficially cemented crust by bioturbation or intermittent current action.

8.3.3 Beaches and other intertidal sediment bodies

Sandy beaches of the tropics are commonly cemented between high and low water marks to produce *beachrock* (Figure 8.7). These rocks have planar laminations, in units normally 10–100 mm in thickness, which dip to seaward at 5° to 15°. Cementation is assumed to have taken place *in situ* beneath a thin sediment cover. The cements are normally fibrous aragonite crystals which may be isopachous (Figure 8.3*D*), or at grain contacts where a meniscus of liquid would

Figure 8.7 Beachrock. Hammer 0.5 m. West Petherbridge Reef, Great Barrier Reef, Australia

be held by capillary forces during a draining of the interstitial water at low tide. Impermanent water saturation (vadose marine setting in this case) may be expected to develop several characteristic features (Figure 8.8):

(i) Meniscus cements are concentrated at grain contacts
(ii) The uneven cements precipitated within this meniscus of liquid result in pore rounding, and the crystals typically have blunt terminations due to undernourishment at their tips
(iii) Gravitational cements develop in a pendant attitude on the under-surfaces of grains—

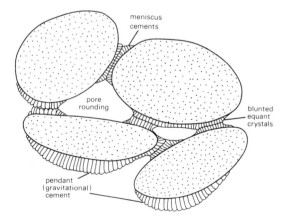

Figure 8.8 Meniscus cement fabrics

these cements may have a mamilated or botryoidal texture, reminiscent of dripstone textures in speleothem deposits

(iv) Drapestone cements occur on the upper surfaces of grains due to the dripping of water from overlying grains during drainage.

Less commonly, tropical beachrock cements have a peloidal, micritic or fibrous Mg calcite composition.

Beachrock cements are a consequence of the rise in ionic concentration resulting from the evaporation of sea water as it drains through the beach at low tide. Some workers feel that the $CaCO_3$ for tropical beachrock cement is derived from freshwater dissolution of carbonate sediments on the land area, but the weight of evidence is against this. The beaches of some tropical volcanic islands have grains that are solely non-carbonate in origin (e.g. olivine) and yet they still can be cemented by aragonite which could only be derived directly from the sea, as no other $CaCO_3$ source is available. Some small islands with beachrock have no fresh water, and global beachrock distribution appears to have no relation to rainfall patterns. Further, the aragonite cements of beachrocks have a high sodium content which is commensurate with seawater origin.

Protected beaches are more prone to beachrock formation, since the grains are stable for lengthy periods. Certain sediment outbuilding during storms may form a deposit unaffected by normal waves, allowing lithification to set in. The stabilization of beaches by algae has led several workers to conclude a causal relationship between algae and littoral lithification, as seems to be the case in the growth of the algal stromatolites of Shark Bay, West Australia (Figure 8.9).

Beachrock formation is very rapid by geological standards of diagenesis. In populated areas many beachrocks have bottle fragments incorporated in them, and on some Indian Ocean coral islands the natives make annual harvests of beachrock for building stone.

Cemented beaches are rare outside the tropics, but those few found in temperate zones normally have cements of blocky crystals of calcite (low Mg), the $CaCO_3$ being derived from freshwater solution of nearby terrestrial limesands or limestones.

There are two other intertidal environments where lithification is induced by evaporation of sea water, organic activity or both: the ridges of coral shingle on the margins of reef flats, and the intertidal sand flats of hypersaline coasts. The

Figure 8.10 Cemented (and partially eroded) forests of coral shingle ('Bassett edges'). Beds 200 mm thick. Intertidal, Low Isles, Great Barrier Reef, Australia. From Scoffin and McLean (1978)

Figure 8.9 Cemented algal stromatolites. Intertidal, Shark Bay, West Australia. Photograph courtesy of Roy McGregor

windward sides of many modern coral reefs, expecially in the Pacific ocean, have large crescent-shaped ridges (or ramparts) of coarse coral shingle banked intertidally and supratidally in series parallel to the shore (Figures 8.10, 14.4). In profile these ridges have an asymmetric wave form with a steep leeward side dipping between 40° and 60° and a gradual seaward dip of about 10°. These ridges commonly pond water in intertidal moats on the reef flat, and these waters drain slowly through the ridges during low tide. Unlike the water bathing most ocean-facing beaches, this ponded water can be very variable in composition, ranging from high through normal to low salinity depending upon evaporation and rainfall. Also, these ponded waters may drain through organic-rich mangrove swamps on route to the ridges. The coral fragments are cemented by micritic and peloidal Mg calcite (10–15 mol% $MgCO_3$) which develops a banded and mamillated dripstone fabric (Figures 8.11, 8.12).

Cementation has been observed within intertidal sand flats in the Persian Gulf and the Bahamas. Salinities are elevated to four times normal in these settings. On the very shallowly seaward-dipping slopes, cemented lumps deve-

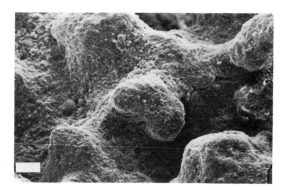

Figure 8.12 Mamillated texture of micritic Mg calcite cement of Figure 8.11. SEM. Scale 100 μm. Nymph Island, Great Barrier Reef, Australia

lop a few centimetres below the surface. These lumps may show characteristic anastomosing shapes, suggesting that small organisms (e.g. worms living in the sediment) may promote lithification. Progressive lithification causes coalescence of lumps into hard nodular crusts or sheets a few centimetres thick 5–30 cm below the surface. The cement of these intertidal lumps and crusts may be fibrous aragonite or micritic Mg calcite (10–15 mol% $MgCO_3$).

8.3.4 Supratidal zone

Of special interest is the diagenesis in the supratidal zones of arid regions, for here evaporation of sea water can bring about the precipitation of a range of carbonate, sulphate and halide salts. The theoretical sequence of salt precipitation from sea water evaporated to dryness is shown in Figure 8.13. The theoretical evaporite succession shown on the right of Figure 8.13 is rarely complete in the rock record (the bittern salts are often missing and halite sequence depleted) as it is very difficult to evaporate to total dryness if the atmosphere has any humidity at all. Also, a totally closed system is geologically unusual, so in the geological column there is an over-representation of the less soluble salts.

In the SE Persian Gulf, where average rainfall is 37 mm/yr and evaporation 1240 mm/yr, there is a broad, windswept, flat coastal belt that lies

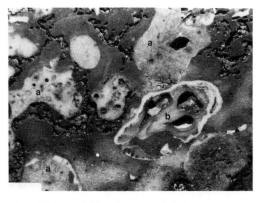

Figure 8.11 Coral (a) and gastropod (b) fragments cemented by peloidal, micritic Mg calcite (14 mol% $MgCO_3$). Scale 10 mm. Recent, high intertidal, Nymph Island, Great Barrier Reef, Australia

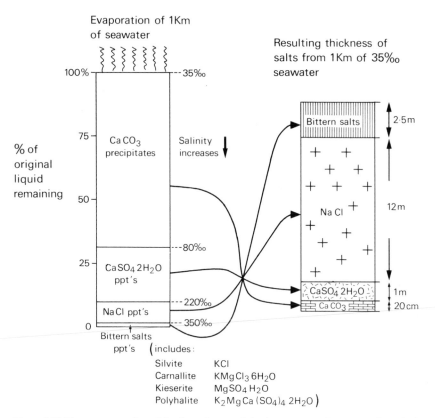

Figure 8.13 The sequence of precipitating salts as salinity increases on the evaporation of 1 km of sea water and the resulting succession of precipitated salts showing their approximate thicknesses

between the dunes of the desert and the intertidal zone flanking the sea. These unvegetated arid plains are known as *sabkhas* from the Arabic word for salt flat (Figure 8.14). The sabkhas have been built by progradation of near-shore and supratidal sediments during the Holocene. Algal laminites are typical in the intertidal zone (Figure 8.15). The supratidal areas are only rarely flooded with sea water during exceptional storms; however, sea water is brought close to the sabkha surface by capillary action and concentrated by evaporation. The brines are concentrated from a chlorinity (g Cl/litre brine) of 21 g/l in the lagoon to about 100 g/l in the intertidal algal mat to over 150 g/l in the supratidal sabkha (Figure 8.16).

The seaward progradation of the sabkha over the last few thousand years (c. 2 m/year) has produced a shallowing upwards sequence (c. 1 m thick) of deposits that consists of lagoonal sediments overlain by intertidal algal laminites, which are in turn overlain by supratidal sediments (Figure 8.16).

Some aragonite is precipitated as small needles in the lagoon, and even more during the early stages of concentration of brines, both within the sabkha sediments and also on its surface. Gypsum ($CaSO_4 . 2H_2O$) precipitates as small lozenge-shaped crystals just beneath the surface algal mat in the intertidal sediments. Anhydrite ($CaSO_4$) forms firstly by the dehydration of gypsum. This process goes by heating or by

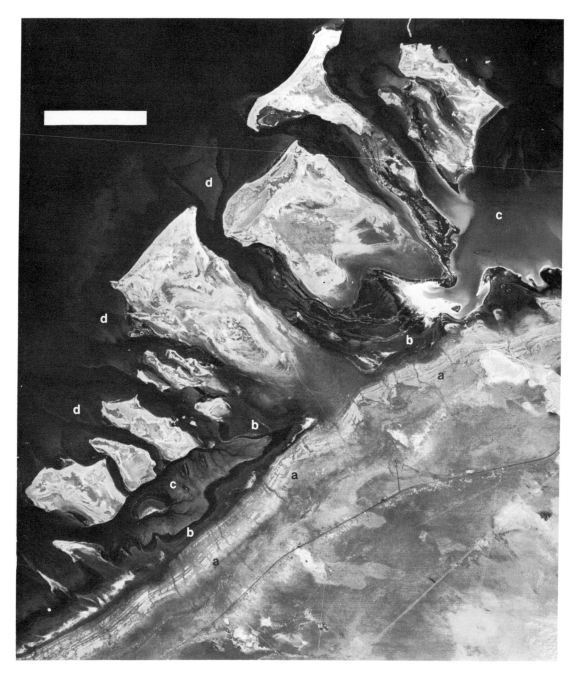

Figure 8.14 Satellite image of part of the Trucial Coast, Persian Gulf: *a*, sabkha; *b*, intertidal algal mat and tidal flats; *c*, shallow lagoons; *d*, ooid shoals in ebb tidal delta. Scale 5 km. (Image processed by ERSAC, Peel House, Ladywell, Livingston, Scotland.)

Figure 8.15 Aerial view of dark intertidal algal mat separating shallow lagoon (upper position of photograph) from the supratidal sabkha, Trucial coast, Persian Gulf. Photograph courtesy of Bob Parks

immersing gypsum in a very saline environment. Anhydrite can then precipitate directly on these nuclei. The anhydrite occurs as irregular nodules or wavy bands (*enterolithic* folds); the buckling results from the expansion of the salts. The extraction from the brines of large quantities of calcium during aragonite and gypsum precipitation raises the Mg/Ca ratio from lagoonal levels of 3:1 to greater than 10:1 in the sabkha, at which point dolomite can form (see Figure 10.1). In brines with high Mg/Ca ratios, *protodolomite* forms, which has an excess of $CaCO_3$ and shows only 40–95% ordering. The precipitation of sulphate salts also removes the SO_4^{2-} ions from solution which are believed to inhibit dolomite formation. On the landward side of the sabkha, the Mg/Ca ratio falls back to 5:1 as the Mg of solutions is depleted due to the formation of the magnesium-rich salts, dolomite and magnesite ($MgCO_3$). Fresh groundwater is also introduced on the landward side of the sabkha, and this helps to lower the Mg/Ca ratio to 5:1 or lower. Here dolomites may be replaced by calcite (a process known as dedolomitization or calcitization), and the fresh water can hydrate some of the diagenetic anhydrite back to gypsum.

Celestite ($SrSO_4$) forms in small quantities within the sabkha from the strontium released during the dolomitization of aragonite (aragonite muds here possess about 9000 ppm Sr and the dolomite contains less than about 600 ppm Sr).

Halite (NaCl) occurs as ephemeral crusts on the sabkha surface. These very soluble crystals are regularly removed during surface flooding induced by storms or very high wind-reinforced tides.

8.4 Marine neomorphism

Neomorphism (Folk, 1965) is the transformation between one mineral and itself or a polymorph. The term indicates that older crystals have been consumed and replaced by new crystals of essentially similar chemical composition (though trace elements and isotopic compositions may change). The new crystals may be larger or smaller than, or just differ in shape from, the previous ones.

There are two types of neomorphism that prevail in the marine environment; one, fairly common and probably controlled by organic activity, is the process of degrading neomorphism or micritization; the other, very rare (though widespread in the freshwater realm), is the alteration of aragonite and Mg calcite grains to blocky sparry calcite low in magnesium (aggrading neomorphism).

Marine degrading neomorphism (micritization). The process of micritization is the partial or total alteration of grains to a homogeneous microcrystalline (micritic) fabric. The alteration normally proceeds centripetally (from the outside inwards); it is not an encrustation or coating, but a replacement of the outer portions of the grains giving them a chalky perimeter. This alteration is seen in skeletal non-skeletal and, aragonitic and calcitic grains alike. The original crystalline textures of the grains are destroyed on total micritization, so that we can only guess at the origin of the grain from its surface morphology. There has been a correlation drawn between the localization of this micritization and

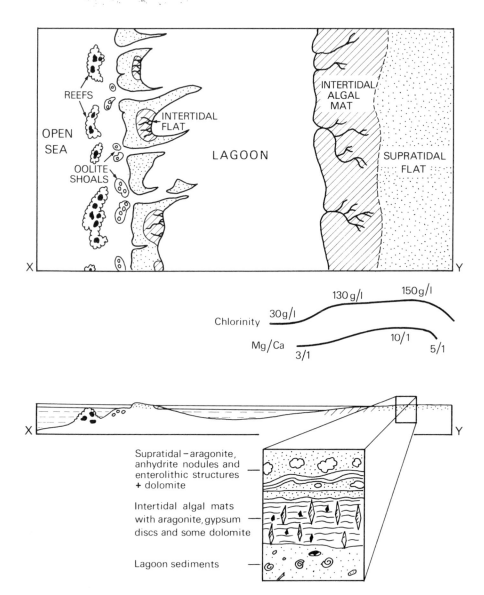

Figure 8.16 Plan and profile sketch of coastal region of SE Persian Gulf. With time the sabkha has prograded over the intertidal and subtidal deposits

the distribution of organics in the original grain. Bathurst (1966) noticed that centripetal micritization appeared to result from the repeated sequence of microborings (by algae or fungi) into the grain perimeter. The microscopic holes would be vacated on the death of the borers, and the fine crystals of micrite (aragonite or Mg calcite) would precipitate within these holes (perhaps aided by bacterial action). Later, renewed boring and micrite fillings would penetrate and extend this micritic rind (Figure 6.2). Micritized grains are particularly abundant in lagoons where algal mats stabilize the sediment. The limited analyses conducted on the chemistry of micritized rinds indicate an enrichment in $\delta^{13}C$ of the micrite relative to the host grain. This suggests that the boring organisms selectively utilized ^{12}C, creating a micro-environment enriched in ^{13}C from which the micrite precipitated.

Marine aggrading neomorphism. Since inorganic aragonite and Mg calcite are precipitated in equilibrium with sea water, it is unlikely that they will change to low-Mg calcite while in the marine environment, and it is this process in the fresh-water setting that normally brings about an increase in crystal size during transformation to sparry calcite. However, most skeletal $CaCO_3$ is precipitated in equilibrium with organic fluids, not sea water, and so mineralogical and textural changes could be expected on death of the organism and decay of its soft tissue. In fact, the change to coarse sparry crystals of calcite or aragonite is very rare in sea water though it has been reported in a few (more commonly deeper-water) areas, including peri-platform oozes exposed in cliffs in deep water off the Bahama Banks, *Halimeda* debris in the deep fore-reef off N. Jamaica, skeletal fragments on deep banks in the Gulf of Mexico, and shells in shallow saline lagoons in the Persian Gulf.

Selected reading

Alexandersson, T. (1969) Recent littoral and sublittoral high-Mg calcite lithification in the Mediterranean. *Sedimentology* 12, 47–61.

Assereto, R.L.A.M. and Kendall, C.G. St. C. (1977) Nature, origin and classification of peritidal tepee structures and related breccias. *Sedimentology* 24, 153–210.

Bathurst, R.G.C. (1966) Boring algae, micrite envelopes and lithification of molluscan biosparites. *Geol. J.* 5, 15–32.

Bathurst, R.G.C. (1974) Marine diagenesis of shallow water calcium carbonate sediments. *Ann. Rev. Earth Planet. Sci.* 2, 257–274.

Broecker, W.S. (1974) *Chemical Oceanography.* Harcourt Brace Jovanovich, New York.

Bromley, R.G. (1979) Hardground diagenesis. In Fairbridge, R.W. and Bourgeois, J. (eds.), *Encyclopedia of Sedimentology*, Dowen, Hutchinson and Ross, Stroudsburg, 397–400.

Choquette, P.W. (1968) Marine diagenesis of shallow marine lime-mud sediments: insights from O^{18} and C^{13} data. *Science* 161, 1130–1132.

Davies, G.R. (1977) Former magnesium calcite and aragonite submarine cements in upper Palaeozoic reefs of the Canadian Arctic : a summary. *Geology* 5, 11–15.

Dravis, J. (1979) Rapid and widespread generation of recent oolitic hardgrounds on a high energy Bahamian Platform, Eleuthera Bank, Bahamas. *J. Sed. Petrol.* 49, 195–208.

Fischer, A.G. and Garrison, R.E. (1967) Carbonate lithification on the sea floor. *J. Geol.* 75, 488–496.

Folk, R.L. (1965, 1975) See p. 131.

Fürsich, F.T. (1979) Genesis environments and ecology of Jurassic hardgrounds. *N. Jb. Geol. Palaont.* 158, 1–63.

Garrison, R.E. (1981) Diagenesis of oceanic carbonate sediments : a review of the DSDP perspective. In Warme, J.E., Douglas, R.G. and Winterer, E.L. (eds.) *The Deep Sea Drilling Project : a Decade of Progress*, SEPM Sp. Pub. 32, 181–207.

Ginsburg, R.N. (1957) Early diagenesis and lithification of shallow water carbonate sediments in South Florida. In R.J. LeBlanc and J.G. Breeding (eds.), *Regional Aspects of Carbonate Deposition*, SEPM Spec. Pub. 5, 80–100.

Ginsburg, R.N. and Schroeder, J.H. (1973) Growth and submarine fossilization of algal cup reefs, Bermuda. *Sedimentology* 20, 575–614.

Given, R.K. and Wilkinson, B.H. (1985) Kinetic control of morphology composition and mineralogy of abiotic sedimentary carbonates. *J. Sed. Petrol.* 55, 109–119.

Harris, P.M., Kendall, C. G. St. C. and Lerche, I. (1985) Carbonate cementation—a brief review. In Schneidermann, N. and Harris, P.M. (eds.), *Carbonate Cements*, SEPM Sp. Pub. 36, 79–95.

James, N.P., Ginsburg, R.N., Marszalek, D.S. and Choquette, P.W. (1976) Facies and fabric specificity of early subsea cements in shallow Belize (British Honduras) reefs. *J. Sed. Petrol.* 46, 523–544.

Kinsman, D.J.J. (1969) Interpretation of Sr^{2+} concentrations in carbonate minerals and rocks. *J. Sed. Petrol.* 39, 486–508.

Krebs, W. (1969) Early void-filling cementation in Devonian fore-reef limestones (Germany). *Sedimentology* 12, 279–299.

Land, L.S. and Goreau, T.F. (1970) Submarine lithification of Jamaican reefs. *J. Sed. Petrol.* 40, 457–462.

Lighty, R.G. (1985) Preservation of internal reef porosity and diagenetic sealing of submerged early Holocene Barrier reef, southeast Florida shelf. In Schneidermann, N. and Harris, P.M. (eds.), *Carbonate Cements*, SEPM Sp. Pub. 36, 123–151.

Longman, H.W. (1982) See p. 131.

MacIntyre, I.G. (1985) Submarine cements—the peloidal question. In Schneidermann, N. and Harris, R. M. (eds.), *Carbonate Cements*, SEPM Sp. Pub. 36, 109–116.

Marshall, J. D. and Ashton, M. (1980) Isotopic and trace element evidence for submarine lithification of hardgrounds in the Jurassic of eastern England. *Sedimentology* 27, 271–289.

Mazzullo, S.J. (1980) Calcite pseudospar replacive of marine acicular aragonite, and implications for aragonite cement diagenesis. *J. Sed. Petrol.* **50**, 409–422.

Milliman, J.D. (1974) Precipitation and cementation of deep-sea carbonate sediments. In Inderbitzen, A.L., (ed.), *Deep Sea Sediments*, Plenum, New York, 463–476.

Morse, J.W., Zullig, J.J., Bernstein, L.D., Millero, F.J., Milne, P., Mucci, A. and Choppin, G.R. (1985) Chemistry of calcium carbonate rich shallow water sediments in the Bahamas. *Am. J. Sci.* **285**, 147–185.

Neumann, A.C. (1965) Processes of recent carbonate sedimentation in Harrington Sound, Bermuda. *Bull. Mar. Sci.* **15**, 987–1035.

Pierson, B.J. and Shinn, E.A. (1985) Cement distribution and carbonate mineral stabilization in Pleistocene limestones of Hogsty Reef, Bahamas. In Schneidermann, N. and Harris, P.M. (eds.), *Carbonate Cements*, SEPM Sp. Pub. **36**, 153–168.

Purdy, E.G. (1968) Carbonate diagenesis: an environmental survey. *Geologica Romana* **7**, 183–228.

Purser, B.H. (1969) Syn-sedimentary marine lithification of Middle Jurassic limestones in the Paris Basin. *Sedimentology* **12**, 205–230.

Sandberg, P. (1985) Aragonite cements and their occurrence in ancient limestones. In Schneidermann, N. and Harris, P.M. (eds.), *Carbonate Cements*, SEPM Sp. Pub. **36**, 33–57.

Schlager, W. and James, N.P. (1978) Low magnesim calcite limestones forming at the deep sea floor, Tongue of the Ocean, Bahamas. *Sedimentology* **25**, 675–702.

Schneidermann, N. and Harris, P.M. (eds.), (1985) *Carbonate Cements*. SEPM Spec. Pub. **36**.

Schroeder, J. H. (1972) Fabric and sequences of submarine carbonate cements in Holocene Bermuda Cup reefs. *Geol. Rdsch.* **61**, 708–730.

Scoffin, T.P. and McLean, R.F. (1978) Exposed limestone of the northern province of the Great Barrier Reef. *Phil. Trans. R. Soc. Lond.* **A291**, 119–138.

Scoffin, T.P. and Stoddart, D.R. (1983) Beachrock and intertidal cements. In Goudie, A.S. and Pye, K. (eds.), *Chemical Sediments and Geomorphology*, Academic Press, London, 401–425.

Shearman, D.J. (1966) Origin of marine evaporites by diagenesis. *Trans. Inst. Mining Met.* (B). **75**, 208–215.

Shinn, E.A. (1969) Submarine lithification of Holocene carbonate sediments in the Persian Gulf. *Sedimentology* **12**, 109–144.

Taylor, J.C.M. and Illing, L.W. (1969) Holocene intertidal calcium carbonate cementation. Qatar, Persian Gulf. *Sedimentology* **12**, 69–107.

9 Meteoric and burial diagenesis

Meteoric environments become established in marine carbonate sediments on emergence of the sea-bed in a moist climate (evaporites may develop initially on emergence in an arid climate). This emergence initially will expose reefal, lagoonal, beach or tidal-bar sediments, from which aeolian deposits may be generated. Meteoric waters are generally of low ionic strength. Ca levels are variable but Mg and Na are usually deficient. The meteoric vadose zone lies above the phreatic zone of permanent water saturation (see Figure 8.1). When the common marine carbonate minerals, aragonite and Mg calcite, come into contact with meteoric water they are unstable and undergo alteration to calcite low in Mg by various diagenetic processes, here grouped under the general term *chemical stabilization*.

9.1 Vadose zone

Near-surface meteoric water is undersaturated with $CaCO_3$ due to atmospheric CO_2 augmented by soil CO_2. Initially, dissolution occurs with the less stable aragonite leached before calcite. The waters may quickly reach equilibrium to become saturated, and precipitation of calcite (low in Mg) cement starts through evaporation or degassing. The vadose zone can thus be divided into two parts which represent the end members (solution and precipitation) of a continuous spectrum. Climate plays a very important role. In dry regions diagenesis is slow, whereas solution and grain neomorphism occur more rapidly in humid climates, partly because of the abundance of fresh water and partly because a thick soil zone develops in a humid climate. The large-scale products of the removal and addition of $CaCO_3$ during vadose diagenesis in carbonate terrains are karst solution and associated speleothem deposition in moist climates, and caliche deposition within soils in arid climates. These products will be described in section 12.1. Within the body of the emerged marine carbonate sediments we may expect removal of some aragonite grains

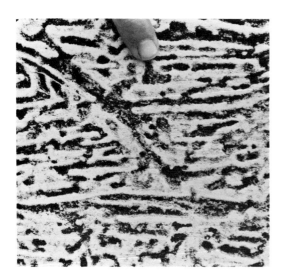

Figure 9.1 Preferential cementation of fine-grained layers of burrowed Pleistocene oolite. Miami, USA

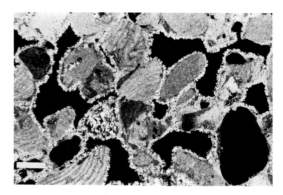

Figure 9.2 Isopachous bladed calcite cement. Thin section Xn. Scale 1 mm. Tertiary, Barcelona, Spain. Photograph courtesy Mateo Esteban

and the precipitation of small crystals of sparry calcite cements, particularly at grain contacts where liquids are held in the meniscus position. As well as meniscus cements with their character-istic blunt terminations, we may see pendant cements arranged predominantly on the under-surfaces of grains, textures similar to those found in the marine vadose setting (Figure 8.8), but now the cement is small equant crystals of calcite (low in Mg) (Figure 5.6). Water is held for longer periods in fine-grained layers where the capillary forces are greater, so cementation is consequent-ly more pervasive in such layers (Figure 9.1).

9.2 Phreatic zone
The phreatic zone of permanent water is the zone where major changes in the mineralogy and texture of the original marine sediment take place. There is an undersaturated zone near the level of the water-table where solution is preva-lent, and below this in the zone of active circul-ation of saturated water, calcite precipitates and unstable grains are neomorphosed to calcite (a process sometimes called calcitization). The cal-cite cement occurs as isopachous bladed fringes

(Figure 9.2) and equant mosaics (Figure 9.3). Generally, crystal size increases towards the pore centres. Echinoderm fragments develop calcitic syntaxial overgrowths (Figure 4.19). Deeper into the phreatic zone the water is saturated with $CaCO_3$ but stagnant, and insufficient new ions are supplied for significant cementation to take place, though neomorphism of aragonite and Mg calcite to calcite may continue here, especi-ally if temperature rises.

We can summarize the mineral stabilization of shallow-water Quaternary limestones in the

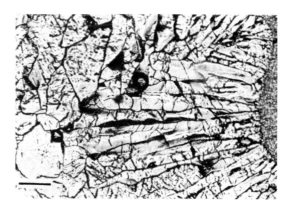

Figure 9.3 Coarse sparry calcite cement, bladed crystals overgrown by an equant mosaic. Thin section Xn. Scale 0.2 mm. Jurassic, Skye, Scotland. Photograph courtesy Julian Andrews

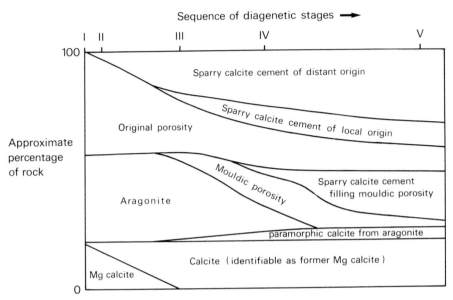

Figure 9.4 Sequential stages in the stabilization (calcitization) of a marine carbonate sand consisting of aragonite and Mg calcite. After Land *et al.* (1967)

phreatic freshwater environment as five progressive stages (Figure 9.4):

  (i)   Unconsolidated sediment of original composition (aragonite, Mg calcite)
  (ii) Limestone consisting of primary skeletal minerals, Mg calcite and aragonite, but cemented by calcite at grain contacts
  (iii) Limestones consisting only of calcite and aragonite, commonly enclosed in fringes of calcite cement, in which Mg calcite has been replaced by calcite
  (iv) Limestone in the process of losing aragonite by solution and neomorphism
  (v)   Stabilized limestone consisting only of calcite.

Note that in Figure 9.4 some calcite cement is derived from outside the zone of lithification (allochthonous), probably by solution at the soil profile, and some cement is autochthonous, being derived from local aragonite grains. Both sources dramatically reduce the porosity of the rock.

9.3 Transformation of aragonite and Mg calcite to calcite

Aragonite and Mg calcite of marine origin in the form of skeletal grains, and the inorganic precipitates of mud, ooids and cements, undergo neomorphic transformations to calcite once removed from the sea. The speed of this change and the resultant texture vary according to the chemistry and flow of the interstitial fluids, and the nature of the original crystals.

Aragonite may alter directly to calcite in the dry state (*inversion*), though the process requires temperatures above about 400 °C to proceed within a reasonable geological time, and is unlikely to have occurred in normal limestones. Most mineral transformations in limestones take place in an aqueous medium.

9.3.1 Aragonite transformation to calcite
Long-term (*c.* 10^7 years) preservation of aragonite in sedimentary carbonates occurs very rarely, but when found the original aragonite grains are seen to be sealed from surrounding

porewaters. This impermeable seal may be afforded by encrusting cements, enveloping shales or even thin organic films around crystals.

There are two varieties of the change from aragonite to calcite which may be considered end members of the one process of dissolution/precipitation. In the first variety the aragonite changes to calcite but traces of the micro-architecture of the original grain are preserved (Figure 9.5). At the other extreme, the entire grain appears to have dissolved, leaving a mould which was later filled by pore-filling calcite cement (Figure 9.6).

Where the transformation has retained the microarchitecture, we believe that the dissolution/precipitation was on an exceedingly fine scale, almost at the level of molecule for molecule across a thin solution film in which aragonite is just soluble and calcite insoluble. Ions leave one surface, cross the film and deposit in a new lattice structure on the neighbouring surface. We can imagine this process by picturing a man digging a trench and throwing the earth over his shoulder to fill the hole behind him with each new spadeload. The extent of the alteration in texture between the original aragonite and the final calcite may relate to the width of this film and the rate of transport of ions within it (i.e. to what extent the system is open or closed). When aragonite is stabilized to calcite, the strontium levels in the $CaCO_3$ fall from perhaps 6000 to 200 ppm, though the Mg, Mn, Fe levels may rise. The transfer relates to the ease with which the ions can be incorporated into a rhombohedral rather than orthorhombic crystal structure (see section 1.2). These subtractions and additions require a degree of openness to the system, but the retention of fine structural detail argues in favour of a nearly closed system.

Observations of aragonite grains that have apparently been caught in the act of calcitization allow us to inspect closely the interface of the old and new mineral. Where the two minerals abut directly against each other with a gap smaller than the resolution of the electron microscope (c.

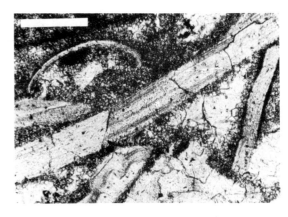

Figure 9.5 Molluscan fragment (*a*) altered to coarse sparry calcite but retaining vestiges of original microarchitecture. Thin section, ppl. Scale 0.5 mm. Jurassic, Skye, Scotland

Figure 9.6 Molluscan fragments preserved as sparry calcite filled moulds. The outlines of the shells are defined by micrite envelopes. Thin section, ppl. Scale 0.5 mm. Jurassic, Eigg, Scotland

10 nm), some fine detail of the original texture is preserved in the new mineral and the trace element and isotope chemistry is not widely different across the mineral boundary. In other examples of partially altered aragonite grains, the two mineral phases are separated by a porous chalky zone. Although gross structural features may survive, the fine detail of the original architecture is lost in the course of such a transformation; and further, trace element variation before and after is now significant. Within a very narrow film, porewaters are isolated and will rapidly attain a steady state of saturation with respect to aragonite. Dissolution rate will then be controlled by the rate at which Ca^{2+} and CO_3^{2-} ions are taken out of solution by calcite precipitation. The more porewaters can effect a thorough exchange, then the wider will be the solution film or chalky zone, since further dissolution can proceed without necessitating calcite precipitation. Where hydrologic factors permit still greater mixing between porewaters and solution film, the entire aragonite may be removed by dissolution and the ions transported well away. Thus at high flow rates and lower pH, immediately below a soil for example, dissolved ions may be completely removed and little or no precipitation takes place. At slightly lower flow rates, precipitation of some calcite cements may take place in nearby intergranular voids or recently created moulds.

It may happen that flow rates or pH values change during calcitization, in which case it is possible to conceive of a fabric containing patches showing good retention of the original microarchitecture intimately associated with clear sparry patches.

We note that within the one rock, some former aragonite skeletons undergo dissolution/precipitation on a microscale so that some microstructure is preserved, while neighbouring different species undergo total dissolution to a mould.

Although calcitization of aragonite (grains or cements) may retain some vestiges of the original

arrangement of crystals, it is not possible for calcite (rhombohedral) to truly paramorphically replace aragonite (orthorhombic). The initial neomorphic reactions (particularly under conditions of slow alteration) occur along crystal defects in the aragonite such as dislocations, twins and stacking faults (many of these defects may be of organic origin). These sites favour calcite nucleation, and the new mineral grows as engulfing structures in aragonite, without topotactic relations (i.e. no lattice directions coincide). The calcite crystals develop a modulated structure (micro- (10 nm) lamellar structure), perhaps related to the incorporation of Mg^{2+} and Fe^{2+} into the new calcite lattice. A second, much rarer, type of replacement occurs within aragonite, which shows mottled microtexture with twins still clearly visible, with local orientation relations ((010) aragonite = $(11\bar{2}0)$ calcite). Two considerations account for the lack of structural distortion which we might expect to see in neomorphic calcite after a change from aragonite of density 2.94 to calcite density 2.71. Firstly, the change is most likely not on a molecule for molecule basis but rather on a volume for volume basis, with the 8.5% excess $CaCO_3$ being transported away by the solution film. Secondly, most aragonite grains have a lower bulk density than 2.94, with small fluid-filled pores and organic matter contained in the grain between and within crystals.

Evidence for the aragonitic composition of the precursor grains or cements has been itemized (in order of decreasing reliability) by Sandberg (1975, 1983).

(i) Aragonite preserved
(ii) Mosaic of generally irregular calcite spar containing oriented aragonite relics (Figure 9.8)
(iii) Mosaic of calcite as (ii), but no contained aragonite relics, yet the Sr^{2+} content is elevated
(iv) Calcite mosaic as (iii) but with low Sr^{2+}
(v) Mould or subsequently-filled mould.

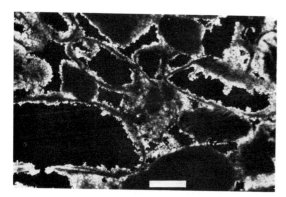

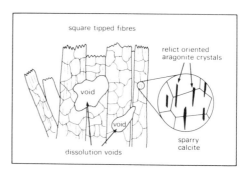

Figure 9.8 Calcitization of aragonite cements. After Folk and Assereto (1976)

Figure 9.7 Micrite envelopes left after the dissolution of grains. The envelopes are preserved by a thin layer of fine cement crystals. Thin section, Xn. Scale 0.2 mm. Tertiary, Barcelona, Spain. Photograph courtesy Mateo Esteban

The calcite mosaic of calcitized mollusc shells is often brownish and pseudopleochroic on account of the organic (or graphite) inclusions concentrated along former growth lines. The pseudopleochroism is caused by the scattering of light by inclusions that have a different refractive index from their medium.

The total dissolution of an aragonite grain will only leave a recognizable void if there is a stable envelope around the grain that resisted solution and acted as a mould (Figure 9.7). This durable coat may have been an early fringe of calcite cement crystals or lithified micrite that encircled the unstable grain and remained intact throughout aragonite dissolution. Commonly the mould is preserved by a rind of micrite, which may be a coating on the original grain (such as a recrystallized algal encrustation), or a micritic replacement of the perimeter of the original grain (micrite envelope) which owes its origin to centripetal micritization (aided perhaps by microorganisms) of the rim. Collapsed micrite envelopes attest to the former void stage.

Some calcitized aragonite cements show ghosts of the external morphology of splays of square-tipped and feather terminations to the former fibres (Figure 9.8); others have a botryoidal texture reminiscent of reef cavity botryoidal aragonite cements. Their marine origin is indicated by their association with internal sediments, and their original aragonitic composition supported by minute aragonite inclusions and the high strontium contents. These botryoids can be replaced by a mosaic of calcite crystals that cross-cut the original radiating fabric or develop columnar calcite crystals with undulose extinction, wholly or partly replacing fans of acicular aragonite.

9.3.2 Mg calcite to calcite transformation

The alteration of Mg calcite to stable calcite takes place by a process of leaching of the Mg^{2+} called *incongruent dissolution*, which leaves the microarchitecture of the grain unaffected (at the level of petrological microscope examination). The Mg content of the grain falls from values of say 10 to 20 mol% $MgCO_3$ to 1.5–4 mol% $MgCO_3$. (There are only one or two reported examples of total dissolution of Mg calcite grains giving a mould in the manner of aragonite transformation.) The exsolved Mg^{2+} may go to from the microdolomite rhombs that are sometimes seen by SEM as inclusions in calcitized Mg calcites.

The solubilities of the different phases of calcium carbonate (aragonite and Mg calcite) are sufficiently similar that at certain saturations the microstructure of the skeletal grains plays a crucial part in the sequence of stabilization.

9.4 Diagenetic fibrous calcites

These are sparry calcite crystals which have a vague fibrous texture or an appearance of large crystalline units containing bundles of fibres whose origins are not easy to explain. It is unlikely that they were originally aragonite, for most transformations of aragonite go to calcite mosaics, even in those near-closed system changes where trace element chemistry is hardly altered.

Some calcite cements are syntaxial overgrowths of fibrous calcite on calcite skeletons (such as those of forminiferans). As there is a progressive and systematic change in the lattice orientation of the fine skeletal crystals which is adopted by the overgrowths, the shell and overgrowths have the appearance of larger crystalline units or bundles of fibres. However, this is not a neomorphic fabric, merely a syntaxial cement.

There is a distinctive calcite texture termed *radiaxial fibrous calcite* which shows a pattern within each crystal of subcrystals that diverge away from the substrate, and the subcrystals have distally convergent *c*-axes with curved cleavages and twin lamellae (Figure 9.9). These composite crystals show undulose extinction with reversed sweeps, and have non-planar

Figure 9.9 Radiaxial fibrous calcite showing curved cleavages and twin lamellae. Thin section, Xn. Scale 1 mm. Carboniferous, Eire. Specimen courtesy Douglas Gillies

boundaries. Radiaxial fibrous calcite is a common cavity cement, especially in ancient reefs where it occurs in banded units which may precede marine coelobite encrustations and may alternate with internal sediments containing marine micro-organisms. Isotope data support a marine origin for some of these radiaxial fibrous calcites, but suggest only an absence of modification since precipitation in others which could have been meteoric in origin. These radiaxial fibrous calcite crystals were once thought to represent a replacement of an earlier acicular cement, but are now considered to have formed by a process of asymmetric growth within calcite crystals undergoing split growth. Radiaxial crystals are composite, and are attempts to assume a spherulitic growth form in diagenetic environments which favour the growth of length-slow calcite. (In length-slow calcite the *c*-axes are normal to crystal elongation, shown by the high relief when crystals are oriented N–S in the microscope field under plane polarized light).

9.5 Neomorphism of ooids

Three types of ooids are common in ancient limestones.

(i) Well-preserved radial-fibrous calcite superimposed on a concentric structure (Figure 9.10*A*)

(ii) Micritic structure of unoriented microcrystalline calcite with a vestige of concentric/radial structure (Figure 9.10*B*)

(iii) A sparry calcite fabric indicative of slow precipitation of calcite from solution in a void (oomouldic pore) during diagenesis (Figure 9.10*C*).

It is thought that preservation of a concentric/radial structure (i) indicates a previous calcitic or Mg calcitic composition, while previous aragonite is indicated by sparry calcite (iii). The original composition of micritic ooids (ii) may have been aragonite or calcite.

Staining of limestones reveals that some ooids are ferroan calcite. Fe-calcitic ooids cannot be

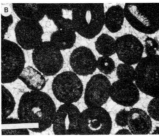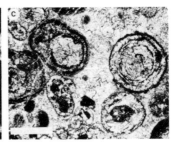

Figure 9.10 (*A*) Ooids with radial-fibrous structure. Thin section ppl. Scale 0.5 mm. Jurassic, Raasay, Scotland. (*B*) Micritic ooids. Thin section, ppl. Scale 0.5 mm. Carboniferous, South Wales. (*C*) Ooids with sparry calcite in concentric layers. Thin section ppl. Scale 0.5 mm. Ordovician, Girvan, Scotland

primary, because their formation requires a reducing environment. They most likely represent original Mg calcite ooids, in which Fe has substituted for some of the Mg during stabilization in a reducing environment in which ferrous iron was available. (The same explanation is applied to skeletal remains that are now Fe calcite in limestones; see section 9.9.1).

We note in marine oolitic limestones of the geological past that there are general changes from concentric/radial dominant ooids to sparry calcite-dominant ooids at specific times. This suggests there were times in the past when marine ooids were principally calcitic and other times (including the present) when they were principally aragonitic. This observation has far reaching consequences regarding the changing composition of the oceans through time (see section 15.1).

9.6 Mixing zone

When marine sediments emerge, the new island develops a lens of fresh interstitial water which floats on the denser interstitial sea water beneath. Ideally this lens is shaped as shown in Figure 8.1, with about 1/32 of its thickness above the sea-level and 31/32 below, on account of the small difference in specific gravity of fresh and salt water. In reality, this body of water has a more irregular shape. It alters its overall form according to rainfall and tide levels and its detailed profile according to the permeability pathways within the sediment. There may be impervious strata or highly porous zones that influence flow; springs of fresh water may emerge under the sea some distance from the land, for example.

At the base of the freshwater body is a narrow zone where fresh and salt waters mix. Some cements precipitate in this brackish area and range from sparry calcites at the fresh end to Mg calcites at the marine end. The waters here are relatively stagnant, and an effect of the slow repeated fluctuations of salinities in this zone is the formation of dolomite at certain intermediate salinities which are slightly undersaturated with calcite and oversaturated with dolomite. The origin of mixing zone dolomites is discussed at greater length in section 10.3.3.

Immediately below the mixing zone is the zone where marine formation (connate) waters are trapped between grains. This marine phreatic zone is stagnant, and little or no diagenesis takes place here until the temperatures and pressures rise significantly after substantial burial.

9.7 Deeper burial setting

A few hundred metres below the ground surface, most rocks are out of the influence of meteoric waters. Their interstitial fluids are not now readily replaced by fresh groundwaters. With accumulation of overburden the pressures and temperatures rise. Increase in temperature aids the precipitation of $CaCO_3$, but there is a finite amount available in the formation waters which is soon spent as they migrate upwards and outwards. The ionic strength is low, precipitation slow, and the crystals of calcite cement are large relative to those that form in near-surface conditions. Blocky crystals of sparry calcite result.

The increase in pressure gives rise to the compaction of the sediments. This can be mechanical, giving breakage of grains, or chemical (pressure dissolution), giving suturing of grains.

Mechanical compaction is rarely manifested in shallow-water limestones, because they are generally partially cemented (and thereby made rigid) early on, in both the marine and meteoric zones. Very few limestones with micrite matrix show crushed grains. The results of mechanical compaction are more evident in mud-free rocks where, for example, broken and crushed ooids or collapsed micrite envelopes are encountered, indicating the lack of framework support once the aragonite grain was dissolved and overburden applied. The limestones in which mechanically compacted grains are present in significant numbers are usually deep-sea deposits that are most likely to have escaped the zones of cementation on the sea-bed and in meteoric waters.

Chemical compaction may commence after about 200 m burial. It affects, firstly, those positions of higher stress at grain contacts. The local increase in elastic strain brings increased solubility and the more soluble phases dissolve; grain-to-grain surface contacts, or sutured interpenetrating grains result (Figure 9.11).

For grains to behave individually and either break or suture at their point contacts, they have to be free of cement. Where grains have supporting cement, a framework is developed and the load is spread. Any pressure dissolution on burial now tends to commence along seams in the rock. These seams develop at right angles to the maximum stress which, except in areas of lateral forces (e.g. fold belts) is normally parallel to the bedding. The seams may begin along thin shale partings, since clay minerals retain liquids at grain (or rock) contacts, which greatly facilitates the transport of ions and favours continued

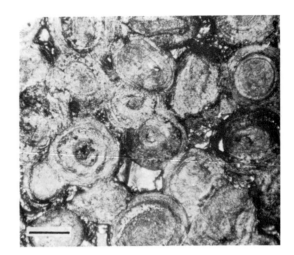

Figure 9.11 Compacted and sutured ooids. Stained peel. Scale 0.5 mm. Jurassic, Cirencester, England

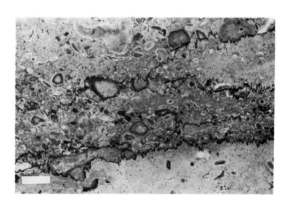

Figure 9.12 Cross-section of stylolites in oncolitic limestone. Scale 5 mm. Jurassic, Paris Basin, France

dissolution. These pressure dissolution seams are called *stylolites*. They often have interpenetrating columns due to the different responses to stress of the two touching crystals (Figure 9.12). Insoluble material within the limestone (such as clay minerals, pyrite, dolomite and organic matter) is concentrated in the seam as *stylocumulate* (Figure 9.13). We usually see that the more insoluble residue there is present, then the less dramatic the interpenetration of stylolite columns. Pressure dissolution puts Ca^{2+} and

Figure 9.13 Dolomite crystals concentrated in a stylolite seam. Thin section, ppl. Scale 0.2 mm. Devonian, Saskatchewan, Canada

CO_3^{2-} ions into aqueous solution, which may precipitate sparry calcite in nearby zones of lower stress as a late post-brittle-fracture cement.

The dissolved ions may be removed from the region of highest stress by diffusion, by fluid flow, or by a combination of both means. If there are permeability barriers (such as clay seams or hardgrounds), then vertical fluid flow may be so restricted that the only means of removal of $CaCO_3$ is by diffusion. In this case, the $CaCO_3$ is likely to precipitate relatively close to the zone of dissolution, for example, half the distance between dissolution seams. We have no textural means of distinguishing between calcite derived by pressure dissolution and late spars from any other deep source, though it is noted in some ancient limestones that the amount of iron in post-burial ferroan calcites falls significantly away from shale-rich dissolution seams. If this

iron was released from the clays at the time of $CaCO_3$ dissolution and incorporated into the precipitating spar, it suggests ionic transport of a few centimetres. For significant pressure-dissolution textural effects to be developed, the rock must, at least initially, be reasonably porous. If the rock were tight, the high levels of supersaturation quickly attained in the very few and very small available pores would inhibit further dissolution at this site.

9.8 Structures generated by compressive and tensional stresses

9.8.1 Stylolites and shear fractures
Logan and Semeniuk (1976) studied the effects of compressive and tensional stresses during the early deformation of limestones. They noted that if stress application exceeds the capacity of rocks to respond by pressure-dissolution, then shear fractures develop. The two processes are pene-contemporaneous; with movement along discontinuities, stylolites become shear fractures and shear fractures become stylolites. The resultant structures develop at various scales, since the stylolite and fracture interfaces can form at all component levels in carbonate rocks; grain to grain, fragment to fragment, or bed to bed. An intergradational suite of limestone bedding structures are produced by dynamic metamorphism involving pressure dissolution and shear fracture, these are termed by Logan and Semeniuk (1976): stylobedding, stylonodular, stylomottled, stylolaminite and stylobreccia (Figure 9.14).

Rocks are usually heterogeneous, so that there is a resolution of stresses along discontinuities; this leads to the formation of weakly developed stylolites at various angles to the predominant set. Conjugate sets bounding rhomboidal units are formed in response to shear stress under conditions of no movement.

The formation of stylocumulate occurs at glide-pressure dissolution surfaces. This may be in discontinuous patches (stylomottled), irre-

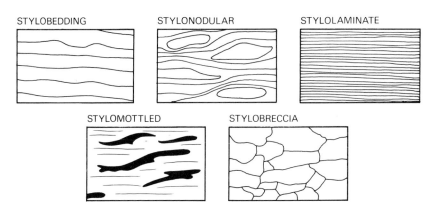

Figure 9.14 Varieties of bedding developed by pressure dissolution seams. After Logan and Semeniuk (1976)

gular elongate patches (stylonodular) or continuous sheets (stylobedding and lamination). Fracture, and perhaps rotation, result in the breccia fabric. Stylolaminite is the final product of pressure-dissolution, being characterized by subparallel stylolite sets and abundant stylocumulate (or reactate) sheets and lenses.

9.8.2 Veins, vugs and breccias

Some veins are replacement features, but most are tensional fissures filled with coarsely crystalline calcite or internal sediment. They occur with sheet or lensoid geometry, and the parallel-sided margins indicate the consolidated nature of the host rocks at the time of fracture. Vein structures may be parallel sheets, rhomboidal to rectangular or breccioid, and the last type grades into a calcite-cemented breccia.

Tensional stresses may result in parting of the host rock along surfaces to form cavities (*strain cavities*) by dilation or rotational deformation. Cavities may be sheet-like, lacy or irregular. Strain-cavity shape and orientation are fundamentally controlled by stress mode and application. They may or may not follow structures in the host rock. The cavities may be enlarged by dissolution or mechanical erosion, with undissolved and eroded fragments providing internal sediment that settles to the floors of cavities, and

the remaining spaces later filled with sparry calcite. Such cavities, with flat floors and irregular roofs, are often termed 'stromatactoid' (see Section 7.2.4). They usually occur in swarms in mounded mudstones and probably developed very shortly after deposition. These distinctive sparry masses (Figures 7.11, 17.6) are thought to represent cavities formed by one or more of the following mechanisms:

(i) Dewatering (or hydraulic jacking)
(ii) Compaction, slumping and downslope creep of consolidated but unlithified sediment
(iii) Compaction and binding of sediment (perhaps by algae) to form crusts, followed by erosion
(iv) Decay and collapse of organic tissue (especially sponges) after partial lithification.

Intraformational breccias are commonly the result of dissolution and collapse of limestone blocks in the subsurface. *Collapse breccias* are common in areas of former evaporite minerals. The more soluble salts dissolve and the surrounding rocks collapse, producing a haphazard accumulation of angular fragments (see Figure 17.22).

Deep burial dolomitization is discussed in section 10.3.4.

9.9 Trace element and oxygen and carbon isotope changes during diagenesis

As described in Chapter 1, strontium is fairly easily taken up in the aragonite structure, and magnesium in the calcite structure. Aragonite precipitated in warm shallow seas is likely to contain between 2500–9500 ppm Sr^{2+} (molluscs c. 2500, corals c. 8000; inorganic aragonite muds and cements c. 8000–9500 ppm Sr^{2+}). In warm shallow seas the common organic groups with calcite skeletons and the inorganically precipitated calcite cements have 12–20 mol% $MgCO_3$.

When the marine sediments of aragonite and Mg calcite are transformed to calcite (low in Mg) during mineral stabilization in the near-surface meteoric realm, where waters are low in Sr and Mg, both Sr and Mg are depleted in the resulting limestone (Sr c. 200 ppm, Mg 0–5 mol% $MgCO_3$). Less radical changes would be expected when stabilizing diagenesis occurs in the closed system of deep burial diagenesis.

Sodium, which is present in modern carbonate sediments to levels of about 3000 ppm, also drops to 200 ppm in ancient limestones after freshwater diagenesis.

Marine carbonate sediments have very low levels of iron and manganese. Fe is present in the ocean but will not enter calcite in the oxidized state (Fe^{3+}), in which it occurs there because of the charge imbalance. It must be reduced to Fe^{2+} to enter the calcite lattice (directly or to substitute for Mg in Mg calcite). Reduction of iron normally takes place with sulphate reduction; pyrite (FeS_2) then readily forms and Fe^{2+} is not available to go into calcite. The principal environment in which Fe^{2+} can enter calcite to form ferroan calcite is after burial, where reducing conditions prevail but no sulphur is present for pyrite genesis. A common diagenetic sequence of cements within limestones is, firstly, a fine-grained early iron-free calcite cement which may have originally precipitated in the sea or the shallow meteoric zone, followed by a few small framboids or cubes of pyrite, followed by coarse-grained crystals of ferroan calcite. Manganese also requires reducing conditions for incorporation into calcite. The distribution of the two elements Fe and Mn in calcite can be plotted using cathodoluminescence and chemical staining techniques.

9.9.1 Ferroan calcite

Calcite that originated either by neomorphism of earlier carbonates or passive precipitation in a reducing (i.e. subsurface) environment may contain ferrous iron in small quantities (c. 1%) which is readily detectable by staining. We note that grains and cements that were precipitated as calcite in oxidizing environments (e.g. brachiopods in the sea, or early cements in the freshwater vadose setting) retain their non-ferroan character through diagenesis, even though Fe^{2+} may later have been available.

Those grains or cements that were originally Mg calcite may (and commonly do) undergo substitution of Fe for Mg in the subsurface (if Fe is available), giving ferroan calcite. Calcite derived by aragonite neomorphism is unlikely to have Fe^{2+} incorporated in it if the transformation was in a near-closed system. The more open the system, with free import and export of ions, then the higher the possibility that calcitized aragonite will be ferroan. It is quite common to

Figure 9.15 Sketch of thin section showing the occurrence of ferroan calcite (hatched) in a hypothetical Jurassic limestone: a, crinoid (formerly Mg calcite); b, micrite envelope of formerly aragonitic mollusc; c, brachiopod (low-Mg calcite); d, peloid (formerly aragonite or low-Mg calcite). Early cement phase is non-ferroan

find that the late stage void-filling sparry calcite within former aragonite moulds is iron-rich (Figure 9.15).

9.9.2 Stable isotopes of carbon and oxygen

As calcium carbonate dissolves during diagenesis, the oxygen and carbon atoms come to equilibrium with those of ambient water. The eventual calcite cement precipitates from a solution to which both sources (supplying fluids and dissolving $CaCO_3$) contributed, and the new carbonate will not, in general, have the same isotopic composition as its precursor. The degree of change will depend on the relative masses of water and calcium carbonate involved, their original isotopic compositions and the temperature of the solution during re-precipitation. Meteoric groundwaters are charged with soil-derived CO_2, which is enriched with the light ^{12}C isotope. When marine sediments of aragonite and Mg calcite are stabilized in the freshwater lens, the light carbon isotope will be incorporated into the precipitating calcite, and $\delta^{13}C$ values for the new limestone will be more negative than those for the original marine sediment. The depletion is most significant near to the exposure surface where the influence of organic fractionation in the soil is greatest. As groundwater percolates down, out of contact with the reservoir of gaseous CO_2 in the soil, the lighter isotope is progressively exhausted during calcite precipitation and $\delta^{13}C$ values increase and thereafter remain fairly constant within the freshwater zone. Diagenetic carbonates such as cements or dolomite formed in the schizohaline zone would show an increase in $\delta^{13}C$ and $\delta^{18}O$ across the salinity gradient. Those cements generated in the relatively closed system of the deep burial environment would reflect the isotopic composition of the original marine sediments, with the higher temperature at depth influencing the oxygen isotope fractionation. Carbon and oxygen isotopic values for carbonates of various origins are given in Figure 9.16.

Because of the large oxygen reservoir available

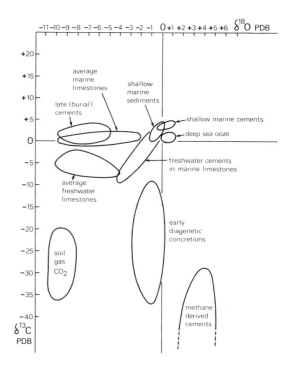

Figure 9.16 $\delta^{13}C$ and $\delta^{18}O$ values for carbonates from various environmental settings. After Hudson (1975)

in meteoric water, oxygen isotope values of neomorphosed calcite are dominated by the meteoric $\delta^{18}O$ signal. Typical $\delta^{18}O$ values for modern meteoric groundwaters and marine sediments are $-3.5‰$ and $-0.5‰$ respectively. The calcite that results on freshwater diagenesis has a $\delta^{18}O$ value of about $-3‰$. There is a slight

Table 9.1 Representative $\delta^{13}C$ and $\delta^{18}O$ values for carbonates of different environmental origins.

	$\delta^{13}C$	$\delta^{18}O_{PDB}$
Carbonate sediment (aragonite and Mg calcite) formed in shallow sea water	$+1‰$	$-0.5‰$
Meteoric groundwater (with soil CO_2)	$-20‰$	$-4‰$
Exposure surface calcite	$-8‰$	$-2‰$
Phreatic zone calcite	$-1‰$	$-3‰$
Deep burial calcite	$+1‰$	$-8‰$

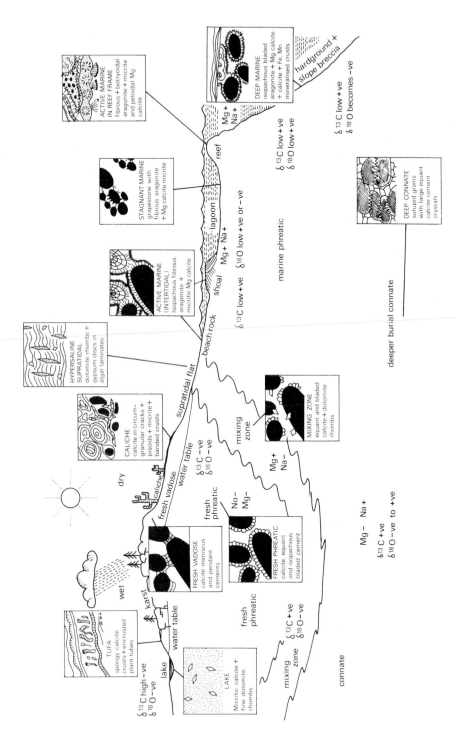

Figure 9.17 Major environments of inorganic calcium carbonate precipitation indicating the typical resultant crystal fabric, $\delta^{13}C$ and $\delta^{18}O$ values, and relative amounts of Na and Mg in the interstitial fluids

positive shift in $\delta^{18}O$ within a metre or so of the subaerial exposure surface, reflecting oxygen isotopic fractionation from evaporation, but otherwise $\delta^{18}O$ values are normally constant through the freshwater lens. Increase in temperature lightens the $\delta^{18}O$ value (c. 1‰ for each 4.3 °C), so the calcite precipitated on deep burial is normally significantly depleted in $\delta^{18}O$ (e.g. $\delta^{18}O = -8‰$ at about 1 km depth). Typical $\delta^{13}C$ and $\delta^{18}O$ values are given in Table 9.1 (see also Figure 9.16).

9.10 Rates of stabilization and diagenetic sequences

We see that each environment of diagenesis has its own chemical signature in the stable calcite. Of critical importance is the fact that diagenesis in the active meteoric setting is an open system resulting in flushing out of Sr^{2+} and Mg^{2+} and a depletion in $\delta^{18}O$ and $\delta^{13}C$ values. The deep burial setting is more likely to be a closed system, with the stable calcites retaining more of the original trace element and isotopic composition. Each setting also has it own diagenetic textural signature (summarized in Figure 9.17). Precipitation is rapid in the concentrated solutions near the surface and develops fine-grained cements (fibres, blades and small equant crystals) which in the vadose zone may show meniscus and pendant textures. These carbonates that undergo rapid stabilization (neomorphism and precipitation of calcite cements) near the surface are less likely to suffer the effects of pressure dissolution on burial. The slower precipitation in more stagnant deeper solutions of lower ionic concentration develops coarser sparry calcite. This slower stabilization may not be brought about until considerable compaction has occurred, resulting in the suturing and interpenetration of grains.

Observations of Quaternary and Tertiary limestones suggest that diagenetic mineral stabilization from aragonite and Mg calcite to calcite is most rapid in the freshwater phreatic zone, with complete stabilization taking about 5000 years;

in the freshwater vadose zone stabilization is slower, taking from 100 000 to 200 000 years depending on rainfall; in the marine phreatic zone, where the minerals have stayed in contact with trapped formation waters, stabilization may take as long as three million years.

Cores through the raised Quaternary reef limestones of Barbados (Matthews, 1968; Allan and Matthews, 1982) display mineralogical, chemical and textural evidence for the diagenetic environments in which the rocks have spent most time (Figure 9.18). Analyses of the intercoralline matrix of the reef limestones revealed the following. The upper 1.5 m has been in the vadose zone for most of the time since deposition, and there is relatively little alteration of the aragonites and Mg calcites. From 1.5 m to a depth of 15.3 m on the cores, the rocks show complete stabilization to calcite with much dissolution and cementation; this results from freshwater phreatic diagenesis. Below 15.3 m, the intercoralline matrix retains much of its original mineralogy with only minor dissolution and cementation. This basal area has suffered only freshwater vadose and marine phreatic diagenesis.

The detailed nature of the diagenetic features recorded in a limestone will vary, not only according to the nature of the diagenetic environments capable of producing their own distinctive petrographic and chemical signatures on the limestone body occupied, but also according to the chronological order in which the limestone body passed through these environments and the time it spent in each.

In general, two contrasting patterns of diagenesis are to be expected (Figure 9.19): one resulting from a transgressive regime in which the marine carbonates move straight to the deep burial setting with trapped formation waters; the other a regressive regime in which the marine carbonates are subjected to exposure, where in an arid climate sabkha diagenesis with evaporite formation may ensue, or in a moist climate, rapid stabilization to calcite takes place in meteoric waters. Transgressive shallow-water carbonates

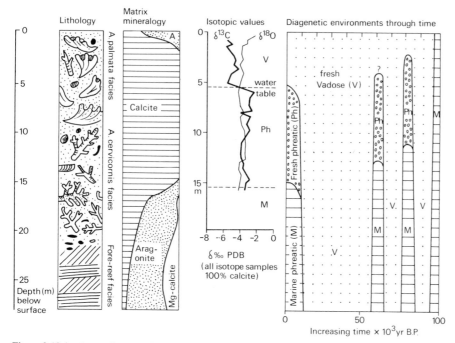

Figure 9.18 Analyses of a core of Pleistocene reef limestone from Barbados showing the lithology, the mineralogy of the matrix, the isotopic composition and the interpreted diagenetic environments occupied by the core over the last 100 000 years. After Matthews (1968) and Allan and Matthews (1982)

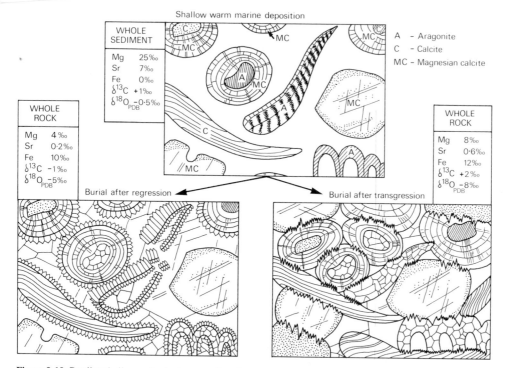

Figure 9.19 Predicted diagenetic textures and rock compositions of shallow marine limestones that suffered burial after regression and burial after transgression

are characterized by overpacking of grains, loss of primary porosity, neomorphism of aragonite grains, ferroan calcite (and dolomite) cements, trace element and isotopic values relatively close to those of original marine sediments which indicate movement from the marine phreatic environment of deposition and diagenesis into the low-oxygen deeper burial connate zone with substantial compaction before cementation. Regressive shallow-water carbonates show a greater variety of diagenetic features including, in arid regions, evaporites and calcretes; in moist climates, extensively leaching of originally aragonitic grains, fine-grained calcite cement as fringes or at grain contacts, some collapsed micrite envelopes, pervasive cementation by blocky sparry calcite, commonly ferroan (and ferroan dolomite), and the whole limestone has relatively depleted $\delta^{18}O$ and $\delta^{13}C$ isotope values and altered trace element values (Figure 9.20). This pattern reflects the replacement of depositional marine phreatic water by meteoric water which dissolved unstable carbonate grains and then deposited stable calcite cements in environments that eventually became increasingly reducing. With the appropriate timing of transgressions and regressions, bodies of stabilized carbonate (phreatic zone) may be sandwiched

between unstabilized carbonates lacking cement (freshwater vadose and marine phreatic zones). Burial of these packets may result in lack of compaction in the partially cemented stabilized phreatic lens zone, and compaction with loss of primary porosity in the surrounding sediments. Primary and leached secondary porosity could then be preserved in the phreatic lens sediments, providing a valuable diagenetic trap for hydrocarbons (see Chapter 18).

9.11 Diagenesis of lime muds

Mud-sized calcite crystals are very common in limestones, either as a matrix between coarser grains, or as the principal component of the rock. In hand specimen, the rock is generally light grey or white on weathered surfaces but dark grey or black on fresh surfaces. It fractures with a rough, splintery or conchoidal fracture; rarely does it split along laminations like a shale. In thin section, the fine sediment normally has a dark, homogeneous, finely granular texture with a brown cast in plane light. The individual crystals are anhedral to subhedral, intersertal, with planar or curved boundaries, usually equant in shape as prisms, rhombs or plates. Size frequency analyses show most crystals fall in the size 1 to 30 μm diameter. The microcrystalline grains 1–4 μm in size are called micrite, and those 4–30 μm in diameter, *microspar*. Carbonate mudstone is the collective term for all microcrystalline calcite from 1 to 30 μm in size, though frequently the term 'micrite' is loosely used for calcites of this size range.

At deposition, carbonate muds may have up to 70% porosity, but micrites are usually dense with less than 5% porosity.

Micrites are formed by the neomorphism of lime mud. Once removed from the sea bed by burial or exposure, the mineralogically unstable aragonite needles and/or small Mg calcite crystals are consumed and cemented by internally and externally derived $CaCO_3$. The finest of crystals in the original mud will no doubt be the quickest to dissolve, either directly on account of

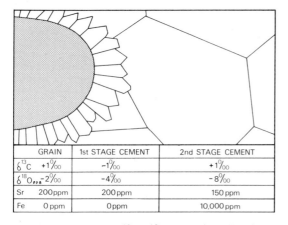

	GRAIN	1st STAGE CEMENT	2nd STAGE CEMENT
$\delta^{13}C$	+1‰	−1‰	+1‰
$\delta^{18}O_{PDB}$	−2‰	−4‰	−8‰
Sr	200 ppm	200 ppm	150 ppm
Fe	0 ppm	0 ppm	10,000 ppm

Figure 9.20 The typical $\delta^{13}C$, $\delta^{18}O$, Sr and Fe values for a grain of marine origin and its early and late (burial) stages of cement

their high surface area to volume ratio, or under the influence of any grain to grain pressures on compaction. Calcite cement would precipitate in optical continuity as overgrowths on original microscopic calcite particles, forming an equant mosaic. Many aragonite needles would be consumed to grow one equant crystal of micrite. Microspar may result from neomorphism and cementation of a mixed mineral (aragonite and calcite) lime mud at the same time as micrite is produced, but in this case the calcite nuclei are fewer and therefore wider apart, so larger crystals grow; alternatively, it may result at a later time by a separate phase of neomorphism during which some micrite crystals grew at the expense of others by an aggrading process.

In a study of Pleistocene mudstones from Bahamas and Florida, Lasemi and Sandberg (1983) show calcitic carbonate mudstones to be of two types: (i) aragonite-dominated precursors; and (ii) calcite-dominated precursors.

Aragonite-dominated precursor (ADP) mudstones may be micrite or more commonly microspar; they contain neomorphic calcite with aragonite relics and pits seen by SEM on prepared polished and etched surfaces. The aragonite relics are distributed similarly in the micrite and the microspar, showing the microspar results from the same one phase of neomorphism (lime mud to calcite mudstone) as does the micrite (a new phase of solution/precipitation to transform micrite into microspar would have removed more of the aragonite relics). This ADP micrite has high Sr (1900 ppm) and lower Mg (200 ppm) compared to those micrites thought to derive from calcite-dominated precursors.

Calcite-dominated precursors (CDP) mudstones generally lack microspar-sized crystals, lack relics and have few pits. Their Mg is high, 3700 ppm, and Sr low, 400 ppm.

Microspar crystals that truncate micrites and grains alike are clearly a late neomorphic feature. Those microspars that are uniform in grain size (often with a loafish form) and grade very smoothly into micrite are most probably of a

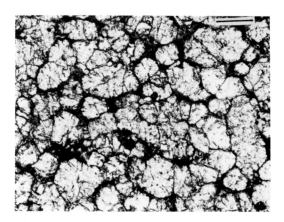

Figure 9.21 Microspar, rich in inclusions and with clay minerals between crystals. Thin section, ppl. Scale 10 μm. Jurassic, Skye, Scotland. Photograph courtesy of Julian Andrews

later neomorphic origin than the micrite. These late microspars are often inclusion-rich and associated with clay minerals (Figure 9.21).

9.12 Diagenesis of deep sea oozes

Deep-sea deposits tend to be uniform over broad areas since there is little change due to the fauna and the site of deposition is below wave base. Unlike most modern shallow-water lime muds, most deep-sea oozes are composed of low Mg calcite, and are therefore chemically stable in sea and fresh waters. Lithification of oozes produces chalk. As they are deposits of the deep sea, it is rare for such sediments to be exposed early in their diagenetic history to meteoric waters, so it is not normally until after significant burial that lithification and porosity reduction commences. Depositional porosity of the ooze is about 70%. On initial burial, water is squeezed out, and some grains are reoriented and deformed, until at about 1 km depth a stable framework is developed, with c. 40% porosity, resisting further mechanical compaction. Chemical compaction then takes over on deeper burial and $CaCO_3$ is transferred from sites of greater to lesser differential stress (i.e. from grain contacts to intergranular pores). If fresh water is flushed into the

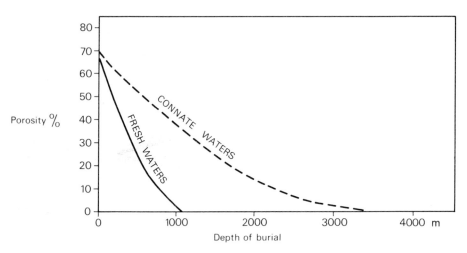

Figure 9.22 Change in porosity on the compaction of deep-sea ooze. Pressure dissolution effects are felt at shallower depth where the interstitial fluid is fresh (low Mg/Ca ratio) rather than connate. After Scholle (1977)

system, lowering the Mg/Ca ratio, then the pressure dissolution effects are felt at a shallower depth (Figure 9.22).

If shelf-edge sediments containing aragonite are rapidly deposited, e.g. by turbidity currents on to a basin floor that is below the aragonite compensation depth, the sediment may be lithified shortly after burial by calcium carbonate (calcite) that was derived from the solution of the unstable aragonite grains.

9.13 Summary of crystal size and shape of diagenetic CaCO$_3$

The common naturally occurring carbonate minerals (aragonite, Mg calcite, calcite and dolomite) exist in three main morphologies—micrite, fibres and coarse equant (sparry) crystals. In meteoric environments the common carbonate is equant calcite. In normal shallow marine settings, micrite and acicular Mg calcite is typically the dominant phase, commonly co-existing with acicular aragonite, whereas in hypersaline supratidal (and lake) settings acicular aragonite predominates. But exceptions, though rare, do exist—e.g. equant calcite is found as a cement in deep cold seas, and acicular forms do occur in freshwater caliches and speleothem deposits;

aragonite also occurs locally in some freshwater caves. Two major factors are believed to explain the general occurrences of the different carbonate minerals and the different morphologies (Figure 9.23): (i) the effect of Mg^{2+} and other ions (notably Na$^+$) in the precipitating waters,

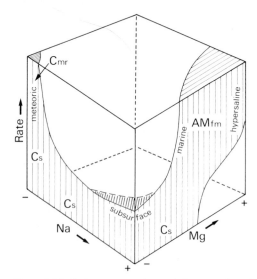

Figure 9.23 Carbonate crystal morphology as a function of rate of crystallization, Na$^+$ and Mg^{2+} content of the solutions. C, calcite; A, aragonite; M, magnesian calcite; s, spar; m, micrite; f, fibres; r, rhombs. After Folk (1974)

and (ii) the rate of crystal growth. These features are controlled by the environment of diagenesis (Figure 9.17). Rapid precipitation is favoured where saturation is high and nuclei abundant at the many interfaces of the near-surface environment:

sea water/air (whitings)
sea water/bottom sediment (hardgrounds)
sea water/sediment/air (beachrock)
fresh water/soil/air (caliche)
fresh water/air (streams and lakes)
fresh water/air/sediment (vadose zone)

and all of these interfaces are characterized by a fine grain size in cement crystals.

Magnesium content is high in marine and hypersaline settings and low in fresh water, and also low in deep burial brines where it is extracted from waters by clay minerals (chlorite and montmorillonite) or precipitated as dolomite, leaving the remaining waters relatively free of Mg^{2+}.

Sodium content is a direct reflection of the salinity. It is high in the sea and in hypersaline environments and remains high in trapped formation (connate) waters, but is low in fresh waters.

Micrite texture is the result of rapid near-surface precipitation by organic influence, evaporation, or chemical reactions causing rapid degassing of CO_2 rapid supersaturation and multiple nucleation.

Fibrous texture is prevalent in aragonites and Mg calcites that form at slightly lower rates of crystallization than do micrites in marine environments having high Mg and Na. Abundant magnesium ions are thought to be the cause of the fibrous development. If Mg^{2+} attaches to the edge of a Ca^{2+} sheet in $CaCO_3$, it will block the sideways growth by causing the CO_3^{2-} sheets above and below to close up to accommodate the smaller ionic radius of Mg. So crystal growth persists more easily along one crystallographic direction normal to the Ca and CO_3 layers (c-axis), giving the high-length-to-breadth (fibrous) form.

Large equant crystals of sparry calcite develop in the subsurface where slow crystal growth rates result in less poisoning by Mg^{2+}, and where organic influences are no longer significant. Slow crystal growth rates also favour the growth of large well-ordered dolomite crystals (limpid) in the subsurface where the Mg/Ca ratio is above 1/2.

Given and Wilkinson (1985) maintained that the major control on both cement mineralogy and crystal form is the rate of crystal growth, with the Mg/Ca ratios of the precipitating solutions being of only indirect significance. They point out that if c-axis growth is enhanced, elongate crystals grow; if it is retarded, equant crystals grow. On c-axis faces the charged surfaces facilitate cation dehydration (the lattice incorporation of Ca) and growth rate is controlled by the local availability of CO_3^{2-} ions. Where CO_3^{2-} is low (because of combination with H^+ to give HCO_3^-) and Ca^{2+} is relatively high (e.g. in a deep cold sea), growth sites on precipitating crystals are starved for carbonate ions and c-axis growth is retarded, giving equant crystals. Elongate crystal habits are found in meteoric vadose and shallow marine settings where CO_2 degassing generates CO_3^{2-} ions by disassociation of HCO_3^-; the system is carbonate-rich, c-axis growth is enhanced and elongate crystals result. Aragonite precipitation is favoured when rates of reactant supply are high; calcite forms when rates are low. On account of the relative rates of dehydration of Ca and Mg ions on different faces of calcite crystals, the amount of Mg incorporated in calcite is controlled by Mg/Ca ratio. The slower the growth rate on the c-axis, the more Mg is expelled from the calcites forming.

Given and Wilkinson (1985) point out that as aragonite cements co-exist with Mg calcite cements in modern reefs (high Mg/Ca), and aragonite co-exists with calcite in some cave deposits (low Mg/Ca), then elevated Mg/Ca ratios do not favour aragonite rather than calcite precipitation as earlier workers have suggested. They maintain that the amount of fluid shear at growing crystal surfaces is the controlling factor. Higher CO_3^{2-} availability gives rise to aragonite, lower availability gives rise to calcite. Higher CO_3^{2-} is available in zones of high hydraulic energy, CO_2 degassing, high evaporation and high saturation.

9.14 Growth of calcite cement and neomorphic spar

In a growing crystal, ions preferentially occupy those sites which result in the greatest possible release of energy. In the example of Figure 9.24, site 1 is energetically favoured until the row is filled, then site 2 commences filling, forming a new row until the face is completed. Depositional energy on a completed face is considerably smaller than that required for the completion of an atomic layer already started.

On a seed crystal there will be areas which are parallel to the developing growth and areas

which are not. Those areas not parallel to the developing faces will generally have higher depositional energies. Growth will occur preferentially on those areas, until all surfaces are parallel to developing crystal faces. Commonly, when growth takes place on a large seed, a number of small crystals develop from the areas of greatest depositional energy. These small subcrystals possess faces which are not quite angularly correct. The subcrystals with the greatest deviation from the correct angles grow faster and coalesce with other subcrystals, until finally a single crystal remains with correct interfacial angles. Once this form has been fully developed, each face has its own specific growth velocity, and crystals enlarge by parallel outward growth from their faces, as indicated by the law of constancy of interfacial angles. Where crystals grow freely into the pore of a fluid they possess *true crystal faces*. When the two crystals impinge on one another, continued

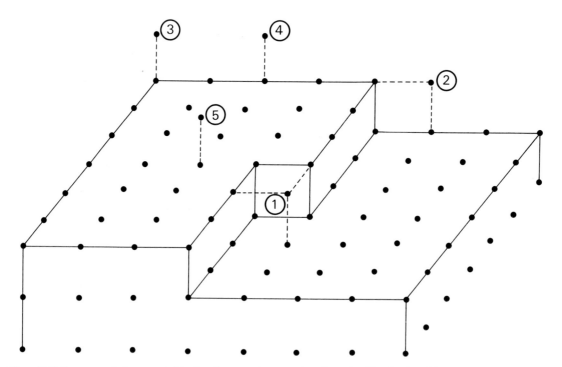

Figure 9.24 Sequence of sites occupied by ions in a growing crystal as determined by the depositional energy. Site 1 is filled before 2 which in turn is filled before 3, then 4, then 5

growth results in loss of faces and the development of *compromise boundaries* between the crystals (Figure 9.25).

The rate of maturation of fabric, that is, how quickly optimum shapes are produced where fastest growth has overtaken other crystals, varies according to the original crystal form.

Crystals with their direction of greatest linear growth oriented normal to the substrate grow fastest, and successfully eliminate crystals of different orientation. On maturing, this gives a general pattern of:

(i) Increase in crystal size away from the substrate

(ii) Longest diameters of crystals normal to the substrate

(iii) Diminution in number of crystals away from substrate

(iv) Any banded zones (e.g. Fe^{2+}- or Mn^{2+}-rich, see below) within crystals meet exactly at the crystal boundaries (Figure 9.25).

Enfacial junctions (Figure 9.25), where one angle of a triple junction is 180°, suggest one crystal stopped growth (preserving a crystal face), and two other crystals, growing later side by side along a natural compromise boundary, confronted this dormant crystal face. Enfacial junctions are common in precipitated sparry calcites where a hiatus in crystal growth is supported by other (chemical) evidence.

Most passively precipitated sparry calcites have planar crystal boundaries, but if growth rates of different crystallographic forms are changed then curved crystal boundaries can be produced. Also, if the growing crystals are irregular, dendritic or split-faced, then an extremely complex pattern of intercrystalline boundaries results.

We may except two types of cement, those which seed on a substrate and those which do not. When cement seeds on a substrate, the orientation of the foundation crystals has a profound control on the initial fabric of cement. For example, calcite overgrowths on the prismatic crystals of ostracod or trilobite fragments are bladed crusts with individual crystals in optical continuity with the foundation crystals, whereas a crinoid ossicle will be coated by one large syntaxial overgrowth crystal. When the first stage is completed, normal competitive growth ensues, controlled by the growth velocities of the various crystallographic forms present. Small seed crystals reach completed faces before a large one, so cement growth stops on an ooid, for example, where it waits for crinoid overgrowth to catch up to its energetic state. In so doing the crinoid overgrowth may engulf the tiny ooid cement fringes and fill the bulk of the pore space.

Growth of cement crystals from a substrate of unoriented crystals, such as in a faecal pellet, or from one of a different mineralogy with no suitable nucleation sites, will show an initial immature fabric of fine crystals with no distinctive features, or orientation, close to the substrate, grading out to the pore centre into larger, fewer, elongate crystals as described earlier for a mature cement fabric.

9.15 Cement stratigraphy

Thin-section studies of intercrystalline boundaries of cement crystals allow us only a limited insight into the sequence of precipitation of

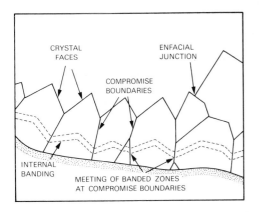

Figure 9.25 Shapes of calcite crystals growing into free space, indicating crystal faces, compromise boundaries and enfacial junctions

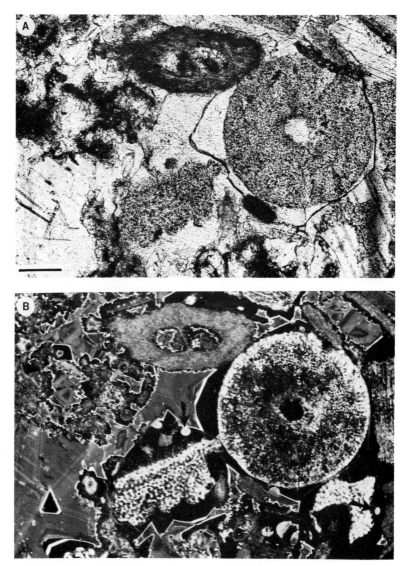

Figure 9.26 Thin section of crinoidal grainstone in plane polarized light (*A*) and under cathodoluminescence (*B*). Note that the sparry cement boundaries as revealed with polarized light do not precisely coincide with the actual margins revealed in cathodoluminescence. The cement crystals show a sequence in luminescence from non-luminescent (zone 1, black) to a thin brightly luminescent zone (zone 2 white) to a dull zone (zone 3 banded grey). The cements are substrate-selective and are large crystals on the crinoids but small on the bryozoan and peloid grains. The round white inclusions (arrowed) of bright calcite in the dark zone 1 cements are casts of sponge spicules which dissolved after zone 1 cement times and the moulds filled with bright zone 2 cement. Scale 0.5 mm. Carboniferous. Derbyshire, England. Photographs courtesy of Gordon Walkden

cements. There are three common techniques for revealing optically the growth patterns *within* crystals which can further our understanding of cement paragenesis; staining, cathodoluminescence, and ultraviolet microscopy. Staining with potassium ferricyanide reveals the small changes in the quantities of ferrous iron incorporated into calcite or dolomite. Electron excitation (cathodoluminescence) and ultraviolet radiation cause those parts of crystals to luminesce which have lattice inhomogeneities, distortion or contain activator impurities, for example Mn (other impurities, such as Fe, Ni and Co, are quenchers and inhibit luminescence). These defects normally relate to changes in the composition or nature (e.g. reducing *v*. oxidizing) of the precipitating solutions, and thus appear as time-correlatable bands within the crystals.

Under favourable conditions it is possible, using these techniques, to relate the timing of cements one to another, and to textural adjustments such as compaction, fracturing and pressure dissolution. In particular, cathodoluminescence and UV microscopy have revealed the importance of dissolution events during cementation where individual crystals have experienced erosion and subsequent repair, a feature not readily detectable by ordinary light microscopy. Cathodoluminescence and UV microscopy may also reveal the earlier existence of grains, fine matrix or cements that have transformed to neomorphic spar.

Studies with cathodoluminescence show that, in general, shallow marine limestones undergo very similar diagenetic changes during progressive burial, which are reflected by a trend in the cements from (1) non-luminescent to (2) bright to (3) dull luminescence (Figure 9.26). This common sequence is thought to represent the evolution of redox potentials in the pore fluids, starting with well-oxidized conditions that inhibit the uptake of the activator ion manganese (they also inhibit the uptake of iron as revealed by the non-ferroan composition of early cements). Reducing conditions followed, allowing

Mn incorporation into cements, but as organic reactions and sulphate reduction locked up available iron, these cements luminesce brightly. Deeper burial produces reducing conditions in which quenching ferrous iron is now available in variable amounts, as is Mn, so dull or occasionally banded luminescence is the consequence.

We may relate bright and dull alternations within cements to cyclic recharge of the freshwater phreatic zone during transgressions/regressions; non-luminescent intervals represent downward penetration of an actively cementing meteoric phreatic lens during regression, and bright bands represent stagnation during transgression. Each successive band shows an overlapping stratigraphic range slightly higher than the last.

9.16 Neomorphic spar

Neomorphic textures may obscure the depositional fabric of the limestone, making interpretations of the environment of deposition exceedingly difficult. If micrite undergoes neomorphic alteration to a mosaic of sparry calcite while, for example, skeletal grains remain unaltered, then a biomicrite may be misinterpreted as a biosparite.

Some of the common characteristic petrographic textures of passively precipitated calcite (planar crystalline boundaries; increase in crystal size away from substrate; longest diameter of crystal normal to the substrate; diminution in number of crystals away from substrate) can equally well apply to neomorphic sparry calcite that nucleated on the perimeter of a grain and grew by replacing the intergranular micrite matrix. Some criteria may help to distinguish between passively precipitated and neomorphic spar:

(i) Neomorphic spar is more typically random in its orientation, since it can nucleate from a multitude of centres, whereas cement must encrust a free surface

(ii) Distinctly banded zones within crystals as

revealed by staining or cathodoluminescence would be uncommon in neomorphic spar

(iii) It is unlikely that two distinctly different generations of spar would result from neomorphic processes

(iv) There would be significantly fewer enfacial junctions in neomorphic spar

(v) Neomorphic spar may contain inclusions as a result of incorporating impurities (e.g. clay minerals, organics) whilst engulfing micrite

(vi) Neomorphic crystals may be separated by impurities that the growing crystals have expelled during crystallization and displaced to line compromise boundaries

(vii) Neomorphic spar, often with euhedral faces, may encroach into grains (e.g. skeletons) whose shape and unaltered internal structure give clear evidence of their origin and thus point to the secondary replacive nature of the spar

(viii) Those sparry patches within micrite which cannot be accounted for by shrinkage, dewatering, differential setting or burrowing, are likely to be neomorphic

(ix) Vague patches of micrite within a sparry mosaic suggest a neomorphic origin for the spar.

In addition to these crystallographic criteria, there are gross textural criteria which may assist the interpretation of sparry calcite in limestone. Features that indicate that the limestone was originally grain-supported (including close packing of grains, and flat floors in partially mud-filled intergranular cavities) suggest that fluids flowed freely between grains from which cement crystals could precipitate. But where grains can be seen to be so loosely packed that they are not in mutual contact, then the rock must originally have been mud-supported and the mud has subsequently recrystallized to spar.

Many alternatives are possible, but in a general sense the trace element and isotope chemistry of a neomorphic spar would approximate more closely to that of the original (normally marine) grains than to a sparry cement which had necessarily precipitated in a more open system.

Selected reading

Allan, J.R. and Matthews, R.K. (1977) Carbon and oxygen isotopes as diagenetic and stratigraphic tools: surface and subsurface data, Barbados, West Indies. *Geology* **5**, 16–20.

Allan, J.R. and Matthews, R.K. (1982) Isotopic signatures associated with early meteoric diagenesis. *Sedimentology* **29**, 797–817.

Aissaoui, D.M. (1985) Botryoidal aragonite and its diagenesis. *Sedimentology* **32**, 345–361.

Bathurst, R.G.C. (1958) Diagenetic fabrics in some British Dinantian limestones. *Liverpool Manchester Geol. J.* **2**, 11–36.

Bathurst, R.G.C. (1959) The cavernous structure of some Mississippian *Stromatactis* reefs in Lancashire, England. *J. Geol.* **67**, 506–521.

Bathurst, R.G.C. (1966) Boring algae, micrite envelopes and lithification of molluscan biosparites. *Geol. J.* **5**, 15–32.

Bathurst, R.G.C. (1979) Diagenesis in carbonate sediments: a review. *Geol. Rdsch.* **68**, 848–855.

Bathurst, R.G.C. (1980) Deep crustal diagenesis in limestones. *Revista del Instituto de Investigaciones Geologicas Diputacion Provincial Universidad de Barcelona* **34**, 89–100.

Bathurst, R.G.C. (1980) Lithification of carbonate sediments. *Sci. Prog.* **66**, 451–477.

Bathurst, R.G.C. (1981) Early diagenesis of carbonate sediments. In Parker, A. and Sellwood, B.W. (eds.), *Sediment Diagenesis*, Reidel, Dordrecht, 349–378.

Bathurst, R.G.C. (1983) Neomorphic spar versus cement in some Jurassic grainstones: significance for evaluation of porosity evolution and compaction. *J. Geol. Soc. London* **140**, 229–237.

Bricker, O.P. (ed.) (1971) *Carbonate Cements*. The Johns Hopkins University Studies in Geology, **19**.

Chilingar, G.V., Bissell, H.J. and Wolf, K.H. (1967) Diagenesis of carbonate rocks. In Larson, G. and Chilingar, G.V. (eds.), *Diagenesis in Sediments*, Elsevier, Amsterdam, 179–322.

Clark, D.N. (1980) The diagenesis of Zechstein carbonate sediments. *Contr. Sedimentol.* **9**, 167–203.

Cullis, C.G. (1904) The mineralogical changes observed in the cores of the Funafuti boring. In *Coral Reef Report. The Atoll of Funafuti*, **14**, 392–420. Royal Society, London.

Dickson, J.A.D. (1984) Diagenesis of shallow marine carbonates. In Brenchley, P.J. and Williams, B.P.J. (eds.), *Sedimentology: Recent Developments and Applied Aspects*, Blackwell, Oxford, 173–188.

Dickson, J.A.D. and Coleman, M.L. (1980) Changes in carbon and oxygen isotope composition during limestone diagenesis. *Sedimentology* **27**, 107–118.

Dravis, J.J. and Yurewicz, D.A. (1985) Enhanced carbonate

petrography using fluorescence microscopy. *J. Sed. Petrol.* **55**, 795–804.

Dunham, R.J. (1969) Early vadose silt in Townsend (reef), New Mexico. In *Depositional Environments in Carbonate Rocks: a Symposium*, SEPM Sp. Pub. **14**, 139–181.

Dunham, R.J. (1969) Vadose pisolite in the Capitan Reef (Permian), New Mexico and Texas. In *Depositional Environments in Carbonate Rocks: a Symposium*, SEPM Sp. Pub. **14**, 182–191.

Folk, R.L. (1965) Some aspects of recrystallisation in ancient limestones. In Pray, L.C. and Murray, R.C. (eds.), *Dolomitisation and Limestone diagenesis*, SEPM Spec. Pub. **13**, 14–48.

Folk, R.L. (1974) The natural history of crystalline calcium carbonate: effect of magnesium content and salinity. *J. Sed. Petrol.* **44**, 40–53.

Folk, R.L. and Assereto, R.L.A.M. (1976) Comparative fabrics of length-slow and length-fast calcite and calcitized aragonite in a Holocene speleothem Carlsbad caverns, New Mexico. *J. Sed. Petrol.* **46**, 486–496.

Friedman, G.M. (1964) Early diagenesis and lithification in carbonate sediments. *J. Sed. Petrol.* **34**, 777–813.

Garrison, R.E. and Kennedy, W.J. (1977) Origin of solution seams and flaser structure in Upper Cretaceous chalks of southern England. *Sed. Geol.* **19**, 107–137.

Given, R.K. and Wilkinson, B.H. (1985) See p. 105.

Heckel, P.H. (1983) Diagenetic model for carbonate rocks in mid continent Pennsylvanian eustatic cyclothems. *J. Sed. Petrol.* **53**, 753–759.

Hudson, J.D. (1962) Pseudo-pleochroic calcite in recrystallized shell limestone. *Geol. Mag.* **99**, 492–500.

Hudson, J.D. (1977) Stable isotopes and limestone lithification. *J. Geol. Soc. London* **133**, 637–660.

Humphrey, J.D., Ransom, K.L. and Matthews, R.K. (1986) Early meteoric diagenetic control of Upper Smackover production, Oaks Field, Louisiana. *Am. Ass. Petrol. Geol.* **70**, 70–85.

James, N.P. (1974) Diagenesis of scleractinian corals in the subaerial vadose environment. *J. Paleontol.* **48**, 785–799.

James, N.P. and Klappa, C.F. (1983) Petrogenesis of Early Cambrian Reef Limestones, Labrador, Canada. *J. Sed. Petrol.* **53**, 1051–1096.

Kendall, A.C. (1985) Radiaxial fibrous calcite: a reappraisal. In Schneidermann, N. and Harris, P.M. (eds.), *Carbonate Cements*, SEPM Sp. Pub. **36**, 59–77.

Kendall, A.C. and Tucker, M.E. (1973) Radiaxial fibrous calcite: a replacement after acicular carbonate. *Sedimentology* **20**, 365–389.

Land, L.S., MacKenzie, F.T. and Gould, S.J. (1967) Pleistocene history of Bermuda. *Geol. Soc. Am. Bull.* **78**, 993–1006.

Lasemi, Z. and Sandberg, P.A. (1983) Recognition of original mineralogy in ancient micrites. *Am. Ass. Petrol. Geol. Bull.* **67**, 499–500.

Logan, B.W. and Semeniuk, V. (1976) *Dynamic metamorphism; processes and products in Devonian carbonate rocks.*

Canning Basin, Western Australia. Geol. Soc. Australia Sp. Pub. **6**, Sydney.

Lohmann, K.C. and Meyers, W.J. (1977) Macrodolomite inclusions in cloudy prismatic calcites: a proposed criterion for former high-magnesium calcites. *J. Sed. Petrol.* **47**, 1078–1088.

Longman, M.W. (1980) Carbonate diagenetic textures from near-surface diagenetic environments. *Am. Ass. Petrol. Geol. Bull.* **64**, 461–487.

Longman, M.W. (1982) Carbonate diagenesis as a control on stratigraphic traps. *AAPG Education Course Notes* **21**, 1–159.

Matthews, R.K. (1968) Carbonate diagenesis: equilibrium of sedimentary mineralogy to the subaerial environment; coral cap of Barbados, West Indies. *J. Sed. Petrol.* **38**, 1110–1119.

Matthews, R.K. (1974) A process approach to diagenesis of reefs and reef associated limestones. In Laporte, C.F. (eds), *Reefs in Time and Space*, SEPM Sp. Pub. **18**, 234–256.

Meyers, W.J. (1974) Carbonate cement stratigraphy of the Lake Valley formation (Mississippian) Sacramento Mountains, New Mexico. *J. Sed. Petrol.* **44**, 837–861.

Meyers, W.J. and Lohmann, K.C. (1978) Micro-dolomite rich syntaxial cements: proposed meteoric-marine mixing zone phreatic cements from Mississippian limestones, New Mexico. *J. Sed. Petrol.* **48**, 475–488.

Oldershaw, A.E. and Scoffin, T.P. (1967) The source of ferroan and non-ferroan calcite cements in the Halkin and Wenlock Limestones. *Geol. J.* **5**, 309–320.

Pray, L.C. and Murray, R.L. (1965) *Dolomitization and Limestone Diagenesis*. SEPM Sp. Pub. **13**.

Sandberg, P.A. (1975, 1983) See p. 226.

Sandberg, P.A. and Hudson, J.D. (1983) Aragonite relic preservation in Jurassic calcite-replaced bivalves. *Sedimentology* **30**, 879–892.

Scholle, P.A. (1977) Chalk diagenesis and its relation to petroleum exploration—oil from chalks, a modern miracle? *Am. Ass. Petrol. Geol.* **61**, 982–1009.

Shinn, E.A., Halley, R.A., Hudson, J.H. and Lidz, B.H. (1977) Limestone compaction: an enigma. *Geology* **5**, 2124.

Sorby, H.C. (1879) Anniversary address of the president (Structure and Origin of Limestones). *Geol. Soc. Lond. Proc.* **35**, 56–95.

Steinen, R.P. and Matthews, R.K. (1973) Phreatic versus vadose diagenesis: stratigraphy and mineralogy of a cored borehole on Barbados, W.I. *J. Sed. Petrol.* **43**, 1012–1020.

Veizer, J. (1977) Diagenesis of Pre-Quaternary carbonates as indicated by trace element studies. *J. Sed. Petrol.* **47**, 565–581.

Veizer, J. and Demovic, R. (1974) Strontium as a tool in facies analysis. *J. Sed. Petrol.* **44**, 93–115.

Wanless, H.R. (1979) Limestone response to stress: pressure solution and dolomitization. *J. Sed. Petrol.* **49**, 437–462.

Wanless, H.R. (1983) Burial diagenesis in limestones. In Parker, A. and Sellwood, B.W. (eds.), *Sediment Diagenesis*, Reidel, Dordrecht, 379–417.

10 Dolomite

10.1 Nature of the mineral

The dolomite mineral is rhombohedral and has the ideal formula $CaMg(CO_3)_2$, in which calcium and magnesium have equal molar proportions; this is called *stoichiometric*. The crystal is ordered, with a Ca and Mg occupying preferred sites. In the ideal mineral, planes of CO_3 anions alternate with planes of cations with the *c*-axis of the crystal perpendicular to the stacked planes. The Ca and Mg planes themselves alternate. Most naturally occurring dolomites are non-stoichiometric, being mainly Ca-rich, and lack perfect ordering, though some workers believe that they become better ordered through time during repeated neomorphism.

There are several varieties encountered in carbonates. The first variety is characteristic of Holocene dolomites only, being particularly common in modern hypersaline settings. It has an excess of calcium and is poorly ordered. It is referred to as calcian dolomite or protodolomite. This form probably grew in solutions of high ionic strength and rapid crystallization, as the structure has many crystallographic faults and dislocations with abundant trace element substitutions, especially of strontium and sodium. It is metastable and very soluble in comparison to the more ordered varieties.

The bulk of phanerozoic dolomites have less calcium and better ordering than these protodolomites, although they are still metastable in comparison with ideal dolomite. They occur in a range of styles in ancient carbonates, for example as void-filling cement layers alternating with calcite cements; as large scattered euhedral rhombs partially replacing the precursors; as total replacements of precursor carbonates perfectly preserving the original fabric; as a dense mosaic of even-sized rhombs with a micritic sucrosic texture; as coarse clear sparry mosaics commonly with zoned crystals; or as large late-stage crystals with curved faces (saddle or baroque) normally occupying voids and frac-

tures. Where dolomite is fabric-preserving (i.e. volume-conserving transformation) the precipitation will have been slow and the system relatively closed, leading to relatively high Sr and Ca values. Fabric-destructive dolomitization takes place with higher fluid flow rates. In this latter case, the larger-scale dissolution of the precursor calcium carbonate allows the dolomite to grow into the most energetically suitable forms, commonly forming a sucrosic texture of rhombs. Dolomites with abundant crystals having idiomorphic forms retain high intercrystalline porosity. When adjacent dolomite rhombs come into contact, crystal growth stops (*contact inhibition*), since the surface free energy is minimal for the low-index crystal faces. Generally, crystals growing in open voids contain relatively few lattice defects (saddle dolomite is an exception, having a complex array of fault-like defects). But where replacement of a precursor has occurred, a heterogeneous microstructure within crystals usually develops.

Sedimentary dolomite is normally enriched in $\delta^{18}O$, about 3 to 4‰ with respect to co-existing calcite in the range of sedimentary and burial diagenetic temperatures. However, the isotopic composition is, of course, controlled by the chemistry of the latest neomorphic event and by the chemistry of the precursor (aragonite, Mg calcite or dolomite).

Modern marine and hypersaline dolomites have an Sr content of 600 ppm, yet few ancient dolomites have more than 200 ppm even when presumed to be of hypersaline origin. During dolomite stabilization to a more ordered form, Sr is expelled.

10.2 Origin

Most dolomites initially from by replacing a calcium carbonate precursor. A fluid imports Mg, dissolves the precursor phase, precipitates dolomite and exports Ca (plus Sr, ^{13}C and ^{18}O). A high fluid flow is needed. It has been calculated

(Land, 1983) that to completely dolomitize 1 cubic metre of a typical sediment (6.3 mol% $MgCO_3$ and 40% porosity) without any porosity reduction requires:

807   pore volumes normal sea water

8070 pore volumes of 10 times diluted sea water (e.g. mixing zone)

44   pore volumes of hypersaline brine that has precipitated gypsum.

Modern dolomites are forming in many different environments, such as hypersaline supratidal flats, the bottoms of some freshwater lakes, the precipitates of some caves and freshwater springs, and the subsurface where fresh and salt water mix. Temperature, solution composition and concentration, organic compounds, and rate of crystallization are all important controls. Folk and Land (1975) maintained that the most important reactions can be explained relatively simply by a diagram of salinity plotted against Mg/Ca ratio of the depositing solution (Figure 10.1). These data on natural waters show that in a hypersaline environment with high ion concentration (salinity) and rapid crystallization, the Mg/Ca ratio must exceed 5:1 or 10:1 for dolomite to form. In normal marine waters (such as certain deep-sea deposits) dolomite probably forms at Mg/Ca values over 3:1. In some freshwater and low-salinity subsurface waters, dolomite can form at Mg/Ca ratios as low as 1:1 because of the lack of competing ions and generally lower rate of crystallization. The lower the salinity, the easier it is for the ordered structure of dolomite to form.

Experimental work by Baker and Kastner (1981) has shown that the transformation of calcium carbonate to dolomite is retarded, or inhibited, depending upon the concentration of SO_4^{2-} in solution. Aragonite dolomitization is less retarded than calcite dolomitization at similar SO_4^{2-} concentrations. The reaction is thought to be a crystal surface-controlled mechanism. Baker and Kastner (1981) point out that dolomite can form in nature only where SO_4^{2-}

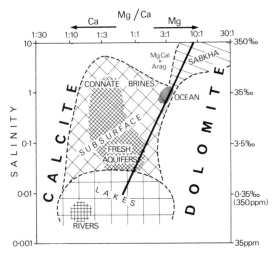

Figure 10.1 Fields of occurrence of common natural waters plotted on graph of salinity v. Mg/Ca ratio. Sabkha waters are highly saline and Mg-rich. Subsurface waters vary from hypersaline to fresh, but commonly contain an excess of Ca over Mg (heavier shading shows most common values). Fields of preferred occurrence of dolomite, aragonite plus magnesian calcite and calcite are also shown. At low salinities with few competing ions and slow crystallization rates dolomite can form at Mg/Ca ratios near 1:1. As salinity rises, it becomes more difficult for ordered dolomite to form, thus requiring higher Mg/Ca ratios. After Folk and Land (1975)

concentrations are low. Dolomite crystals may develop therefore in low-sulphate alkaline lacustrine environments, but not in normal sea water. There are various mechanisms of depleting the SO_4^{2-} ionic strength of sea water to levels that allow dolomite (or, at higher SO_4^{2-} values, protodolomite) to form:

(i) Microbial reduction (as occurs in some fine-grained deep-sea organic-rich sediments)

(ii) Calcium sulphate (gypsum, anhydrite) precipitation (as in a sabkha environment)

(iii) Mixing of sea water with large amounts of fresh water (as in the schizohaline zone around a freshwater lens).

The ammonia produced during SO_4^{2-} reduction may also release Mg^{2+} adsorbed on any silica present in the sediments, thus enhancing the Mg/Ca ratio and favouring dolomite formation.

10.3 Occurrence and mechanisms of formation

10.3.1 Primary dolomites

There is evidence to suggest that dolomite does occur as a primary precipitate, i.e. has nucleated and grown in open water, in a few areas of the world. In the Coorong region of South Australia there are ephemeral lakes where fine-grained whitings containing dolomite have been observed. The accumulating lake floor sediment is a white gelatinous slurry of fine-grained dolomite. The lakes dry out each summer, a dolomitic crust forms on the surface, and evaporite minerals may precipitate, but are flushed out during the wet winter months when the lakes are refilled and some of the dolomites reworked. The indurated crusts which develop during the dry periods have characteristic sedimentary structures: large polygonal cracks, tepees and breccias.

In the Baffin Bay area of Texas, cores of thin beds of pure dolomites interbedded with terrigenous muds provide sedimentological evidence that the carbonate formed on the sea-floor, either as primary dolomite or as a precursor carbonate (such as Mg calcite) that has been totally replaced.

Penecontemporaneous dolomites are found in interstitial waters of sediments on the sea-floor in 1000 m of water west of Baja California. These dolomites (Figure 10.2) do not appear to replace a precursor, but normally post-date pyrite and pre-date glauconite formation. Though SO_4^{2-} is present in the interstitial waters, precipitation of the dolomite rhombs is near the zone of reduction in bioturbated, organic-rich, near-surface sediments.

10.3.2 Hypersaline dolomites

Many supratidal sediments of the tropics contain calcian dolomites as very small rhombs, usually replacing fine-grained aragonite. In arid regions (e.g. the Persian Gulf) this dolomite is usually found within the soft sediment in the intertidal and low supratidal areas of the tidal flats, whereas in humid climates (e.g. the Caribbean) the dolomites occur more commonly as surficial crusts on supratidal flats.

In the Trucial Coast area of the Persian Gulf (Figure 8.14) contemporaneous dolomites occur in sabkha sediments where high Mg/Ca ratios are attained. On the seaward part of the sabkha, infiltration of wind-driven sea water which has high Mg/Ca ratios causes net downward flow through the sediments. The downward flow depends on the permeability of sediments and flooding frequency, which decreases from the strandline and away from tidal channel axes. Consequently, within the area of high Mg/Ca-ratio groundwaters, there is a narrower zone (c. 1 km wide) in which elevated Mg/Ca ratios and high flow rates combine to give optimum conditions for dolomite formation. The dolomite forms as poorly ordered, calcium-rich, minute rhombs in the intertidal sediments (commonly algal mats) as a replacement first of aragonite mud and later of aragonite pellets.

In the moist tropical climate of the Caribbean, hard dolomite (c. 10%) crusts form on exposed supratidal mud flats on the broad low landward flanks of beach ridges and in a similar position on the flanks of channel levees (Figure 10.3). The site of formation is just above (5–10 cm) mean

Figure 10.2 Dolomite rhombs in Recent deep-sea sediments. SEM. Scale 10 μm. 200 mm below the sea-bed in 1000 m water, Baja California, Mexico. Photograph courtesy of Graham Shimmield

Figure 10.3 Dolomite crust (arrowed) on the flanks of tidal channel levée. Andros, Bahamas. Photograph courtesy of Conrad Neumann

Figure 10.4 Dolomite crust (broken on upheaval by the breathing roots of *Avicennia* mangrove) in supratidal setting amongst pin-cushion algal mats (*Scytonema*). Lens cap 50 mm. Sugar Loaf Key, Florida, USA. Photograph courtesy of Julian Andrews

high tide level, where tidal flooding and storm sedimentation is followed by days of subaerial exposure. Surface evaporation during this exposure increases the concentration of dissolved salts near the surface. The Mg/Ca ratio rises to 10:1, perhaps by the fall in Ca levels during $CaCO_3$ and $CaSO_4$ precipitation, but evaporites (such as gypsum and anhydrite) are only rarely preserved (e.g. Bonaire) due to the humid climate. The dolomite, which is thought to be a penecontemporaneous replacement of aragonite in the sediment, occurs as 3 μm rhombs in surface crusts that are often associated with algal laminates, stromatolites and mud cracks (Figure 10.4). Storm erosion can bring about the deposition of an edgewise conglomerate of tabular fragments of dolomite crusts. There is some debate as to whether these dolomitic crusts of supratidal flats of moist climates formed purely as a result of the concentration of sea water and raising of the Mg/Ca ratio, or by the mixing of saline and fresh waters, for small calcian dolomite crystals are found in the subsurface beneath supratidal islands (hammocks) where freshwater lenses are developed.

There are many ancient carbonate rocks in which dolomites replace (with large-scale cross-cutting patterns) normal marine carbonates, many of which are closely associated with hypersaline deposits. These secondary dolomites owe their origin to the active flushing of magnesium-rich water through the porous rocks. There are a variety of ways in which this may be brought about.

Reflux. The specific gravity of sea water increases as the brine is concentrated. Hypersaline waters in a sabkha may have a density of 1.2 kg/m^3 and lagoonal sea water 1.03 kg/m^3. The density difference, plus the head of water in the supratidal zone following storms, may cause the hypersaline brines, with high Mg/Ca ratios, to displace the connate waters and seep slowly downward, dolomitizing the permeable carbonates beneath the lagoon floor (Figure 10.5). An alternative way of getting a head of dense water in the sabkha is to lower the sea-level by eustatic or tectonic means.

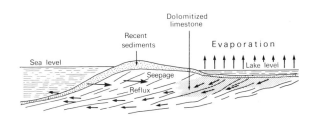

Figure 10.5 Model for dolomitization by seepage reflux from a supratidal lake. After Zenger (1972)

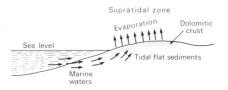

Figure 10.6 Model for dolomitization by evaporative pumping. After Zenger (1972)

Evaporative pumping. During long dry periods, instead of hypersaline waters being pushed from landward to seaward through a column of carbonates by flood recharge, marine waters may be pulled in the other direction by capillary and evaporative action on the sabkha (Figure 10.6). There may be a barrier separating the basin of intense evaporation from the sea, and the subsurface carbonates in this barrier suffer the greatest water flux, bringing about dolomitization. The process of evaporative pumping slows once the basin fills with salts.

10.3.3 *Mixing of fresh and salt water*
Geochemical considerations suggest that a plausible mechanism for dolomite formation is the mixing of fresh and salt waters, though it may be a slow process. This may arise by fresh groundwaters impinging on hypersaline supratidal areas, or it may occur in the mixing zone at the basal perimeter of a freshwater lens (Figures 8.1, 10.7). A solution is produced which

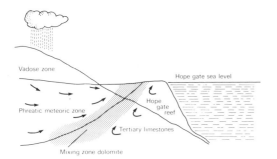

Figure 10.7 Cross-section of the Hope Gate Fm on the north coast of Jamaica showing the mixing of fresh and salt waters. After Land (1973)

is undersaturated with respect to calcite but still supersaturated relative to dolomite. At progressively reduced salinities (isotopic evidence suggests solutions are about 90%–95% fresh groundwater 10%–5% sea water) dolomite is able to nucleate at low Mg/Ca ratios approaching 1:1 (Figure 10.1). Subsurface mixing drastically lowers salinity reducing the concentration of competing ions and slowing crystallization rate, but the Mg/Ca ratio remains high because the amounts of Ca and Mg added by fresh water are very small compared to the large amounts of these cations present in sea water. The dolomite crystals that form are rhombs, normally calcium-rich poorly ordered and up to 50 μm in diameter, and appear to occur more commonly as passively precipitated cements than carbonate replacements. The absence of impurities in the fresher waters may allow clear, inclusion-free rhombs of well-ordered dolomite to form. These *limpid* dolomites are less soluble than most sedimentary dolomites.

10.3.4 *Burial dolomitization*
Dolomitization and dolomite cement can occur on deep burial where interstitial brines can have salinities from 0.1‰ to 200‰. These dolomites may have essentially similar textures to those thought to relate to an evaporative origin (i.e. fine-grained sucrosic or coarse-grained clear mosaic textures). Burial dolomites are often late-stage, and may result from the remobilization of earlier dolomites. Some can be shown to relate directly to pressure dissolution features, others to late-stage voids and fractures. Some apparently developed at the time of flushing of hydrocarbon-associated brines, others during hydrothermal events. These late-stage dolomites are commonly ferroan and can approach ankerite in composition (especially where associated with terrigenous rocks). They are coarsely crystalline, often with strongly curved cleavages and crystal faces, showing undulose extinction (Figure 10.8). Hydrothermal dolomites usually show a sufficient temperature fractionation in

Figure 10.8 Baroque ferroan dolomite (*a*) overlying bladed calcite cement (*b*) which surrounds a fenestellid bryozoan (*c*). Thin section, ppl. Scale 1 mm. Carboniferous, Clitheroe, England. Specimen courtesy of Douglas Gillies

their oxygen isotopic composition to be distinguishable from dolomites formed in near-surface regimes.

Dolomite is uncommon in limestones and chalks that are basinal in origin and well removed from the influence of shallow marine limestones. However, it is not uncommon to find a narrow zone of dolomitization at the basinal margin of a shallow-water limestone, e.g. an upper fore-reef slope. Also, there are some examples of undolomitized talus blocks, derived from such a (now dolomitized) margin incorporated in basinal shales at the foot of the slope. This particular relationship suggests that dolomitization occurred after burial, preferentially affecting the near-surface area. Blocks enveloped in basinal shales may have been sealed off from dolomitizing solutions.

The source of Mg for burial dolomitization may be from shales during compaction (e.g. Mg^{2+} released during montmorillonite to illite transformation). It could also be from the Mg contained in Mg calcites, which occur not only as skeletal grains but also as subsea cements which are especially abundant on fore-reef slopes. It has been estimated that an appropriate reorganization of the Mg in the modern Mg calcite

cements of Jamaica's fore-reef could bring about 30–50% dolomitization of the reef.

Some Mg may be derived from organic components. The regular alternations of calcite laminae and dolomite laminae in ancient algal stromatolites have been explained in this way. Algal filaments in modern stromatolites are seen to concentrate Mg to levels up to four times that of the surrounding waters. A 2 mm thick algal lamina may provide sufficient Mg for the production of a dolomite lamina 1 mm thick.

Patterns of dolomitization are controlled by factors that govern the development of depositional and burial environments, for example:

(i) Palaeogeographic setting of originally permeable limestone units relative to a source of dolomitizing pore fluids (e.g. porous shelf-edge reef between hypersaline lagoon and shale basin, or tidal flat deposits)

(ii) Exposure at unconformities

(iii) Palaeogeographic distribution relative to tectonic highs or regions of subaerial exposure (sites for freshwater recharge)

(iv) Timing of eustatic or tectonic fluctuations controlling movement and evolution of groundwater and connate water

(v) Relationships to palaeogroundwater conduits or water tables.

The petrography of dolomites and porosity development within them are discussed further in section 18.1.4.

Selected reading

Badiozamani, K. (1973) The Dorag dolomitization model application to the middle Ordovician of Wisconsin. *J. Sed. Petrol.* **43**, 965–984.

Baker, P.A. and Kastner, M. (1981) Constraints on the formation of sedimentary dolomite. *Science* **213**, 214–216.

Davies, G.R. (1979) Dolomite reservoir rocks: processes, controls, porosity development. In *Geology of Carbonate Porosity*, AAPG Education Short Course Notes, **11**, C1–C17.

Deffeyes, K.S., Lucia, F.J. and Weyl, P.K. (1965) Dolomitization of Recent and Plio-Pleistocene sediments by marine evaporite waters in Bonaire, Netherlands Antilles. In Pray, L.C. and Murray, R.C. (eds.) *Dolomitization and Lime-*

stone Diagenesis—A Symposium, SEPM Sp. Pub. **13**, 71–88.

Folk, R.L. and Land, L.S. (1975) Mg/Ca ratio and salinity: two controls over crystallisation of dolomite. *Am. Ass. Petrol. Geol. Bull.* **59**, 60–68.

Gebelein, C.D. *et al.* (1980) Subsurface dolomitization beneath the tidal flats of central West Andros Island, Bahamas. In Zenger, D.H., Dunham, J.B. and Ethington, R.C. (eds.) *Concepts and Models of Dolomitization.* SEPM Sp. Pub. **28**, 31–49.

Hsü, K.J. (1967) Chemistry of dolomite formation. In Chilingar, G.V., Bissell, H.J. and Fairbridge, R.W. (eds.) *Carbonate Rocks: Physical and Chemical Aspects*, Elsevier, Amsterdam, 169–191.

Hsü, K.J. and Siegenthaler, C. (1969) Preliminary experiments and hydrodynamic movement induced by evaporation and their bearing on the dolomite problem. *Sedimentology* **12**, 11–25.

Illing, L.V., Wells, A.J. and Taylor, J.C.M. (1965) Penecontemporory dolomite in the Persian Gulf. In Pray, L.C. and Murray, R.C. (eds.), *Dolomitization and Limestone Diagenesis*, SEPM Spec. Pub. **13**, 89–111.

Land, L.S. (1973) Holocene meteoric dolomitization of Pleistocene limestones north Jamaica. *Sedimentology* **20**,

411–422.

Land, L.S. (1980) The isotopic and trace element geochemistry of dolomite: the state of the art. In Zenger, D.H., Dunham, J.B. and Ethington, R.L. (eds.), *Concepts and Models of Dolomitization*, SEPM Sp. Pub. **28**, 87–110.

Land, L.S. (1983) *Dolomitization*. AAPG Education Course Note Series **24**, 1–20.

Radke, B.M. and Mathis, R.L. (1980) On the formation and occurrence of saddle dolomite. *J. Sed. Petrol.* **50**, 1149–1168.

Shinn, E.A., Ginsburg, R.N. and Lloyd, R.M. (1965) Recent supratidal dolomite from Andros Island Bahamas. In Pray, L.C. and Murray, R.C. (eds.), *Dolomitization and Limestone Diagenesis*, SEPM Sp. Pub. **13**, 112–123.

Ward, and Halley, R.B. (1985) Dolomitization in a mixing zone of near seawater composition, Late Pleistocene, northeastern Yucatan Peninsula. *J. Sed. Petrol.* **55**, 407–420.

Zenger, D.H. (1972) Dolomitization and uniformitarianism. *J. Geol. Educ.* **20**, 107–124.

Zenger, D.H., Dunham, J.B. and Ethington, R.L. (eds.) (1980) *Concepts and Models of Dolomitization*, SEPM Sp. Pub. **28**, 320.

11 Diagenesis of impure limestones and the formation of bedding

11.1 Organic-rich calcareous shales

As organic matter is especially abundant in fine-grained sediments, it plays an important role in the subsurface diagenesis of calcareous shales. Diagenetic processes associated with organic matter decay fall into depth-related zones which can be interpreted from the chemistry of the calcareous concretions.

Zone 1. The topmost centimetre or so below the sea-bed is kept oxygenated by downward diffusion of dissolved oxygen from the depositional waters. Oxidation of organic matter by bacteria produces isotopically light CO_2 ($\delta^{13}C$ c. $-25‰$)

Zone 2. Below this uppermost zone interstitial water is stagnant and anoxic, and bacteria (*Desulphovibro*) reduce sulphate anions. This sulphate reduction produces bicarbonate with depleted $\delta^{13}C$ ($-25‰$) and hydrogen sulphide. The reaction reaches a peak about 0.5 m below the sea-bed where metal sulphides and calcium carbonate may precipitate. The porewater sul-

phate is gradually exhausted with depth, and the reaction ceases about 15 m below the surface. Siderite may form in this zone if sulphate is locally excluded.

Zone 3. Once the sulphate is exhausted, organic fermentation (oxidation of organic matter by the oxygen contained within the organic carbon compounds, generating CO_2 and CH_4) occurs along with methanogenesis by CO_2 reduction, at depths from about 15 m to 1000 m. The methanogenesis fractionates the carbon isotopes, leading to a very light methane ($\delta^{13}C = -90$ to $-60‰$) and heavy dissolved carbon dioxide ($\delta^{13}C$ c. $+15‰$). Ferrous iron may now precipitate with carbonate at depth to give isotopically heavy ferroan calcite, ferroan dolomite, ankerite or siderite. If the methane generated escapes to the surface (perhaps along steep fractures) it may be oxidized by bacteria which contribute ^{12}C-enriched CO_2 to the dissolved carbon, bringing about the precipitation of aragonite or Mg-calcite crust cements (Figure 8.5) exceptionally light in $\delta^{13}C$ ($c. -50‰$). CO_2 reduction also favours carbonate precipitation since it raises pH. The resultant surface hardgrounds are concentrated at pockmarks, large (100–1000 m diameter) dish-shaped hollows in the sea-bed that are produced by escaping gas.

Zone 4. As suitable organic matter for fermentation is exhausted at depths greater than about 1 km and the temperature rises, the $\delta^{13}C$ values in any precipitating carbonate reflect the abiotic processes (such as decarboxylation—the expulsion of CO_2 from organic matter) and become progressively heavier (to about $-6‰$). Most porewaters are expelled by this stage.

Zone 5. Between about 2.5 km and 7 km (i.e. at temperatures of 70 °C to 200 °C) hydrocarbons are generated, clay mineral diagenesis may commence, involving montmorillonite conversion to illite, and water is lost from interlayer positions in clay minerals.

Zone 6. Below about 7 km (temperature > 200 °C) truly metamorphic reactions commence.

11.2 Concretions and nodules

These terms are often used synonymously. Most writers consider nodules to be the smaller, but both may be spheroidal, ovoid or irregular primary aggregations which have a different composition from the host rock. Their structure indicates formation by precipitation from an aqueous solution within the host rock. Concretions (and nodules) thus grew in place; either during sedimentation, shortly after sedimentation but during the early stages of compaction, or after compaction. Most ancient concretions grew below the sediment–water interface in the marine phreatic realm before much compaction. Concretions are mainly segregations of the minor constituents of the rock in which they are found, for example, chert nodules in chalk, calcium carbonate or siderite concretions in sandstones or shales. Free energy is less if these minor constituents cluster together as an aggregate rather than remaining finely disseminated through the sediment.

The bacterial processes of sulphate reduction and ammonia formation are important sources of excess HCO_3 in sediment porewaters which can bring about the precipitation of $CaCO_3$. The precipitates may aggregate in pre-existing voids, such as geodes, or in zones of greater permeability such as burrows (for example the *Thalassinoides*-shaped chert nodules in chalk (Figure 11.1), and calcareous nodules in marls (calcareous shales)). They may aggregate around a nucleus of a skeleton or fragment of organic matter, or may grow within pore spaces but then physically displace the surrounding host sediment.

Calcareous concretions in sandstones may be 50 mm–1 m in diameter and are roughly spher-

Figure 11.1 *Thalassinoides* in chalk; some burrows are replaced by flint nodules. Scale 100 mm. Cretaceous, Mons Klint, Denmark

Figure 11.2 Calcareous concretions in cross-bedded sandstones. Jurassic, Skye, Scotland

Figure 11.3 Calcareous concretions in bituminous shales. Hammer 300 mm. Jurassic, Whitby, England

ical (Figure 11.2). Bedding features commonly pass through the concretions into the surrounding rock without distortion at the interface, suggesting a post-consolidation origin for such structures. Most calcareous concretions in sandstones owe their origin solely to localized cementation in a porous sand. They are often found to be concentrated at one stratigraphic horizon, which suggests a hydrological and/or E_h control on the cementation.

Calcareous concretions in shale are oval to spherical, somewhat flattened in shape parallel to the bedding (Figure 11.3). Most are calcitic, with or without pyrite crystals, others are sideritic. Many, though not all, contain nuclei of fossils, which are uncompacted relative to the same species in the surrounding shales, indicating the pre-compaction formation of the concretion. Diffusion of calcium from the surrounding sea water and reaction with ammoniated fatty acid may result in a localized concentration of calcium soap. With time this would break down to $CaCO_3$ and hydrocarbons. Both the decrease in carbonate away from the nucleus and the convergence of internal laminations suggests compaction was coeval with concretion growth.

The shapes of concretions probably relates to the permeability anisotropy of the original sediment, which is why sandstones have rounder concretions than shales, which have disc-shaped forms.

The pyritic margin of concretions indicates an early origin. Pyrite forms by bacterial reduction of porewater sulphates, and trapped interstitial sea water could form only approximately 0.3% pyrite sulphur by the utilization of all its sulphur. So these concretions with much higher levels of pyrite at their margins must have formed in an open system close enough to the sediment surface to allow the porewater system to be replenished by diffusion from sea water. Siderite, on the other hand, requires a CO_2 partial pressure higher than that of normal sea water, and its occurrence implies a closed system.

Septarian nodules are oblate spheroids with radiating, usually spar-filled cracks that widen towards the centre and die out near the margin, crossed by a series of cracks concentric with the margin (Figure 11.4). This form results from case hardening of the exterior during concretion formation, accompanied by dehydration and shrinkage of the interior. Later calcite crystals precipitated in the cracks. It has been suggested that these structures were originally gel-like in constituency, and formed in highly porous water-laden sediment.

Cone-in-cone structures are distinctive features found in certain shale beds which owe their name to the pattern of vertically stacked cones occurring in sheets parallel to bedding, or radiating around large calcareous concretions. Detailed examination shows that in many cases the structure is actually a series not of nested cones but of spirals. Internally, the cones normally consist of fibres arranged parallel to the axis of the cone. These sheets of calcite fibres (sometimes called 'beef') owe their origin to crystal growth in a stress field. The shale layers probably separated initially by hydraulic jacking; as water was injected into the beds, calcite crystals precipitated on the free surfaces. The force of

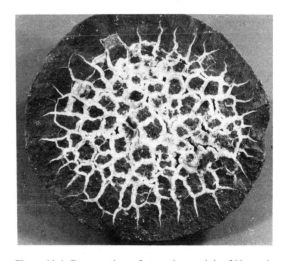

Figure 11.4 Cross-section of septarian nodule, 200 mm in diameter. Carboniferous, Fife, Scotland

Figure 11.5 Radiating concretions in dolomite (possibly a replacement of gypsum). Scale 100 mm. Permian, Sunderland, England

growing crystals kept apart the two sides and resulted in the formation of cone-in-cone structures.

There are some concretion structures that occur in limestones and dolomites which, on account of their distinctive radiating and concentric patterns and stratigraphic associations, are thought to represent replacements of bedded evaporite deposits. The 'cannonball' concretions of the Permian Limestones of North-East England (Figure 11.5) are examples.

11.3 Bedding in limestones

As most carbonate sediments are intrabasinal in origin, they do not necessarily require transportation to their sites of deposition. Consequently, limestones on the whole have fewer traction current structures than sandstones. There are, of course, areas of carbonate deposition where

hydraulic energy is high, and grains are shifted, sorted and deposited in characteristic bedforms. For example, calcareous aeolianites show typical large-scale tabular-planar and trough cross-bedding; lower beach calcarenites show small to medium tabular festoon cross-bedding; limestone turbidites show graded beds with scoured surfaces.

However, many limestones, especially those thought to have deposited in quiet-water areas below wave base, show exceedingly regular parallel bedding. Beds may extend for up to 1 km or more. The planar form of the bedding surfaces and their lateral continuity is surprising in the light of the apparent irregularity of most modern carbonate sea-beds (e.g. Figures 6.15, 6.17).

The regular and commonly cyclic nature of these bedding planes is not completely understood. They may simply represent small breaks (diastems) in deposition, or they may be the manifestation of a diagenetic phenomenon such as pressure-dissolution. The bedding planes may be stylolites, which can be seen to pass laterally into thin seams of shale. The seams themselves may represent concentrations of the less soluble components of the limestones (*stylocumulates*) and/or new insoluble minerals (*reactates*, such as dolomite, mica and iron oxides) created in this narrow zone during the pressure dissolution process. Whatever their nature, it is difficult to judge how much dissolution of limestone has occurred, as the original distribution of insolubles is not known, though guesses can be made on the thickness of limestone lost where it is possible to match features of known size and shape above and below the seam. Some dissolution seams follow lithological inhomogeneities, but others clearly do not. We need to explain what controls the location and spacing of those bedding planes identified as regionally developed pressure-dissolution seams which do not have lithological control. It has been argued that lithostatic pressure is translated into dissolution at one seam (or zone of sutured grains) until most nearby pores are sealed and fluids in the vicinity of suturing become too saturated for further dissolution, at which point another seam starts to develop some centimetres above where porosity levels permit the release of dissolved ions. An alternative explanation is that changes in the rate of sedimentation created variations in the permeability of a homogeneous deposit because of unequal duration of exposure of sediments to near-surface diagenetic environments. This could cause a secondary (diagenetic) vertical heterogeneity in the final composition of an initially uniform accumulation, of which pressure-dissolution could then take advantage. Bioturbation may blur this heterogeneity but not perhaps erase it altogether.

There are examples of surfaces representing submarine hardgrounds in the middle of beds that are defined by pressure-dissolution seam bedding planes. The hardgrounds themselves do not mark what we would call the bedding planes; it would seem that the early cemented layers resisted pressure dissolution and perhaps inhibited the migration of fluids. Sutured grains and stylolites developed some centimetres above and below these cemented horizons.

Argillaceous limestones are more apt to be irregular and nodular, as limey layers pinch and swell or separate into lenticular nodular bodies lying parallel to the bedding (Figure 11.6). This nodular character can in some cases be related to bioturbation; this develops inhomogeneities in the permeability of the sediment which can result in distinctive packing and even early cementation of burrows. The inhomogeneities in packing or lithification cause differential mechanical and chemical compaction. Insoluble residues of pressure dissolution are concentrated between the nodular layers.

Regular alternations of limestone and shale beds (Figure 11.7) may be laterally continuous over hundreds of square kilometres. Many such alternations are fundamentally primary in origin, as revealed by the manner in which one lithology fills the uppermost burrows in the

Figure 11.6 Nodular bedded argillaceous limestones. Hammer 300 mm. Silurian, Much Wenlock, England

Figure 11.7 Regular limestone/shale alternations. Jurassic, Lyme Regis, Dorset, England

distinctly different underlying lithology. The cyclic alternations could originate by variations in the rate of lime production or terrigenous input, by being under climatic or tectonic control. On burial, chemical compaction would accentuate even minor differences in composition between the bands; insoluble clays would concentrate in dissolution seams in the more shaly portions, and dissolved calcium carbonate would migrate to cement (and thus enrich in $CaCO_3$) the neighbouring more limey bands.

11.4 Common replacement minerals

11.4.1 Chert
Siliceous organisms such as radiolarians, diatoms and sponges consist of opal, an isotropic amorphous variety of quartz with up to 10% water. During chert formation biogenic opal is dissolved and reprecipitated as finely crystalline cristobalite, or opal-CT, which inverts to quartz. During the growth of the quartz crystals limestone may be replaced.

Chert commonly occurs as nodules in limestones. These aggregates of silica may be concentrated at particular horizons and they may initially form in areas of slightly different interstitial water chemistry or permeability, for example, in burrows or skeletal cavities. Chert

nodules (flints) are particularly abundant in pelagic limestones such as the Upper Cretaceous chalk of Britain.

11.4.2 Phosphorites
The phosphorus content of sea water is at its maximum between 30 and 500 m depth and is especially high where phosphate-rich waters are upwelling adjacent to shallow shelves in the Trade Wind Belts. Evidence from phosphorite rocks suggests that locally in these zones of high P_2O_5, phosphate minerals precipitate interstitially and replace carbonate grains at and just below the sediment–water interface where phosphorus-rich organic matter decays. The common phosphate minerals are hydroxyl- and fluor-apatite, but a whole spectrum of carbonate-rich apatites exists. The phosphorite rock may have a texture identical to that of a shallow-water limestone, indicating a slow process of replacement operating in a relatively closed system.

Some modern coral islands have a veneer of phosphorite which forms by the subaerial replacement and cementation of carbonate grains by phosphate derived from overlying accumulations of guano. Such occurrences relate to populations of nesting migratory sea-birds,

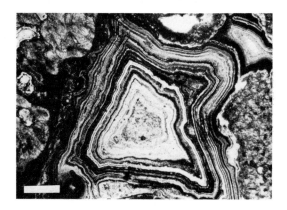

Figure 11.8 Banded phosphate cement filling pores between coral fragments. Thin section, ppl. Scale 0.5 mm. Recent, Suwarrow Atoll, Cook Islands, Pacific

whose phosphorus-rich droppings build the guano encrustations. These insular phosphates typically have 16% to 30% P_2O_5 and result from the replacement of shallow-water limestone grains such as *Halimeda*, benthic foraminiferans and corals, and the precipitation of intergranular banded phosphatic cements (Figure 11.8). Phosphatic oolites can be formed within caves if the percolating solutions are rich in phosphorus.

There is a connection between phosphate occurrence and the mica mineral glauconite, both tending to be found in horizons of reduced sedimentation.

11.4.3 Iron minerals

Geothite FeO(OH) and *haematite* F_2O_3 are present mainly as ooids and impregnations and replacements of fossils in Phanerozoic sedimentary ironstones. The replacement may have been very shortly after deposition. *Chamosite* $3(Fe, Mg)O.(Al, Fe)_2O_3.2SiO_2.nH_2O$ also commonly occurs as ooids within a matrix of calcite or siderite. The ferrous silicate is thought to form first as a mixed gel which converts to chamosite within the reducing environment just below the sea-bed. The chamositic ooids must have been soft, for many are preserved in a squashed state (spastolith) in ironstone. An alternative origin for the ooids is by the replacement of calcareous ooids, with the iron derived from interbedded organic-rich muds. *Siderite* ($FeCO_3$) can occur as very fine-grained crystals or as coarse rhombs or spherulites which may replace calcite and chamosite in limestones and ironstones. Siderite is common in calcareous concretions in shales,

especially those of freshwater origin. Siderite crystals (sometimes oxidized to goethite) are often found as late-stage cements in calcareous sandstones.

Selected reading

Boles, J.R., Landis, C.A. and Dale, P. (1985) The Moeraki boulders—anatomy of some septarian concretions. *J. Sed. Petrol.* **55**, 398–406.

Calvert, S.E. (1983) Sedimentary geochemistry of silicon. In Aston, S.R. (ed.), *Silicon Geochemistry and Biogeochemistry*, Academic Press, New York, 143–186.

Einsele, G. and Seilacher, A. (eds.), (1982) *Cyclic and Event Stratigraphy*. Springer Verlag, Berlin, 536.

Heath, G.R. and Moberley, R.M. (1971) Cherts from the western Pacific Leg 7, Deep Sea Drilling Project. In Winterer, E.L. *et al.* (eds.), *Initial Reports DSDP 7*, 991–1008.

Hudson, J.D. (1978) Concretions, isotopes and the diagenetic history of the Oxford Clay (Jurassic) of central England. *Sedimentology* **25**, 339–370.

Kennedy, W.J. and Garrison, R.E. (1975) Morphology and genesis of nodular chalks and hardgrounds in the Upper Cretaceous of southern England. *Sedimentology* **22**, 311–386.

Marshall, J.D. (1982) Isotopic composition of displacive fibrous calcite veins: reversals in pore-water composition trends during burial diagenesis. *J. Sed. Petrol.* **52**, 615–630.

Raiswell, R.W. (1971) The growth of Cambrian and Liassic concretions. *Sedimentology* **17**, 147–171.

Raiswell, R.W. (1976) The microbiological formation of carbonate concretions in the Upper Lias of north east England. *Chem. Geol.* **18**, 227–244.

Raiswell, R.W., Brimblecombe, P., Dent, D.L. and Liss, P.S. (1980) *Environmental Chemistry*, Edward Arnold, London.

Simonson, B.M. (1985) Sedimentology of cherts in the Early Proterozoic, Wishart Formation, Quebec-Newfoundland, Canada. *Sedimentology* **32**, 23–40.

Stoddart, D.R. and Scoffin, T.P. (1983) Phosphate rock on coral reef islands. In Goudie, A.S. and Pye, K. (eds.), *Chemical Sediments and Geomorphology*, Academic Press, London, 369–400.

Part 5 Carbonate environments

Calcium carbonate sediments are being deposited today in a wide range of environments; in the deep or shallow, cold or warm waters of the oceans and, to a much lesser extent, in lakes and rivers, and soils, caves and dunes on land. This chapter will describe the areal distribution and nature of sediment types in these different environmental settings and indicate, with examples, the characteristic rocks that form there. I will pay greatest attention to those environments that are volumetrically the most significant in $CaCO_3$ deposition. The chapters that follow are arranged geographically for convenience, progressing from land out to the deep sea. Chapter 12 is devoted to terrestrial carbonates. Chapter 13, on the marine environments, follows with an introductory comparison between temperate and tropical carbonates. Chapter 14 on tropical marine depositional environments is subdivided, essentially according to water depth, as follows:

(i) High- and low-hydraulic-energy littoral deposits, which include beaches, storm ridges and tidal flats

(ii) Platforms, which include epeiric seas, continental shelves and mid-ocean banks and stretch from low-water mark to the edge of the continental shelf, and are subdivided into restricted platform (c. 0–25 m), open platform (c. 10–200 m) and reef and sand-shoal rimmed platform margins (c. 0–50 m)

(iii) Platform slope-basin margins, which includes slope deposits beyond the platform margin (c. 50–1500 m)

(iv) Deep-sea basins (c. 200–4500 m).

In nature, the accumulations are not distinct, isolated entities, but merge laterally one into another.

In order to simplify a comparison of the vast amount of information now known about carbonate sediments in these tropical marine environments, each environment is described in terms of (a) physical setting and geometry of accumulating sediment, (b) sedimentary/biogenic structure, (c) biota, (d) grain composition and textures, (e) diagenetic overprint, and (f) facies associations.

12 Terrestrial carbonates

The distribution of modern carbonates of terrestrial origin relates firstly to the distribution of ancient rocks (themselves normally carbonates) at or near the surface that on dissolution provide the ions for calcium carbonate precipitation, and secondly, to the prevailing climate and local organic activity which can bring about this precipitation. Carbonate sediments of terrestrial origin are not common relative to marine carbonates, and, when formed, generally have a low preservation potential.

12.1 Subaerial exposure surfaces
The exposure of calcareous rocks and sediments to the environment of meteoric water results in a zone of weathering in which some $CaCO_3$ will be dissolved and eroded, giving *karst* geomorphological features, and locally some $CaCO_3$ will precipitate on the surface as *speleothem* (cave) and *caliche* (soil) deposits. The deposition is essentially diagenetic, being a remobilization and reprecipitation of $CaCO_3$ rather than the introduction of new $CaCO_3$ to the area. The zone of

weathering can vary in thickness from a few millimetres to tens of metres depending upon the climate, the organic activity, the nature of the host rock and the duration of meteoric exposure.

The hydrological zones in which these dissolution and precipitation events take place are shown schematically in Figure 12.1. The band of infiltration at the top of the vadose zone has active waters which may have high atmospheric or biogenic CO_2 levels and thus cause $CaCO_3$ dissolution, giving solution pipes and vertical caves; or, if the CO_2 levels are lowered by degassing or plant uptake, they may cause $CaCO_3$ precipitation within soil and rock interstices. As the waters percolate down into the lower vadose zone they reach equilibrium, and little or no dissolution occurs. Eventually precipitation of cements at grain contacts may occur. At the bottom of the vadose zone, just above the phreatic water-table, the saturated water loses CO_2 as it enters air-filled caves and there is intense carbonate precipitation, giving the characteristic speleothem deposits of caves: *stalactites*, *stalagmites*, *dripstones*, *flowstones* and *globoids* (cave pearls). The upper phreatic zone is marked by the development of subhorizontal caves as a result of hydraulic erosion and dissolution due to increasing hydrostatic pressure. Collapse breccias occur in this zone, and some local precipitation of speleothems. At greater depths in the phreatic zone the waters become stagnant and eventually grade into connate (formation) waters.

12.1.1 Karst erosion and speleothem deposits

The karst setting is one of dissolution of calcium carbonate, generating a distinctive landscape. The solution, which is normally more rapid in the humid tropics because of the increased acidity derived from the rapid decay of overlying vegetation, usually starts along joints and faults. Characteristic landforms result, including networks of furrows and sharp crests called *lapies*, and small funnel-shaped hollows called *dolines* (or swallow holes) which may result from the collapse of limestone into subterranean caverns. Where two or more dolines coalesce they produce an *uvala*, which is normally 100–300 m in diameter. Larger steep-sided isolated depressions floored with alluvium are termed *poljes*. These solution hollows lie between small conical hills, though in areas of extreme weathering, tower karst may result, in which steep-sided isolated remnants of limestone project from a flat alluvium-coated plain (Figure 12.2).

The insoluble residues left by the dissolution of impure carbonate rocks accumulate as soils, for example terra rossa and laterites. Subterranean landforms of pipes, vugs, and caves are also generated, which may contain collapse breccias and speleothem deposits. Precipitation from flowing water gives laminated flowstones (Figure 12.3) which have concentric layers of

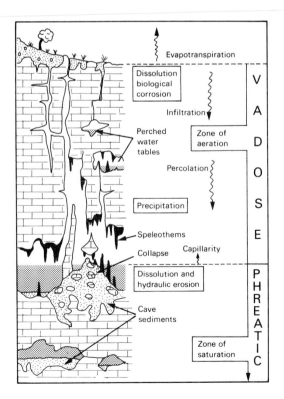

Figure 12.1 Mature karst profile showing the hydrological zones. After Esteban and Klappa (1983)

Figure 12.2 Tower karst, South China. Photograph courtesy of Colin Scrutton

Figure 12.3 Cross-section of banded flowstone from a cave in Carboniferous Limestone. Scale 10 mm. Somerset, England

calcite crystals oriented radially to the long axes of the stalactite cores they envelop. Locally, in splash cups, where water is frequently agitated, concentrically zoned grains called globoids or cave pearls develop. Speleothems are normally calcitic in limestone caves, though precipitation of aragonite and dolomite are known.

12.1.2 Caliche

In the mature stages of karst development, especially in the more arid regions, the soil may be rich in calcium carbonate and become a caliche or calcrete deposit. Caliche is a body resulting from the epigenetic accumulation of calcium carbonate (as calcite) in unconsolidated sediments under conditions derived from soil processes in climates where moisture is deficient during all seasons. The following sequence of caliche formation is common:

(i) Chemical and physical weathering of host carbonate rock.

(ii) Pedogenesis (soil development) by the accumulation of insoluble residue and humus.

(iii) Accumulation of CaCO$_3$ within soil by the evaporation of saturated porewaters drawn to the surface by capillary forces. The deposition is initially as a chalky substance but the soil progressively loses porosity and permeability as CaCO$_3$ precipitation extends, calcifying biological constituents such as rootlets (*rhizoliths* or *rhizoids*), faecal pellets, insect eggs and pupae, and fungal growths (*Microcodium* aggregates). Vertical water movements and taproot growth produce vertically oriented carbonate nodules, but on more complete calcification water moves horizontally and thin platy horizons develop with horizontal rhizoids. Pervasive calcite accumulation leads to a point when soil organisms are no longer viable and the soil profile is

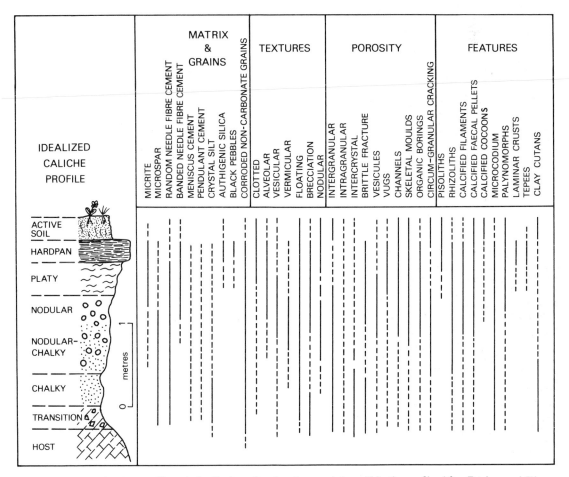

Figure 12.4 Idealized caliche profile and distribution of major characteristics within the profile. After Esteban and Klappa (1983)

consolidated and a surface crust forms, termed *hardpan*.

(iv) A reworking phase may develop in which the lithified caliche profile is brecciated by weathering and pedoturbation from renewed plant and animal activity.

An idealized caliche profile is shown in Figure 12.4. The vertical zonation has, from bottom to top, transition from host rock containing vestiges of original structures; white, friable, chalky and nodular chalky zone; subvertical nodular-crumbly zone; subhorizontal platy zone; compact crust or hardpan; active soil.

The recognition of exposure surfaces in the sedimentary record is most important, for not only do they point to periods of non-deposition and erosion during the unconformity stage, they represent a phase of regression within the basin of deposition as a whole.

Apart from the macro-features of karst erosion and caliche deposition already described, caliche profiles contain distinctive petrographic textures which can be seen in thin section. These are as follows:

(i) Clotted, mottled and peloidal micrite with spar-filled circumgranular and intergranular cracks and channels (Figure 12.5)—the clotted texture results from crumbly frac-

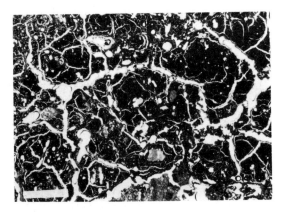

Figure 12.5 Thin section of caliche showing clotted micritic texture and circum-granular cracks. Ppl. Scale 0.5 mm. Recent, Calpe, Spain

ture of dense micrite and the cracking results from repeated wetting and drying

(ii) Calcite (low in magnesium) cements precipitate at points where percolating water is retained by capillary forces longest, giving meniscus cements at grain contacts and pendant or gravitational cements on the undersurfaces of grains—the meniscus cements commonly show blunt crystal terminations due to mineral starvation at the water–air interface

(iii) Microstalactitic crusts of banded calcite cements

(iv) Subhorizontal micritic to microsparitic carbonate laminae forming an irregular brownish crust or rind, common in hardpan

(v) Nodular and brecciated micrite commonly showing relic sedimentary structures of host rock in the transitional zone

(vi) Rhizoids, which are root moulds, root casts, root tubules and root concretions, all millimetres to centimetres in diameter, but which may be tens of centimetres long

(vii) *Alveolar* texture, which is a network of anastomosing micrite walls commonly enclosing a sparry calcite—this fabric is formed by coalesced rhizoids

(viii) Random needle fibres of calcites arranged in bands

(ix) Tangential needle fibres of calcites arranged in bands

(x) Elongate petal-shaped calcite prism groups in spherical sheets with hollow centres, called *Microcodium*—these precipitates result from the calcification of mycorrhizae, which are symbiotic associations between soil fungi and cortical cells of higher plant roots

(xi) Caliche glaebules which include pisoids, caliche ooids, peloids and concretions. The *in-situ* formation of these 'particles' is indicated by the fitted polygonal structure of pisoids and caliche ooids, their downward elongation, and the inclusions of silt perched in the upper parts of concentric growth layers.

Caliche deposits may migrate downslope under gravity, and a concentric zonation of wedge-shaped caliche lithofacies results around limestone highs. Breccias occur adjacent to ridges where slopes are steep; these may give way to pisoid-rich caliches which grade into ooid-rich caliches. Soils are thickest on the lower flanks of ridges, and thin towards remnant limestone crests.

12.1.3 Springs, streams and rivers

There are very few $CaCO_3$ accumulations of volumetric significance in flowing fresh water. Streams and rivers are usually undersaturated with $CaCO_3$, and freshwater organisms, like snails, often suffer some skeletal dissolution during life. Where the fresh water drains through calcareous rocks or sediments it may become saturated with $CaCO_3$, and under special conditions some $CaCO_3$ may then precipitate out. The two common settings for precipitation are (i) at springs where heating and CO_2 expulsion on atmospheric exposure may be aided by the biochemical activity of plants (usually green and blue-green algae and mosses, Figures 12.6, 12.7) and (ii) at waterfalls and cascades where turbulence drives off CO_2 (Figure 12.8). These precipitates are called *travertine*. The terms *tufa* or *calcareous tufa* are often used for the more

Figure 12.6 Calcareous tufa associated with mosses growing at a spring in a Jurassic limestone cliff. Scale 1 m. Recent, Lyme Regis, Dorset, England

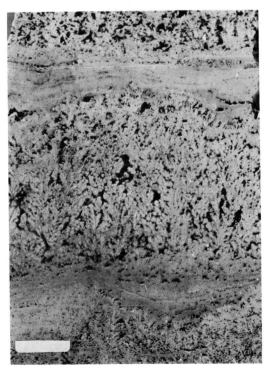

Figure 12.7 Cross-section of calcareous tufa. Scale 20 mm. Locality unknown

F

Figure 12.8 Dome-shaped growths of travertine in river cascades, N. Jamaica

Figure 12.9 Travertine accumulation in pools and dams associated with hot springs. Scale 1 m. Recent, Yellowstone, USA. Photograph courtesy of R. Jemielita

porous, spongy varieties that are associated with mosses and algae. The dense, banded deposits, chiefly of inorganic origin and closely related to speleothem crusts, are sometimes referred to as *sinter*. The $CaCO_3$ of these deposits is normally calcite low in magnesium. The crystals vary in length from a few microns to millimetres, and occur as crusts around plant stems and leaves or else in patterns of radial growth within fine laminae.

Excessive precipitation of $CaCO_3$ at cascades can encrust trapped plant debris and a calcareous dam may result. The dams spread laterally as they pond water upstream. On preservation, these travertine deposits are disposed as arcuate lenses oriented normal to the palaeoflow within fluvial deposits. These travertine accumulations

are controlled by drainage pattern, gradient, discharge rate and floral association.

At hot springs, whose locations are usually controlled by contemporary tectonics, horizontal sheets of travertine accumulate in pools while sub-vertical sheets form at dams (Figure 12.9). These deposits contain a variety of minerals, with aragonite and low-magnesium calcite being common. In some localities the agitated water in hot-spring pools generates ooids and pisoids which have cortices made of minute tangentially oriented aragonite crystals. These ooids become incorporated in the horizontal sheets of travertine.

12.2 Lacustrine carbonates

Lakes that deposit calcium carbonate sediment can be separated into two broad types: *freshwater lakes*, which are normally perennial and occur mainly in temperate humid climates, and *saline lakes*, which are normally ephemeral and occur mainly in hot arid climates.

12.2.1 Freshwater lakes

Examples are Lake Zürich and Lake Constance in Europe and Green Lake, New York, USA. Hardwater lakes have between 1000 and 5000 ppm dissolved solids. The surface waters are usually saturated with respect to $CaCO_3$, at least during summer. The calcium carbonate (normally low-Mg calcite) precipitates from surface waters due to high temperatures and CO_2 loss. This precipitation may be induced by CO_2 uptake during the photosynthetic activity of planktonic algae. Provided these calcite crystals are not swamped by large quantities of terrigenous sediment transported into the lake, a chalky deposit will accumulate. Thin, alternating layers (varves) of fine-grained calcite-rich and clay-mineral-rich sediments are produced as a result of summer and winter deposition. These laminations will be preserved provided there is no infaunal bioturbation. In deep lakes ($> 30 \, m$) the low temperatures at depth, and abundant decaying organic matter, may promote solution of the fine $CaCO_3$ in undersaturated bottom waters.

The marginal areas of freshwater lakes contain coarse carbonate particles of allogenic origin as well as the authogenic chalky deposits just described. The allogenic carbonates include reworked carbonates plus organic secretions. The animal skeletal remains include the shells of freshwater ostracods, bivalves and gastropods. Charophytic algae such as *Chara* produce calcareous tubules and calcified reproductive bodies. Stromatolitic accretions of banded carbonate formed by the activities of filamentous blue-green algae occur in freshwater lakes, and locally, where currents are strong, algal nodules or oncolites, 5–$300 \, mm$ in diameter, can form. Blue-green and green algae may promote the formation of upright calcareous frameworks that encrust the margins of lakes or grow as discrete lenses and cones up to several metres in diameter.

12.2.2 Saline lakes

Examples are Death Valley, California, the Great Salt Lake, Utah, and the Dead Sea. Saline lakes are normally formed in hydrologically restricted basins (commonly fault-controlled) in which water outflow is restricted and evaporation exceeds inflow. These conditions are ideally

met in orographic (rain-shadow) deserts where nearby mountains act as precipitation traps and the valley floors are arid. Saline lakes can form in temperate humid regions only where the water supplied is derived from the leaching of evaporitic rocks. Ephemeral saline lakes that dry up at least once every few years are termed *playa* lakes, or playas when dry (Figure 12.10). The sediments of these intermontane basins normally show a concentric facies zonation (Figure 12.10). At the margins are the coalescing wedges of alluvial fans of coarse gravels with braided channel deposits. Mounds and sheets of travertine may occur at the toes of fans where springs emerge. The marginal immature terrigenous sediments are cemented by caliche crusts, and pass into planar and wavy laminated sands of the sand flat. These in turn grade laterally into the carbonate-rich mud-flat deposits which show desiccation cracks and saline efflorescent crusts. At the centre of the basin, the saline lake deposits laminations of carbonates and gypsum, and, if, very saline, halite. Periodically the basins are flooded and the lakes expand, forming saline mud flats with some resedimentation of surface crusts. Over a long period the lake then dries out to give a playa stage during which salts precipitate. Thus one storm (flood) creates a couplet of mud overlain by salts. Repeated storms give alternating laminae. The amount of carbonate formed depends on the initial $HCO_3/Ca + Mg$ ratio; when molar ratios are near unity, much carbonate can precipitate. The mineral form of $CaCO_3$ that precipitates appears to relate to the Mg/Ca ratio of the lake water. Magnesium is enriched in the residual waters as carbonate precipitation proceeds, so that initially, at Mg/Ca < 2, low-Mg calcite precipitates; at Mg/Ca $= 2$–7, Mg calcite forms; at Mg/Ca $= 7$–12, Mg calcite and protodolomite form, and at Mg/Ca > 12, aragonite and possibly magnesite ($MgCO_3$) precipitate.

Rarely, in waters of high alkalinity, *vaterite* (μ-$CaCO_3$) and monohydrocalcite ($CaCO_3.H_2O$) occur. At extreme concentrations

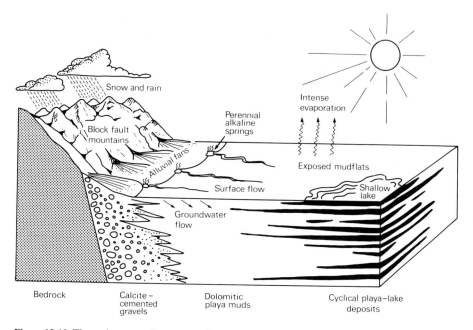

Figure 12.10 The carbonate sediments associated with an arid intermontane basin. After Eugster and Hardie (1978)

(e.g. 300 000 ppm dissolved solids) and under conditions of low sulphate and pH = 9, sodium carbonate and bicarbonate minerals, such as trona NaHCO$_3$. Na$_2$CO$_3$. 2H$_2$O, nahcolite NaHCO$_3$, and natron Na$_2$CO$_3$. 10H$_2$O, can form in playa lakes.

Perennial saline lakes are usually quite deep and are constantly fed by rivers and springs. The evaporation rate is high, though the spring water itself may be saline after draining through evaporitic rocks. Evaporite minerals continuously form at the surface and sink to the lake floor where dense brine accumulates. In the Dead Sea, precipitation of minute crystals of aragonite occurs in irregular cyclic phases apparently triggered by increased temperatures at the end of summer. Such mass precipitations cause a spectacular whitening of the water, and white laminae are formed in the sediment. Gypsum (CaSO$_4$. 2H$_2$O) crystals also form in the surface waters of the Dead Sea but these crystals are reduced by bacteria to hydrogen sulphide and calcite as they reach the anaerobic environment

at the deep lake bottom. The carbonate deposits of the Great Salt Lake of Utah include numerous aragonitic ooids accumulating in the agitated near-shore waters.

12.3 Aeolian carbonates

Quaternary carbonate dunes are found close to many carbonate shorelines and, rarely, adjacent to saline lakes. The sediment of coastal dunes is transported by strong and persistent onshore winds from beaches. The dunes and beaches thus have similar grains; generally rounded, well-sorted, polished, sand-sized grains of skeletal remains and ooids; though dunes may also contain land snails and land plants. Coastal carbonate dunes occur as transverse dune ridges parallel to the shoreline. These ridges are made of coalesced lobate or parabolic sand bodies which may be hundreds of metres in diameter and tens of metres in amplitude. The coastal dunes on spits interfinger to seaward with beach sediments and to landward with lagoonal sediments. Interior dunes bordering saline lakes are usually

Figure 12.11 Cliffs of high-angle cross-bedded Pleistocene aeolianites. Note intertidal erosion notch at sea-level. Scale 1 m. Abaco, Bahamas

transverse or barchan forms. In cross-section, aeolian carbonates show large-scale cross-stratification (Figure 12.11) with high angle (30°) foresets dipping chiefly to landward. The bedding, which consists of alternating fine and coarse laminae, may be tabular-planar, wedge-planar or of festoon trough type. Ripple marks, where present, are normally aligned parallel to the dip of the dune foresets. The tops of carbonate dunes often show signs of karst erosion and the development of a soil horizon (Figure 12.12),

Figure 12.12 Soils filling solution pipes in Pleistocene aeolianite. Cliff 3 m high. Bermuda

the constituents of which may be wind-derived. Plants may stabilize dunes and contribute to soil formation. Plant roots are commonly preserved in aeolianites as rhizoids.

Calcareous dune sands show typical vadose diagenetic fabrics; solution of unstable (mainly aragonite) grains and precipitation of calcite at grain contacts.

Selected reading

Dean, W.E. and Fouch, T.D. (1983) Lacustrine environment. In Scholle, P.A., Bebout, D.G. and Moore, C.H. (eds.) *Carbonate Depositional Environments*, Am. Ass. Petrol. Geol. Mem. **33**, 97–130.

Esteban, M. and Klappa, C.F. (1983) Subaerial exposure environment. In Scholle, P.A. and Bebout, D.G. and Moore, C.H. (eds.) *Carbonate Depositional Environments*, Am. Ass. Petrol. Geol. Mem. **33**, 1–54.

Eugster, H.P. and Hardie, L.A. (1978) Saline lakes. In Lerman, A. (ed.), *Lakes: Chemistry, Geology, Physics*, Springer Verlag, Berlin, 237–293.

Goudie, A.S. and Pye, K. (1983) (eds.), *Chemical Sediments and Geomorphology*. Academic Press, London.

Hardie, L.A., Smoot, J.P. and Eugster, H.P. (1978) Saline lakes and their deposits: a sedimentological approach. In Matter, A. and Tucker, M.E. (eds.), *Modern and Ancient Lake Sediments*, Int. Ass. Sedimentol. Spec. Pub. **2**, 7–41.

Harrison, R.S. and Steinen, R.P. (1978) Subaerial crusts, caliche profiles and breccia horizons; comparison of some Holocene and Mississippian exposure surfaces, Barbados and Kentucky. *Geol. Soc. Amer. Bull.* **89**, 385–396.

Irion, G. and Müller, G. (1968) Mineralogy, petrology and chemical composition of some calcareous tufa from the Schwäbische Alb, Germany. In Müller, G. and Friedman, G.M. (eds.), *Carbonate Sedimentology in Central Europe*, Springer Verlag, Berlin, 157–171.

Jakucs, L. (1977) *Morphogenetics of Karst Regions*, John Wiley & Sons, New York.

Julia, R. (1983) Travertines. In Scholle, P.A., Bebout, D.G. and Moore, C.H. (eds.), *Carbonate Depositional Environments*, Am. Ass. Petrol. Geol. Mem. **33**, 64–72.

James, N.P. (1972) Holocene and Pleistocene calcareous crust (caliche) profiles: criteria for subaerial exposure. *J. Sed. Petrol.* **42**, 817–836.

Kelts, K. and Hsü, K.J. (1978) Freshwater carbonate sedimentation. In Lerman, A. (ed.), *Lakes: Chemistry, Geology, Physics*, Springer Verlag, Berlin, 297–323.

Klappa, C.F. (1980) Rhizoliths in terrestrial carbonates: classification, recognition genesis and significance. *Sedimentology* **27**, 613–629.

Leeder, M.R. (1975) Pedogenic carbonates and flood sediment accretion rates: a quantitative model for alluvial arid zone lithofacies. *Geol. Mag.* **112**, 257–270.

Legrand, H.E. and Stringfield, V.T. (1973) Karst hydrology—a review. *J. Hydrology* **20**, 97–120.

Marker, M.E. (1971) Waterfall tufas: a facet of karst geomorphology. *Z. Geomorphol. Sub Band* **12**, 138–152.

Matter, A. and Tucker, M.E. (eds.) (1978) *Modern and Ancient Lake Sediments*. Int. Ass. Sedimentol. Sp. Pub. **2**.

McKee, E.D. and Ward, W.C. (1983) Eolian environment. In Scholle, P.A., Bebout, D.G. and Moore, C.H. (eds.), *Carbonate Depositional Environments*, Am. Ass. Petrol. Geol. Mem. **33**, 131–170.

Neev, D. and Emery, K.O. (1967) The Dead Sea: depositional processes and environments of evaporites. *Israel Geol. Surv. Bull.* **41**, 1–47.

Scholle, P.A. and Kinsman, D.J.J. (1974) Aragonitic and high-magnesium calcite caliche from the Persian Gulf—a modern analog for the Permian of Texas and New Mexico. *J. Sed. Petrol.* **44**, 904–916.

Thrailkill, J. (1968) Chemical and hydrologic factors in the excavation of limestone caves. *Geol. Soc. Amer. Bull.* **79**, 19–46.

Walkden, G.M. (1974) Palaeokarstic surfaces in Upper Visean (Carboniferous) limestones of the Derbyshire Block, England. *J. Sed. Petrol.* **44**, 1232–1247.

13 Marine carbonates: temperate seas

The bulk of modern carbonate sediments form in shallow seas in the tropics, but where terrigenous input is low, carbonate sediments may form in sufficient abundance to build limestones in high latitudes.

13.1 Carbonate grain associations in shallow seas

When we look at the compositions of carbonate sediments from modern open shelf seas we note broad skeletal grain associations. One group contains mainly benthonic formaminiferans, molluscs, barnacles, bryozoans and calcareous red algae (with echinoderms, ostracods, sponge spicules and worm tubes in relatively minor quantities). This group has been termed *foramol* (Lees and Buller, 1972) and the assemblage is typical of temperate-water carbonates. The other group may contain any of the foramol constituent, but also contains significant contributions from corals and calcareous green algae. This group is called *chlorozoan*, and the assemblage occurs in warm tropical shallow seas. Temperature and salinity appear to control which of these two groups occurs on continental shelves (Figure 13.1). For the chlorozoan assemblage the minimum and maximum annual temperatures must not fall below 15 °C and 26 °C respectively. The salinity tolerance range of the normal chlorozoan association is approximately 31‰ to 40‰. Once these temperature and salinity values are exceeded, the chlorozoan/foramol boundary appears to be influenced by both temperature

and salinity in such a way that high temperature compensates for low salinity, and vice versa. Thus the foramol association, the normal one in cooler waters, extends into the warm waters of low latitudes when the salinity is too low for development of the chlorozoan association. A third skeletal association, termed *chloralgal*, which has calcareous green algae but no corals, is characteristic of areas where the salinity range is more extreme than on open platforms.

As already indicated, non-skeletal grains are restricted to relatively warm seas. They occur in two associations; in one, peloids are the only non-skeletal grains represented, in the other, ooids and/or aggregates are also present. The relationship between temperatures, salinities and the distribution of these non-skeletal grain associations is shown in Figure 13.2.

Carbonate muds of organic origin may occur with chlorozoan or foramol assemblages (though they are generally rare in temperate seas). Carbonate muds of inorganic origin appear to occur in the ooid/aggregate field of distribution. The ooid/aggregate association exists where salinity always exceeds 35.8‰, even if temperatures are high. The zones of maximum salinity of oceanic waters lie at about 25 °N and 25 °S of the equator in the trade-wind regions where annual evaporation is greater than precipitation. The highest maximum and minimum isotherms for surface waters are found on the western sides of the oceans, since the surface waters are heated as

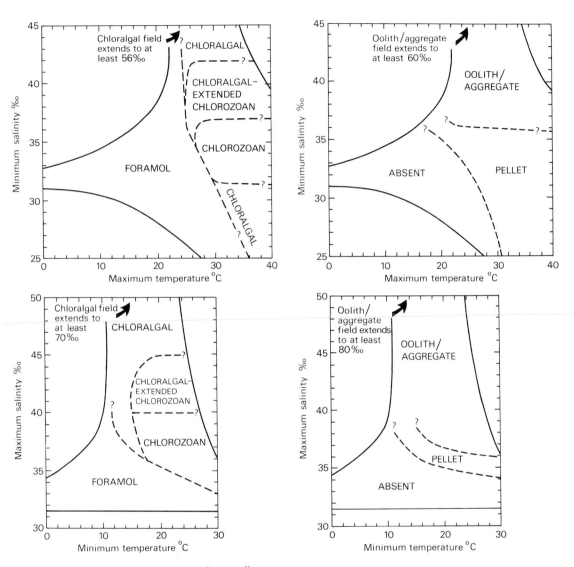

Figure 13.1 Salinity and temperature annual ranges diagram pair for skeletal grain associations in modern shelf carbonate sediments. After Lees (1975)

Figure 13.2 Salinity and temperature annual ranges diagram pair for non-skeletal grain associations in modern shelf carbonate sediments. After Lees (1975)

they flow from east to west in the equatorial currents.

These temperature and salinity limits apply to most grain associations in shallow seas (0–100 m). Some anomalies do exist, especially in enclosed or semi-enclosed seas, but here especially the other major controls on biogeography must be taken into account. For example, migration barriers may have restricted faunal/floral reappearance after the last glacial low sea-level.

Table 13.1 Tropical *v.* temperate shallow water (< 100 m) carbonate sediments.

	Tropical	Temperate
Grain size	Muds, sands, gravels	Sands and gravels
Non-skeletal grains (e.g. ooids, aggregates, peloids)	Abundant	Absent
Mineralogy	Aragonite dominant	Calcite dominant
Sea-bed lithification	Common locally (e.g. beachrock, reefs, hardgrounds)	Absent
Shallow-water reefs	Abundant	Absent
Major skeletal groups	Calcareous green algae Calcareous red algae Corals Molluscs Benthic foraminiferans Echinoderms	Barnacles Calcareous red algae Bryozoans Molluscs Benthic forminiferans Echinoderms Serpulids
Landward flanking non-carbonate facies	Deltaic and coastal terrigenous sediments; evaporites in arid regions	Coastal terrigenous sediments may include lag gravels and fine sediments of glacial origin
Seaward flanking deposits	Wedging deposits of talus and debris flows near windward reef environments, gravity flows of ooids, mud and skeletal grains interfinger with periplatform carbonates on leeward margins	Gravity flows and slumps of skeletal grains grade into periplatform sediments with glauconite. No marked distinction between windward and leeward margins
Bank edge profile	Commonly steep mesa-like profile maintained by sea-bed lithification and reef growth	Normally convex profile with gentle slopes

13.2 Tropical versus temperate shallow-water carbonate sediments

The observed differences between tropical and temperate shallow-water (< 100 m) carbonate sediments are summarized in Table 13.1. The principal sedimentological differences between the warm and cold water realms result from the higher degree of $CaCO_3$ supersaturation in the shallow tropics compared to temperate seas of similar depth. This difference in water chemistry affects $CaCO_3$ production, stability of very fine-grained $CaCO_3$ sediments, and lithification of the sea-bed.

13.2.1 CaCO₃ production
Inorganic grains, for example ooids, aggregates, peloids and mud, are produced only in warm

shallow seas. Though individual groups of organisms may not have significantly different rates of production of skeletal $CaCO_3$ in the two realms, overall $CaCO_3$ production in the shallow tropics vastly outweighs that from cold waters at similar depths. The greater abundance and diversity of calcareous organisms (coupled with the inorganic production) in the tropics accounts for the observed difference.

13.2.2 Carbonate mud stability
There are very few areas of significant carbonate mud accumulation in temperate seas. Doubtless skeletal grains break down either by abrasion or by the decomposition and removal of supportive organic matrix between crystallites within skeletons, but the scarcity of these breakdown pro-

ducts suggests they are dissolved in the cold waters. On the contrary, carbonate mud accumulates in abundance in sheltered, shallow, warm, seas, especially in areas of elevated salinity.

13.2.3 Lithification of the sea-bed

The high degree of $CaCO_3$ supersaturation promotes the lithification of the sea-bed in the shallow tropics at positions of high water flux, stable sea-bed and low sedimentation rates. These hard surfaces form ideal substrates for colonization by epilithic organisms, but in temperate seas, where there is no sea-bed lithification, epilithic growth depends on bedrock outcrops for suitable substrates. Unlike the tropics, where hard substrates may continue to form, the rock outcrops of temperate seas eventually are buried and the dominant skeletal production shifts to the flora and fauna that live on and in the loose sediment. Consequently, in temperate seas epilithic skeletal production may be expected to persist only in coastal environments. The sediment pile resulting from a transgression would contain skeletal remains that show a vertical transition from rock-dwelling to sand-dwelling assemblages.

The high production of $CaCO_3$ at platform margins in the tropics, in conjunction with the damming effect of elevated rim reefs and the retention of steep slopes by subsea cements at this position, help to maintain the characteristic mesa-like profiles of many tropical bank and shelf margins (e.g. the Bahamas). This profile may be asymmetric, with steeper windward margins and gentler leeward slopes. In colder seas where carbonate-covered banks occur but lack the significantly higher production and stability of the margins, the slopes are gently convex, with similar angles on windward and leeward sides, and banks (e.g. Rockall) have shallowly domed profiles.

Present-day warm and cold-water marine carbonate sediments may pass laterally into non-carbonate facies. Facies of tropical carbonates may flank deltaic and coastal terrigenous sediments, and, in arid regions, neighbour evaporite deposits, whereas modern temperate carbonates are more likely to be associated with poorly sorted terrigenous sediments of glacial origin.

13.3 Temperate seas

Examples of temperate carbonate sediments west of Britain at latitude 57° N. The continental shelf west of the British Isles faces the southwesterly swells of the North Atlantic. In the north and west of Scotland and Ireland, major rivers are few and the majority of the exposed rocks are crystalline, of metamorphic and igneous origin. Gravels and sands of solely skeletal carbonates accumulate on beaches, in aeolian dunes and in offshore banks and ribbons, where they mingle with some terrigenous sediments of reworked glacial origin. Nearshore there are sharp variations in physical conditions, substrate types and terrigenous supply, and these are reflected in the faunal/floral assemblages and sediment lithologies. Offshore, physical gradients are more gradual and facies patterns are more regular.

Figure 13.3 Temperate beach deposit of molluscan and barnacle fragments. Scale 2 mm. Coll, Scotland

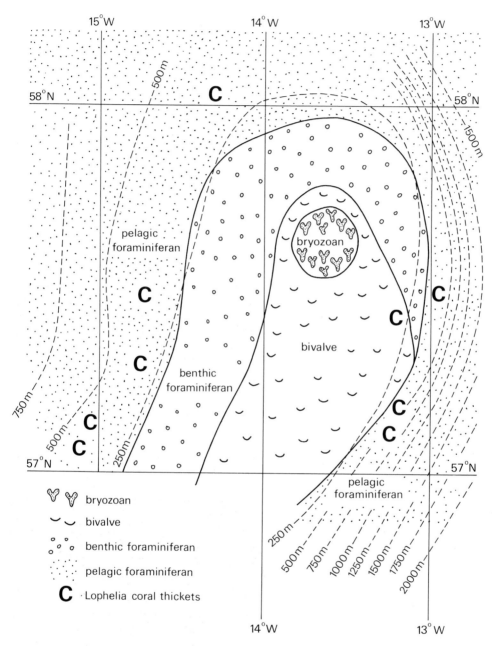

Figure 13.4 Lithofacies distribution, Rockall Bank, N. Atlantic. After Scoffin *et al.* (1980)

13.3.1 Rocky shores (< 20 m depth)

Barnacles, bivalves, gastropods and echinoid fragments constitute the bulk of the gravel-sized shelly deposits that accumulate on the high-energy beaches neighbouring rocky shores (Figure 13.3), and in the near-shore blankets of sand swept into ripples by waves and tidal currents or locally sheltered by kelp forests. Where wave action is reduced but current action enhanced, such as in the vicinity of sounds between islands, thick banks (*maerl*) of branching calcareous red algal grains (e.g. *Phaematolithon calcareum*) accumulate (Figures 4.53, 4.54).

13.3.2 Continental shelf (10 to 200 m depth)

Areas exposed to high-energy waves and currents have rock substrates supporting epilithic organism such as barnacles, molluscs, echinoderms, bryozoans and serpulids, and their abraded skeletal fragments produce quantities of gravel that accumulate nearby in mega-rippled banks. In the more sheltered areas, bioturbated sand and silt substrates abound, supporting an epifauna and infauna of mainly molluscs, benthic foraminiferans and echinoids which contribute coarse and fine grains to a poorly sorted, mixed terrigenous and calcareous, sediment. Generally carbonate percentage increases with hydraulic energy from about 40–60% in sheltered areas to > 80% in exposed areas. The principal grains of these carbonates are sand- and gravel sized. Muds are absent. The dominant mineralogy of the skeletons is calcite (c. 50%), with Mg calcite and aragonite roughly equal (c. 25% each).

13.3.3 Offshore bank (70 to 400 m water depth— e.g. Rockall Bank, N. Atlantic)

On this mid-ocean high-latitude bank, physical conditions vary gradually in a symmetrical pattern related to water depth. So the carbonate sediments on Rockall Bank have a relatively simple concentric distribution pattern (Figure 13.4). In the shallow central area,

71–100 m depth, rippled gravels of bryozoan and serpulid fragments predominate around the basalt outcrops and boulders (Figure 4.24). These give way below the photic limit to bioturbated and microbored sands and gravels rich in mollusc, echinoderm and benthic foraminiferan remains at 100 to 200 m depth. The transfer in dominance from benthic to planktonic foraminiferans takes place at 200 to 300 m water depth, where numerous foraminiferan tests are impregnated with diagenetic glauconite, a mica with the formula $K(Fe^{2+}, Mg, Al)_2 Si_4 O_{10}(OH)_2$. In the peripheral zone, 200–400 m depth, thickets (c.

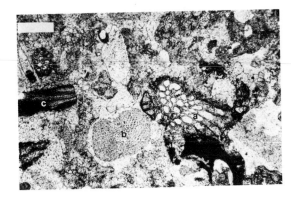

Figure 13.5 Thin section of temperate limestone containing bryozoan (*a*), echinoderm (*b*) and barnacle (*c*) fragments. Ppl. Scale 0.5 mm. Tertiary, Waitomo, New Zealand

Figure 13.6 Banks of bryozoan debris. Scale 1 m. Palaeocene. Stevns Klint, Denmark

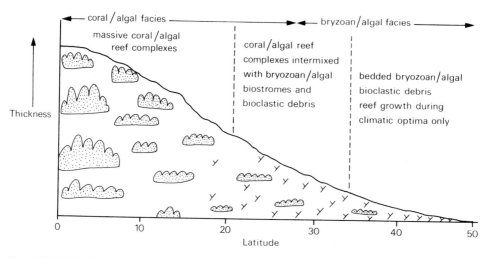

Figure 13.7 Skeletal assemblages on NW Pacific sea-mounts in tropical and temperate latitudes. After McKenzie *et al.* (1980)

20 m diameter, 1 m elevation) of *Lophelia pertusa* corals are patchily distributed on the planktonic foraminiferal ooze (Figure 4.31).

Ancient examples of temperate water limestones are rare. The Tertiary limestones of the Waitomo region of New Zealand provide an example of barnacle- and bryozoan-rich grainstones with sparry calcite cements (Figure 13.5) which represent shallow marine high-latitude deposition. The limestones of the Cretaceous–Tertiary boundary near Stevns Klint, Denmark, include thick banks of bryozoan debris (Figure 13.6), and local *Lophelia* coral thickets indicative of moderately deep cold water.

13.4 Sea-mounts

Submerged mid-ocean volcanic edifices provide ideal terrigenous-free, open-water locations for many lime-secreting organisms to live. We can observe the changing skeletal assemblages with latitude along N–S oriented island chains such as the Emperor sea-mounts in the North-Western Pacific (Figure 13.7). The high-latitude shallow-water deposits are characterized by rhodoliths of encrusting calcareous red algae and bryozoans, with sand grains of red algae, bryozoans, benthic

foraminiferans and molluscs. Low-latitude shallow-water deposits are characterized by coral reefs with red algal encrustations; sand grains are rich in corals, calcareous green algae *Halimeda*, molluscs and benthic foraminiferans.

The distinctions are less clearcut in the deeper sub-photic waters where bryozoans, molluscs, echinoderms, brachiopods and benthic foraminiferans are found at depths between 100–300 m over wide latitudinal ranges.

Selected reading

Chave, K.E. (1967) Recent carbonate sediments—an unconventional view. *A.G.I. Counc. Educ. Geol. Sci. Short Rev.* **7**, 200–204.

Lees, A. (1975) Possible influence of salinity and temperature on modern shelf carbonate sedimentation. *Mar. Geol.* **19**, 159–198.

Lees, A. and Buller, A.T. (1972) Modern temperate-water and warm-water shelf carbonate sediments contrasted. *Marine Geol.* **13**, M67–M73.

McKenzie, J., Bernoulli, D. and Schlanger, S.O. (1980) Shallow-water carbonate sediments from the Emperor Seamounts: their diagenesis and paleogeographic significance. In Jackson, E.D., Koisumi, I. *et al.* (eds.), *Initial Reports of the Deep Sea Drilling Project* **55**, 415–455.

Nelson, C.S. (1978) Temperate shelf carbonate sediments in the Cainozoic of New Zealand. *Sedimentology* **25**, 737–771.

Pilkey, O.H., Blackwelder, B.W., Doyle, C.J., Estes, E. and Terlecky, P.M. (1967) Aspects of carbonate sedimentation of the Atlantic continental shelf off the South United States. *J. Sed. Petrol.* **37**, 744.

Rodgers, J. (1957) The distribution of marine carbonate sediments: a review. In LeBlanc, R.J. and Breeding, J.G. (eds.), *Regional Aspects of Carbonate Deposition*, SEPM Sp. Pub. **5**, 15–79.

Scoffin, T.P., Alexandersson, E.T., Bowes, G.E., Clokie, J.J., Farrow, G.E. and Milliman, J.D. (1980) Recent, temperate, sub-photic, carbonate sedimentation: Rockall Bank,

Northeast Atlantic, *J. Sed. Petrol.* **50**, 331–356.

Summerhayes, C.P. (1969) Recent sedimentation around northernmost New Zealand. *N.Z.J. Geol. Geophys.* **12**, 172–207.

Teichert, C. (1958) Cold- and deep-water coral banks. *Am. Ass. Petroleum Geologists Bull.* **42**, 1064–1082.

Wass, R.E., Conolly, J.R. and MacIntyre, J. (1970) Bryozoan carbonate sand continuous along southern Australia. *Mar. Geol.* **9**, 63–73.

14. Marine carbonates: tropical seas

14.1 Littoral zones

The littoral zone is that related to the shore, and the term is loosely synonymous with 'intertidal', the zone between high- and low-water mean tide levels. It is flanked by the supralittoral (supratidal) above, and the sublittoral (subtidal) below. Littoral carbonate deposits can be split into two types: those formed in areas of high hydraulic energy (sand beaches, storm ridges etc.) and those formed in areas of low hydraulic energy (tidal flats).

14.1.1 High-energy littoral deposits

Setting and geometry. This zone ranges from the shallow subtidal shoreface to the supratidal level at the top of beach berms and ridges. These positions face open water waves, tidal and long-shore currents, and develop a characteristic profile and suit of sediments (Figures 14.1, 14.2). The foreshore may have a relatively steep angle of dip to seaward of 7–20°.

In areas of rapid carbonate production and relatively low tidal range (< 3 m), onshore transport builds barrier beaches and islands, particularly on low-gradient shelves adjacent to low-relief coastal plains, such as Abu Dhabi on the Trucial coast of the Persian Gulf (Figure 8.14). Barrier islands are rectilinear and parallel the coast, sheltering shallow lagoons to landward. The islands are separated by tidal channels which are deeper and wider in regions of higher tidal range (2–4 m) where *flood and ebb tidal deltas* may form at the channel mouths (Figures 14.1, 14.3). Tidal deltaic deposits may build up into the littoral zone. They have arcuate lobe and tear-drop plan morphologies, and maximum diameters of several hundred metres. Storm surges cut through the barrier island, creating sluiceways, and build lobes of sediment into the lagoon, known as *washovers* and *spillovers*. Washover fans are generally thin tabular bodies (100mm to 1m in thickness), elongate to semicircular in plan, a few hundred metres in width, oriented normal to the shoreline. Though built by storms, they are typical of the low-energy environment of the lagoon. Sands of barrier islands are easily transported by onshore winds to build narrow strips of coastal dunes.

When ocean waves crash on the windward margins of coral reefs, their energy is lost, and coarse coral debris accumulates as arcuate ridges and tongues of rubble at the windward side of the reef flat (Figure 14.4). Sand-sized sediment may be carried over the reef flat and dropped in the lagoon or back-reef area as prograding wedges of coarse back-reef sand. It may pile against storm ridges to build reef flat islands (triangular or ribbon-shaped 'motu', so common on atolls (Figure 14.5, see also Figure 14.37); or it may be carried laterally along the shallow flanks of the reef by longshore drift and eventually be dumped as horns or spits on the reef flanks or as leeward reef-flat islands where opposing wave-induced currents converge (Figure 14.6). On atolls, these sandy island develop initially at the sharp bends in the perimeter outline where wave convergence is prevalent (see Figure 14.45). On platform reefs, in trade wind belts, isolated sand cays or

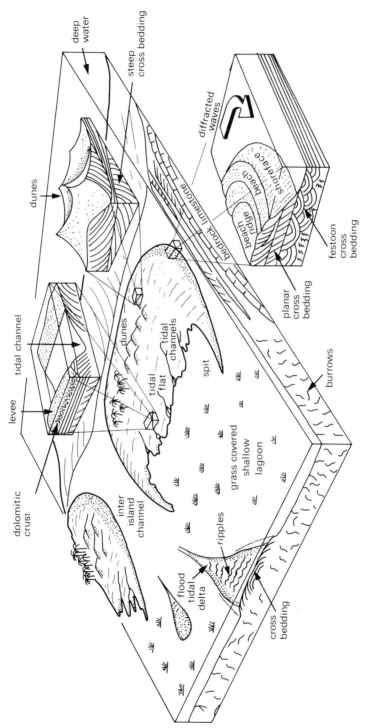

Figure 14.1 Barrier islands showing associated sedimentary structures

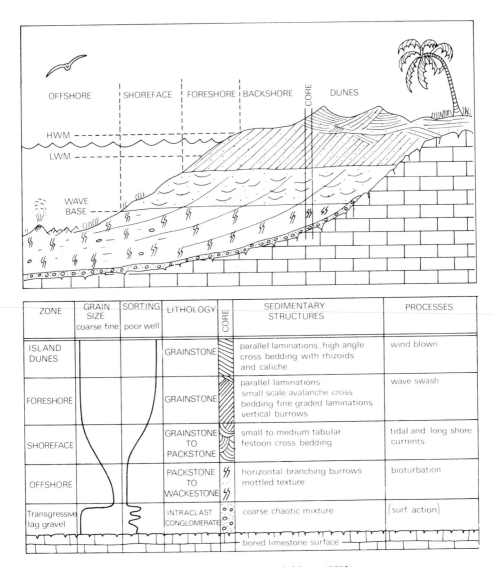

Figure 14.2 Model of beach sediments. After Inden and Moore (1983)

elongate sandy spits build to leeward, again by wave convergence.

Sedimentary/biogenic structures. The lower foreshore zones are characterized by small-scale festoon cross-bedding oriented parallel to the shoreline. The upper foreshore deposits are thick-bedded planar cross-bedded accretionary units which dip gently seaward (7° to 20°) (Figures 14.1, 14.2). These upper foreshore sands may have small pore spaces (vugs) formed by trapped or escaping gas bubbles. Berm crests form plane beds lying horizontally or with gentle landward dips, and the higher dunes typically have thick sets of planar and trough cross beds (Figure 14.1). Washover fans usually have

Figure 14.3 Flood tidal deltas and tidal channels between platform margin islands, Bahamas. Air photo courtesy of Conrad Neumann

Figure 14.4 Tongue of coral shingle (rampart) on the windward reef flat advancing over mangroves and eroded cemented rampart foresets. Hammer (arrowed) 300 mm. Turtle III Reef. Great Barrier Reef, Australia

Figure 14.5 Reef flat islands (motu) with flanking sediment horns. Rarotonga, Cook Islands, Pacific

scoured lower contacts, and consist of horizontal plane laminations in cross-section. Tidal channels are characterized by erosional bases, and on lateral migration they are filled with coarse basal lag deposits overlain by large-scale planar and trough cross-bedded fining-upward sands. Tidal deltas generally have arcuate or tear-drop plan morphologies, and the most common bed forms of mega-ripples and sandwaves produce trough planar cross-stratification internally

Figure 14.6 Spit of sand developed by wave convergence on leeward side of reef. Southeasterly trade winds blow from top right of photograph. West Petherbridge Reef, Great Barrier Reef, Australia

Figure 14.7 Cross-bedded tidal bar sands overlying oyster beds. Pleistocene, Nicosia, Cyprus. Interestingly these shallow-water carbonate sands consist almost exclusively of reworked Tertiary planktonic foraminiferans. Photograph courtesy of Jean McCallum

(Figure 14.7). Traction current structures are normally well preserved, punctuated perhaps by sparse vertical burrows of crabs, molluscs or worms. The arcuate tongues of coarse corals on the windward sides of reef flats (Figure 14.4) have an asymmetric wave profile with the steep face dipping at up to 60° to landward. Storms develop discrete ridges which are separated on reef flats by moats of ponded water. Cementation and partial erosion of these coral debris ridges produce jaggedly protruding beds

termed 'bassett edges' by geomorphologists (Figure 8.10).

Biota. Few organisms survive the turbulent water and mobile substrate of the beach environment. Some active infaunal and epifaunal macroorganisms can cope with the excessive sedimentation, such as certain molluscs, crustaceans and worms.

Grain composition and texture. Beaches and barrier islands built by onshore transport will contain grains derived from the nearby high-energy subtidal environment, that is, normally whole and fragmented skeletal grains such as molluscs, benthic foraminiferans, calcareous green and red algae, and corals, locally ooids and intraclasts, rarely pellets.

The grains are texturally mature to supermature, being well sorted, rounded and probably polished, and may show textural inversion, such as fragmented rounded particles.

Diagenetic overprint. Tropical beaches are commonly penecontemporaneously cemented in the zone between high and low tide levels by acicular aragonite and/or micrite Mg calcite (section 8.3.3). Large seaward-dipping slabs of beachrock are formed, which are undercut by strong wave and current action, causing collapse, breakage and reworking into tabular cobble- to pebble-sized beachrock clasts.

The topmost portion of an undisturbed beach can develop a thin cover of soil in which characteristic pedogenic structures, including caliche, form (section 12.1.2). The foreshore and backshore sediments are then capped by iron-stained laminated subaerial crusts containing nodules, pisolites, coated and micritized clasts, circumgranular cracks and vadose cements.

Facies association. Though seen as narrow strips surrounding islands during deposition, beaches prograde over subtidal deposits to build sheet-like cross-bedded accumulations. Landward facies equivalents are tidal flats, and aeolian, coastal plain or alluvial fan deposits, depending upon climate and hinterland relief. Seaward facies are the subtidal sediments of restricted lagoons and open platforms.

14.1.2 Low-energy littoral deposits

Setting and geometry. As the name suggests, tidal flats have low relief. They are dissected by tidal channels which drain to seaward, and have been described as a river delta turned wrong side out with the sea as the 'river' supplying sediment to the channelled flats (the 'delta'). This channelled zone separates a broad supratidal zone to landward from a seaward shallow intertidal–subtidal marine zone. The landward supratidal zone of

arid regions (e.g. the Persian Gulf) is a broad flat zone of accumulation of lime sands and muds and evaporite minerals where little life exists (sabkha); in humid regions (e.g. the Bahamas), rainfall ensures the survival of algal growths, and the zone is called the inland algal marsh. The channelled zone is broadly similar in most regions; the sinuous channels narrow and branch landward and are flanked by channel banks and levees (Figures 14.1, 14.8, 10.3). The levees discontinuously enclose broad low-relief depressions or ponds, which may be flooded at each tide with water supplied by a channel branch. The tidal channels may be permanently filled

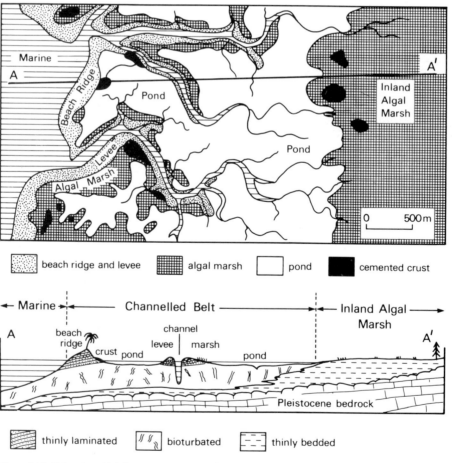

Figure 14.8 Bahamian tidal flat environments. After Shinn *et al.* (1969)

Figure 14.9 Dried-up tidal channel in the intertidal algal mat zone. Stake 1.5 m high. Trucial Coast, Persian Gulf. Photograph courtesy Bob Parks

with water, having over a metre's relief from floor to bank top; they may be abandoned and filled with sediment; or they may have low relief and have only irregular periods when active (Figure 14.9). The seaward margin of the tidal flat joins the shallow lagoonal waters at a beach or mud flat. The beaches are usually backed by storm ridges which slope into intertidal ponds. Lobes of beach-derived sediment accumulate as beach-ridge washover fans after storms. In a broad sense, the sedimentary facies parallel the shoreline with belts of progressively greater atmospheric exposure occurring to landward. But in detail this broad trend may be complicated by the dissection of the area by tidal channels with channel and levee deposits, as well as beach-ridge washover fans lying crudely normal to the shoreline.

The numerous subenvironments, which exist in very close proximity with only small changes in elevation, are produced by the interplay between the frequency of exposure (or flooding) and frequency of sedimentation. These environments are characterized by sediments of distinct structure, texture and composition, and by a distinctive biota which adapts to and modifies the accumulating sediment (Figure 14.10).

Sedimentary/biogenic structures. Tidal channel deposits have a scoured base overlain by coarse sand and gravel lag deposits and edgewise conglomerates (usually transported fragments of penecontemporaneous cemented crust), which in turn are covered with fining-upwards cross-bedded sands which grade into ripple and wavy-bedded sands. The channel-bank top deposits of the levees have horizontal thin laminations, with fenestral pores created by horizontal cracking of laminae by shrinkage on desiccation and entrapment of gas from rotting algae (Figure 14.11).

Intertidal algal laminites and stromatolites vary in form according to the sediment supply, current and wave energy, tidal range, degree of exposure and dominant algal species (Figure 4.47). Varieties of laterally linked hemispheroids are the most common forms of stromatolites (Figure 14.12). Well-laminated sediments with fine laminar fenestral pores characterize areas of smooth mat in the lower intertidal zone. Poorly laminated sediments with an irregular fenestral fabric produced beneath pustular mats characterize the middle to upper intertidal zone. In the higher, more indurated, supratidal zone, film mats are associated with aragonitic crusts, and blister mats are produced by the disruption of deposition fabrics by authigenic gypsum crystals. The striking vertically stacked hemispheroids (Figure 8.9) occur in higher-energy restricted areas with high tidal range. Algal laminites are frequently desiccated, producing wrinkled, cracked, curled and chipped mats, distinctive polygonal mud cracks, sheet cracks and mud flake conglomerates (Figure 14.13). Supratidal algal marsh deposits show thick laminations of dark organic-rich sediment and light lime-mud layers (overbank deposits from tidal channels), which are locally disrupted by vertical and branched burrows of worms, shrimps, crabs and insects, and also by roots of shrubs and grasses.

In arid regions the intertidal precipitation of interstitial acicular arogonite cement produces pans of thin crusts overlying loose sediment.

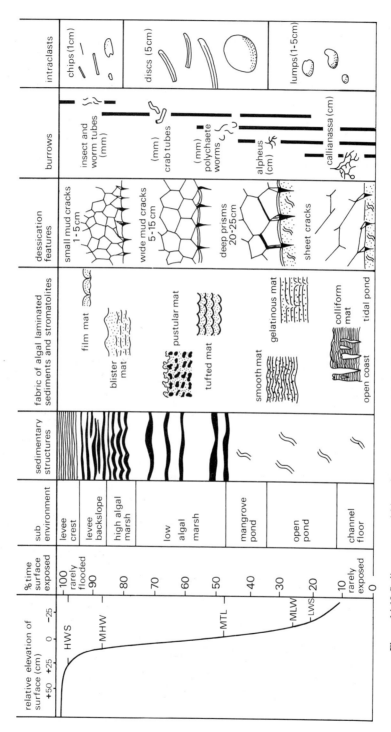

Figure 14.10 Sedimentary and biogenic structures associated with different elevations in the tidal zone. After Hardie (1977)

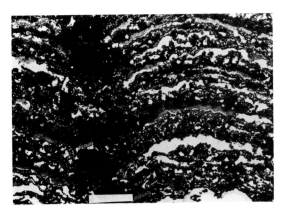

Figure 14.11 Fenestral cavities (white) in laterally linked hemispheroids. Scale 10 mm. Tertiary, Alicante, Spain

Figure 14.13 Imbricate mud flake conglomerate overgrown with arborescent algae and stromatolites. Scale 10 mm. Triassic, Somerset, England

These crusts crack into large polygons which, on expansion, due to crystallization forces, thrust over each other at their edges, producing tepee structures. Cemented, buckled intertidal algal mats create convex seaward arcuate ridges. In some high intertidal and supratidal settings, smooth to irregular laminated aragonitic crusts develop dripstone fabrics on rocky substrates.

Evaporite minerals produced in arid supratidal settings form characteristic diagenetic

Fig. 14.12 Laterally-linked hemispheroidal stromatolites. Hammer 300 mm. Jurassic, Skye, Scotland

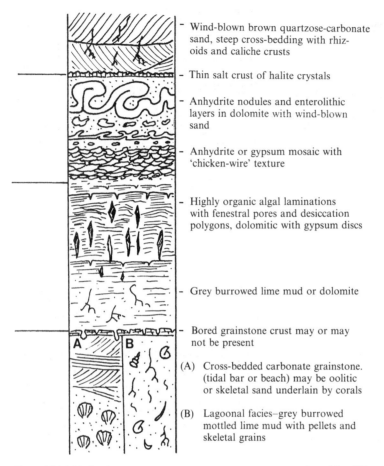

Wind-blown brown quartzose-carbonate sand, steep cross-bedding with rhiz-oids and caliche crusts

Thin salt crust of halite crystals

Anhydrite nodules and enterolithic layers in dolomite with wind-blown sand

Anhydrite or gypsum mosaic with 'chicken-wire' texture

Highly organic algal laminations with fenestral pores and desiccation polygons, dolomitic with gypsum discs

Grey burrowed lime mud or dolomite

Bored grainstone crust may or may not be present

(A) Cross-bedded carbonate grainstone. (tidal bar or beach) may be oolitic or skeletal sand underlain by corals

(B) Lagoonal facies–grey burrowed mottled lime mud with pellets and skeletal grains

Figure 14.14 Shallowing-upwards sequence in an arid tidalflat setting. After Shinn (1983)

structures such as nodular, chicken-wire and enterolithic anhydrite (Figure 14.14).

Biota. The tropical littoral setting has a range of salinities from brackish (20‰) to hypersaline (50‰); consequently it supports only a restricted, euryhaline biota. Plants include a range of lime-secreting and sediment-binding filamentous blue-green algae such as *Lyngbya, schizothrix* and *Scytonema.* Green algae such as *Batophora* and *Penicillus* (calcareous) are found only in the low intertidal zones, as are sea-grasses such as *Thalassia, Syringodium* and *Cymodocea.* Halophyte grasses, shrubs and man-groves occur in the high intertidal and supratidal areas, and may shelter and support distinctive assemblages of molluscs. Gastropods such as *Batillaria* graze in large numbers on mucilagi-nous algae in the low intertidal zone and produce vast quantities of faecal pellets. Infaunal shrimps, crabs, worms and insects burrow in the soft littoral and supralittoral sediments.

Grain composition and texture. The low-energy littoral deposits are characterized by poorly sorted sands, silts and muds. Some are indigen-ous, others are derived by storms and high tides from the nearby marine setting, and include pellets, intraclasts and ooids, with skeletal fragments such as benthic foraminiferans, molluscs and calcareous green algae also common. Most other grains are authigenic, including aragonite mud, minute dolomite rhombs and a variety of evaporite minerals in arid settings. Some grains may be supplied by wind action: carbonate sand grains from the seaward beach, and, in arid regions, siliciclastic grains from nearby deserts.

Diagenetic overprint. The diagenesis of this zone is described in sections 8.3.3 and 8.3.4, and illustrated in Figure 14.14. Arid littoral coasts develop aragonite-cemented crusts, gypsum occurs as a mush and disc-shaped crystals within algal laminites, (Figure 14.15) and dolomite rhombs replace aragonitic faecal pellets and mud, anhydrite nodules and enterolithic layers (Figure 14.16) and other evaporite minerals including celestite, huntite, magnesite, nesquehonite, halite and polyhalite are also common.

Evaporite minerals do not form in moist climates, but dolomite crusts are produced on low supratidal flanks of levees and beach ridges.

Facies associations. The algal laminites and evaporites are easily recognized within limestone beds (see Figure 17.22) and are diagnostic of inter- and supratidal environments. They represent the borders of the marine basin of deposition and allow the interpretation of the surrounding lithologies in some kind of logical sequence. The neighbouring facies are the same as those for the high-energy littoral zone, i.e. to landward, dunes, soil horizons, coastal plain deposits, alluvial fans; to seaward, subtidal deposits of restricted lagoons or open platforms.

The common vertical succession found is a shoaling-upwards sequence which represents passage from reduced grey subtidal deposits, usually intensely burrowed and with marine fossils, into oxidized tan or brown inter- and supratidal deposits with algal laminations, fenestral pores, mud cracks and evidence of evaporites probably capped by terrestrial deposits (Figure 14.14).

Figure 14.15 Section cut into Recent intertidal algal laminite (dark) containing gypsum crystals (*g*). Scale (large divisions) 50 mm. Trucial Coast, Persian Gulf. Photo courtesy of Bob Parks

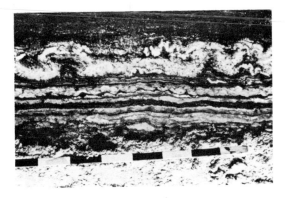

Figure 14.16 Cross-section of Recent enterolithic folding in layers of anhydrite. Scale divisions 100 mm. Trucial coast, Persian Gulf. Photo courtesy of Bob Parks

14.2 Restricted platforms

Geometry and setting. These totally or partially enclosed shallow bodies of water (5–25 m deep) normally have slow water circulation, which leads to long residence times and consequently abnormal salinities, depleted nutrients and extremes of temperature. The restriction that reduces hydraulic energy may be a physical barrier such as reefs, islands or sand shoals, or the damping effect created by vast expanses of shallow water.

The plan morphology of this environment is governed by the structure of the embayment. For example, it may be roughly rectilinear, as in a lagoon encompassed by land on one side and a barrier reef or chain of barrier islands on the other; or roughly circular, as within the confines of the reef rim on an atoll. In three dimensions the deposits have a sheet-like or blanket configuration.

Examples include the central sheltered areas of the Great Bahama Bank; Florida Bay; Gulf of Batabano, Cuba; Shark Bay, West Australia; and the Java Sea.

Sedimentary/biogenic structures. Traction current structures are rare in this calm setting. Most of the sea-bed is hummocky, with pits, hollows and bumps resulting from the extensive bioturbation by crustaceans, worms, molluscs and echinoderms. The accumulating sediment may show well-defined burrows (e.g. *Thalassinoides* Figure 14.17) or it may be mottled or homogenized. Sediment within burrows is frequently seen to have a different grain size or packing to the host sediment. Some burrows have linings of fine agglutinated sediment, some are filled or lined

Figure 14.17 *Thalassinoides* burrows in restricted platform wackestones. The burrows stand out as they once contained ferroan dolomite which has been de-dolomitized, causing ferruginous staining. Hammer head 150 mm across. Jurassic, Paris Basin, France

with faecal pellets. Fine millimetre-scale lamination characterizes deposits of anaerobic settings. Coarser (tens of centimetres) alternations of limestone and shale indicate cyclic variations in calcium carbonate and terrigenous sediment supply. Storm wave reworking of the muddy sediments creates thin widespread grainstone layers containing reworked shells of mud-dwelling fauna. Marine vegetation, particularly marine grasses and algal mats, flourishes in this setting. Thick grass beds can trap enough fine sediment from suspension to build and stabilize banks of mud.' These may have 1 to 5m relief and a mound or sinuous ridge shape. On burial, burrows and moulds of marine-grass rhizomes may escape compaction, to be preserved as vertical and anastomosing cavities.

Biota. The restricted shelf setting is characterized by biota with low diversity and large populations, caused by the ability of one or two well-adapted (euryhaline) organisms to succeed and multiply in a stressed environment where competition from other organisms is reduced.

The dominant skeletal animal groups are epifaunal and infaunal molluscs, benthic foraminiferans, and ostracods. Dwarf individuals and aberrant growth forms attest to the adverse conditions, and the common microbored, micritized and encrusted particles point to slow accumulation rates.

Calcareous green algae (such as *Halimeda* and *Penicillus*) are present, but not in such luxuriant growths as on the open platform.

Grain composition and texture. The sediments of this low-energy restricted setting are typically poorly sorted, and contain carbonate mud of inorganic or organic origin, terrigenous mud in near-land locations, faecal pellets, peloids, intraclasts, and a limited range of skeletal components. Many of the sturdy skeletons are deposited whole and articulated. These sediments are destined to become wackestones with common mudstones and packstones, and local pellet and intraclast grainstones.

Diagenetic imprint. Marine cementation is represented chiefly by incipient lithification in the aggregation of particles such as faecal pellets and grapestones. The patchy and mottled texture produced by burrowing may be accentuated on compaction to produce a nodular or flaser bedded structure, especially striking where there are admixtures of clay minerals. Dolomitized restricted shelf limestones are common in the record, locally with burrows preferentially affected (Figure 14.17). The dolomitization is probably attributable to seepage reflux or mixing-zone processes related to the nearby subaerial deposits. Ancient restricted shelf limestones are occasionally found with replacement chert nodules.

Facies associations. This shallow setting, with little or no sea-bed slope, can have a monotonous expanse of one lithology. On the other hand, minor changes in depositional topography cause subtle changes in litho- and biofacies so that a mosaic of facies with somewhat random transitions result. Laterally equivalent facies include, in the direction of open water, belts of skeletal grainstones and packstones passing into platform margin reef complexes, and sand shoals consisting of skeletal grains and ooids, and in the landward direction, terrigenous deltas, beaches and tidal-flat sediments.

Within the relatively monotonous sequences of subtidal bioturbated fossiliferous wackestone, intercalations can occur, for example, the mudstone lenses representing former grass-trapped mounds of mud, and thin interbedded horizons of skeletal grainstone, the washed-in storm deposits of spillover lobes from nearby barrier beaches.

Restricted-shelf facies is dominantly a blanket of moderate to poorly fossiliferous, bioturbated wackestone or mudstone which, with continuous sedimentation under a constant sea-level, will develop a shallowing upwards sequence into light, bedded, littoral sediments above. Periodic movements of sea relative to land on the gentle slope of the inner platform will generate cycles of shallowing-upward sequences. An ideal cycle will comprise four units (Figure 14.18): a thin basal high-energy unit records the initial transgression over pre-existing deposits; this may be a lag gravel or conglomerate rich in lithoclasts. The next unit is the dark bioturbated wackestone or mudstone of the restricted shelf facies, perhaps with some fine terrigenous admixtures. Beds will be massive, mottled or nodular and of irregular thickness. Seaward progradation of the nearby shoreline produces a stacking of progressively shallower facies, or lagoonal accumulation may be purely vertical behind a protective barrier. Either way, the deposits build up to the new sea-level, and in sheltered low-energy zones typical tidal-flat algal laminites or mangrove marshes develop, whereas in high-energy zones coarse cleanly-washed laminated beach deposits result.

The top of the cycle will contain supratidal laminated dolomites, flat pebble breccias, and/or evaporites and may be capped by dunes, terrestrial shales or caliche. Deepening-upward cycles passing from intertidal to subtidal units

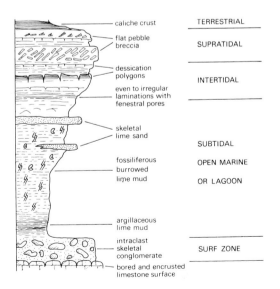

Figure 14.18 Shallowing-upwards sequence in a moist climate

above, representing repeated slow transgressions, are less common in the geological record.

14.3 Open platforms

Setting and geometry. This environment is located from the middle to the edge of the platform or shelf, or in an open lagoon where water is well circulated. The sea water is of salinity, temperature and nutrients typical of the shallow tropics, as it is well exchanged with ocean water. Depth range is from about 10 to 200 m, so much of the sea-bed is below fair-weather wave base. The open platform setting can suffer a wide range of hydraulic conditions: if the platform is rimmed, then large, though relatively shallow, areas will be sheltered from the full effects of the open-water waves. Nevertheless, tidal currents and storm wave action will

still be effective in these calm zones, circulating water and periodically reworking the deposits. If, on the other hand, the platform is not rimmed, but slopes continuously seaward to the basin (as in a ramp), open-water waves will travel further across the platform and spend their energy closer to land. (The high-energy sand bodies of ramps will be considered later with the genetically similar platform margin sand shoals.)

The facies in this setting normally occur as parallel-sided belts related to bathimetric contours and distance from shore or break in slope (e.g. Belize, Florida; Figures 14.19 and 14.20), though irregular topography, such as patch reefs or depressions, may create local anomalies in facies patterns (e.g. Great Barrier Reef, Australia; Figure 14.21). The three-dimensional configuration will be sheet-like with even subsidence, whereas a wedge of sediment develops if subsidence is significantly greater on one side of the platform, or if sediment builds up to sea-level across a stable sloping platform.

Sedimentary and biogenic structures. Bioturbation structures are again the feature of this mid-shelf sea-bed, with horizontal, inclined and vertical, single and branched burrows common, together with traces of epi- and intrastratal crawling. On burial these deposits will be light to dark, mottled or nodular, unlaminated sediments. Sea-grass beds are not as widespread as in the restricted platform zone, though mucilaginous mats of filamentous or coccoid algae, and diatoms, are often encountered on sea-beds that are not too frequently stirred by burrowers. These sticky surficial mats trap grains but do not build laminated structures in this setting, as the organic films are disrupted and consumed by the infauna. Wind-forced currents and storm surges can entrain and transport sediment to depths of 100 m. The resultant winnowed horizons of coarser debris with medium to small-scale (possibly hummocky) cross-stratification would punctuate the essentially sand- and silt-rich shelf deposits.

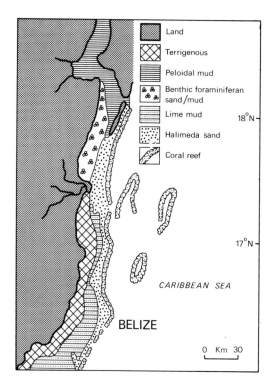

Figure 14.19 Lithofacies belts on the Belize shelf margin. After Wilson and Jordan (1983)

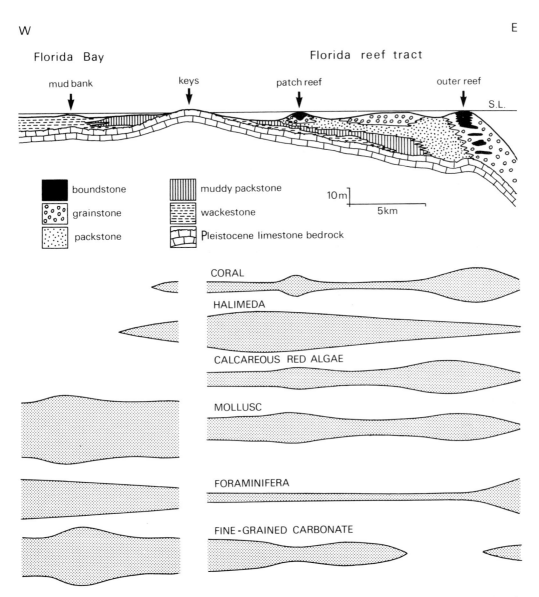

Figure 14.20 Cross-section of Florida shelf margin showing lithofacies distribution and (below) the distribution of constituent grains in surface sediments After Enos and Perkins (1977) and Ginsburg (1956)

Traction current structures produced by waves and tides in the inshore zones of ramps are similar in origin and structure to those formed in the platform margin zone, discussed in the next section.

Patch reefs are prevalent on open platforms.

They vary in diameter from a few metres (Figure 14.22) to a few kilometres (Figure 14.23), and most rise from a sea-bed generally less than 50 m deep up to the surface. The larger patch reefs may enclose a shallow lagoon. The reef framework initially inherits the

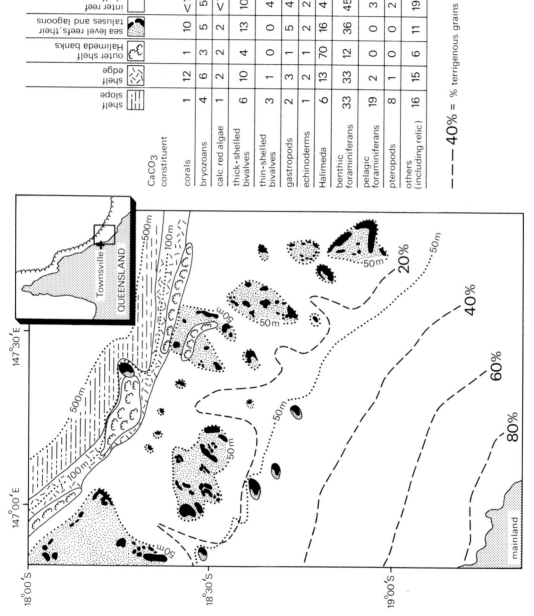

$CaCO_3$ constituent	shelf slope	shelf edge	outer shelf Halimeda banks	sea level reefs, their taluses and lagoons	inter reef shelf
corals	1	12	1	10	<1
bryozoans	4	6	3	5	5
calc. red algae	1	2	2	2	<1
thick-shelled bivalves	6	10	4	13	10
thin-shelled bivalves	3	1	0	0	4
gastropods	2	3	1	5	4
echinoderms	1	2	1	2	2
Halimeda	6	13	70	16	4
benthic foraminiferans	33	33	12	36	45
pelagic foraminiferans	19	2	0	0	3
pteropods	8	1	0	0	2
others (including relic)	16	15	6	11	19

— — 40% = % terrigenous grains

Figure 14.21 Lithofacies distribution, and their component composition, for the central region of the Great Barrier Reef of Australia. After Scoffin and Tudhope (1985)

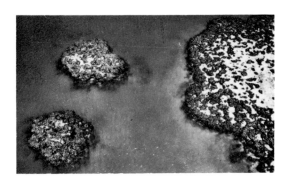

Figure 14.22 Patch reefs whose tops are within 2 m of the sea surface and bases at 18 m depth. Coral growth is best at the rims; central areas become progressively sandy when the reef approaches sea-level. The two patches on the left are approximately 25 m in diameter. North Lagoon, Bermuda

Figure 14.23 Patch (or platform) reefs, many with small islands, Pelau Seribu, Java Sea, Indonesia. Reefs are roughly 1 km wide

configuration of the rocky foundations on which it builds (see section 14.4.2). Once the reef reaches sea-level, the principal growth direction is lateral, and the shape develops in harmony with the prevailing conditions (mature). Where hydraulic conditions are uniform, small patch reefs develop a radial symmetry with a narrow halo of reef-derived sediment a few metres wide, but where the winds prevail from one direction, they develop an elongation to leeward by growing over sediment spread downwind in spits and horns from the reef flanks (Figure 14.6).

If reef growth lags behind sea-level rise, then it retains the form of its antecedent topography for a longer period (immature). We notice a gradual change across a seaward-tilting shelf such as that of north Queensland, Australia, from mature reefs inshore to immature reefs offshore (Figure 14.24).

Where normal sea-water vigorously circulates right up to the shoreline, coral and coralline algal reefs fringe the rocky coast and commonly have a discrete lunate plan form around headlands, as active sediment movement prohibits their development in bays (Figure 14.25).

Biota. Open platforms have an abundant and diverse sand-dwelling fauna and flora of stenohaline forms (i.e. those with low tolerance to salinity varying from that of normal sea water).

Molluscs are common, and generally thick-shelled and robust in the high-energy settings and more delicate in deep calm waters. Infaunal molluscs are particularly abundant. Benthic foraminiferans occur in large numbers, living on the surface sediment and attached to soft algae and sea-grasses. They are the dominant component of the mid-shelf sediments of the Great Barrier Reef province of Australia, for example. Echninoderms, bryozoans and solitary corals add (usually minor) contributions of skeletal material to the sediments. Soft corals and sponges contribute sclerites and spicules to the very fine fraction of deposits.

Calcareous green algae (e.g. *Halimeda* and *Penicillus*) abound in this setting and their disaggregated skeletons contribute mud-sized aragonite to the sediments. Luxuriant *Halimeda* growths between 20 and 100 m depth in areas of nutrients upwelling may build elongate banks of coarse segments 20 m thick on the outer shelf (Figure 14.21). Calcareous red algae encrust coarse debris and, where currents are strong, may form rhodoliths.

Patch reefs have a primary framework of scleractinian corals (e.g. *Acropora*, *Millepora*, *Porites* and faviids) and a secondary framework

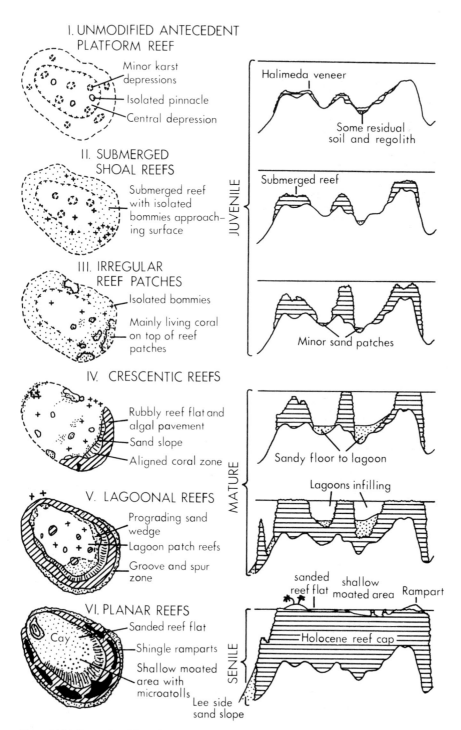

Figure 14.24 Examples of juvenile, mature and senile platform reefs found on the Great Barrier Reef of Australia. Juvenile forms have a configuration that most closely follows that of the antecedent topography. Mature and senile reefs have a high sediment production relative to sea-level rise and consequently mask the form of their pre-Holocene foundations. After Hopley (1982)

Figure 14.25 Aerial photograph of the west coast of Barbados. Modern fringing reefs extend from coastal prominences. The low-relief terrace on land extends to the right of the photograph up to a distinctive cliff line (arrowed) which marks the edge of an earlier (Pleistocene) reefal development (see Figures 14.40, 14.42)

rich in calcareous red algae, bryozoans, encrusting foraminiferans such as *Homotrema* and *Gypsina*, molluscs (particularly oysters and vermetid gastropods) and serpulids. Boring molluscs (*Lithophaga*) are common, and boring sponges may provide a large quantity of silt-size sediment chips eroded from the exposed framework.

Grain composition and texture. The bulk of modern tropical open-platform sediments are skeletal and peloidal grainstones and packstones. *Halimeda* (calcareous green algae), benthic foraminiferans and molluscs are the dominant calcareous organisms, with corals and calcareous red algae common near to reefs and rocky substrates. Clay-sized particles are not especially abundant today in open shelves; any clays produced here are kept in suspension by burrowers and flushed out by tidal currents to accumulate in the sinks of deeper waters or restricted bays. On the south Florida shelf (Figure 14.20) fine sediments are concentrated in the deeper fore-reef and the shallow sheltered Florida Bay area. If the hinterland has significant relief, terrigenous sands and clays accumulate near-shore as fining-outward belts (Figure 14.21). Grain size preference of certain

deposit feeders and burrowers may cause a biological sorting of the surface sediment, but usually the subsurface deposits are well mixed into poorly-sorted homogeneous accumulations. Normally poorly-sorted coarse epilithic fragments form the patch reef flanking sediments.

Diagenetic overprint. The open-platform sea-bed sediments have relatively stagnant interstitial marine waters. Marine cementation is rare, except in the stable inner interstices of patch reefs where aragonite and Mg calcite may precipitate.

Pellets and intraclasts are not as abundant as in the inner and outer platform positions. Slow sedimentation can result in a degree of mineralization of grains by iron, manganese and phosphorus-rich minerals, or glauconite in the deeper parts of the open platform.

Facies associations. Widespread deposits of skeletal and peloidal grainstones, packstones and argillaceous wackestones characterize fossil open platform limestones. The strata range from highly nodular beds, through beds with irregular wavy surfaces and uneven thicknesses to homogeneous massive, parallel-bedded units. Limestone–shale alternations result where biogenic activity was insufficient to obscure cyclical variations in calcium carbonate and terrigenous input. Scattered within these low-energy facies are the boundstone masses of patch reefs (Figure 14.26), some with flanking wedge-shaped beds of reef-derived sediment, and the multiple thin amalgamated storm beds that increase in thickness and abundance upwards.

To landward, these open platform deposits interfinger with the calcareous or terrigenous sands of the high-energy littoral zone or the finer accumulations of the restricted platform and tidal flat belts. On rimmed platforms, marginal shoals of ooid and skeletal grainstones, or reef complexes, constitute the seaward flanks, but where the platforms slope steadily into the deep bathyal zones, peri-platform sediments (a mixture of pelagic oozes and washed-off platform sediments) take over.

Figure 14.26 Quarry face of lensed patch reef in argillaceous nodular limestone-shale alternations typical of open platform deposition. Bilateral symmetry of reef suggests uniform depositional conditions (see text, section 17.3). The argillaceous off-reef sediment has compacted 20% more than the massive reef. Hammer (arrowed) 300 mm. Silurian, Much Wenlock, England

14.4 Platform margins: non-rimmed and rimmed

Platform margins are adjacent to a significant steepening in basinward slope. This steepening may be tectonically controlled (e.g. rift margin), it may relate to an erosional feature formed during periods of lower sea-level, or it may be the basinward limit of an accretionary sediment wedge. In modern tropical seas we normally associate this position with the edge of the continental shelf. As cold, deep, nutrient-rich ocean waters are drawn up on the platform edge they are heated and agitated by wave action, which drives off CO_2, aiding the precipitation of $CaCO_3$. Lime production, both organic and inorganic, is generally higher in this shallow tropical platform margin zone than in any other, so the edge commonly has an elevated rim built of bodies of sand or of reefs right up to sea-level. Outside the tropics, where lime production is lower, shelf edges are not characterized by elevated rims.

Non-rimmed open carbonate platforms (or ramps) are gently seaward-dipping surfaces which lack a continuous elevated rim to act as an energy barrier. As a consequence, open-water waves are able to propagate across much of the platform. Thus the break in slope at the seaward edge is a relatively broad area of gradual change compared to the sharp precipitous slope breaks of rimmed platforms.

These gradual slope breaks occur where carbonate production has been insufficient to keep up with relative sea-level rise, and they may contain sediments such as ooids or reef frameworks which are drowned shallow-water features. The inability of platform margin deposits to keep pace with sea-level rise can be due to slower production, caused by a detrimental climatic change or excessive off-bank siltation at the moment the platform was flooded during the transgression, or to tectonic forces, causing a marked increase in the rate of platform edge subsidence.

The sedimentary/biogenic structures, biota, sediment compositions and facies association of non-rimmed margins are the same as those described earlier for typical open platforms, though there may be relict platform-margin shallow-water structures and grains that have been preserved during drowning. The slow sedimentation rate will be reflected in the abundance of iron, manganese and phosphorus minerals coating or replacing grains, and the abundance of glauconite fillings of foraminiferan tests.

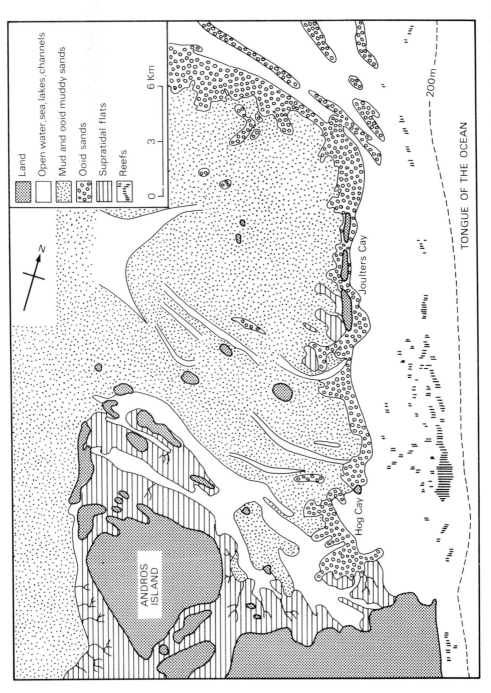

Figure 14.27 Depositional environments in the vicinity of Joulters Cays on the north-eastern margin of the Great Bahama Bank. After Purdy and Imbrie (1965)

G

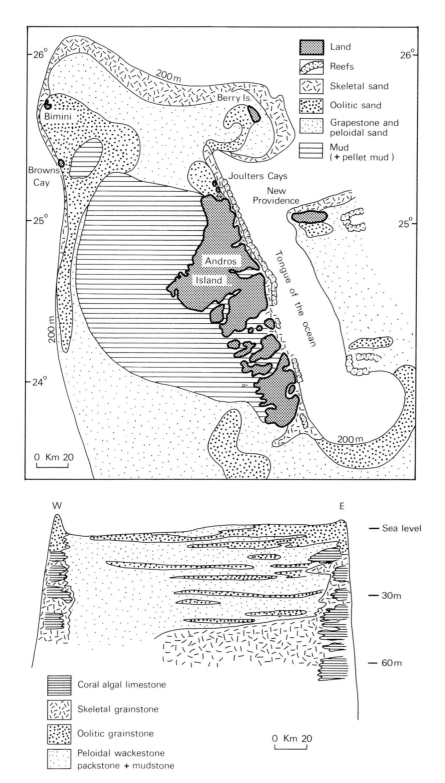

Figure 14.28 Lithofacies of the Great Bahama Bank and east–west profile based on core analyses. After Purdy (1963) and Beach and Ginsburg (1980)

Platform margins on mid-ocean banks and continental shelves face the open ocean, but can be disposed to windward or leeward. Leeward, open and tide-dominated tropical platform margins are more frequently rimmed by sand shoals than by reefs. The sands may be rich in skeletons, peloids, aggregates or ooids. Ooid shoals are generally tidally driven, whereas non-ooid shoals are formed as a result of intermittent storm-generated sand transport. Windward margins are generally steeper than leeward margins and, where they have been characterized at some stage by bare rock expanses, tend to be reef-rimmed. The break in slope position is ideal for the growth of these epilithic skeletal edifices, for not only are nutrient levels high, but any loose sediment generated which could swamp and kill off the sessile reef-builders can readily be funnelled off the platform, through passes in the rim, out to deeper water.

Sand shoal margins and reefal margins will be discussed separately, though they can occur in close proximity, as for example near Joulters Cays, Bahamas (Figure 14.27).

14.4.1 Sand-shoal margins

Setting and geometry. The manufacture of new grains in the 0–5 m depth range on the rim of a platform margin helps to maintain the break in slope. Platform margin sand bodies have been extensively studied on the Bahama Banks (Figure 14.28) where three major types of ooid sand bodies are distinguished: (i) *Tidal bar belts* are oriented perpendicular to the shelf margin, parallel to the flow of strong tidal currents (> 1000 mm/s). They are well developed at the cul-de-sac ends of deep embayments (such as the Tongue of the Ocean and Exuma Sound): individual ribbon-like bars are up to 20 km long and 1 to 1.5 km wide (Figure 14.29). (ii) *Marine sand belts* develop parallel to the windward and leeward bank edges, normal to tidal flow, which may be 500 mm/s but still well above critical threshold levels. These belts range from 1 to 4 km in width and 25 to 75 km in length (Figure 14.30).

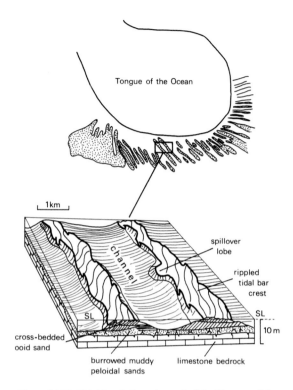

Figure 14.29 Tidal bar belt at the end of the Tongue of the Ocean Embayment, Bahamas, showing structure of bars. After Ball (1967)

(iii) *Tidal deltas* have lobate or tear-drop forms and are generated by tidal currents flowing through gaps between islands (Figure 14.3).

It should be pointed out that shoals of ooids develop in shallow-water high-energy zones that are not necessarily at the margins of a platform, but may be on a gently sloping ramp on the inner part of the platform. In the SE coastal area of the Persian Gulf, ooids form in large ebb-dominated tidal deltas associated with the coastal barrier system (Figures 8.14, 8.16). They also occur on tidal bars in wide channels between islands and on open tidal flats and beaches. In the hypersaline Hamelin Basin of Shark Bay, West Australia, ooids form in the zone of maximum turbulence at the outer margins of sublittoral platform promontories. Here, warm, saline, platform waters (< 3m depth) are in contact with

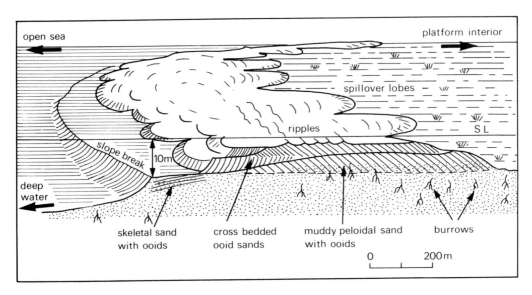

Figure 14.30 Sedimentary structures and grain types typical of marine sand belts on the margins of the Bahama Banks. After Ball (1967)

cooler basin waters. Waves impinge on the platform margin, recharge waters on the platform and move the nuclei of skeletal grains, quartz and pellets. Ooid sands form, and the sedimentary bodies accrete as series of foreset beds in linear ribbons parallel to the shore at depths of 0–2 m.

The prevailing winds influence the direction of extension of platform margin sand bodies. In the Bahamas where trade winds are from the NE, sand transport is mainly off-bank on the west (leeward) of the banks, for example Lily Bank where ooid grainstones swamp Holocene bank slope reefs, and on-bank on the east (windward) of the Banks, e.g. Joulters Cays (Figure 14.27) where grainstone lobes swamp lagoonal muds.

The specific pattern of movement of platform margin sands is also governed by tidal currents and the presence or absence of marginal islands which can, for instance, even in high-energy settings, cause a seaward transport of sand by storm return flows and gravity processes.

Sedimentary and biogenic structures. Tidal-bar belt ribbons are covered with sand waves whose crests are oblique or subparallel to the bar axes. Smaller-scale mega-ripples flank these bed forms. Cross-beds dip perpendicular to the long axes of bars in the bar crests, and parallel to channel axes in channels. The 1–3 km wide channels between the tidal bars are 3–8 m deep and may have sea-grass-covered, burrowed, sand or cemented rock bottoms. In places, small channels cut through tidal bars (perhaps during storms), and build spillover lobes into the broad channels (Figure 14.29). Beds are convex-up in spillovers, and younger beds butt against bedding planes of older beds.

The main bed forms on marine sand belts are symmetrical and asymmetrical sand waves of 10–100 m wavelength and 0.5–4 m amplitude (Figure 14.30). Ripples cover the stoss slopes of the sand waves. Also, shapes similar to barchan dunes lie in chains on the bank margins, migrating to leeward over a firm, nearly bare, rock platform. The marine sand belts are maintained by daily tidal flow, but they are also significantly influenced by storms which are responsible for channels normal to the belt axis and the spillover lobes of sediment at the channel mouths (Figure 14.30). Cross-beds dip perpendicular to the belt's long axis, with largest sets at the base, and dipping predominantly away from deeper or more open water.

Tidal deltas are also dominated by sand-wave, mega-ripple and ripple bed forms. The migration of these lobes takes place during storms when faster-than-normal currents surge through the island passes.

Three varieties of internal structure predominate in all of these ooid shoals.

(i) *Avalanche* deposits have cross-bedding with angle-of-repose lee slopes (*c.* 30°). Individual beds may be graded and coarser particles are concentrated in wedges down the dip (Figure 14.31). The grains in these cross-beds were deposited under gravity and have relatively loose packing.

These cross-beds represent normal flow on the lee side of ripples and delta-like embankments forming along the sides of channels.

(ii) *Accretion* deposits have gently sloping, curved cross-bedding, less than the angle of repose (< 30°) without down-dip sorting (Figure 14.31). High-velocity currents (or storms) were involved in their formation, and grains are tightly packed.

Both avalanche and accretion cross-bedding can show two (180°) opposing directions of dip which represent flood- and ebb-tide structures. Ripple form may be preserved at the top of the sets or, at high accumulation sites, ripple drift lamination is preserved. Cross-ripples (sets oriented at 90° to each other) are common on channel edge bars and form by competing tidal and wind driven currents.

(iii) *Sheet* deposits are flat or gently dipping

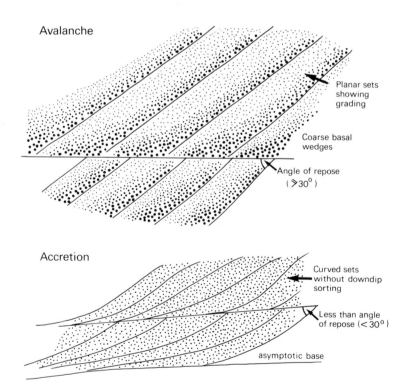

Figure 14.31 Cross-sections of avalanche and accretion structures in ooid shoal deposits

strata parallel to the underlying truncation surfaces. These form during upper flow regimes on exposed flats (beaches).

Bar interiors may show alternations of avalanche and accretionary cross-bedding capped by sheet laminations on the bar crest. On the crests of active ooid shoals, the grains are clean and well-sorted. Where ooids mix with lagoonal muddy sediments on the flanks of active bars, the sediments are poorly sorted and commonly bioturbated.

Laterally persistent ooid flats develop flat-bedded sequences which are cut by low-flow-regime tidal channels. Laterally migrating meandering tidal channels produce a vertical sequence that indicates a decrease in flow energy and competency. The base of the channel deposit is a lag gravel of shells and intraclasts. This may be covered by flat-bedded, high-flow-regime oolites, or pass directly into planar and trough cross-bedded oolitic limestone. Individual cross-beds are graded, and they thicken and coarsen downslope in a manner typical of avalanching. The cross-beds give way vertically to wavy-bedded, rippled, oolitic limestone capped by channel-top flatbedded wackestones and mudstones.

At the flanks of active ooid shoals and in wide channels, where sedimentation is low but currents swift and supersaturation high, the surface grains can lithify and hardgrounds form (Figure 6.10). Tepee structures develop at the junction of polygonal slabs on hardground surfaces. Storm reworking of hardground layers creates layers of coarse intraclasts, which will be interbedded with grainstones of similar composition.

Cemented substrates support an epilithic fauna such as corals, sponges, bryozoans, oysters and, locally, stromatolites. If the sea-bed remains bare of sediment for a considerable time, patch reefs will grow, but if lateral shifting of channels allows only brief bare rock exposure at one site, then a bed of epilithic organisms (*biostrome*) will result beneath the cross-bedded sands of the migrating active shoal.

Ooid shoals that become inactive, perhaps due to a rapid sea-level rise, become relict and stabilized by sea-grasses. Fine sediment is trapped and mixed in with the well-sorted sands by crustacean burrowing, which also destroys the original cross-laminations.

Biota. The mobile sands of the platform margin shoals are inhospitable to most of the macrobenthos. From the air, the active sand shoals are clearly white against the darker, more organic-rich, lagoonal deposits they border. Less active portions of the sand bodies may have a veneer of vegetation in which molluscs and foraminiferans live. Hardgrounds are encrusted with epilithic and endolithic organisms, as described earlier.

Grain composition and texture. The sediments of an active platform margin sand shoal are clean, well-sorted and rounded ooids or skeletal grains with minor admixtures of peloids and aggregates. These deposits will ultimately become parallel and cross-bedded grainstones. Inactive marginal shoals develop a grainstone or packstone microfacies.

Diagenetic overprint. During periods of sediment stability (i.e. lack of active shoal migration and intense bioturbation), fringes of radially oriented aragonite needles, precipitated at the sea-bed, cement grains into friable crusts and hardgrounds (Figure 6.10). This sea-bed lithification inhibits mechanical erosion and also stabilizes steep slopes on the flanks of ooid shoals. Marine cemented grains escape the effects of chemical compaction on burial, and hardground layers within the grainstone sequence significantly retard the vertical flow of interstitial fluids during later diagenesis. Ooid shoals build up to and above mean sea-level, and these sediments are frequently exposed to meteoric waters during a slight relative lowering of sea-level. Once an island emerges, fresh water can be trapped in rock interstices beneath as a discrete sub-island lens. Vadose and phreatic freshwater stabilization and mixing-zone diagenesis will ensue.

Facies associations. On a broad scale the facies are in belts paralleling the platform margins, though complexities arise as a result to topographic irregularities and localized depocentres. Ooid grainstones are commonly flanked to seaward by skeletal grainstones or peri-platform sediments of platform and pelagic mixtures and, on the sheltered platform side, by ooid packstones which give way to peloidal packstones and skeletal or peloidal wackestones (Figure 14.28).

Regular changes in relative sea-level across a wide gently sloping platform results in the production of numerous shallowing-upward cycles. A typical cycle will have a transgressive basal lag of coarse shells or lithoclasts on the basal subaerial exposure surface. Initially, increasing water depth creates a subtidal lagoonal environment in which restricted wackestones and mudstones accumulate. Improved circulation allows growth of a more varied biota which may include an infauna, allowing the sediment to become bioturbated. Lime production is eventually so active in these platform margin settings that carbonate sediments accumulate at greater rates than the rate of relative subsidence, so waters shoal and agitation is increased. Ooids form in areas of strong tidal flow. Ooid shoals grade upwards from accretion and cross-rippled bar

deposits to laminated beach deposits. Dunes with steep platformward-dipping foresets may cap the sequence.

14.4.2 Reef-rimmed margins

Setting and geometry. Many tropical platform margins are rimmed by coral reefs which grow up to sea-level. Reef-building corals have specific light, temperature, sedimentation and substrate requirements for healthy growth in normal sea water. These conditions restrict them to tropical latitudes where their principal occurrences are on elevated rocky foundations on the warmer western sides of oceans (Figure 14.32). The best

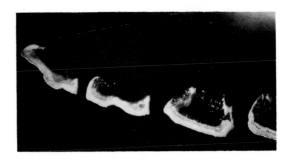

Figure 14.33 Ribbon reefs (with horns of flanking sediments) separated by deep passes. The outer barrier reefs of the Northen Great Barrier Reefs, Australia. The open Pacific Ocean is to bottom of photograph and the Queensland Shelf to the top. Reefs are roughly 1 km wide and 6 km long

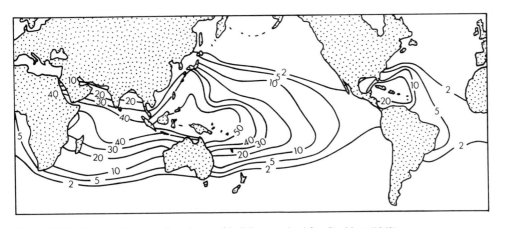

Figure 14.32 Number of genera of modern reef-building corals. After Stoddart (1969)

development of platform margin reefs is on the windward side of the platform where agitation brings nutrients and disperses sediment. The reefs are not normally laterally continuous for more than a few kilometres along the line of the break in slope. Commonly elongate ribbons of reefs are separated by relatively deep passes (10–50 m) through which tides mix ocean and lagoonal waters and platform sediments migrate seawards (Figure 14.33). Reefs that enclose a landward lagoon are called *barrier reefs*.

The form of platform margin reefs is governed by several interrelated factors:

(i) The configuration of the foundation on which the reefs grow—the antecedent topography

(ii) The tectonic setting and global sea-level changes

(iii) The prevailing physical conditions (waves, tides, storms, climate and inorganic precipitation of $CaCO_3$)

(iv) The nature of the dominant organisms.

The reef morphology is influenced by the antecedent topography principally during its initial stages (immaturity) of growth. After a prolonged period of stable growth (maturity), the pattern of sedimentation on and around the reef and the nature of skeletal growth take over to dominate the configuration (Figure 14.24). As the sea has only been at its present level for a few thousand years (section 15.4) very few modern reefs have reached the maturity stage. Most have configurations that reflect the form of the foundations: e.g. karst, fluvial, tidal delta (Figure 14.34), spillover lobes (Figure 14.35), and barrier islands.

An idealized cross-section of facies in a typical mature platform margin reef is shown in Figure 14.36. The key element is the reef framework; without this, the reef complex would not exist. The framework initiates the rim and supplies large quantities of sediment to the fore-reef and back-reef. However, although it is the focal point of living reefs, the framework is not well

preserved and as little as 10% of a fossil reef complex may be *in-situ* framework.

The reef framework consists of sessile, calcareous, massive and branching organisms, usually with parts of their surfaces encrusted one to another. During growth this framework is open

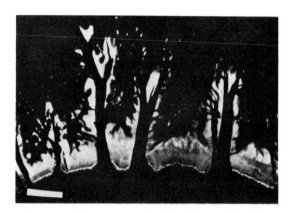

Figure 14.34 Tidal delta pattern of reefs. Outer barrier, Northern Great Barrier Reef, Australia. Open Pacific Ocean is to bottom of photograph. Scale 1 km

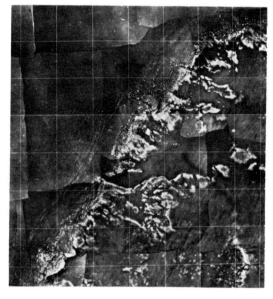

Figure 14.35 Aerial photograph of reef shapes resembling spillover lobes, washover fans and flood tidal deltas on Bermuda Atoll's NW rim

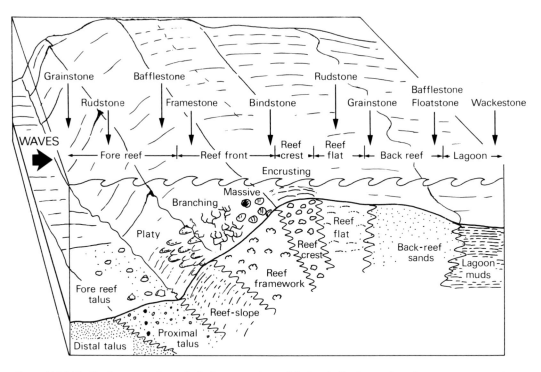

Figure 14.36 Idealized cross-section of platform margin reef facies, indicating reef environment zones and nature of accumulating sediment. After James (1979) and Longman (1981)

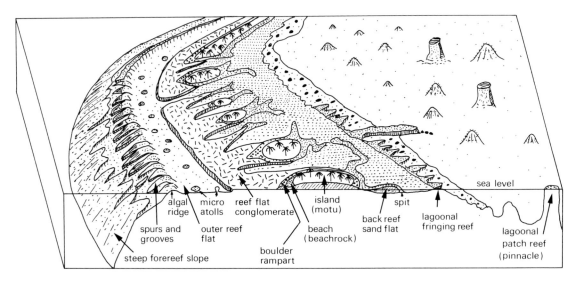

Figure 14.37 Schematic diagram of the morphological features found on an Indo-Pacific atoll. After Battistini *et al.* (1975)

and water easily flushes through it, but within the deeper recesses, sediments of reef debris settle out within framework cavities and are cemented by encrusting coelobites and marine cements (section 7.2). The framework is weakened by bio-erosion and the pounding of waves, parts are broken, some sediment is moved back over the reef framework by waves and currents to give the back-reef sands, and some falls down the front of the reef by gravity to give proximal and distal talus deposits.

This general arrangement of facies (Figure 14.36) is found on most living and fossil platform margin reefs. However, modern reefs also show a variety of intricate surface morphological features, some of which are inherited, some presently developing in response to prevailing conditions. Figure 14.37 indicates a selection of surface features commonly found on Indo-Pacific reefs. Modern fore-reefs are normally terraced and their seawardmost slope may be precipitously steep. The submarine terracing results from the reef foundations either forming by earlier growth up to a former sea-level or being reduced by planation down to a former

Figure 14.38 Spurs and grooves on the seaward margin of a fringing reef. Rarotonga, Cook Islands, Pacific Ocean. Spurs between 5 and 30 m wide

sea-level. These terraces are overgrown by little more than veneers of Holocene corals, and they may be cut by seaward-sloping channels. Debris is carried off the reef via these channels (grooves), while corals, preferring to colonize the silt-free prominences, enhance the relief of the intervening spurs (Figure 14.38).

Spurs and *grooves* require a slope for their formation but may owe their configuration to one or a combination of causes.

(i) The grooves originated by dissolution of the foundation limestone during exposure to the atmosphere in the Pleistocene at times of low sea-level, in a manner similar to lapies today. Subsequently, when the sea transgressed over these channelled limestones, corals and coralline algae preferentially colonized the elevated ridges.

(ii) The grooves are purely erosional, gouged by the to-and-fro motion of sand and gravel under the influence of waves and gravity, the regular spacing of the channels being a function of the waves' characteristics.

(iii) The spurs are purely constructional, formed by the in-place growth of corals and algae in ecologically controlled, regularly spaced, seaward projections. Some reefs show a relationship between the angle of wave impingement and spur-and-groove orientation which does suggest a direction response of the coral growth to the physical setting.

The reef crest is the highest part of the reef at any stage in its growth and is usually subjected to intense wave turbulence. Only a few encrusting coral species can tolerate these conditions. Where the crest is deeper, and in zones of lower hydraulic energy, communities of branching corals live. Encrusting calcareous red algae are especially abundant on the reef crest at the intertidal position, perhaps due to the relief from the pressure of grazing fish in the surf zone. The common genera of algae found in these pink algal ridges are *Porolithon, Neogoniolithon, Lithophyllum* and *Lithothamnium*. Along with encrusting formaniferans, vermetid gastropods and some encrusting corals (for example *Mille-pora*), the algae build a compact boundstone made of encrusting layers which is normally well cemented shortly after growth. Surge channels through the algal ridge supply water to the reef flat, and with time these channels may be roofed over by rapid algal accretion.

The reef flat extends lagoonwards of the algal ridge (Figure 4.50). It is a shallow pavement normally less than 2 m deep, with scattered corals and a thin cover of sand. Normal wave energy is low on the reef flat, though the area is subjected to tidal currents and storm waves. The reef flat has a patchy cover of tongues and arcuate ridges of coarse coral debris, representing separate storm deposits. These ramparts of conglomerate, and algal ridges pond sea water at low tide into moats in which coral microatolls grow (Figure 14.39).

Coral reef islands (*motu*) develop on high banks of coral conglomerate and at places where opposing wave sets converge, causing a drop in hydraulic energy and accumulation of loose sand. The sands of these coral-island beaches can be piled into supratidal ridges by storms, blown to form land dunes by the prevailing winds, or stabilized in the intertidal position by lithification into beach rock. In many sheltered intertidal zones, mangroves grow around coral island coasts, bringing about the trapping of fine carbonate sediments and the accumulation of peats.

Tidal currents flow in channels between reef flat islands, and these channels may support unusual rolling algal, and even coral, skeletal growths. Rhodoliths, discrete spheroidal structures made of encrusting or branching calcareous red algae (Figure 4.55), and coralliths, similar skeletal structures built by corals, have all-round

Figure 14.39 Coral (*Porites*) microatolls (*c.* 1 m diam.) on the reef flat of Low Isles, Great Barrier Reef, Australia, during an exceptionally low tide. Domed corals build up to the level of ponded water, the tops die and growth continues in a lateral direction only

peripheral growth which is maintained by periodic rolling.

Most reef-derived sands are swept over the reef flat to build back-reef deposits within the lagoon or back-reef area. The prograding wedges of these sediments characteristically develop a lobed plan morphology which is moulded by the dominant wave pattern. These deposits are locally covered with corals, forming a fringing reef on the lagoon side of the reef flat. Steep-sided patch or pinnacle reefs grow up to sea-level in the sheltered lagoon (Figure 14.37).

Sedimentary/biogenic structures. The fore-reef sediments accumulate on ledges and at the foot of the reef slope as wedging beds of poorly sorted talus. Beds of the distal talus sands often show grading and basal scour. The framework itself is an anastomosing network of rigid encrusting skeletons with organic and inorganic cement, as described in section 7.2. It is intimately associated with broken framework pieces and the skeletal debris of reef-dwellers. Storm action easily breaks the thinly branched skeletons of shallow zones, while the massive corals survive. In the Caribbean, for example, the branching corals *Acropora cervicornis* and *Porites porites*, which grow relatively quickly, producing dense thickets, are broken during storms into piles of rod-shaped branches which accumulate around the undisturbed erect massive skeletons of *Montastrea annularis* and *Diploria strigosa* (Figure 7.6). The sediments of the reef top are principally coarse, unbedded storm accumulations of coral boulders. Locally, the broken coral branches are imbricated and ridge interiors have a crude cross-bedding (Figures 8.10, 14.4). Beaches and dunes of coral-reef islands show distinctive cross-bedding, as described earlier for the sand shoal rims. The flanks of reefs develop sands and gravel horns and spits with planar stratification, while tides and storm surges build tidal deltas, spillover lobes and washover fans of reef-derived sands between reefs and on their leeward margins. The deposits of the lagoon have a blanket geometry and consist of generally fine, poorly sorted, sands locally trapped and stabilized by sea-grasses and algal mats and extensively burrowed.

Biota. Healthy reefs typically have luxuriant growths of primary and secondary frame-building organisms such as corals, calcareous red algae, bryozoans, oysters, encrusting foraminiferans, serpulids, vermetid gastropods and sponges. A large variety of skeletal and soft-bodied organisms live attached to, or loosely upon, this framework. Attached organisms include calcareous green algae (e.g. *Halimeda*), gorgonians, and byssally attached bivalves; and free-living reef dwellers include gastropods, echinoids, ophiuroids, crinoids, crustaceans and benthic foraminiferans. These skeletal remains contribute to the reefal sediment but not to the rigid framework. Reef framework and cemented internal deposits are penetrated by a range of endolithic organisms, particularly bivalves, sponges, worms and filamentous blue-green algae.

Reef organisms are characteristically zoned according to depth, light, wave energy and siltation rate. Different species have different tolerances to these variables, seen clearly in the modern and Pleistocene corals of Barbados reefs (Figure 14.40), and one species may develop different growth forms in response to these physical parameters. Generic diversity is greatest in the mid-water depth (5–30 m) on the reef-front; the more stressed settings, e.g. deep fore-reef, reef-crest, reef-flat, have a lower diversity of macrobenthos.

We frequently notice a succession of communities in vertical sections of ancient reefs. Four stages of development have been recognised: stabilization, colonization, diversification and domination. The stabilization stage is represented by piles of skeletal debris which have been colonized by animals and plants with holdfasts which bound the raised substrate. The second stage represents the initial colonization by the

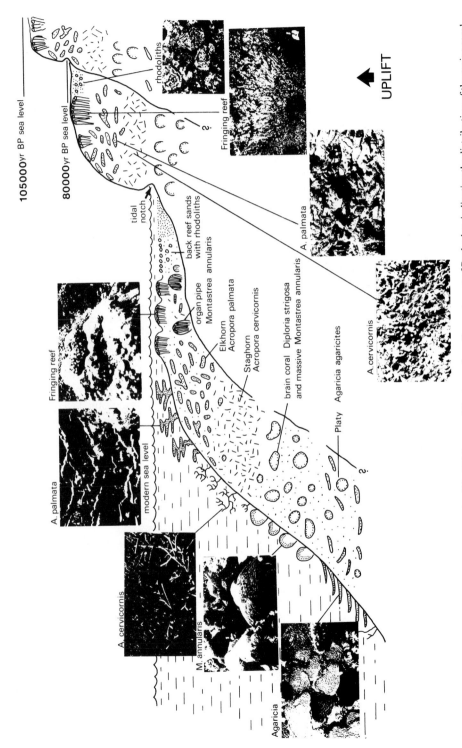

Figure 14.40 Schematic cross-section of modern and uplifted Pleistocene fringing reefs on the west coast of Barbados, indicating the distribution of the major coral species

reef-building animals. There may be only a few species of builders, but they characteristically are types capable of coping with high sedimentation rates. The diversification stage is when upward building proceeded in earnest and lateral facies developed. At this stage there is a wide variety of taxa and growth forms. The relief of the reef is now sufficient to modify the surrounding sedimentation and the reef itself develops a zonation since its margins now reach from shallow to deepwater. The domination or climax stage is usually represented by a few taxa of limited growth habit, generally encrusting. There is a debate as to whether the community succession is intrinsically controlled by the organisms, which gradually alter the ecological setting, with, for example, the structure responding to specific reproduction strategies, or whether the control is extrinsic, reflecting a progressive replacement of deep-water communities by shallower ones as the reef builds into more turbulent shallow water.

Grain compositions and texture. There is considerable variability in the composition of reef-related sediments (Table 14.1). On reef tops and in very close proximity to reef framework (normally within a few hundred metres) the skeletal remains of epilithic frame-building and frame-dwelling organisms abound (e.g. corals, calcareous red algae). Where the source of sediment is sandy substrates, as in inter-reef or lagoonal situations, benthic formaniferans, molluscs and calcareous green algae are dominant. Micritized grains of unknown origin are also common near to platform margin reefs.

Distal deposits are fine, show moderate to good sorting, and eventually form packstones. Typically, the slopes of the reef front are characterized by poorly sorted mixtures of very coarse talus made of fragments of cemented reef framework and finer reef debris. These deposits will ultimately form mixtures of boundstones, grainstones and packstones. The internal sediments of the framework have been described earlier. They are fine and commonly show grading in partially filled cavities. Reef-crest, reef-flat and back-reef sediments are coarse, moderately sorted grainstones, while lagoonal sediments are generally fine, poorly sorted wackestones.

Diagenetic overprint. Marine lithification of reefs (section 8.3.1) is common, particularly in those areas of constant water flux such as on the windward margin. The zone of active cementation appears to be confined to the outer metre of the reef surface. There is relatively less lithified framework and rubble during periods of especially rapid reef growth or rubble sedimentation. Conversely, hiatuses allow the formation of pavement-like reef-framework crusts.

Table 14.1 The grain composition of reef-associated sediments from different parts of the world.

Component	Caribbean (Jamaica) reef/lagoon		Pacific Atoll (Suwarrow) reef/lagoon		Great Barrier Reef, Australia reef/inter-reef shelf		Bahama Banks margin/interior	
Coral	23	14	28	5	17	1	11	0
Mollusc	12	13	9	5	18	26	19	8
Benthic foraminiferans	6	11	18	23	19	42	14	8
Calcareous red algae	17	8	14	2	8	0	16	0
Calcareous green algae (mainly *Halimeda*)	24	28	16	62	23	8	21	16
Other skeletal	14	8	10	3	11	19	4	2
Non-skeletal (includes micritized grains)	4	18	5	0	4	4	15	66

Reef cements include fringes, fans and botry-oids of acicular aragonite crystals, and blades, micrite and peloidal micrite of Mg calcite (see section 8.3.1). Open voids have isopachous or equant cements, whereas more confined voids commonly show much larger and irregular crystals. Syntaxial acicular aragonite is often found within coral skeletal cavities, and norm-ally predates Mg calcite cement where both are present. Mg calcite cements tend to form, in reefal areas of high hydraulic energy and/or low sedimentation, as dense crusts in the outer chambers of coral skeletons, and thus may preserve internal skeletal porosity.

Back-reef storm deposits and coral cays are the highest in the reef complex, and with pro-longed emergence can develop freshwater lenses which will bring about mineral stabilization. This diagenesis results in the dissolution of aragonite skeletons, such as corals, the alteration of Mg calcite to calcite and the precipitation of calcite (and locally dolomite formation). In regions of high rainfall, extensive leaching can produce networks of caves (Figure 14.41) in the vadose zone of raised reef limestones.

The rigid skeletal framework, strengthened by marine cements, produces a massive structure which does not compact like the surrounding mechanically deposited sediments. The ana-stomosing framework also inhibits the compac-tion of internal sediments, so delicate peloidal textures are normally well preserved in shelter cavities. However, this framework rigidity may cause the reef to behave in a brittle manner during later diagenesis, resulting in extensive fracturing. Periodic adjustments of the frame-work during compaction brings about the depo-sition of multiple generations of any loose inter-nal sediment within original and diagenetic cavities.

Facies association. The arrangement of facies shown in Figure 14.36 is common for most platform margin reefs. Though the *in-situ* reef framework (or core) may be poorly represented

Figure 14.41 Cavernous raised reef limestone. Inner margin of raised Miocene reef, Mangaia, Cook Islands, Pacific. Photograph courtesy of David Stoddart

in the fossilized limestone, there is usually a clear distinction between the sloping wedges of con-glomeratic fore-reef talus deposits and the more horizontal back-reef sands, allowing the former position of the zone of maximum production (the core) to be deduced. The interplay of calcium carbonate accretion, vertical tectonic move-ments and eustatic sea-level change causes basic trends in the migration of the laterally equivalent facies. In this discussion I will use the expression '*relative* sea-level change' to indicate the net response of eustatic fluctuations, regional uplift and subsidence, and reef growth.

(i) *A relative lowering of sea-level* terminates the growth of the uppermost shallow-water corals by their exposure, but growth may continue down at the new lower level. If relative sea-level falls intermittently, with stillstand periods when marginal reefs can form, a terraced effect results, and when the relative sea-level is continually falling, then the oldest reef will be exposed at the top and the terraces become progressively younger lower down.

Barbados in the lesser Antilles of the Caribbean Sea is located close to the junction of two colliding plates of the Earth's crust, and is being uplifted on a fore-arc ridge by as much as 3 mm/year. The glacio-eustatic sea-level changes of the Pleistocene have punctuated this steady rise of the island so that now a sequence of Pleistocene reef limestones caps the deep-water Pliocene and earlier sediments (Figure 14.42). The terraces (which on Barbados are well developed only on the leeward side of the island) are progressively younger (with one or two exceptions), from 700 000 years BP at the top to 60 000 years BP near to modern sea-level. The cliffs at the front of each terrace normally show signs of former coastal erosion and consist of a shallowing-upwards succession of reef-building corals which represent one prograding increment of reef growth during a relative sea-level stillstand (Figure 14.40). The flat terrace surfaces, presently covered with sugar-cane fields, represent the extent of the reef flat and back-reef sands

facies at the close of each sea-level phase (Figure 14.25).

(ii) *A relative rise of sea-level* will have different effects upon a reef, depending upon whether or not $CaCO_3$ production can keep pace with the marine transgression (Figure 14.43). If the rate of $CaCO_3$ production exceeds the rate of transgression the reef will build upwards until sea-level is reached, and continued expansion will be purely lateral. But if the rates of reef growth and rising sea-level are in balance, then extension will be essentially vertical, building a thick reefal accumulation. As the $CaCO_3$ production is most rapid at the rim, then a deep-water back-reef lagoon will develop with continued sea-level rise. Atolls develop in this manner.

When sea-level rise is too rapid for the reef growth to keep pace, the reef core may retreat landward over the back-reef talus, developing a transgressive reef. However, in this situation it is perhaps more common for the old reef to cease growth and become drowned; any later reef growth starts anew at a separate site some distance landward from the abandoned reef (Figure 14.44)

14.4.3 Atolls: a special type of reef-rimmed platform

Atolls are annular reefs with deep central lagoons (Figure 14.45). They are formed by the

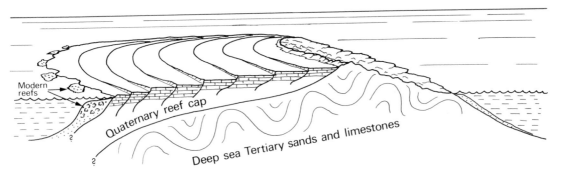

Figure 14.42 Schematic cross-section of Barbados Island showing the terraced Quaternary reefs capping deep-sea Tertiary sands and limestones. In general the reef terraces are younger at lower levels

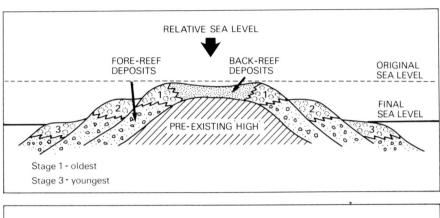

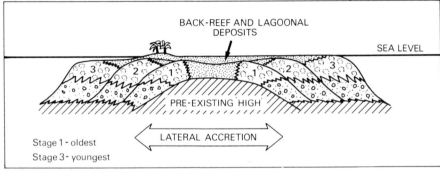

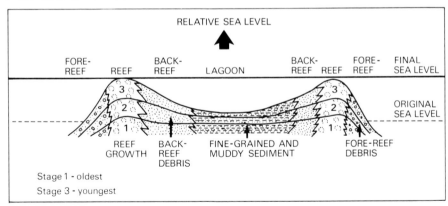

Figure 14.43 Responses of reef growth to regression, stable sea-level and transgression. After Longman (1981)

continued upward and seaward growth of reef-builders while the foundations subside. Where mid-ocean volcanic islands reach sea-level in the warm tropics, fringing reefs build on the rocky shores. With time, as the volcanic foundations cool and contract, the islands subside, subjecting the reefs to a relative sea-level rise. The initial rates of subsidence (first 2 Ma) of mid-ocean ridges are 0.2 mm per year and for mature ocean crust the rate is 0.02 mm per year. Under favourable conditions the reefs grow upwards at a pace equal to that of the foundation subsidence, and

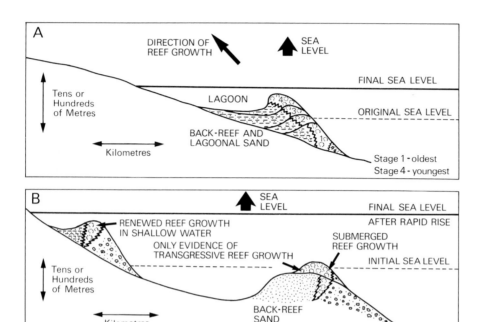

Figure 14.44 Responses of reef growth when sea-level rise exceeds the rate of reef growth. After Longman (1981)

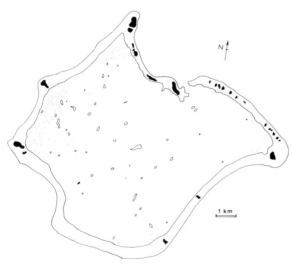

Figure 14.45 Suwarrow atoll, Cook Islands, Pacific

as the volcanic cone subsides, become separated from the coast by a progressively deepening lagoon. This is the barrier reef stage. The old volcano is lowered and dissected by subsidence and erosion until eventually it sinks below sea-level and an atoll is born (Figure 14.46). Charles Darwin put forward his theory of atoll evolution by subsidence of volcanic foundations in 1842, but it was not until 1951, when basalt was reached at 1267 m depth in a borehole through Enewetak Atoll in the Pacific Ocean, that the subsidence theory was confirmed. The limestones recovered were all of shallow-water origin, demonstrating both subsidence of the atoll and upward growth of shallow-water corals since Eocene time, approximately 49 million years BP.

We can see the lateral expression of this

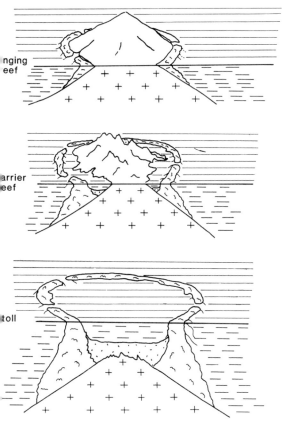

Figure 14.46 The evolution of an atoll via fringing and barrier reef stages by the subsidence of the volcanic foundations

Figure 14.47 Distribution and ages of atolls, barrier and fringing reefs on the Society Island Chain

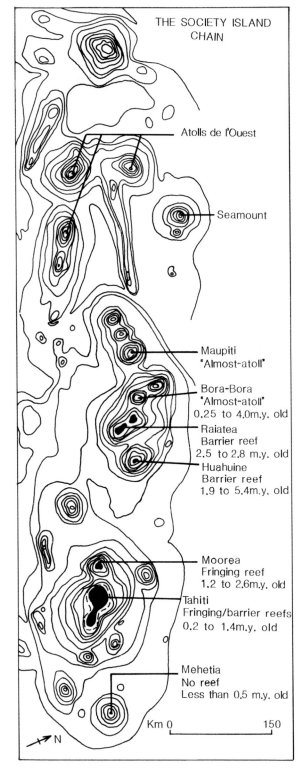

THE SOCIETY ISLAND CHAIN

Atolls de l'Ouest

Seamount

Maupiti "Almost-atoll"

Bora-Bora "Almost-atoll" 0.25 to 4.0m.y. old

Raiatea Barrier reef 2.5 to 2.8 m.y. old

Huahuine Barrier reef 1.9 to 5.4m.y. old

Moorea Fringing reef 1.2 to 2.6m.y. old

Tahiti Fringing/barrier reefs 0.2 to 1.4m.y. old

Mehetia No reef Less than 0.5 m.y. old

Km 0   150

N

subsidence on volcanic island chains, which owe their origins to the migration of the oceanic crustal plate over relatively fixed magma sources or 'hot spots', e.g. the Hawaiian and Society Island chains. The reefal development along the Society chain shows the fringing–barrier–atoll trend in a northwesterly direction away from the present igneous centre as the volcanic islands progressively cool and subside with age (Figure 14.47).

In reality, the subsidence trend is rarely so regular and simple along volcanic island chains, because of the loading effects associated with vulcanism. When a volcanic island builds on the oceanic crust, the lithosphere starts to sag and a wide (tens of kilometres) moat is created around the island. Any atolls located in this zone of depression would subside more rapidly than normal. The lithosphere behaves elastically, and the moating (subsidence) is accompanied by a much less pronounced peripheral bulging (uplift), so that any atolls located at the zone of arching would suffer a vertical movement (of some tens of metres), the reverse of the normal

(cooling) trend, and may be raised above sea-level. Mangaia in the Cook islands of the southern Pacific ocean is a good example of a coral reef raised by lithospheric flexuring. Mangaia has an eroded volcanic core, 17 Ma old, surrounded by high exposed coral reefs of Miocene to Pleistocene age (Figure 14.41). The uplift of this island occurred about 1.5 Ma ago, when nearby Raratonga erupted and built a large volcanic edifice which loaded the immediate lithosphere, causing the arching of the lithosphere in the vicinity of Mangaia.

So we see in general that mid-ocean volcanic islands subside as they cool, and the coral reefs that fringe the shores develop into atolls. If the edifice migrates on the drifting ocean crust out of the tropics into colder seas, then the rate of calcium carbonate deposition may become slower than the subsidence and a drowned atoll results (Figure 14.48). The latitude at which growth rate is unable to keep pace with subsidence has been termed the Darwin Point. For the North Pacific the Darwin Point is at 28 °N on the Hawaiian island chain at Kure atoll. North of

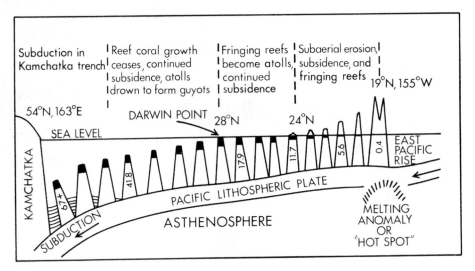

Figure 14.48 Schematic illustration of the Hawaiian–Emperor chain migrating on the Pacific plate towards the Kamchatka trench. At a latitude of 28 °N (the Darwin Point) reef growth slows to a rate that cannot keep up with subsidence, and guyots result. After Grigg (1982)

this point, the volcanic chain is submerged, and cold-water carbonates now veneer the drowned coral reefs. Eventually these carbonate-covered volcanic edifices, carried on the drifting ocean crust, may be engulfed in a subduction zone. The oldest sea-mounts in the Pacific ocean are Cretaceous in age, and have elevated reefal rims constructed of rudists.

Though we can account for the characteristic profile of atolls (raised coral framework rims and central lagoonal depressions) by the interaction of peripheral reef growth and foundation subsidence, it is possible that the surface 'dish' morphology was enhanced by freshwater dissolution when the limestone was exposed to the atmosphere during times of lowered sea-level. Experimentation with acid on limestone blocks and studies of karst landforms (Purdy 1974) have shown that during emergence the rim of a limestone platform suffers less dissolution than the interior (though some local residual towers may remain prominent). Such karst development might be expected to have occurred several times on atolls and limestone shelves during periods of low sea-level in the Pleistocene. On re-advance of the sea (interglacial) over the limestone platform, carbonate production, especially coral reef growth, would be greatest on the elevated rims and prominent knolls (Figure 14.49). Several morphological features of modern reefs, includ-

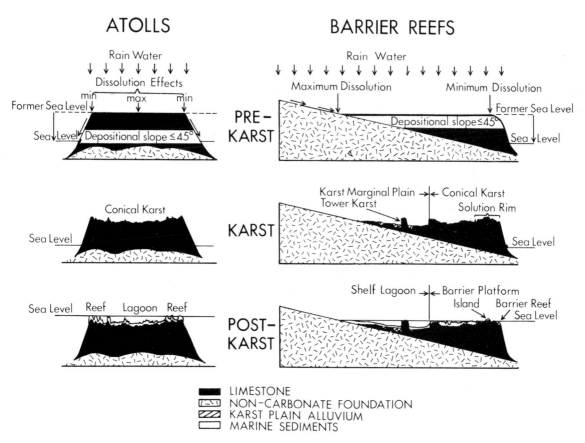

Figure 14.49 Diagrammatic evolution of atolls and barrier reefs according to antecedent karst theory. The sequences begin with subaerial exposure and terminate with depositional consequences of a drowned karst topography. After Purdy (1974)

Table 14.2 Major types of submarine mass transport on slopes and suggested criteria for their recognition. After Cook and Mullins (1983).

Types of mass transport	Cross-section	Internal mechanical behaviour	Transport mechanism and dominant sediment support	Sedimentary structures and bed geometry
Rockfall			Freefall and rolling single blocks.	Grain-supported framework, variable matrix, disorganized. May be elongate parallel to slope and narrow perpendicular to slope.
Slide translational (glide)		Elastic	Shear failure along discrete shear planes subparallel to underlying beds.	Bedding may be undeformed and parallel to underlying beds or deformed, especially at base and margins. Hummocky, slightly convex at top. 10s to 1000s of metres wide and long.
Slide rotational (slump)			Shear failure along discrete concave-up shear planes accompanied by rotation of slide.	Bedding may be undeformed. Upper and lower contacts commonly deformed. Internal bedding at angular discordance to enclosing strata. Size variable.
Debris flow		Plastic	Shear distributed throughout the sediment mass. Clasts supported above base of bed by cohesive strength of mudmatrix and clast buoyancy.	Clasts matrix supported; clasts may exhibit random fabric thoughout the bed or oriented subparallel especially at base and top of flow units. Normal and inverse grading possible. Sheet to channel shaped bodies cms to several 10s of metres thick and 100s to 1000s of metres long.
Grain flow			Cohesionless sediment supported by dispersive pressure.	Massive; clast A-axis parallel to flow and imbricate upstream, inverse grading may occur near base. Scours on base and flat top.
Fluidized flow		Fluid	Cohesionless sediment supported by upward motion of escaping pore fluid.	Dewatering structures, sandstone dykes, flame and load structures, convolute bedding, homogenized sediment.
Turbidity current flow			Clasts supported by fluid turbulence.	Bouma sequences; sole markings on base, good grading, laminations and ripples. Millimetres to several 10s of cm thick, 10s to 1000s of metres in length, width variable.

ing lagoons, reef rim passes, spurs and grooves, patch reefs and faroes (annular reefs on atoll margins) have been explained by a karst land-form control on reef foundations.

14.5 Platform slope–basin margins

Setting and geometry. The zone between the platform margin and basin is characterized by a slope which can be gentle (0.5°) or steep (90°). The slope decreases in grade with depth and merges imperceptibly with the abyssal zone, tens or hundreds of km from the platform margin. Carbonate platform slopes tend to be steeper than terrigenous platform slopes, since the CaCO₃ deposits frequently show signs of synde-positional lithification. Carbonate slope deposits are transitional from the rapidly produced shallow-water platform carbonates to the slow rain of fine-grained pelagic sediments in the basin. The break in slope at the platform edge commonly occurs at a marginal escarpment; this passes basinwards into talus slope, gullied slope, base of slope apron, basin margin and basin. Gentle accreting slopes which merge with the basin floor are termed 'depositional slopes', whereas steep slopes with a submarine escarp-ment across which sediment is transported from shallow to deep water, without significant depo-sition on the slope itself, are termed 'by-pass slopes' (Figure 14.50).

The rim may be reefal or sand-shoal, and its form varies according to tectonics, dominant organisms, submarine lithification, the presence of platform margin islands which influence hy-draulic forces at the margin, sea-level changes, and antecedent topography.

Mass-movement processes under gravity are the dominant modes of mobilization, transport and deposition in the slope environment. The gravity-induced processes include rockfall, slides, slumps and sediment gravity flows (Table 14.2), which are subdivided according to their internal mechanical behaviour. The mass flows of debris, mud and grain flows behave

plastically, whereas liquefied flows, fluidized flows and turbidity current flows behave as viscous fluids. These deposits grade into one another, one type transforms into another and several may be found together.

Sediment input on carbonate slopes is usually along a line source (or numerous closely-spaced small gullies) rather than the point source of a canyon typical of terrigenous slopes. The debris apron has an overall wedge shape as opposed to the cone which results from the channel-fan system. A slope–base of slope apron–basin model is characterized by a transition from slide to mass flow to fluidal flow deposition.

Sedimentary/biogenic structures. The slope set-ting and its instability are indicated by geopetals at an angle to the bedding, slumps and deformed beds, talus blocks, breccias, imbrication, graded beds, Bouma sequences, and sole markings.

Characteristic sedimentary structures are as-sociated with the different types of mass trans-port deposit which are described in more length in the following section on grain composition and texture.

Biogenic structures are rare in the coarse slope deposits, but during calm episodes, when fine-grained sediment accumulates, an infauna, dominantly of worms and crustaceans, can surv-ive, producing burrows within the sediment and feeding traces on the sea-bed. Preserved burrows may be branched and spiral, such as these of the trace fossils *Chondrites* and *Zoophycos,* and feeding trails are recorded on bedding planes as spoked, reticulated and meandrine patterns.

Biota. Most of this zone lies below the photic zone, so living algae are absent. The episodic deluges of sediments are detrimental to most benthos, and only in stable areas of slow sedi-mentation are bottom-dwellers common. These locations are the sites of possible sea-bed lithific-ation, so sessile epilithic organisms such as sponges, alcyonarians and deep-water stony corals are found in scattered communities (e.g. on the lithified mounds or 'lithoherms', at 700 m

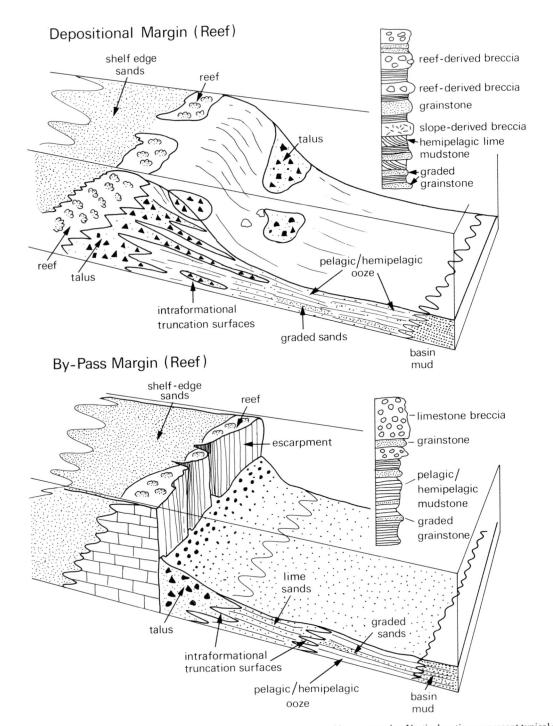

Figure 14.50 Reef rimmed platform margins that have depositional and by-pass modes. Vertical sections represent typical slope accumulations. After McIlreath and James (1979)

depth in the Florida Straits (Figure 6.11). Thickets of corals, such as *Oculina varicosa* (50–125 m depth) and *Lophelia pertusa* (Figure 4.31) (200 and 1000 m depth) provide a habitat for crustaceans, ophiuroids, crinoids, bivalves, brachiopods, echinoids, anemones, bryozoans and worms. Deep-water epilithic organisms also grow on the blocks of reef talus that accumulate on the slope.

Skeletons of pelagic organisms accumulate as sediments fall from suspension. These organisms will be discussed in the later section on the basin setting.

Grain composition and texture. Slope deposits originate in three ways (i) platform edge accumulations, e.g. reefal sediments, ooids and muds, washed off the platform; (ii) resedimented slope deposits, and (iii) pelagic rain falling from suspension.

(i) Reefal sediment includes loose debris channelled down grooves to spread out on the fore-reef slope, and pieces of shallow-water reef framework that have become unstable and dislodged by asymmetric growth and by biological and physical erosion. The coarse talus does not travel far from the escarpment and forms a narrow apron at the slope top. Sand-shoal platform margins provide debris for slope sedimentation, especially on the leeward sides of platforms. Platform sand sediment is deposited by gravity on windward slopes where platform-edge islands interrupt the normal on-platform accumulation by the prevailing windward transport. Ebb tides also transfer loose sediment from platform margins to the slope setting. Off-platform sand transport occurs as sharp pulses when platforms are initially flooded during sea-level rise, and at the pre-emergence stage during sea-level fall. When platforms are exposed, relatively little sediment is shed off the margins. Also, when platforms are well covered, by, for example, 10–20 m of sea water, then sea-grasses and algal mats effectively stabilize the sands and

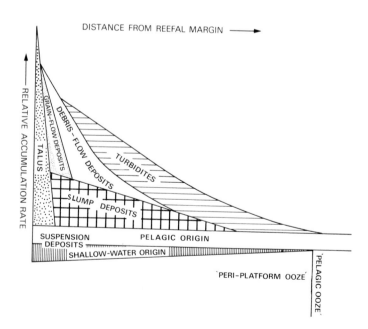

Figure 14.51 Relative sediment contributions by different transport processes on fore-reef carbonate slopes with varying distance from reef-bound basin margin. After Enos and Moore (1983)

muds, reducing their supply to the margins throughout normal wave and tidal conditions, though not during storms.

(ii) The rockfall, slide and gravity-flow deposits indicated in Table 4.2 progressively supersede one another down the platform slopes (Figure 14.51). Rockfalls include the coarse talus derived from steep reef fronts or limestone escarpments (Figure 14.52). The blocks, which

normally show signs of marine cementation, accumulate in chaotic deposits that form narrow wedges at the base of the escarpment. Slides can be translational (glide) or rotational (slump). The shear plane of a translational slide is along a planar or gently undulating surface parallel to underlying beds. Rotational slides (slumps) have concave-up (listric) shear planes (Figure 14.53) and a backward rotation of the slumped body.

Figure 14.52 Sawn quarry face revealing exposure of fore-reef talus blocks composed of massive stromatoporoids cemented by a fibrous (marine) cement. Devonian, Wirbelau, Germany

Figure 14.54 Buckling and *in-situ* brecciation of platy nodular limestones produced by slope creep within differentially lithified nodular lime muds. Lens cap 50 mm. Cambrian, Central North Greenland. Photograph courtesy of Jon Ineson, reproduced with permission of Greenland Geological Survey

Figure 14.53 Laminated dolomitic lime mudstones with small-scale discontinuities produced by draping of minor slump scars. Scar surfaces have low-angle listric form. Lens cap 50 mm. Cambrian, Central North Greenland. Photograph courtesy of Jon Ineson, reproduced with permission of Greenland Geological Survey

Figure 14.55 Slump folding in carbonate slope deposits. Cliff face 3 m. Tertiary, Cyprus. Photograph courtesy of Simon Eaton

The lime-muds of the slope facies are prone to downslope creep (Figure 14.54). Slump folding is common (Figure 14.55). Slumps require steep slopes, rapid sedimentation, fine-grained sediment and lack of cement. The slump folds show no mixing of grains on account of the general cohesion of the slumped body, but we note mixing of lithologies by the juxtaposition of successive allochthonous slump masses.

Sediment gravity flows are distinguished by the forces that support the grains during the downslope movement. In debris flows the larger grains are supported by matrix; in grain flows the sediment is supported by grain collisions; in liquefied flow the cohesionless sediment is supported by upward displacement of fluid as grains settle. The support in fluidized flow is similar, being by upward motion of escaping pore fluids. In turbidity current flow the sediment is supported by the upwards component of fluid turbulence.

Debris flows form breccias or megabreccias (Figures 14.56, 14.57) on slopes of about 1°. Such deposits occur in sheets or lenticular masses 0.5 m to tens of metres thick, and extend tens of kilometres basinwards. The lower boundaries are sharp and usually conformable. Clasts normally float in a matrix, though clast-support is common. Sorting is very poor. Clast orientation is normally chaotic, though particles near the base commonly parallel the base. Downslope imbrication of clasts is reported. The breccias may be polymict, i.e. made up of clasts from various sources, containing reefal debris, frag-

Figure 14.56 Graded carbonate debris flow with turbidite top. Incipient incorporation of unconsolidated lime mud into debris flow base at lower left. Hammer 300 mm. Jurassic, Al Ajal, Oman. Photograph courtesy of David Cooper

Figure 14.57 Slope-derived clast-supported limestone conglomerate composed of angular platy slabs of laminated lime mudstone in a wackestone matrix, probably deposited from a high-density sediment gravity flow. Clast fabric crudely parallel to bedding and shows normal grading at the top passing into a laminated grainstone. Lens cap 50 mm. Cambrian, Central North Greenland. Photograph courtesy of Jon Ineson, reproduced with permission of Greenland, Geological Survey

ments of cemented shoal and even tidal flat deposits, individual skeletons and intraclasts. Muddy intraclasts increase basinwards and may plastically deform to give a flaser breccia fabric. Where lateral displacement is slight, internal breccias result which are oligomict with closely fitted angular clasts. These breccia beds are the result of metastably packed sediments becoming differentially cemented and then sloughing away downslope by failure in uncemented layers. There is then a strong similarity between breccia clasts and cemented nodules of thin-bedded sands. The clasts are angular and do not show signs of abrasion (Figure 14.54).

Grain flows, which behave as either a plastic or a highly viscous fluid, need very high slopes to be generated and maintained, and are rare. They show grading which is normally inverse; clasts 'float' near to the top of the deposit, grain

Figure 14.58 Graded radiolarian wackestone turbidite deposits with parallel laminated (locally rippled) bases. Replacement chert forms ribbons in centre of beds. Lens cap 50 mm. Jurassic, W. Hanya, Oman. Photograph courtesy of David Cooper

orientations are parallel to the flow direction, and injection structures occur at the base of the deposit.

Carbonate turbidites spread many kilometres into the basin. The deposits are well bedded and characteristically have sharp planar bases which may or may not truncate the underlying units (Figure 14.58). Bouma divisions A,B,C,D and E (Figure 14.59) may be present within the turbidite beds, though in some carbonate turbidite sequences the D and E divisions are omitted, whereas in the more distal turbidites it is the A and B divisions that are commonly absent. Sole markings, such as flute casts (Figure 14.60) are found but not widely reported.

If carbonate sand shoals form the platform margin, then grain flows and turbidites and debris flows with calcarenite clasts are the dominant slope sediment. But if the platform is reef-rimmed, coarse breccias of debris flows are the main resedimented deposit.

(iii) Two types of suspension deposit occur in

Figure 14.60 Conjugate parabolic, with subordinate asymmetrical, flute casts on base of calciturbidite. Lens cap 50 mm. Jurassic, W. Nayid, Oman. Photograph courtesy of David Cooper

the slope setting; peri-platform ooze and pelagic ooze. Peri-platform ooze is a mixture of storm-generated shelf-derived mud and pelagic mud. Fine-grained platform sediments are dominantly of aragonite composition, whereas most pelagic

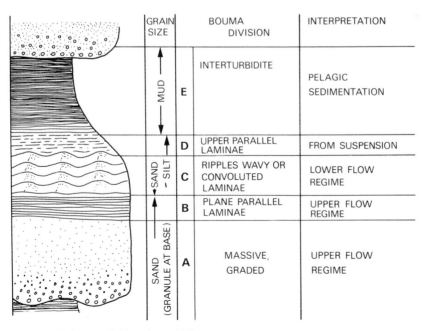

GRAIN SIZE		BOUMA DIVISION	INTERPRETATION
MUD	E	INTERTURBIDITE	PELAGIC SEDIMENTATION
SAND – SILT	D	UPPER PARALLEL LAMINAE	FROM SUSPENSION
	C	RIPPLES WAVY OR CONVOLUTED LAMINAE	LOWER FLOW REGIME
	B	PLANE PARALLEL LAMINAE	UPPER FLOW REGIME
SAND (GRANULE AT BASE)	A	MASSIVE, GRADED	UPPER FLOW REGIME

Figure 14.59 Bouma divisions for turbidites

skeletons are calcite (the major exception is pteropods). Increases in the abundance of mixed-composition peri-platform ooze deposits in an interbedded succession with normal pelagic oozes may represent cycles in the flooding of the platform. Slope deposits of peri-platform ooze are monotonous, dark grey, fine-grained, lime mudstones, that are thinly bedded with flat planar contacts and internal microlaminations. Shale alternations are common and nodular bedding can occur. Modern carbonate muds of pelagic origin contain planktonic foraminiferans, pteropods, juvenile planktonic bivalves, and coccoliths. Other material from suspension includes biogenic silica, terrigenous mud and pyroclastic material. These deposits are generally dark-coloured, contain fine laminations or are bioturbated, and occur in thick structureless beds. They will be discussed further in the section dealing with basins.

Diagenetic overprint. A wide spectrum of diagenetic textures is possible in this setting which ranges from shallow turbulent waters to deep calm waters. Talus breccias commonly contain boulders showing evidence of marine cement in the form of Mg calcite peloidal micrite or crusts of aragonite. These boulders themselves may be cemented together by crusts of marine cements (Figure 14.52) at the escarpment base.

Further down the slope, hardgrounds are present in areas of slow sedimentation. The marine cement will inhibit the mechanical and chemical compaction of these layers, whereas uncemented bands may later show considerable suturing of grains after deep burial. Some areas of incipient marine cementation can develop a nodular or, with synsedimentary movement, a brecciated, texture. The inter-nodular sediment may show considerable pressure dissolution on compaction, giving a flaser bedded structure. Aragonite marine cements are less common at depth and calcite cements become more depleted in Mg^{2+} with depth. In areas of slow sedimentation, glauconite may precipitate, especially

within foraminiferal tests. Iron manganese and phosphatic salts precipitate as reddened crusts on hardground surfaces in this bathyal setting. Fine-grained organic-rich calcareous sediments may develop framboids of pyrite during SO_4^{2-} reduction, and also fine rhombs of authigenic dolomite.

Facies associations. The style of carbonate sedimentation is a function of the abruptness of the margin-to-basin transition and the nature of the shallow portion of the margin. Where slopes are gentle and decrease basinward to merge with the flat basin floor, depositional margins develop; but where slopes are steep so sediments are transported directly from shallow to deep water, a by-pass margin develops. Each type may have reefal shallow-water deposits or lime-sand shoal deposits at the adjacent platform edge.

Depositional margins with shallow-water reefs (Figure 14.50) have a narrow zone of peri-platform talus, but many of the allochthonous deposits generated high on the slope are deposited far down the slope. The mass movements that transport this debris may by-pass the zone immediately seaward of the peri-platform talus leaving only hemipelagic sediments to accumulate here. Where shallow-water lime sands flank the slope, sedimentation is active all along the slope profile. Turbidites and grain flows are the predominant transport mechanisms whereas debris sheets are rare. Hardgrounds, nodular beds and *in-situ* breccias are common on these slopes. By-pass margins adjacent to shallow-water reefs are characterized by a debris apron near the base of the escarpment composed of a wedge of reefal talus (Figure 14.50). These talus deposits may interdigitate along strike with carbonate submarine fans deposited from channels in the escarpment. If the shallow-water margin facies is lime-sand on a by-pass margin, then the peri-platform talus will be predominantly lime-sand intercalated with lime-mud. Any limestone blocks present may be cemented platform sediments derived from the submarine cliff.

14.6 Basins

Setting and geometry. Basinal limestones are normally deposited in deep water (*c.* 200 m to 4500 m), well removed from terrigenous supply. The carbonate sediments that accumulate here are of two types: (i) oozes that result from the accumulation of planktonic skeletons, and (ii) sediments derived from the platform margin and slope.

In modern oceans, calcareous oozes are widespread and fairly monotonous, producing blanket deposits of well-bedded chalks (firmly consolidated oozes) (Figure 14.61) and basinal limestones (well-lithified oozes). Lithification increases with age and depth of burial. Siliceous oozes undergo similar progressive consolidation during diagenesis, from ooze (radiolarite or diatomite) to porcellanite and eventually to chert. Platform-derived sediments can spread many kilometres on to the basin floor, but are most prolific in linear prisms at the foot of the platform slope or as cones and fans of sediment at canyon mouths. Sediments derived from the platform margin and slope have been described in the previous section and will receive only minor attention here.

Oozes accumulate today in those parts of the oceans where the plankton thrives in abundance and where the sea-bed lies above the carbonate

Figure 14.61 Well-bedded chalks. Cliff 4 m high, Tertiary, Cyprus

compensation depth. The controls on the production of pelagic organisms in surface waters are nutrient supply from upwelling deeper water, water temperature, light and salinity. These controls in turn are dependent upon climate and patterns of ocean circulation. Most present-day calcareous plankton production is in warm surface waters of tropical and temperate seas. Some planktonic organisms can tolerate a wide range of temperatures and salinities and are found in polar surface waters and in low salinity areas such as the Black Sea (salinity 17‰). Siliceous plankton is concentrated in areas of cooler surface waters and high nutrient supply (e.g. Antarctic and equatorial divergences).

Basinal sediments accumulate at very low rates (e.g. 10–30 mm per 1000 years) compared to shallow-water deposits (e.g. tens of cm to a few m per 1000 years). If less than 25% of the size fraction greater than 5 μm of the basin sediments is of terrigenous, volcanogenic and/or platform origin we define the sediments as *pelagic*, but if these constituents occur in abundances greater than 25% then the deposits are said to be *hemipelagic*. There are pelagic limestones which were deposited in relatively shallow waters; for example, much of the Upper Cretaceous chalk of western Europe accumulated on sea-floors between 50 and 400 m depth. Unlike deep-sea basinal limestones, these relatively shallow chalks contain abundant benthonic skeletal remains, but were clearly deposited well away from terrigenous sources during widespread transgressions.

The distribution and accumulation of deep-sea carbonates are a function of the rate of supply versus dissolution. As ocean waters deepen they become colder, richer in dissolved CO_2 and progressively undersaturated with respect to calcium carbonate. Fine pelagic particles dissolve as they fall through the water column and rest on the deep sea-bed. Aragonite is dissolved at shallower depths than calcite (Figure 14.62). For example, at present in the North Atlantic Ocean, aragonite dissolves at

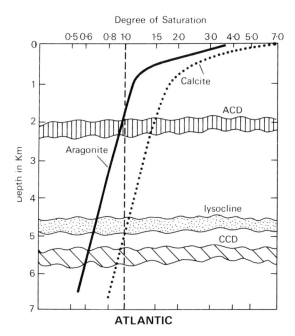

Figure 14.62 Degree of saturation of sea water with respect to aragonite and calcite in the Atlantic Ocean. The lysocline marks the top of a zone of greatly increased rates of dissolution. *ACD* and *CCD* are the aragonite and calcite compensation depths respectively. After Broecker (1974)

2 km and calcite at 5 km depth (these depths have varied through time and between oceans). The level within the ocean where calcite dissolution greatly increases is known as the *lysocline*, and the depths below which no aragonite and calcite pelagic sediments accumulate are known as the aragonite and calcite compensation depths. Thus, there is a depth zone within which aragonite dissolves and calcite does not. A carbonate may be thermodynamically soluble in the solution with which it is in contact, that is, its solubility product is greater than the ion activity product of calcium and carbonate ions in solution, but it may still not dissolve at a measurable rate. One of the reasons for this is that the carbonate particles may be coated in a protective organic membrane. Some fine pelagic grains escape dissolution by being incorporated in faecal pellets (of, for example, zooplankton)

which descend to the sea-floor more rapidly than do individual nanoplankton fragments. Also, carbonate grains swept on to the floor of the basin by turbidity currents may be rapidly buried on a sea-bed below the calcite compensation depth, and thus escape dissolution by undersaturated sea water.

Sedimentary/biogenic structures. Large-scale sedimentary structures are rare in pelagic deposits, though locally large channels, slumps and mounds are recorded (Figure 14.63). Small-scale sedimentary structures include rhythmic bedding marked by alternations of clay-rich and clay-poor sediment, zones of chert nodules and alternating carbonate turbidites and pelagic layers. Nodular bedding, flaser bedding and *in-situ* brecciation occur, but are essentially of diagenetic origin. Carbonate turbidites show typical Bouma divisions. Grading is most apparent in the coarser proximal turbidites. Deep-sea currents (e.g. contourites) are capable of producing ripples and winnowing sea-floor sands.

Fine laminations are only well preserved in basinal limestones in areas of poor circulation where oxygen, and hence biogenic activity, is minimal. These deposits of stagnant sea-beds are normally dark and organic-rich. Light colours,

Figure 14.63 Large bedded mounds (*a*) and probable channels with truncated bases (*b*), in chalk. The bedding structures are accentuated by dark bands of chert nodules. Cliff about 70 m high. Cretaceous, Etretat, France

more biogenic structures and fewer preserved sedimentary structures result from stronger circulation.

Well-preserved infaunal burrows and epi- and intrastratal feeding traces are common in pelagic limestones. The large branching burrow *Thalassinoides* is more common in shelf pelagic limestones than deep basins where the deposit-feeding burrow systems of *Planolites*, *Chondrites* and *Zoophycos* occur.

Biota. The skeletal benthic macro-organisms likely to be found in well-oxygenated deep-sea deposits include echinoderms, sponges, crustaceans and deep-water corals. Bryozoans, serpulids and certain agglutinated foraminiferans encrust hardground surfaces. In areas of poor circulation deep-sea benthos is represented mainly by trace fossils, since soft-bodied organisms can sustain themselves in water ten times more deficient in oxygen than that required by skeletal groups. Body fossils of macro-organisms are more common in shelf pelagic limestones than in deep-sea settings. Calcareous planktonic organisms present in modern oceans include foraminiferans, with globigerinids (Figures 4.6, 4.7) the dominant group, which are mainly calcitic ($0-5$ mol% $MgCO_3$); pteropods (Figures 4.15, 4.16) which are planktonic gastropods with an aragonitic shell; and coccolithophores (Figure 4.70) which are minute unicellular algae that produce a skeleton consisting of shields (coccoliths) of tiny calcite crystals (< 1 mol% $MgCO_3$). Other pelagic organisms whose calcareous skeletons contribute (in minor proportions) to deep-sea deposits include planktonic ostracods and pelecypods and nektonic molluscs such as *Nautilus*, *Sepia* and *Spirula*. The quantitatively important siliceous plankton includes radiolaria (protozoa) (Figure 4.69) and diatoms (single-called algae) (Figure 4.71).

Calcareous plankton was not always as abundant in the past as it is now. Coccolithophores evolved during the Jurassic and tended to replace the thin-shelled planktonic bivalves and

ostracods, whereas planktonic foraminiferans did not become widespread until the early Cretaceous. Planktonic calcareous nanofossils were not present during the Palaeozoic, and deep-sea limestones formed during this era were build mainly of very fine platform-derived carbonate grains which accumulated with some nektonic macrofossils, such as cephalopods, and some pelagic skeletons including ostracods, calcispheres, thin-shelled bivalves and cricoconarids (e.g. styliolinids and tentaculities). Mesozoic basinal limestones contain ammonites, belemnites, planktonic echinoderms, sponge spicules, bivalves (especially *Inoceramus* and *Halobia*), brachiopods, ostracods, calcispheres and calpionellids. Ammonites (dominantly aragonite) in many basinal limestones show skeletal dissolution (commonly a mould was formed on the sea-bed and was filled with fine marine sediments), while surrounding calcite (e.g. echinoderm) skeletons are well preserved. The calcitic portions of ammonite skeletons (e.g. aptychi—the plates closing the aperture of the outer chamber) were not affected by dissolution and are disproportionally preserved in some limestones (e.g. the Aptychus Limestones of the Tethyan Mesozoic) which are presumed to have been deposited at depths between the aragonite and calcite compensation depths.

Grain composition and texture. Deep-sea carbonates are normally extremely fine-grained with many nanofossil fragments less than $1 \mu m$ in diameter. Chalks are essentially calcitic and may consist entirely of a poorly-sorted mixture of coccolith ($0.5-20 \mu m$) (Figure 14.64) and planktonic foraminiferan ($25-100 \mu m$) remains. The polymodal grain size distributions have peaks corresponding to the average size of the dominant constituents and their breakdown products. The surface of these skeletons is commonly dull on account of a degree of etching by the cold deep water. Detrital terrigenous components, mostly clays and silts of platform, volcanogenic and wind-blown origins, may constitute $1-50\%$

Figure 14.64 Scanning electron microscope photograph of chalk showing fragments of weakly cemented coccoliths. Scale 7 μm. Cretaceous, Swanage, England

of the sediment. Terrigenous rich chalks are usually called marls. Silica occurs as very fine terrigenous quartz particles, disseminated sponge spicules, or in discrete aggregates as chert nodules. Chert nodules and beds are most prevalent where siliceous organisms were abundant, either in the water column as planktonic tests (radiolarians and diatoms), or on the sea-bed (sponges). Silica is stable at depths deeper than calcite, and so siliceous oozes accumulate at depths below the CCD and, on burial, alter to bedded cherts. Where dissolution of carbonate occurs on the sea-bed and sedimentation is very slow, a residual clay results.

Carbonate turbidites contain platform-derived particles such as ooids, muds and benthic skeletons which have a range of mineralogies: aragonite, Mg calcite and calcite. Slope-derived turbidites tend to be of pelagic origin, and are hence primarily calcitic in composition.

Diagenetic overprint. Calcium carbonate grains are susceptible to dissolution in the cold, CO_2-rich waters of the deep oceans. Above the calcite compensation depth, aragonite skeletons may be leached on the sea-bed to leave moulds in the firm sediment. This $CaCO_3$ may precipitate locally, in

some places around fossils, forming nodules. Generally, sea-bed lithification is uncommon in the deep sea, but under certain conditions nodules or hardgrounds do form. Hardground formation is favoured by long contact with sea water, and occurs mostly in areas of slow sedimentation or current winnowing. Thus, hardgrounds are most abundant on topographic highs or restricted straits (especially at times of relatively lowered sea-level). The calcite cements of hardgrounds are progressively Mg-poor with descending depth (12 mol% $MgCO_3$ at 500 m, 3 mol% $MgCO_3$ at 2000 m). Calcium phosphate, glauconite and iron and manganese salts also precipitate in hardgrounds. Fossils examples of these settings commonly show multiple hardgrounds with significant amounts of time (10^5 years) representing each lithification surface. These *condensed* sequences often show zones of banded, rust-coloured iron staining that gradually intensifies towards the hardground surface. The hardground surfaces are sharp and commonly show truncation features, organic encrustations and endolith boreholes. Marine lithification may differentially cement burrow fillings which can lead to a nodular texture. If the cemented portions are later exhumed by current winnowing, a pebble bed can result.

The essentially low-Mg calcite composition of most pelagic sediments gives them a chemical stability early in their history, unlike platform or platform-derived carbonates of mixed mineralogies. Consequently, it is not until deep burial that significant lithification of an ooze into a chalk takes place. Deep burial produces mechanical and chemical compaction effects, such as crushing of delicate shells, and suturing of grains. Compaction effects are not seen in hardgrounds. The original shapes of burrows are well preserved in the hardground horizons, but deformed by compaction into flattened forms in the adjacent uncemented beds. Chemical compaction of a nodular sea-bed produces pressure dissolution stringers in the matrix and creates a flaser texture to the bedding.

Carbonate turbidites, consisting originally of aragonite and Mg calcite, are prone to leaching of unstable minerals and also to dolomitization by Mg-rich waters during diagenesis. Examination of deep-sea cores commonly reveals the presence of early non-ferroan calcite cement in relatively young calciturbidites that clearly have had no freshwater influence, whereas cement is absent where aragonite fossils are still preserved. It is interpreted from this relationship that the early non-ferroan calcite cemented sediments were deposited below the aragonite lysocline.

Basinal limestones are commonly replaced by chert during diagenesis on account of remobilization of the biogenic silica present in this setting supplied by siliceous plankton and sponges.

Facies associations. Basinal sediments are commonly thick, laterally extensively and monotonous. They may grade laterally and vertically into bedded chert or deep-water terrigenous sediments. Near the basin margin they are interbedded with platform slope deposits. In small restricted basins in areas of high evaporation, evaporite minerals may precipitate from sea water and accumulate in association with pelagic sediments. This happened, for example, in the Miocene of the Mediterranean, where beds of gypsum, anhydrite and halite occur with basinal marls, and in the Permian Basin of west Texas, where anhydrite, halite and sylvite were deposited in water hundreds of metres deep to accumulate in layers overlying dark basinal limestones.

Selected reading

Littoral zone

Butler, G.P., Harris, P.M. and Kendall, C.G.St.C. (1982) Recent evaporites from the Abu Dhabi coastal flats. In *Depositional and Diagenetic Spectra of Evaporites: a core workshop*, SEPM Core Workshop **3**, 33–64.

Ginsburg, R.N. (ed.) (1975) *Tidal Deposits. A Casebook of Recent Examples and Fossil Counterparts.* Springer Verlag, New York.

Hardie, L.A. (ed.) (1977) *Sedimentation on the Modern Carbonate Tidal Flats of N.W. Andros Island, Bahamas.* Johns Hopkins Press, Baltimore.

Inden, R.F. and Moore, C.H. (1983) Beach environment. In Scholle, P.A., Bebout, D.G. and Moore, C.H. (eds.), *Carbonate Depositional Environments*, Am. Ass. Petrol. Geol. Mem **33**, 211–265.

Kendall, C.G.St.G. and Skipwith, P.A. D'E. (1969) Geomorphology of a Recent shallow-water carbonate province: Khor al Bazam, Trucial Coast, southwest Persian Gulf. *Geol. Soc. Am. Bull.* **80**, 865–891.

Kinsman, D.J.J. (1969) Modes of formation, sedimentary associations and diagnostic features of shallow-water and supratidal evaporites. *Amer. Ass. Petrol. Geol. Bull.* **53**, 830–840.

Kirkland, D.W. and Evans, R. (1973) *Marine Evaporites: Origins, Diagenesis and Geochemistry.* Benchmark Papers in Geology. Dowden, Hutchinson & Ross, Stroudsburg.

Logan, B.W. (ed.) (1974) Evolution and diagenesis of Quaternary carbonate sequences, Shark Bay, Western Australia. *Am. Ass. Petrol. Geol. Mem.* **22**, 358.

Patterson, R.J. and Kinsman, D.J.J. (1982) Formation of diagentic dolomite in coastal sabkha along Arabian (Persian) Gulf. *Am. Assoc. Petrol. Geol. Bull.* **66**, 28–43.

Purser, B.H. (ed.) (1973) *The Persian Gulf: Holocene Carbonate Sedimentation and Diagenesis in a Shallow Epicontinental Sea.* Springer Verlag, Berlin.

Schreiber, B.C. (1986) Arid shorelines and evaporites. In Reading, H.G. (ed.), *Sedimentary Environments and Facies*, Blackwell, Oxford.

Shearman, D.J. (1982) Evaporites of coastal sabkhas. In Dean, W.E. and Schreiber, B.C. (eds.), *Marine Evaporites*, SEPM Short Course. **4**, 6–42.

Shinn, E.A. (1983) Tidal flat environment. In Scholle, P.A., Bebout, D.G. and Moore, C.H. (eds.), *Carbonate Depositional Environments*, Am. Ass. Petrol. Geol. Mem. **33**, 171–210.

Shinn, E.A., Lloyd, R.M. and Ginsburg, R.N. (1969) Anatomy of a modern carbonate tidal flat, Andros Island, Bahamas. *J. Sed. Petrol.* **39**, 1202–1228.

Warren, J.K. and Kendall, C.G.St.C. (1985) Comparison of sequences formed in marine sabkha (subaerial) and salina (subaqueous) settings—Modern and ancient. *Am. Ass. Petrol. Geol. Bull.* **69**, 1013–1023.

Wright, V.P. (1984) Peritidal carbonate facies models: a review. *Geol. J.* **19**, 309–325.

Platforms

Ahr, W.M. (1973) The carbonate ramp: an alternative to the shelf model. *Gulf. Coast Ass. Geol. Soc. Trans.* **23**, 221–225.

Ball, M.M., Shinn, E.A. and Stockman, K.W. (1967) The geologic effects of hurricane Donna in south Florida. *J. Geol.* **75**, 583–597.

Broecker, W.S. and Takahashi, T. (1966) Calcium carbonate precipitation on the Bahama Banks. *J. Geophys. Res.* **71**, 1575–1602.

Degens, E.T. and Ross, D.A. (eds.) (1974) *The Black Sea—Geology, Chemistry and Biology.* Am. Ass. Petrol. Geol. Mem. **20**.

Enos, P. (1983) Shelf environment. In Scholle, P.A., Bebout, D.G. and Moore, C.H. (Eds.), *Carbonate Depositional*

Environments, Am. Assoc. Petrol. Geol. Mem. **33**, 267–295.

Enos, P. and Perkins, R.D. (1977) See p. 76.

Fürsich, F.T. (1973) *Thalassinoides* and the origin of nodular limestone in the Corallian Beds (Upper Jurassic) of southern England. *Neues Jb. Geol. Paläont. Mh.* **3**, 136–156.

Ginsburg, R.N. (1956) See p. 76.

Ginsburg, R.N. and James, N.P. (1974) Holocene carbonate sediments of continental shelves. In Burk, C.A. and Drake, C.C. (eds.), *The Geology of Continental Margins*, Springer Verlag, Berlin, 137–155.

Hallam, A. (ed.) (1967) Depth indicators in marine sedimentary environments. *Marine Geol.* **5**, 5/6, 327–567.

Illing, L.V. (1954) Bahamian calcareous sands. *Am. Ass. Petrol. Geologists Bull.* **38**, 1–95.

James, N.P. (1979) Shallowing-upwards sequences in carbonates. In Walker, R.G. (ed.), *Facies Models*, Geoscience Canada Reprint Series 1, 126–136.

Maxwell, W.G.H. (1968) *Atlas of the Great Barrier Reef.*, Elsevier, Amsterdam.

Maxwell, W.G.H. (1973) Sediments of the Great Barrier Reef Province. In Jones, O.A. and Endean, R. (eds.), *Biology and Geology of Coral Reefs, 1.* Geology **1**, 299–346.

Neumann, A.C. and Land, L.S. (1975) Lime mud deposition and calcareous algae in the Bight of Abaco, Bahamas: a budget. *J. Sed. Petrol.* **45**, 763–786.

Newell, N.D., Rigby, J.K., Whiteman, A.J. and Bradley, J.S. (1951) Shoal water geology and environments eastern Andros Island, Bahamas. *Bull. Amer. Mus. Nat. Hist.* **97**, 1–30.

Newell, N.A.D. and Rigby, J.K. (1957) Geological studies on the Great Bahama Bank. In Le Blanc and Breeding, J.G. (eds.), *Regional Aspects of Carbonate Deposition*, SEPM Sp. Pub. **5**, 15–79.

Purdy, E.G. (1963) Recent calcium carbonate facies of the Great Bahama Bank. *J. Geol.* **71**, 334–355.

Purdy, E.G. and Imbrie, J. (1965) Carbonate sediments, Great Bahama Bank: a guidebook for fieldtrip no. 2. *Geol. Soc. Am. Convention*, Nov. 1964.

Scoffin, T.P. and Tudhope, A.W. (1985) Sedimentary environments of the Central Region of the Great Barrier Reef of Australia. *Coral Reefs* **4**, 81–93.

Wantland, K.K. and Pusey, W.C. (eds.) (1975) *Belize Shelf-Carbonate Sediments, Clastic Sediments and Ecology*, A.A.P.G. Studies in Geology **2**, Tulsa.

Wilson, J.L. and Jordan, C. (1983) Middle Shelf environment. In Scholle, P.A., Bebout, D.G. and Moore, C.H. (eds.), *Carbonate Depositional Environments*, Am. Ass. Petrol. Geol. Mem. **33**, 297–343.

Platform margins: sand shoals

Ball, M.M. (1967) Carbonate sand bodies of Florida and the Bahamas. *J. Sed. Petrol.* **37**, 556–591.

Beach, D.K. and Ginsburg, R.N. (1980) Facies Succession, Plio-Pleistocene carbonates, northwestern Great Bahama Bank. *Am. Assoc. Petrol. Geol. Bull.* **64**, 1634–1642.

Harris, P.M. (1979) Facies anatomy and diagenesis of a Bahamian ooid shoal. *Sedimenta.* **7**, University of Miami.

Hine, A.C. (1977) Lily Bank, Bahamas: history of an active oolite sand shoal. *J. Sed. Petrol.* **47**, 1554–1582.

Imbrie, J. and Buchanan, H. (1965) Sedimentary structures in modern carbonate sands of the Bahamas. In Middleton, G.V. (ed.), *Primary Sedimentary Structures and their Hydrodynamic Interpretation*, SEPM Sp. Pub. **12**, 149–172.

Platform margins: reefs

Battistini, R. *et al.* (1975) Éléments de terminologie recifale indopacifique. *Tethys* **7**, 1–111.

Bloom, A.L. (1974) Geomorphology of reef complexes. In *Reefs in Space and Time*, SEPM Sp. Pub. **18**, 1–8.

Darwin, C.R. (1842) *The Structure and Distribution of Coral Reefs.* Smith, Elder and Co., London.

Emery, K.O., Tracey, Jr. J.I. and Ladd, H.S. (1954) Geology of Bikini and nearby atolls. *US Geol. Surv. Prof. Papers* **260-A**: 1–265.

Frost, S.H., Weiss, M.P. and Saunders, J.B. (1977) *Reefs and Related Carbonates—Ecology and Sedimentology.* Amer. Ass. Petrol. Geol. Studies in Geology **4**, 421.

Geister, J. (1983) Holocene West Indian coral reefs: geomorphology, ecology and facies. *Facies* **9**, 173–284.

Goreau, T.F. (1959) The ecology of Jamaican coral reefs. I Species composition and zonation. *Ecology* **40**, 67–89.

Goreau, T.P. and Goreau, N.I. (1973) The ecology of Jamaican Coral Reefs. II Geomorphology, zonation and sedimentary phases. *Bull. Mar. Sci.* **23**, 399–404.

Grigg, R.W. (1982) Darwin point: a threshold for atoll formation. *Coral Reefs* **1**, 29–34.

Heckel, P.H. (1974) Carbonate buildups in the geologic record: a review. In Laporte, L.F. (ed.), *Reefs in Time and Space*, SEPM Sp. Pub. **18**, 90–154.

Hopley, D. (1982) See p. 88.

Hoskin, C.M. (1963) Recent carbonate sedimentation on Alacran Reef, Yucatan, Mexico. *National Academy of Sciences—National Research Council Pub.* **1089**, 1–160.

James, N.P. (1979) Reefs. In Walker, R.G. (ed.), *Facies Models*, Geoscience Canada Reprint Series 1, 121–133.

James, N.P. (1983) Reef environment. In Scholle, P.A., Bebout, D.G. and Moore, C.H. (eds.), *Carbonate Depositional Environments*, Am. Ass. Petrol. Geol. Mem. **33**, 345–440.

James, N.P. and MacIntyre, I.G. (1985) Carbonate depositional environments, Modern and ancient, Part 1. Reefs, zonation, depositional facies and diagenesis. *Colorado School of Mines Quart.* **80**, No. 3.

Kornicker, L.S. and Boyd, D.W. (1962) Shallow water geology and environments of Alacran reef complex Compeche Bank, Mexico. *Am. Assoc. Petrol. Geol. Bull.* **46**, 640–673.

Ladd, H., Tracey, J., Gross, G.M. (1970) Deep drilling on Midway atoll. *US Geol. Survey. Prof. Paper.* **680-A**, 1–22.

Laporte, L.F. (ed.) (1974) *Reefs in Time and Space.* SEPM. Sp. Pub. **18**, 256.

Logan, B.W. (1969) Coral reefs and banks, Yucatan Shelf, Mexico. *Am. Ass. Petrol. Geol. Mem.* **11**, 129–198.

Longman, M.W. (1981) A process approach to recognizing facies of reef complexes. In Toomey, D.F. (ed.), *European*

Fossil Reef Models. SEPM Sp. Pub. **30**, 9–40.

Maiklem, W.R. (1970) Carbonate sediments in the Capricorn Reef Complex Great Barrier Reef, Australia. *J. Sed. Petrol.* **40**, 55–80.

MacNeil, F.S. (1954) The shape of atolls: an inheritance from subaerial erosion forms. *Amer. J. Sci.* **2522**, 402–27.

Maxwell, W.G.H. and Swinchatt, J.P. (1970) Great Barrier Reef: variation in a terrigenous-carbonate province. *Geol. Soc. Am. Bull.* **81**, 691–724.

McKee, E.D. (1956) Geology of Kapingamarangi Atoll, Caroline Islands. *Atoll Res. Bull.* **50**, 1–38.

McKee, E.D., Chronie, J. and Leopold, E.B. (1959) Sedimentary belts in the lagoon of Kapingamarangi Atoll. *Am. Assoc. Petrol. Geol. Bull.* **43**, 501–562.

McNutt, M. and Menard, H.W. (1978) Lithospheric flexure and uplifted atolls. *J. Geophys. Res.* **83**, 1206–1212.

Newell, N.D. (1971) An outline history of tropical organic reefs. *Amer. Mus. Novitates* **2465**, 1–37.

Purdy, E.G. (1974) Reef configurations: cause and effect. In Laporte, L.F. (ed.) *Reefs in Time and Space*, SEPM Sp. Pub. **18**, 9–76.

Rosen, B.R. (1971) Principal features of reef coral ecology in shallow water environments of Mahe, Seychelles. In Stoddart, D.R. and Yonge, C.M. (eds.) *Regional Variation in Indian Ocean Coral Reefs*, Symp. Zool. Soc. London **28**, 163–183.

Rosen, B.R. (1971) The distribution of reef coral genera in the Indian Ocean. In Stoddart, D.R. and Yonge, C.M. (eds.) *Regional Variation in Indian Ocean Coral Reefs*, Symp. Zool. Soc. London, **28**, 263–299.

Scoffin, T.P. and Dixon, J.E. (1983) The distribution and structure of coral reefs: one hundred years since Darwin. *Biol. J.* **20**, 11–38.

Stoddart, D.R. (1969) Ecology and morphology of recent coral reefs. *Biol. Reviews* **44**, 433–498.

Tracey, Jr. J.I., Ladd, H.S. and Hoffmeister, J.E. (1948) Reefs of Bikini, Marshall Islands. *Bull. Geol. Soc. Am.* **59**, 861–887.

Vaughan, T.W. (1911) Physical conditions under which Palaeozoic coral reefs were formed. *Geol. Soc. Amer. Bull.* **22**, 238–252.

Zankl, H. (1971) Upper Triassic carbonate facies in the northern Limestone Alps. In *Sedimentology of Parts of Central Europe Guidebook*, VIII Int. Sediment. Congress 1971, Heidelberg, 147–185.

Platform slope: basin margins

Crevello, P.D. and Schlager, W. (1980) Carbonate debris sheets and turbidites, Exuma Sound, Bahamas. *J. Sed. Petrol.* **50**, 1121–1148.

Cook, H.E. (1979) Ancient continental slope sequences and their value in understanding modern slope development. In Doyle, L.J. and Pilkey, O.H. (eds.), *Geology of Continental Slopes*, SEPM Sp. Pub. **27**, 287–305.

Cook, H.E., McDaniel, P.N., Mountjoy, E.W. and Pray, L.C. (1972) Allochthonous carbonate debris flows at Devonian bank ("reef") margins Alberta, Canada. *Bull. Can. Petrol. Geol.* **20**, 439–497.

Cook, H.E. and Mullins, H.T. (1983) Basin margin environ-ment. In Scholle, P.A. Bebout, D.G. and Moore, C.H. (eds.) *Carbonate Depositional Environments.* Am. Ass. Petrol. Geol. Mem. **33**, 539–617.

Cook, H.E., Hine, A.C. and Mullins, H.T. (1983) Platform margins and deep water carbonates. SEPM. *Short Course* **12**.

Doyle, L.J. and Pilkey, O.H. (eds.) (1979) Geology of continental slopes. SEPM Sp. Pub. **27**, 374.

Enos, P. and Moore, C.H. (1983) Fore-reef slope environment. In Scholle, P.A., Bebout, D.G. and Moore, C.H. (eds.) *Carbonate depositional environments.* Am. Ass. Petrol. Geol. Mem. **33**, 507–537.

Goreau, T.F. and Land, L.S. (1974) Fore-reef morphology and depositional processes, North Jamaica. In Laporte, L.F. (ed.) *Reefs in Time and Space.* SEPM Sp. Pub. **18**, 77–89.

Halley, R.B., Harris, P.M. and Hine, A.C. (1983) Bank margin environment. In Scholle, P.A., Bebout, D.G. and Moore, C.H. (eds.) *Carbonate depositional environments.* Am. Ass. Petrol. Geol. Mem. **33**, 463–506.

Hine, A.C. and Neumann, A.C. (1977) Shallow carbonate bank margin growth and structure, Little Bahama Bank, Bahamas. *Am. Ass. Petrol. Geol. Bull.* **61**, 376–406.

James, N.P. and Ginsburg, R.N. (1979) The seaward margin of Belize Barrier and atoll reefs. *Int. Ass. Sed. Spec. Pub.* **3**.

McIlreath, I.A. and James, N.P. (1979) Carbonate Slopes. In Walker, R.G. (ed.), *Facies Models*, Geoscience Canada Reprint Series 1, 133–149.

Mullins, H.T. and Neumann, A.C. (1979) Deep carbonate bank margin structure and sedimentation in the northern Bahamas. In Doyle, L.J. and Pilkey, O.H. (eds.) *Geology of Continental Slopes.* SEPM Sp. Pub. **27**, 165–192.

Neumann, A.C., Kofoed, J.W. and Keller, G.H. (1977) Lithoherms in the Straits of Florida. *Geology* **5**, 4–10.

Stanley, D.J. and Moore, G.T. (eds.) (1982) *The shelfbreak: critical interface on continental margins.* SEPM Sp. Pub. **33**, 467.

Basins

Berger, W.H. (1974) Deep sea sedimentation. In Burk, C.A. and Drake, C.L. (eds.) *The Geology of Continental Margins*, Springer Verlag, Berlin, 213–241.

Berger, W.H. (1976) Biogenous deep-sea sediments: production preservation and interpretation. In Riley, J.P. and Chester, R. (eds.) *Treatise on Chemical Oceanography*, **5**, Academic Press, London, 265–388.

Broecker, W.S. (1974) See p. 105.

Cook, H.E. and Enos, P. (eds.) (1977) *Deep Water Carbonate Environments.* SEPM Sp. Pub. **25**, 336p.

Funnel, B.M. and Riedel, W.R. (eds.) (1971) *The Micropaleontology of Oceans.* Cambridge University Press.

Garrison, R.E. and Fischer, A.G. (1969) Deep water limestones and radiolarites of the Alpine Jurassic. In Friedman, G.M. (ed.) *Depositional Environments in Carbonate Rocks.* SEPM Sp. Pub. **14**, 20–56.

Hancock, J.M. (1975) The petrology of the chalk. *Proc. Geol. Ass. Lond,* **86**, 499–535.

Hay, W.W. (ed.) (1964) *Studies in Paleo-oceanography.* SEPM Sp. Pub. **20**.

Heezen, B.C. and Hollister, C.D. (1971). *The Face of the Deep*. Oxford University Press, New York.

Hsü, K.J. and Jenkyns, H.C. (eds.) (1974) *Pelagic Sediments on Land and under Sea*. Spec. Pub. Int. Ass. Sedimentologists **1**, Blackwell, Oxford, 447.

Kennedy, W.J. and Juignet, P. (1974) Carbonate banks and slump beds in the Upper Cretaceous (Upper Turonian—Santonian) of Haute Normandie, France. *Sedimentology* **21**, 1–42.

Schlager, W. and Chermak, A. (1979) Sediment facies of platform-basin transition. Tongue of the Ocean, Bahamas. In Doyle, L.J. and Pilkey, O.H. (eds.) *Geology of Continental Slopes*, SEPM Sp. Pub. **27**, 193–208.

Scholle, P.A., Arthur, M.A. and Ekdale, A.A. (1983) Pelagic environment. In Scholle, P.A., Bebout, D.G. and Moore, C.H. (eds.) *Carbonate Depositional Environments*. Am. Ass. Petrol. Geol. Mem. **33**, 619–691.

Part 6 Ancient limestones

15 A note on uniformitarianism

Geologists study modern depositional environments in order to aid the interpretation of ancient deposits. But how typical are modern carbonate accumulations of those throughout the geological past? Are we able to recognize and plot the trends of any significant variations through time?

15.1 Long-term (secular) changes in sea-level and climate

Processes within the Earth's interior influence sea-levels by changing the Earth's surface configuration, and may simultaneously affect the atmosphere and therefore climates through vul-

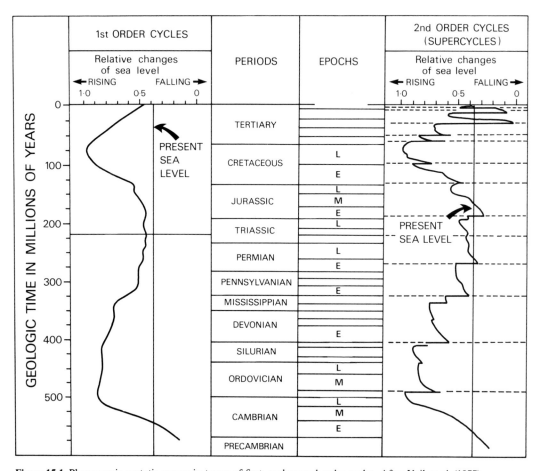

Figure 15.1 Phanerozoic eustatic curves in terms of first- and second-order cycles. After Vail *et al.* (1977)

canism. Long-term sea-level fluctuations are related to changes in volume of mid-oceanic ridges engendered by variations in rates of ocean floor spreading. So, great transgressions correlate with accelerated spreading rates. If spreading were to cease and the ridge system were allowed to cool for 70 Ma, sea-level would be lowered by 500 m and a vast regression would ensue. When continents collide, the crustal shortening at the convergent zone results in a relative increase in ocean area, and sea-level falls, but this effect is cancelled to an extent by the greater influx of sediment into the oceans at times of the continental uplifts, raising sea-level. World-wide correlatable patterns of sedimentary onlaps and offlaps are detected and dated by stratigraphic interpretations of seismic profiles across the world's continental margins. This allows the construction of relative global sea-levels through time (Figure 15.1). The character and composition of the oceans is fundamentally different during these periods of high or low global sea-level, as summarized below.

15.1.1 Features associated with high sea-level

 (i) Continents are submerged, giving wide epeiric seas.
 (ii) Large-scale extraction of $CaCO_3$ from the sea occurs, (a) by greater skeletal production in shallow waters, (b) by increased calcareous ooze deposition. Bicarbonate influx, from the smaller land area, decreases.
 (iii) Competition for available $CaCO_3$ leads to a rise in the carbonate compensation depth (CCD), the level of the sea-floor below which dissolution of calcite exceeds supply.
 (iv) Ocean temperatures are higher and more uniform. This moderation in climate is due to the high relative thermal inertia of water, the linking of seas and a reduction in the 'continentality' of climate.
 (v) The 'greenhouse climate' has low temperature gradients along latitudes, and oceans are warm throughout. Ocean circulation is

sluggish, the oceans are more prone to anoxia and pelagic diversity is high.
 (vi) $CaCO_3$ solubility increases due to the higher levels of dissolved CO_2 in deep waters associated with oxygen deficiency.
 (vii) Submarine weathering of mid-ocean basalts removes Mg from sea water during the conversion of plagioclase and mafic minerals to chlorite and epidote. This lowers the Mg/Ca ratio in sea water, favouring calcite over aragonite in inorganic precipitation.
 (viii) Submarine weathering of mid-ocean basalts liberates H^+ and Ca^{2+} ions, which on reaction with bicarbonate ions drive CO_2 into the atmosphere (greenhouse effect). The increase in atmospheric and oceanic CO_2 due to this process (and to the decrease in photosynthesis) leads to a favouring of calcite over aragonite in inorganic precipitation.

15.1.2 Features associated with low sea-level

 (i) Continents are emerged.
 (ii) Global increase in 'continentality' leads to a deterioration of climate.
 (iii) Colder climatic intervals ('icehouse climate') lead to increased circulation rates, better oxygenation of the oceans and lower diversity of pelagic organisms.
 (iv) With emergent land, carbonates are eroded, sulphides oxidized and evaporites precipitated.
 (v) Increased photosynthesis on land (and lower rates of submarine weathering) depresses atmospheric and oceanic CO_2 pressures, which favour aragonite over calcite in inorganic precipitation in the sea.
 (vi) Larger land area gives higher terrigenous sedimentation, though this is compensated by the low temperatures and low rainfall which reduce the rate of subaerial weathering and land erosion.

We are presently in a period of relatively low sea-level because of the decrease in the volume of the mid-ocean ridge system (*c.* 300 m below the Cretaceous sea) and low global temperatures (*c.* 10 °C below Cretaceous average temperatures), so we may expect the present abundance of marine $CaCO_3$ sediment and the mineralogy of its abiotic constituents to be fundamentally different from those periods in the past when sea-level and global temperatures were relatively high.

Using chemical and microscopic textural criteria, we can identify the original mineralogy of inorganic $CaCO_3$ and note that marine cements and ooids have changed in composition through geological time, oscillating between calcite-dominated and aragonite-dominated varieties. These oscillations correlate with major rhythms in relative sea-level during the Phanerozoic (Figure 15.2). During sea-level highs, calcite is the dominant polymorph of inorganic $CaCO_3$ precipitated. Low relative sea-levels, as today, are characterized by a dominance of aragonite ooids and marine cements.

Shorter wavelength rhythms of sea-level fluctuations are recognized (e.g. the variation in diversity of pelagic biotas correlates with a 32-Ma rhythm in sea-level oscillation—Fisher and Arthur, 1977). The underlying cause of these sea-level rhythms appears to be inner earth processes, as is confirmed by the correlation between the polarity of the Earth's magnetic field and the incidence of periods of transgression and regression. It is important to realize that dramatic changes can affect climate, and therefore calcium carbonate production and deposition, over a very short period. During major global changes there may be positive feedback mechanisms, such as albedo and greenhouse effects, which can compound a trend and greatly accelerate a rate of climatic change, leading to extreme conditions. It is these sudden changes which can cause widespread exterminations and long-lasting facies changes.

Apart from appreciating where the 20th century fits into secular changes in sedimentation patterns related to sea-level oscillations, we real-

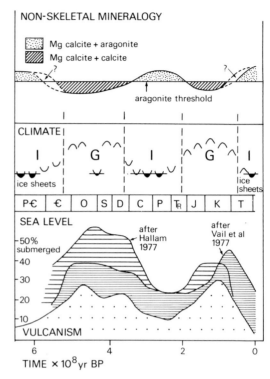

Figure 15.2 Inferred first-order cycles in non-skeletal carbonate mineralogy involving oscillations above and below and apparent aragonite threshold. These cycles are compared with the major cycles of Phanerozoic climate, sea-level and volcanic activity. I, icehouse; G, greenhouse effects. After Sandberg (1983)

ize that we are also at a particular point in organic evolution and continent/ocean development, which influence the trends of carbonate deposition.

15.2 Organic evolution

The major organism groups and, hence the nature and mineralogical composition of the sediment, differ at different times in geological history. Figure 4.1 gives a summary of the diversity, abundance and composition of the principal groups of calcareous marine organisms. There were two major bursts in the evolution of metazoans, one at the start of the Cambrian and another in the early Ordovician. The skeletal planktonic microorganisms have become significant contributors to carbonate sediments only since Cretaceous times. But in the last 100 million years they comprise about two-thirds of world-wide carbonate deposition.

One particular carbonate niche, the reef, has been occupied by different frame-building sessile skeletal organisms through the Phanerozoic (Figure 7.5). The extinction, and emergence, of different reef-builders has been related to the critical stages in the plate tectonic evolution of the globe. If organisms capable of building large, robust, branching or massive skeletons were not available, reefs which could grow in the zone of constant wave-induced turbulence would not exist. The absence of reefs, which could grow up to sea-level on exposed platform margins, would have a profound effect on the facies evolution of the whole platform.

15.3 Continental drift

Underlying global changes may be damped or reinforced by the geographic configuration of the continents around the globe, which influences ocean circulation and climate. For example, the general high sea-level during the Cretaceous was reinforced by the absence of any polar land masses on which ice caps could develop at that time.

During the creation of a new ocean, the trailing margins of the divergent continents pass through various sequences of sediment accumulation, depending upon the latitude and climate. A simple model of tropical passive margin sediment development is as follows.

After cratonic rifting, young ocean basins are invaded by marine waters from pre-existing oceans. Carbonate accumulation commences at zones, such as the margins of isolated faulted blocks, where terrigenous supply is low. Poor circulation in small basins encourages evaporite formation if the climate is arid. In moist climates, freshwater drainage at this initial stage is away from the new ocean, but with time thermal contraction brings about a drainage reversal, rivers flow into the basin, and the carbonates are progressively swamped by prograding terrigen-

ous sediments. After prolonged erosion the hinterland relief is subdued, the terrigenous supply is depleted and carbonate sedimentation may again take over.

As carbonate sediment type relates closely to water temperature, the deposits on continental margins, or the flanks of mid-ocean volcanic islands, will undergo a characteristic evolution depending upon whether that portion of the tectonic plate is migrating into or out of tropical seas (sections 13.4, 14.4.3).

15.4 Glacio-eustatic sea-level changes

Over the last two million years, polar ice sheets have expanded during cold *glacial* periods and abstracted water from the oceans. Each major glacial advance (there were at least four in the Pleistocene) caused a worldwide (eustatic) lowering of sea-level by about 140 m. (If all the water locked up in our present ice caps were to melt, sea-level would rise about 60 m above the present position.) The warm *interglacial* periods saw a retreat of ice and a consequent rise in sea-level to one similar to that of today. During the progressive cooling of a glacial period there were brief warm interludes known as *interstadials*.

The last interglacial period was about 125 000 years ago, when reefs and other shallow-water carbonates built deposits up to a sea-level comparable to today's. During the subsequent glacial

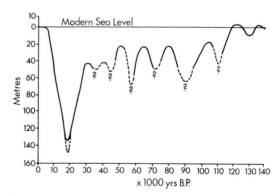

Figure 15.3 Pattern of sea-level changes over the last 140 000 years. After Hopley (1982)

advance, sea-level fell, and these (and earlier shallow-water interglacial deposits) were exposed to the atmosphere. Terrestrial erosional and depositional features developed on the newly exposed land. In the tropics, this meant the generation of karst landforms and the deposition of fluvial, aeolian and pedogenic sediments. The most recent glacial cycle is represented by the sea-level curve for the last 140 000 years shown in Figure 15.3. Though sea-level was raised for four or five interstadial periods, when marine conditions prevailed briefly up to − 20 m, it is clear from this curve that much of our shallow platforms was undergoing fresh water erosion for most of the last 120 000 years, and that the latest (uninterrupted) phase of marine carbonate deposition on platforms has lasted only about 15 000 years. This last marine advance (Holocene) has deposited carbonate sediments unconformably on top of eroded last interglacial (or interstadial) marine deposits, or, with variable amounts of reworking, on top of fluvial or aeolian sediments that accumulated during the glacial period.

The brevity of the Holocene shelf sedimentation in comparison with the prolonged recent period of exposure means that many of the physiographic features of the continental shelf and shelf edge relate not to the prevailing regime but to a previous, mainly erosional, phase. The modern sediments are relatively thin veneers on the pre-Holocene surface. As a result, such morphological features as erosional terraces, karst features, strandlines, levees, aeolian dunes and fossil fringing reefs may still persist and dominate the superficial contemporary forms.

Holocene sea-level rise has been very rapid (averaging 140 m in 20 000 years but reaching 14 mm per year) and some shelf facies (e.g. certain ooid shoals and reefs) have been unable to keep pace with the deepening water. But, since little time has elapsed since this drowning, many of these former shallower deposits are not yet covered by deeper facies in equilibrium with the new regime.

15.5 Catastrophic events

There are sedimentation events which are infrequent and of short duration, but which have a profound effect on the nature of the accumulation. Tropical storms (hurricanes, cyclones, typhoons) have wind speeds well over 100 km per hour, generating high waves and surges of banked-up water which can swiftly transport vast quantities of sediment. Approximately 80 tropical storms have affected the Bahama Banks during the last century. Platform sand shoals in the direct path of a hurricane are mobilized, creating new sand waves and spillover structures. These new bed forms, however, may not move for a further 10, 20 or even 100 years, until the next direct strike by a hurricane. Though very short on a geological timescale, this interval is long with respect to a human lifetime.

Most organisms (especially shallow-water sessile forms) are very sensitive to environmental changes. The organisms thrive within certain tolerance limits of temperature (e.g. most reef-crest corals have a temperature tolerance of about 19 ° to 30 °C), turbulence, salinity, turbidity, exposure to the atmosphere, etc., but it requires only a very brief period of time when the critical threshold is exceeded for wholesale extermination to occur and carbonate production of the region to drop to near zero. The sort of catastrophic events that can affect reef organisms include, for example, one month of exceptionally turbid and low-salinity water following freak monsoonal floods; one week of exceptionally warm (35 °C) surface sea water during the El Niño phenomenon which occurs about every seven years in the South Pacific Ocean; one day of heavy rain in coincidence with a period of very low tides; one afternoon of storm waves during the passing of a hurricane.

Individual field studies may not perceive the significance of the dramatic rare event. However, with increasing quantitative records on a monitoring basis and with improved means of data storage and retrieval, we can start to appreciate the importance of the infrequent environmental phenomena and let the principle of 'catastrophic uniformitarianism' rule.

15.6 Preservation potential and bias in observations

There are many shallow-water carbonate depositional environments where soft organisms, such as filamentous algae and sea-grasses, play a major role in sedimentation and yet leave no record of their former presence after burial. Even skeletons have widely differing mechanical and chemical durabilities, causing potential anomalies between the component compositions of living and fossil assemblages.

Our observations of modern carbonate environments have naturally focused on those readily accessible areas having calm, warm and shallow seas. But here the sediments may be a long way, in time and distance, from the moment and place of fossilization. A carbonate grain may spend over a thousand years between its initial precipitation and ultimate fossilization, during which time, for example, it may be broken in half by a crustacean; swept by a storm into a sand wave; enmeshed in an algal mat; bored by microborers; ingested, pulverized and excreted by a fish; pelletized by a gastropod; buried by prograding intertidal silts; exhumed by a burrowing shrimp; trapped by and eventually buried amongst grass blades. The grain could undergo all or part of such a cycle many times before finally coming to rest, and our field examination attempting to document the characteristic processes prevailing in the environment may be at any point in this complex array of events during the grain's history. It is particularly important that we include subsurface material collected from shallow cores in our observations of modern sedimentation, for this sediment is perhaps the closest to representing this environment in the rock record.

Improved technology will eventually also enable us to freely observe and sample those parts currently difficult to investigate, such as a shallow lagoon floor during a hurricane, the deep fore-reef of a remote atoll, or the diagenetic realm of the deep subsurface.

Selected reading

Fischer, A.G. and Arthur, M.A. (1977) Secular variations in the pelagic realm. In Cook, H.E. and Enos, P. (eds.) *Deep Water Carbonate Environments.* SEPM Sp. Pub. **25**, 19–50.

Given, R.K. and Lohmann, K.C. (1985) Derivation of the original isotopic composition of Permian marine cements. *J. Sed. Petrol.* **55**, 430–439.

Hays, J.D. and Pitman, W.C. (1973) Lithosphere plate motions, sea-level changes and climatic and ecological consequences. *Nature, London* **246**, 18–22.

Hopley, D. (1982) See p. 88.

MacKenzie, F.T. and Pigott, J.D. (1981) Tectonic controls of Phanerozoic sedimentary rock cycling. *J. Geol. Soc. London* **138**, 183–196.

Newell, N.D. (1972) The evolution of reefs. *Sci. Amer.* **226**, 54–65.

Sandberg, P.A. (1975) New interpretations of Great Salt Lake ooids and of ancient non-skeletal carbonate mineralogy. *Sedimentology* **22**, 497–537.

Sandberg, P.A. (1983) An oscillating trend in Phanerozoic non-skeletal carbonate mineralogy. *Nature, London* **305**, 19–22.

Stoddart, D.R. (1973) Coral reefs: The last two million years. *Geography* **58**, 313–323.

Vail, P.R., Mitchum, R.M. Jr. and Thomson, S. (1977) Global cycles of relative changes in sea level. In *Seismic Stratigraphy—Applications to Hydrocarbon Exploration. Am. Ass. Petrol. Geol. Mem.* **26**, 83–98.

Wilkinson, B.H., Owen, R.M. and Carroll, A.R. (1985) Submarine hydrothermal weathering, global eustasy, and carbonate polymorphism in Phanerozoic marine oolites. *J. Sed. Petrol.* **55**, 171–183.

16 Controls on carbonate facies patterns

The pattern of carbonate facies that develops depends on slope, climate, relative sea level and geological age.

The tectonic setting influences shoreline orientations and slope gradients, relative to sea-level, and also the possible supply of terrigenous sediment, which will also affect facies patterns. The climate influences the distribution of organisms and abiotic carbonate constituents by governing sea-level, sea composition, circulation,

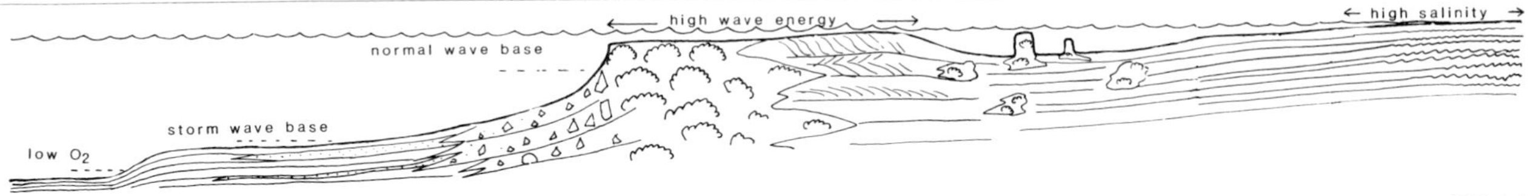

Figure 16.1 Idealized facies distribution on a mature carbonate platform and basin. After Wilson (1974)

	Deep Basin	Shallow Basin	Basin Margin	Platform Slope	Platform Reef	Margin Sands	Open Platform	Restricted Platform	Tidal flats and Sabkha
PROFILE GEOMETRY	Wide belt, central subsidence gives saucer-shaped profile	Wide belt	Narrow belt, prism of gently sloping beds (possible mounds)	Narrow belt, prism of sloping wedging beds and basin in-prograding ebb-tide lobes	Narrow belt, massive mounds (with interfingering or escarpment edge)	Narrow belt, of bars and platform-prograding storm and flood-tide lobes (with channels)	Wide belt, blanket-sediments with scattered massive mounds	Wide belt in thin cycles	Wide belt in thin cycles (with narrow channels)
SEDIMENTARY AND BIOGENIC STRUCTURES	Very thin laminations, rhythmic bedding	Well-segregated thin to medium beds, marked bioturbation, turbidites with Bouma sequences, rhythmic bedding	Beds and lenses of graded sediments, distal gravity flow deposits, Bouma sequences	Large blocks in wedging beds. Slumps, slides proximal gravity flow deposits	Massive open framework of branching, encrusting, organisms	Medium to thick massive parallel and cross-bedded units. Cross-bedding tabular and trough. Lag deposits in channels	Medium thickness massive beds with marked bioturbation (by crustaceans, bivalves, worms)	Medium thickness massive beds with marked bioturbation (by crustaceans and worms)	Fine laminations with fenestral pores, cross-bedded sands in channels, platy conglomerates, tepees. Stromatolites and algal laminites
BIOTA	Exclusively nektonic–pelagic	Pelagic with diverse stenohaline shelly infauna and epifauna	Skeletal debris derived from platform plus some pelagic and benthic	Skeletal debris derived from platform plus some benthic	Framebuilding colonies in situ with associated epilithic fauna and flora	Few living forms in this active zone. Pockets and lenses of abraded skeletal remains	Diverse stenohaline fauna and flora, infauna and epifauna/flora abundant. Framebuilder on patch reefs	Very limited euryhaline fauna and flora. High numbers of few types Stunted forms common	Virtually no indigenous fauna, filamentous algae common
GRAINS	Lime mud and sand (ooze)	Lime mud and sand	Fine skeletal sand and lime mud	Reef and skeletal debris of angular to rounded boulders, gravel and sand	Skeletal framework plus reef and skeletal debris of boulders gravel and sand. Lime mud (+ sand) internal sediment within framework	Well-sorted, well-rounded ooid and skeletal sands, some intraclasts	Poorly sorted skeletal and peloidal sands. Some intraclasts	Poorly sorted lime mud and peloidal sands	Peloidal muds with authigenic evaporite minerals
DIAGENETIC OVERPRINT	Below CCD carbonate ooze dissolves	Rare local incipient sea-bed lithification	Rare local incipient sea-bed lithification, local chert	Local incipient sea-bed lithification of sandy substrates can give breccias and nodular bedding	Marine cements in framework. Prone to exposure and meteoric diagenesis and to late dolomitization	Local marine cemented sea-bed crusts and hardgrounds. Prone to exposure and meteoric diagenesis	Local intraclasts (grapestones)	Prone to early dolomitization	Calcareous and dolomitic crusts, gypsum mush, nodular anhydrite with enterolithic folds, collapse breccias. Mouldic porosity after evaporites
COLOUR	Dark grey, black, brown, red	Dark grey-white	Dark grey-white	Dark grey-white	Medium grey	Light grey to white	Dark to light grey	Dark to light grey	Grey, brown, yellow, red
LITHOLOGY	Calcareous, bituminous, shale, marl, (may have evaporites)	Fossiliferous wackestone and mudstone in well segregated beds	Fossiliferous wackestone and mudstone	Skeletal wackestone, packstone and grainstone plus reef rudstone and floatstone	Boundstone. Pockets of grainstone, packstone wackestone, mudstone	Ooid and skeletal grainstone	Skeletal, peloidal, (rare intraclasts) grainstone, packstone and wackestone	Peloidal wackestone, mudstone	Irregularly laminated dolomite mudstone and anhydrite

hydraulic energy and so on. The geological age is important, since at different times in the past different organic groups have been dominant, and also long-term (secular) variations have influenced ocean composition and global sea-level.

Shallow-water carbonate depositional rates are very rapid where conditions are favourable, e.g. 1 m per 1000 years; this can cause widespread shoreline progradation. The critical zone for rapid production is where the photic zone and wave-base intersect a seaward-sloping bottom far enough from land so that terrigenous sediment and fresh water will not inhibit organic growth. This rapid carbonate production on the upper part of a gentle seaward slope has a positive feedback response, for it maintains a break in slope. New growth builds seaward and a prograding body of carbonate sediment develops. Concurrent fill-in of the lagoon, between the platform margin and land, occurs by restricted marine or evaporite deposits, and eventually a level platform with a steep basinward margin slope is created on the original gentle slope. The basin receives relatively little

sediment, yet subsides rapidly compared to the platform. Also, the fine basinal sediments tend to compact more than the platform deposits, further enhancing the relief between platform and basin.

Stable conditions following a marine transgression over a gently seaward dipping slope (ramp) will bring about the evolution from a simple pattern of nearshore sands and offshore muds into a mature carbonate platform with differentiated facies, as shown in Figure 16.1. Not every carbonate province of the past will show all these facies belts side by side as represented in this idealized arrangement, though normally sufficient evidence will be available to recognise palaeoshorelines and palaeoslopes. The vertical arrangement of the facies that we see in geological sections can help us to interpret the sequence of events and the major trends in tectonic, climatic and sea-level evolution of the area.

16.1 Relative sea-level changes

As platform carbonates deposit at or very near to sea-level, limestone facies types provide accurate

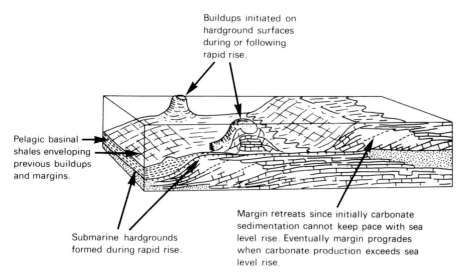

Buildups initiated on hardground surfaces during or following rapid rise.

Pelagic basinal shales enveloping previous buildups and margins.

Submarine hardgrounds formed during rapid rise.

Margin retreats since initially carbonate sedimentation cannot keep pace with sea level rise. Eventually margin progrades when carbonate production exceeds sea level rise.

Figure 16.2 Responses of carbonate platform margins to a relative sea-level rise which at first exceeds the margin's carbonate growth potential and then at least matches the growth potential. After Kendal and Schlager (1981)

gauges of sea-level changes during the past. World-wide changes in relative sea-level (the sum of eustatic sea-level changes, sedimentation and crustal movements) have occurred repeatedly and cyclically through geological time producing characteristic responses in carbonates.

16.1.1 Sea level rise greatly exceeds carbonate accretion

If $CaCO_3$ deposition cannot keep pace with relative sea-level rise, shallow-water deposition stops, hardgrounds and condensed sequences may occur, and deep-water facies may cover the platform (Figure 16.2). The slope break is not characterized by a specific facies, though it may contain sedimentary structures indicative of instability. The basinal deposition is condensed and starved as carbonate supply is reduced. The high-energy deposits are now close to shore, and ramp facies patterns are developed. It has been pointed out that drowned carbonate platforms represent something of a paradox (Figure 16.3), since our measured rates of carbonate production are so much faster (e.g. 5 mm per year for modern reef growth) than our estimates of rates of relative sea-level rise (e.g. 0.02 mm per year for mature ocean crust subsidence). However, most of our estimates of relative sea-level rise are based on averages over fairly long periods; all that is required is a short-term pulse of sea-level rise which is equivalent to about the depth of the photic zone (c. 100 m), for this will greatly retard the production of carbonate by the principal groups of organisms. Rapid sea-level rises can occur by tectonic subsidence (e.g. transform faulting), glacio-eustatic processes, rapid desiccation of ocean basins and submarine volcanic outpourings. Effects which slow organic growth include drift to higher latitudes, salinity changes to very fresh or very saline, temperature effects such as El Niño, and flooding of the platform to give dirty (clay-rich) waters. Superimposition of several effects leading in the same direction could be enough to cause platform drowning.

A rapid relative rise in sea-level produces a characteristic response from the carbonate sediment, usually in three phases. Firstly, the carbonate accumulation lags behind the rising sea.

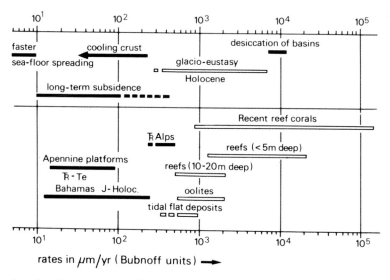

Figure 16.3 The paradox of platform drowning is illustrated by a comparison of rates of relative sea-level rise (upper part of graph) and rates of growth and sediment accumulation (lower part). Holocene rate, open bars; pre-Holocene rates, solid bars. All Holocene rates are one to several orders of magnitude higher than those of the geological record. After Schlager (1981)

After initial drowning, and perhaps setback of growth by inimical platform waters, reef and platform sediments enter a *start-up* phase. Gradually carbonate accumulation exceeds the rate of sea-level rise and the reef and platform build to sea-level during a *catch-up* phase. The final phase is the *keep-up* phase when accumulation closely matches the rate of rise and the top of the reef or platform remains at, or very close to, sea-level.

16.1.2 Sea-level exceeds carbonate accretion

When sea-level rise exceeds by only a small amount the platform carbonate accumulation, several possibilities arise. The facies belts retreat progressively landward (onlap). However, this rarely happens in a smoothly gradual manner for reefs. A reefal margin is more likely to retreat in steps. The growth potential of a reefal rim is normally the highest for all the platform facies, so the rim may survive a slow transgression and even enhance its relief above the rest of the platform for a while, forming a deep lagoon. But when sea-level rise exceeds even reefal growth potential, the reef eventually will be killed, and, as the back-reef area is low or flat, a new reef cannot develop until a long way shorewards, where optimum shallow-water conditions are establishing (Figure 14.44). Relatively little sediment is transported seaward, and so slope and basin deposits are thin.

16.1.3 Sea-level rise equals carbonate accretion

When sea-level rise and carbonate accretion have similar rates, the facies remain in more or less the same geographical position as the deposits thicken. In detail, the environments produce carbonate sediments at different rates. As the rim growth rate normally dominates, it enlarges and expands over neighbouring facies. The platform top may become filled and essentially flat, close to sea-level. The relief between the platform and basin becomes pronounced and the adjacent slope changes from a depositional to bypass mode.

16.1.4 Sea-level rise smaller than carbonate accretion

When relative sea-level rise is outpaced by carbonate accretion, the platform facies prograde seaward over older deposits. The rim builds out over adjacent slope deposits which, because of oversupply, are characterized by thick accumulations of resedimented sands and conglomerates. The platform slope steepens with progradation. Excess platform sedimentation causes sea water circulation to be locally restricted so that evaporites deposit in platform lagoons. Also, local exposure surfaces may develop with consequential freshwater diagenesis, karst development and pedogenesis.

16.1.5 Sea-level rise much smaller than carbonate accretion

Emergent carbonate platforms result from a rapid lowering of sea-level, rather than excess carbonate production. The carbonate 'factory' is now shut down and again the basin is starved of sediment. Semi-enclosed basins suffer evaporite deposition, but in open-marine basins land-derived clastic sediments may deposit, having bypassed the platform and slope. Some shallow-water deposits, including reefs, may develop part-way down the former platform slope. The bulk of the platform is exposed and suffers atmospheric conditions. Limestones undergo freshwater diagenesis, and under favourable climatic conditions aeolian clastics may encroach on the landward margin of the carbonate platform.

16.2 Sea-level oscillations

Oscillating sea-level changes across gently inclined platforms can generate cycles containing repetitive sequences of carbonate rock types spread over wide areas. We frequently encounter shallowing upwards cycles representing a regressive record of open marine to tidal and supratidal accumulation (section 14.2). Where relative sea-level changes are more extreme and perhaps accompanied by climatic changes, the depositional cycles may alternate between carbonate (high sea-level) and clastic (low sea-level) phases.

16.3 Reconstruction of depositional setting

When interpreting the environments of deposition of sequence of carbonate rocks and reconstructing a picture of the depositional and diagenetic history of the area, we draw on a range of evidence which includes:

(i) The arrangement of the lithofacies (e.g. shoaling upward cycles)
(ii) The configuration of the sediment bodies, including the nature of bedding (e.g. massive reef rocks flanked by wedging beds of talus
(iii) The sedimentary and biogenic structures present (e.g. trough cross-bedding and laterally linked hemispheroidal stromatolites)
(iv) The size, texture and composition of the component grains (e.g. coarse, well-sorted, intraclasts)
(v) The biota and the style of its preservation (e.g. calcareous red algae in an encrusting habit on a framework)
(vi) Diagenetic petrographic textures (e.g. fibrous rays of calcite cement crystals containing micro-dolomite rhomb inclusions)
(vii) Chemical composition of specific components (e.g. strongly negative $\delta^{13}C$ values of a cement fringe).

The intriguing feature of carbonate sedimentary rocks is that though all these aspects, macro- and micro-, go towards building a picture, it may be the presence of just one small character (e.g. a distinctive fossil, a gypsum pseudomorph, a caliche profile) that conveys the essence of the depositional setting and then allows the neighbouring rocks to be set into an environmental or tectonic pattern.

Selected reading

Beach, D.K. and Ginsburg, R.N. (1980) Facies successions, Plio-Pleistocene carbonates, Northwestern Great Bahama Bank. *Am. Ass. Petrol. Geol. Bull.* **64**, 1634–1642.

Cloud, P.C. (1952) Facies relationships of organic reefs. *Am. Ass. Petrol. Geol. Bull.* **36**, 2125–2149.

Fisher, J.H. (ed.) (1977) *Reefs and Evaporites: Concepts and Depositional Models.* Am. Ass. Petrol. Geol. Studies in Geology **5**.

James, N.P. (1977) Introduction to carbonate facies models. *Geoscience Canada* **4**, No. 3, 123–125.

Kendal, C.G.St.C. and Schlager, W. (1981) Carbonates and relative changes in sea level. *Mar. Geol.* **44**, 181–212.

Laporte, L.F. (1969) Recognition of a transgressive carbonate sequence within an epeiric sea: Helderberg Group (Lower Devonian) of New York State. In Friedman, G.M. (ed.), *Depositional Environments in Carbonate Rocks*, SEPM Sp. Pub. **14**, 98–119.

Longman, M.W. (1981) A process approach to recognizing facies of reef complexes. In Toomey, D.G. (ed.) *European Fossil Reef Models*, SEPM Sp. Pub. **30**, 9–40.

Mesolella, K.J. Sealy, H.A. and Matthews, R.K. (1970) Facies geometries within Pleistocene reefs on Barbados, West Indies. *Am. Assoc. Petrol. Geol. Bull.* **54**, 1890–1917.

Playford, P.E. (1980) Devonian 'Great Barrier Reef' of Canning Basin, Western Australia. *Am. Assoc. Petrol. Geol.* **64**, 814–840.

Read, J.F. (1982) Carbonate platforms of passive (extensional) continental margins: types, characteristics and evolution. *Tectonophys.* **81**, 195–212.

Schlager, W. (1981) The paradox of drowned reefs and carbonate platforms. *Geol. Soc. Am. Bull.* **92**, 197–211.

Schlanger, S.O. (1981) Shallow-water limestones in oceanic basins as tectonic and paleoceanographic indicators. In Warme, J.E., Douglas, R.G. and Winterer, E.L. (eds.) *The Deep Sea Drilling Project: a Decade of Progress*, SEPM Sp. Pub. **32**, 209–226.

Stanton, R.J. (1967) Factors controlling shape and internal facies distribution of organic carbonate buildups. *Am. Assoc. Petrol. Geol. Bull.* **51**, 2462–2467.

Tucker, M.E. (1985) Shallow-marine carbonate facies and facies models. In Brenchley, P.J. and Williams, B.P.J. (eds.), *Sedimentology: Recent Developments and Applied Aspects*, Blackwell, Oxford, 147–169.

Wilson, J.L. (1974) Characteristics of carbonate platform margins. *Am. Assoc. Petrol. Geol. Bull.* **58**, 810–824.

17 Examples of facies sequences

In the sections on carbonate depositional environments some examples of ancient limestones were presented to illustrate the sedimentary structural and petrographic characteristics of particular environments. In this section some sequences of limestone types are presented to illustrate facies patterns. It should be stressed that each carbonate province offers its own special characteristics, and countless varieties exist; for example, reefs of each different geological period have different types of frameworks, and hence associated sediments, simply because new reef-building metazoans were evolving. In this book I have had to be selective, but have tried to include the more common facies associations and to give a spread of geological ages in the examples. The reader is referred to Wilson (1975) for a comprehensive treatment of carbonate facies throughout geological history. The examples chosen here are:

(i) Prograding reef complex—Permian, West Texas and New Mexico (section 17.1)
(ii) Foreslope mud mounds—Dinantian, British Isles (section 17.2)
(iii) Shallowing-upwards carbonate platform with patch reefs—Wenlock, Silurian, England (section 17.3)
(iv) Lime-sand shoal cycles—Jurassic, Paris Basin, France (section 17.4)
(v) Shallowing-upwards tidal flat deposits—Purbeck, England (section 17.5)

Other examples of facies patterns are described later, in Chapters 18 and 19 dealing with economic aspects of carbonates.

17.1 Permian Reef Complex, Guadalupe Mountains USA

The Permian Reef Complex and associated sediments of the Guadalupe Mountains of New Mexico and West Texas, USA, have been extensively studied, partly because they reveal, in excellent exposures, classical basin to slope to

Table 17.1 Summary of facies and environments of the Permian rocks of West Texas. After Selley (1985).

Facies name	Description	Environment
Bernal	Red siltstone	Continental
Chalk Bluff	Laminated gypsum and dolomite wackestone	Sabkha evaporite
Carlsbad	Dolomite wackestone, algal stromatolites, peloidal dolomites	Restricted shelf
	Cross-bedded skeletal dolomitic grainstones	Exposed shelf margin
Capitan	Skeletal wackestones and boundstones	Reef or shelf margin
	Major slope-bedded wackestones and breccias	Slope margin
Delaware	Radiolarian black shales	Starved basin
	Fine-grained sandstones	turbidites

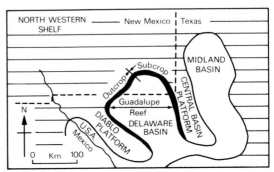

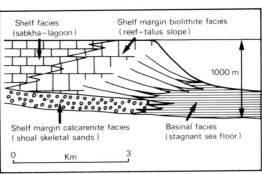

Figure 17.1 The disposition of basins and shelf in the Upper Permian of Texas and New Mexico. The cross-section shows the lateral transition from shelf facies (Bernal Chalk Bluff and Carlsbad) through shelf margin facies (Capitan) into basinal facies (Delaware). After Selley (1985)

platform facies, and partly because similar rocks of equivalent age further along the strike in the subsurface are oil-bearing. There are still, however, differing views on the precise origins of these rocks.

The facies and environmental interpretations are summarized in Table 17.1. Unlike modern atolls or banks, which have a lagoon or platform within a rim of coral framework that grows out towards the deep ocean, the reefs of this Permian complex grew on an epicontinental platform and were distributed around the rim of a deep mediterranean sea (Delaware Basin) which overflowed the basin, covering shallow, but extensive, areas of evaporation outside the basin and behind the reef (Figure 17.1). There are three provinces that are stratigraphically equivalent but contain dissimilar rocks: these are (i) the Delaware Basin; (ii) the narrow margin of the shelf; and (iii) the broad shelf area outside (landward of) the marginal zone.

17.1.1 The Delaware Basin

The Delaware Basin (Figure 17.1) is about 200 km long and 120 km wide. It contains thinly-bedded fine-grained grey sandstones and minor amounts of black bituminous limestone reaching a maximum of 2.5 km thickness. The sandstones are uniform in texture and composition, consisting of well-sorted, angular, fine (< 0.1 mm) quartz grains. Fossils are rare. The limestones are fine-grained, dark, laminated and cherty, with rare thin, fine-grained, graded beds of turbidite origin. These dark laminated sediments represent deposition in a shallow poorly-oxygenated basin. They are overlain by thousands of metres of anhydrite and gypsum, the upper part of which spreads beyond the basin limits. Towards the basin margin, the dark mudstones are cut by channels which are filled mainly with contorted deposits of silicified reef fossils. At the basin edge there are beds of coarse platform-derived clasts and fossils which alternate with massive beds of crinoidal debris and lime mudstones. Bioturbation structures occur at the basin edge, but are reduced in occurrence towards the basin centre. Thick-shelled benthic organisms are restricted to the basin edge, and include crinoids, brachiopods, fusulinid foraminiferans, bryozoans and echinoids. All fossils are well-worn, broken and usually disarticulated, indicating transportation. These fossils give way to a zone at the basin margin with thinly calcified or non-calcified organisms, such as holothurians, ostracods, bivalves, textularid foraminiferans, siliceous sponges and soft-bodied burrowers, representing a zone of moderately to poorly oxygenated water. Pelagic organisms are also most common at the basin edge (where production was probably greater), and include conodonts, radiolarians, ammonoids, and remains of sharks and true fish.

The inclination of the slope sediments suggests a water depth of about 500 m within a few kilometres of the platform margin. Sequences of mass flow deposits thin from about 33 m to 6 m in thickness from the platform edge to 23 km into the basin. At the basin margin, beds show basal erosion, grading, and scour indicative of swift downslope currents, and contain much disarticulated platform-derived skeletal debris. These are carbonate turbidites which show a proximal to distal transition, in which

(i) Beds thin basinwards
(ii) Beds show better grading basinwards
(iii) Dominant grain size decreases basinwards
(iv) Laminations and ripples increase in abundance basinwards
(v) Scoured channels and washouts decrease basinwards
(vi) Wackestones become dominant over packstones basinwards.

Bouma divisions are present, but the lower divisions tend to occupy troughs and so are less prominent than B, C and D divisions, which are common both within and between channels.

Wavy bedding structures in the slope limestones indicate differential loading and intrastratal flow before lithification. Many thin-bedded black limestones display intraformational deformation caused by penecontemporaneous creep and slump of bottom sediments. At places, recumbent folds pass into glide planes which may cut across bedding planes. Intrastratal flow in partially lithified basin limestones has resulted in local brecciation.

17.1.2 Margin of the shelf

The dark basinal deposits give way to light-coloured carbonates of the platform margin. Massive inclined beds of dolomitic breccia and grainstone grade from the reef to the basinal sediments. The beds thin from 20–30 m to 2 m thick at the foot of the slope. Many large blocks of reef rock and consolidated fore-reef detritus occur in comparatively fine sediments at the foot of the slope. Dolomitization is widespread but patchy. Interbedded sandstones contain few reef blocks or skeletal remains, supporting the view that the sandstones were deposited during times of little contribution from the reef, but relatively great terrigenous input, which probably spilled over the reef from the shelf area. The periods of sandstone deposition may represent lowered sea-level, though this does not appear to be supported by evidence of emergence or appropriate facies changes in the carbonates.

The massive Capitan carbonates, up to 600 m thick, form a more or less continuous narrow rim around the Delaware Basin for a distance of about 600 km. The lower two-thirds of these massive carbonates is reef talus, over which the reef front migrated basinwards for more than 5 km during later stages of carbonate deposition. The massive Capitan reef rocks are fine-grained white limestones containing well-preserved fossils, many of which are *in situ*, with large quantities of fibrous and sparry calcite cement within and between grains and framework. *In-situ* framework is not widespread, but it increases in abundance up through the succession from 5% to 60% of the rock. Where seen, it contains a mixture of frame-building and binding organisms which include calcareous sponges,

bryozoans, calcareous red, green and blue-green alge (*Parachaetetes, Hedstroemia, Girvanella* and stromatolites), bladed phylloid algae, and binding organisms of uncertain affinities, *Archeolithoporella* (probably a red alga), *Collenella* (algal, but not a stromatolite), *Tubiphytes* (alga or hydrozoan) and *Solenopora texana* (now thought to be a bryozoan, not a red alga). Skeletal debris collects amongst the framework, and in addition to fragments of the above, contains brachiopods, fusulinid and other benthic foraminiferans, bivalves, gastropods, echinoderms, ostracods and cephalopods. The fauna and flora suggest growth on stable and firm substrates within well-oxygenated, warm, clear, shallow seas of normal salinity. The greater dominance of algae towards the top of the Capitan limestone suggests a shallowing of water towards the end of reef growth.

The reef rock consists of a large proportion of inorganic cement, reaching up to 80% of the rock volume in places. These cements are all now

Figure 17.2 Thin section showing bands of radiating fibrous cement growing over pisoids. Reef facies. Ppl. Scale 2 mm. Permian, West Texas, USA

calcite, and have a variety of habits: (i) radiating fibres in rays or botryoids, (ii) isopachous fibrous, (iii) isopachous bladed, (iv) syntaxial overgrowths on echinoderm grains, and (v) clear equant crystals.

The fibrous cements are preserved mainly as ghost textures within fine sparry masses (Figure 17.2) and show square-tipped and feather terminations to fibrous crystals, suggesting a composition that was originally aragonite. The first four cement types listed above are frequently found alternating with organic encrustations (such as *Archeolithoporella*, *Tubiphytes* and encrusting foraminiferans) and internal sediment. They are thus considered marine. The reef rock was thus growing as a solid cemented structure on the sea-bed. Fissures within the reefs, occurring parallel to the strike of the shelf edge, contain Permian fossils, and their sides are encrusted with frame-builders such as *Archeolithoporella*, further attesting to the consolidated nature of the rock during deposition. The clear equant sparry cement postdates the other cements and internal sediment, usually being the final fill of vugs. It is thought to be of non-marine origin.

17.1.3 Broad shelf landward of the marginal zone

The back reef area is occupied by a range of carbonates (mainly dolomite), sandstone and evaporite rocks (Table 17.1), which are in beds lying roughly horizontal, i.e. parallel to the original sea-level, which allows us to reconstruct slopes of 20° to 35° for the reef front in Capitan times. Passing shelfward from the reef, the following broad facies are encountered in belts roughly parallel to the shelf edge.

(i) Grainstones and packstones rich in reef-derived organic remains, such as bryozoans, *Tubiphytes*, sponges, echinoderms, gastropods and calcareous algae (though dasycladacean algae are more important here), plus peloids and intraclasts.

(ii) Parallel-bedded skeletal and non-skeletal dolomitic grainstones and packstones, with a low-diversity, restricted biota of mainly dasycladacean algae, with some ostracods, gastropods and benthic foraminiferans Figure 17.3). Non-skeletal grains are peloids, intraclasts and coated grains. A fenestral fabric of algal laminites is common, and parallel beds are also interrupted by abundant tepee structures.

(iii) A dolomitic zone rich in pisoids which are 20–30 mm in size and occur with some peloids, intraclasts, oncoids and dasycladacean algal fragments and foraminiferans. These pisolitic units are laterally impersistent beds associated with abundant tepee structures. Most pisoids are 'clastic' and were freely moving in a subaqueous setting during growth or resedimentation. Some pisolites may show polygonal fitting (Figure 5.7), downward elongation, local perched inclusions, and also in-place, non-algal, accretionary growth, all of which have been cited to suggest a concretionary origin. However, they do not appear to replace precursor sediment and are thought to be of submarine and not caliche origin.

(iv) Dolomitic mudstone with some wackestones and packstones containing intraclasts and peloids and a restricted biota of dasycladacean algae, ostracods, calcispheres and gastropods. There is evidence of former evaporites in the form of nodular moulds of anhydrite and crystal-

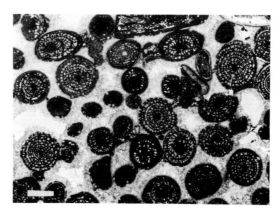

Figure 17.3 Fusulinid foraminiferan grainstone, shelf facies. Thin section. Ppl. Scale 1 mm. Permian, West Texas, USA

shaped moulds of gypsum. Wavy bedding and crinkly laminations suggest former algal mats.

(v) Fine, sand-sized, quartz sandstone with some feldspar grains and local dolomitic cement, that appear similar to the quartz sandstones in the Delaware Basin. Bedding shows parallel to wavy laminations with local low angle cross-sets.

(vi) Extensive deposits of anhydrite and gypsum with some green clayey silt. The bedding is deformed due to the expansion of salts during the hydration of anhydrite to gypsum on modern weathering.

Thus in the back reef facies, (i) there are trends of increasing carbonate towards the shelf margin; (ii) abundance and diversity of skeletal grains increase towards the shelf margin; (iii) carbonates become more poorly sorted and there is an increase in micrite and evaporite traces away from the shelf margin; and (iv) tepees and algal laminated beds are most common in a band a short distance behind the reef. It appears that this zone was perhaps structurally the highest during deposition and contained a restricted biota, with sedimentary and biogenic structures indicative of inter- and supratidal environments. The evaporites shelfwards of this position most probably represent subaqueous precipitation in semi-enclosed pools receiving a fairly constant flow of saline sea water.

17.1.4 Summary
The evaporites and biota suggest a hot arid climate. The facies configuration indicates a 600 m-deep, relatively stagnant basin containing sandstones and dark limestones, surrounded by platform carbonates of reefal and back-reef origin. The reefs grow part-way down the slope as small structures of sponges and algae, strengthened by vast quantities of fibrous aragonite marine cements. The sediments on the fore-reef slope were redeposited as gravity flows and accumulated as wedging beds of talus over which the reef prograded. Carbonate turbidites added to the basin margin sediments. Back-reef sediments were laid down in restricted shallow lagoon and tidal flat settings. They pass away from the reef into evaporites. The shelf and margin carbonates are mainly dolomite, whereas the fore-reef debris and basinal deposits are now calcite.

17.2 Foreslope mud mounds—Dinantian of Europe

There is a distinctive facies in the Lower Carboniferous strata of Europe and North America, consisting of mounds of massive lime mudstones with scattered crinoid and bryozoan fragments. This facies, commonly referred to as Waulsortian, after the town (Waulsort) in Belgium where the facies was first recorded, occurs as a distal slope facies between geosynclinal basins and platform deposits. The mud mounds occur as overlapping stacked structures (Figures 17.4, 17.5), are flanked distally by dark argillaceous, cherty, thin-bedded basinal limestones, and pass landward into lagoonal limestones of peloidal,

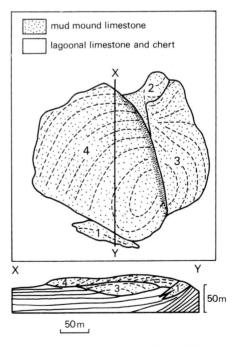

Figure 17.4 Concentric growth lines of Waulsortian mud mound accumulation. Galway, Eire. After Lees (1964)

Figure 17.5 Waulsortian mud mound revealing high angle of growth layers defined by stromatactis sheets, bioclastic layers and thin clay seams. Hammer 500 mm. Carboniferous, Galway, Eire

crinoidal, bryozoan and algal wackestones and grainstones with scattered mud mounds. The Waulsortian facies has been subdivided (Lees and Miller, 1985) into four depth-related phases which span the sub-photic to photic boundary.

Phase D (shallowest)
Coated and micritized grains, fenestellid bryozoans in a sparry calcite-dominated matrix with some fan cements. Locally ooids at the top and evidence (dissolution voids) of emergence.

Phase C
Plurilocular foraminiferans, *Girvanella* algae, gastropods and echinoderms in a dominantly mudstone matrix.

Phase B
Hyalostellid sponges and filamentous algae in a mudstone matrix with stromatactoid and sheet spar cavities (Figure 17.6).

Phase A (deepest)
Fenestellid bryozoans, crinoids, ostracods, bivalves and nautiloids in a sparry calcite matrix.

The beds of phases B and C, which are defined by clay seams or stylolites, show rhythmic development of bioclasts and fabrics which may

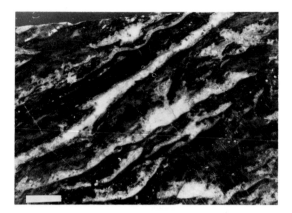

Figure 17.6 Slab revealing sheet-like stromatactis cavities. Scale 10 mm. Carboniferous, Galway, Eire

include striking spar-filled cavities. Towards the base of beds, laterally extensive sheet spar cavities occur which on close inspection show that the roofs and floors can be refitted, indicating a tensional origin in a dewatering mud of gel-like consistency. These cavity types give way to stromatactoid cavities (flat floors and irregular roofs) higher in the bed, where they are associated with the common fenestellid bryozoan sheets. Each bed behaves as a unit and may show internal reorganization of muds, but there is no interchange of sediments between beds and no sign of hardgrounds on the bed surfaces. The carbonate mud is believed to be derived by biological processes and the mud accumulation attained steep slopes (up to 50°) aided by biological mats and early cementation.

17.3 Shallowing-upwards carbonate platform with patch reefs—Much Wenlock Limestone, England

The Much Wenlock Limestone Formation of the Silurian of Shropshire, England, is approximately 30 m thick and represents carbonate deposition on the stable platform of the English Midlands. Figure 17.7 shows a west–east section of the principal limestone outcrop where patch reefs abound. In central Wales, 50 km to the west of the section, the rocks of equivalent age are black

graptolitic shales which represent the Welsh Lower Palaeozoic geosynclinal basin. Near Birmingham, 30 km to the east of Much Wenlock, shallow-water Wenlockian carbonate sediments with patch reefs and tidal flat deposits outcrop with some argillaceous admixtures. The reefs of the Much Wenlock Limestone Formation increase in both number and thickness towards the western margin of the reefal outcrop and then abruptly stop. The deeper-water limestones (Facies F) to the west of the section (Figure 17.7) are thinly bedded, nodular and argillaceous, containing fine, comminuted, skeletal debris with some whole brachiopods, ostracods and trilobites (but no algae) in a mudstone matrix. The fossiliferous grainstone beds of Facies E show evidence of synsedimentary folding, suggesting deposition on a narrow submarine slope immediately basinward of the reefal platform. The platform limestones themselves grade up from the calcareous shales of the underlying formation into nodular argillaceous fossiliferous wackestones. The fossil content of these limestones increases vertically as the nodular horizons become more bedded and change to fossiliferous packstones and grainstones (Figures 17.7, 17.8). The irregular bedded limestone–shale alternations indicate a degree of bioturbation, absence of hardgrounds, and a diagenetic accentuation of primary lime-rich and clay-rich layers by pressure dissolution. The patch reefs, which are roughly 5 m thick and 20 m wide, showing a crude bilateral symmetry (Figure 14.26), do not all start at one horizon but develop at different levels in the succession upon small lenses of coarse crinoidal, bryozoan and coral debris (Figure 17.9). The reefs are massive, with a lensed internal structure and interdigitate margins. They increase in number and lateral extension up the succession (Figure 17.8). Tabulate and rugose corals, stromatoporoids, bryozoans and algae constitute the main part of the reef framework (Figure 17.10) but large quantities of coarse crinoidal debris and fine calcite mudstone are trapped within the struc-

Much Wenlock Limestone Outcrop and Bedded Facies

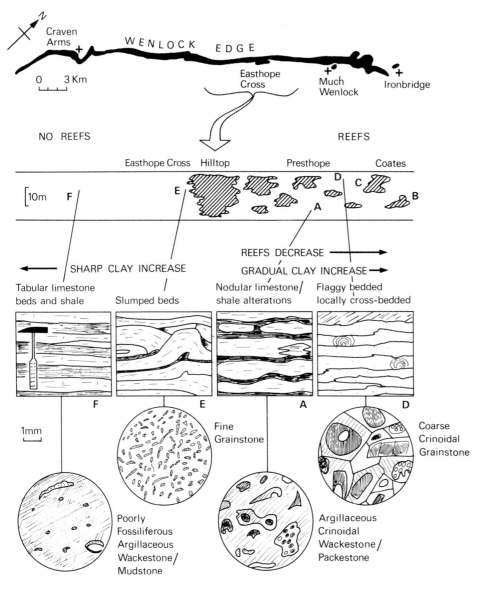

Figure 17.7 Schematic cross-section of the distribution of reefs and the major bedded limestone facies in the Wenlock Limestone. After Scoffin (1971)

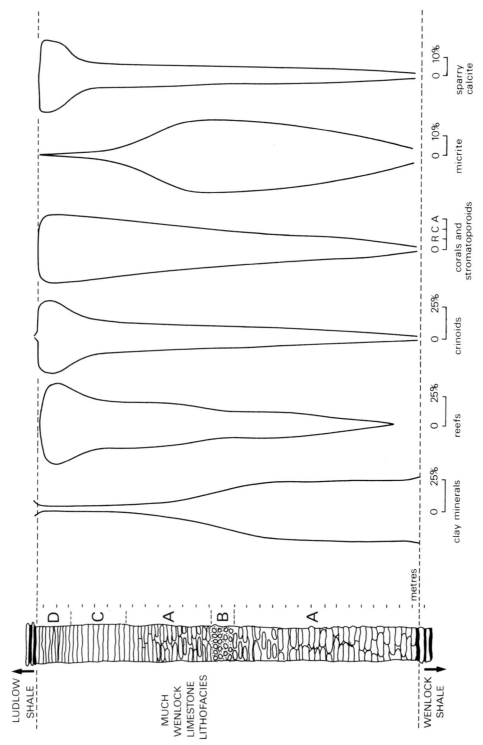

Figure 17.8 Variations in abundance of the main components of the Wenlock Limestone. After Scoffin (1971)

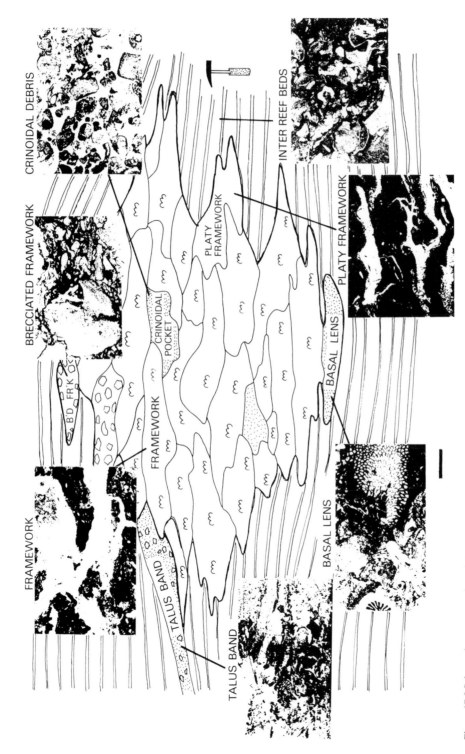

Figure 17.9 Schematic representation of the petrographic character of the reefal sediments of the Wenlock Limestone. All photomicrographs are ppl and of roughly similar scale (bar by basal lens photomicrograph = 2 mm)

ture. Reef-derived fossil debris is most abundant in beds flanking reefs, but wedging bands of talus are rare and extend only a few metres (10–30 m) from the patch reefs (Figure 17.9). These talus bands contain truncated blocks of reef-framework with consolidated interstitial sediment, indicating a degree of marine lithification during reef growth. Ash falls periodically interrupted reef growth, as is indicated by the correlation of bentonites with marked indentations into the reef margins. The growth stages of the reefs can be plotted using the attitudes of encrusting organisms and enveloping argillaceous bands, from which it can be shown that most reefs had a relief above the surrounding sea-floor of only a metre or so. With time and progressive shallowing, terrigenous sediment content was reduced and low-relief reefs dominated the shallow sea-floor. It appears that these hard substrates supported large numbers of crinoids, whose skeletal debris was swept on to the shallow platforms to form coarse, locally cross-bedded, skeletal grainstones at the top of the formation, the crinoids behaving in a similar manner to *Halimeda* plates on modern reefs. The truncation of some reef surfaces at this time, and the rare occurrence of desiccation structures, suggest local emergence at the completion of shallowing.

Figure 17.10 Photograph of stained (methylene blue) peel of Wenlock Limestone reef framework. Banded peloidal micrite masses (*a*), stromatolitic in appearance, encrust bryozoans (*b*) and corals (*c*). Internal sediments include clay-rich micrite (*d*) and late stage (possibly after a vadose dissolution phase) micrite (*e*). Sparry calcite masses (*f*) fill remaining cavity space. Silurian, Much Wenlock, England

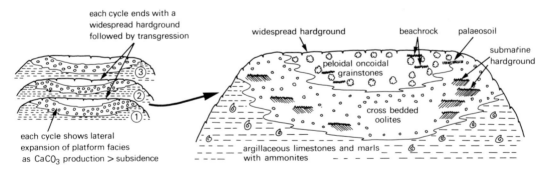

Figure 17.11 Three major cycles of Jurassic platform limestones of the Paris Basin each passing vertically from open water argillaceous limestones, through cross-bedded oolites into lagoonal grainstones

17.4 Platform cycles, Mid-Jurassic, Paris Basin, France

The three major cycles representing essentially the Bajocian, Bathonian and Callovian deposition on the Burgundy Platform of northern France are illustrated in section in Figure 17.11. The platform (*c.* 200 km wide) had low relief (*c.* 20 m) and no well-defined margin. Each shallowing-upwards cycle consists of three major rock units each grading upwards into the other:

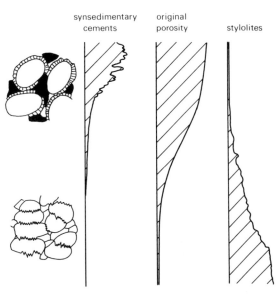

Figure 17.14 Schematic graph showing the increased retention of original porosity at horizons with synsedimentary cements (hardgrounds, beachrock) and loss of primary porosity during the chemical compaction (stylolites) at other horizons. Jurassic, Paris Basin, France

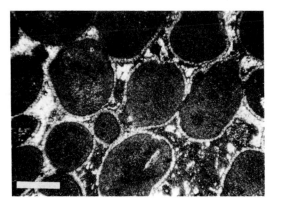

Figure 17.12 12 m-high quarry wall showing accretion cross-bedding of an oolite sand bar capped by horizontal strata of restricted lagoonal origin. Jurassic, Massangis, France

Figure 17.13 Thin section showing isopachous fringe of fibrous cement on peloids preceding micritic internal sediment and hence most possibly marine in origin. Ppl. Scale 0.5 mm. Jurassic, Paris Basin, France

Figure 17.15 Hardground on top of ooid bed showing an encrustation by large flat oyster shell (*a*) and bivalve borings (*b*) which also penetrate the oyster. Coin 20 mm. Jurassic, Paris Basin, France

(i) A basal argillaceous thin-bedded fossiliferous wackestone unit, locally rich in ammonites, overlying hardground

(ii) A middle oolitic-skeletal grainstone unit up to 80 m thick (with local coral patches and biostroms)

(iii) An upper peloidal and oncoidal unit with algal laminations and birdseye structures occupying the platform interior position.

Each major cycle represents an expansion phase of the platform when carbonate production significantly exceeded subsidence. Oolitic/skeletal grainstones, commonly spectacularly cross-bedded (Figure 17.12), prograded laterally across a gently sloping surface (of basinal marls) to form a widespread (up to 150 km) diachronous sheet. Periodically these sand shoals emerged locally forming elongate cays which were affected by vadose diagenesis.

This expanding sand-shoal rim enclosed a shallow sheltered area in which lagoonal deposits formed in minor cycles 1–10 m thick. At the base are bioturbated oncoidal and peloidal muds which grade up into low-angle cross-bedded peloidal, intraclast sands at the top (Figure 9.12).

These Jurassic carbonate sands underwent diagnostic synsedimentary and burial diagenesis. Many of the beds show fibrous, possibly marine cements (Figure 17.13). Locally on the top of the oolites, palaeosoils and associated early sparry calcite cements developed, indicating emergence. The ooids with early cements have retained up to 20% primary porosity. The ooids unaffected by these early cements suffered mechanical and chemical compaction on burial and now have porosities of less than 5% (Figure 17.14). The porous zones with early cements occur at the top of the oolite formation and tend to be located near the platform margin. Within the lagoonal deposits there are thin bands cemented by vadose marine cements, and these represent beachrocks. Those peloidal sands not early cemented suffered considerably compaction and stylolitization. Submarine cements forming hardgrounds are

common, especially at the top of each of the three major cycles. The hardgrounds show some iron mineralization and are colonized by oysters and bored by bivalves, worms and sponges (Figure 17.15).

Those grainstones that underwent emergence have been locally affected by dolomitization. *Thalassinoides* burrows may show selective ferroan dolomitization (Figure 14.17), though in places the rhombs have been calcitized or leached.

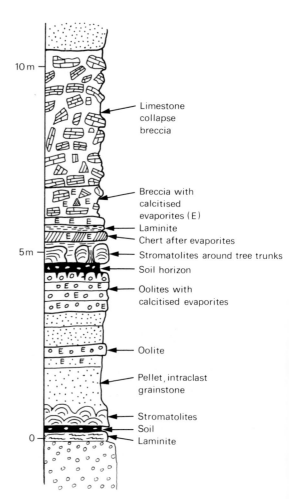

Figure 17.16 Graphic log of the lithologies in the basal Purbeck at Lulworth, Dorset, England. After West (1975)

17.5 Tidal flat deposits, Upper Jurassic, Dorset, England

In the Tithonian of southern England, relative sea-level fall resulted in a change from open, marine, shallow platform deposits of the thick-bedded Portland oolites to the restricted platform and littoral deposits of the Purbeck. The vertical succession is shown in Figures 17.16 and 17.17. The Portland oolite represents deposition

Figure 17.17 Cliffs containing strata of the Portland–Purbeck transition. The lower beds (beneath the geologists) are massive thick-bedded ooidal grainstones representing open marine conditions, the upper beds are algal laminites and peloidal grainstones representing restricted intertidal and supratidal deposits. Mupe, Dorset, England

Figure 17.19 Thin section of algal stromatolitic bands with sparry calcite pseudomorphing former gypsum crystals. Ppl. Scale 2 mm. Jurassic, Lulworth, Dorset, England

Figure 17.18 Algal stromatolite with a central hollow that represents the position of a former silicified tree trunk. Hammer 300 mm. Jurassic, Lulworth, Dorset, England

Figure 17.20 Peloidal grainstone with pseudomorphs after halite. Scale 10 mm. Jurassic, Lulworth, Dorset, England

in clear, shallow, warm waters. Beds are massive, and locally small patch reefs contain abundant oysters, bivalves, *Solenopora* red algae, and bryozoans (Figure 4.60). The thin soils in the Purbeck clearly show emergence, but these are interbedded with laminated algal stromatolites which locally grew around the base of *in-situ* and fallen trees (Figure 17.18). The stromatolites have a domed, banded structure which is very porous. In thin section, sparry calcite patches are clearly seen to be pseudomorphing former gypsum crystals (Figure 17.19). Several horizons contain coarsely crystalline limestones and chert that have replaced anhydrite. The stromatolites and former evaporite minerals are indicative of intertidal deposition in an arid setting, while the tree trunks and soils indicate that only a short time earlier the area was emergent with some fresh groundwaters.

The thinly-bedded overlying deposits are peloidal, ostracod and oncolite grainstones (Figure 2.3*D*), packstones, wackestones and mudstones. Hypersaline conditions are suggested by abundant halite pseudomorphs (Figure 17.20), enterolithic folding, possibly after anhydrite (Figure 17.21) and local tepee structures. In certain areas the thin-bedded lime-

Figure 17.22 The lower portion of the Purbeck succession in which a soil horizon is overlain by a sequence of algal laminites and capped by a collapse breccia. Hammer 300 mm. Jurassic, Lulworth, Dorset, England

stones are disrupted into a chaotic pile of blocks representing a collapse breccia (Figure 17.22) formed by the removal of former evaporite minerals.

Figure 17.21 Thin-bedded argillaceous lime mudstone with white enterolithic folded layers respresenting former anhydrite horizons. Scale 100 mm. Jurassic, Lulworth, Dorset, England

Selected reading

Achauer, C.W. (1969) Origin of Capitan Formation, Guadalupe Mountains, New Mexico and Texas. *Am. Assoc. Petrol. Geol. Bull.* **53**, 2314–2323.

Babcock, J.A. *et al.* (1977) *Upper Guadalupian facies, Permian reef complex, Guadalupe Mountains New Mexico and West Texas.* 1977 Field Conference Guidebook, Permian Basin Section, SEPM Pub. **77–16**.

Dunham, R.J. (1972) *Capitan Reef, New Mexico and Texas: facts and questions to aid interpretation and group discussion.* Permian Basin Section, SEPM Pub. **72–14**.

El-Shahat, A. and West, I.M. (1983) Early and late lithification of aragonitic bivalve beds in the Purbeck Formation

(Upper Jurassic–Lower Cretaceous) of southern England. *Sedimentary Geol.* **35**, 15–41.

Kendall, C.G.St.C. (1969) An environmental reinterpretation of the Permian evaporite/carbonate shelf sediments of the Guadalupe Mountains. *Geol. Soc. Amer. Bull.* **80**, 2503–2526.

Lees, A. (1964) The structure and origin of the Waulsortian (Lower Carboniferous) 'reefs' of west central Eire. *Phil. Trans. Roy. Soc. Lond.* **B247**, 483–531.

Lees, A. and Miller, J. (1985) Facies variation in Waulsortian buildups, Part 2, Mid-Dinantian buildups from Europe and North America. *Geol. J.* **20**, 159–180.

Newell, N.D. (1955) Depositional fabric in Permian reef limestones. *J. Geol.* **63**, 301–309.

Newell, N.D., Rigby, J.K., Fisher, A.G., Whiteman, A.J., Hickox, J.E. and Bradley, J.S. (1953) *The Permian Reef Complex of the Guadalupe Mountains Region, Texas and New Mexico.* W.H. Freeman, San Francisco.

Schwarzacher, W. (1961) Petrology and structure of some lower Carboniferous reefs in northwestern Ireland. *Bull. Amer. Ass. Petrol. Geol.* **45**, 1481–1503.

Scoffin, T.P. (1971) The conditions of growth of the Wenlock reefs of Shropshire (England). *Sedimentology* **17**, 173–219.

Scoffin, T.P. (1972) Cavities in the reefs of the Wenlock Limestone (Mid-Silurian) of Shropshire, England. *Geol. Rdsch.* **61**, 565–578.

Selley, R.C. (1985) See p. 14.

Toomey, D.F. (ed.) (1981) *European Fossil Reef Models.* SEPM Sp. Pub. **30**.

West, I.M. (1975) Evaporites and associated sediments of the basal Purbeck Formation (Upper Jurassic) of Dorset. *Proc. Geol. Ass.* **86**, 205–225.

J

Part 7 Economic aspects

Limestones and dolomites are important reservoirs of minerals. About 40% of the world's oil is produced from carbonate rocks, and valuable deposits of lead, zinc and other metals are found in carbonate host rocks. It is this role as storage reservoirs which will receive greatest attention in this section. The capacity to store water and minerals is related to the abundance of voids (pores) within the host rock.

18 Hydrocarbon reservoirs in carbonate rocks

In this brief account, the aspects to be considered regarding the exploration and production of oil and gas from carbonate rocks are the porosity characteristics and the distribution and geometry of the reservoirs.

18.1 Porosity in carbonates
Porosity (ϕ) is the proportion (expressed as a percentage) of the rock occupied by pores:

$$\phi = \frac{\text{pore volume}}{\text{total volume}} \times 100.$$

It is the interconnected (or effective) porosity rather than the absolute porosity that concerns the oil geologist. Permeability (K) is a measure of the ease with which fluids are transmitted through the rock. The unit of measure is a darcy (D) or millidarcy (mD) (one thousandth of a darcy). One darcy equals a permeability such that one millilitre of fluid, of one centipoise viscosity, flows in one second under a pressure differential of one atmosphere through a porous medium having a cross-sectional area of one square centimetre and a length of one centimetre.

Voids in limestones range in size from less than one micron to metres in diameter. In order of increasing size, voids may be

(i) Within crystals, e.g. fluid inclusions
(ii) Between crystals, e.g. within a skeleton, ooid, peloid or cement fabric

(iii) Between grains, e.g. within a grainstone (these relate to the sorting, packing and shape of grains)
(iv) Within bedded or massive units, e.g. shrinkage cracks, burrows, dewatering structures, borings, and small-scale dissolution features
(v) Within formations, e.g. fissures, and large-scale dissolution features such as karst caverns and collapse breccias.

Pore spaces can conveniently be subdivided into those that originate during deposition (*primary*) and those that develop subsequent to deposition (*secondary*).

18.1.1 Primary and secondary porosity
Primary porosity may be as high as 70% at deposition. Examples of maximum porosity at deposition are: lagoonal muds, 70%; pelagic oozes, 70%; reef framework, 60%; reef debris, 60%; ooid grainstones, 40%. This porosity occurs between and within grains. In muds, the high initial porosity is rapidly reduced by mechanical compaction on early burial to about 40%. In sands the primary porosity is reduced by cementation and chemical compaction. A porosity of 20% is considered high in a limestone; most pre-Tertiary limestones have a porosity less than 3%. To preserve primary porosity, the sediment has to (i) have good initial porosity, (ii) avoid

Table 18.1 Classification of porosity in carbonate rocks.

Porosity type	I Intra-particle	II Inter-particle	III Enhanced primary	IV Inter-crystalline	V Mouldic	VI Vuggy	VII Fracture/breccia	VIII Stylolitic
Common pore size range	0.01–1 mm	0.05–1 mm	0.1–1 mm	0.1–10 μm	0.2–10 mm	1 mm–1 m	0.5 mm–10 mm	0.1 cm width 10 cm–10 m long
Variation in size	Low-moderate	Low	Moderate	Low	Moderate	Large	Moderate-large	Moderate
Pore shape	Chambered, cellular e.g.	Negative of grains	Enlarged and irregular versions of I, II	Prisms and thin sheets	Positive of grains	Irregular	Parallel or conjugate sets of thin sheets	Parallel-sided along short columns normal to the seam: seam usually parallel to bed
Fabric selectivity	Yes	Yes	Yes	Variable	Yes	No	No	Variable
Time of origin	Deposition	Deposition	Early diagenesis	Early/late diagenesis	Early/late diagenesis	Early/late diagenesis	Post-lithification and burial	Post-lithification and burial
Relationship with permeability	Poor	Moderate	Moderate	Good	Poor	Poor-moderate	Good	Moderate-good
Relative recovery efficiency (for 0–20% porosity)	Very low 0–5%	Coarse 45–55% fine 20%	45–60%	50–60%	10–50% depending on connections between pores	15–30%	15%	15%
Anisotropy of pore system	Isotropic	Variable: traction current structures → anisotropic; mixed, bioturbated sediments → isotropic	Isotropic to anisotropic (as II)	Isotropic	Isotropic on fine scale but strongly anisotropic at the scale of laminae or beds	Variable but large caverns normally anisotropic	Strongly anisotropic	Strongly anisotropic
Abundance in the major carbonate reservoirs	Very rare	Common	Common	Rare/common	Rare/common	Common	Common	Very rare

early total cementation, and (iii) avoid mechanical and chemical compaction.

As we noted earlier in the diagenesis section, cementation of carbonates is most rapid in sediments exposed to abundant fresh water (particularly the phreatic zone). Consequently, the preservation of primary intergranular and intragranular porosity is favoured, firstly in shallow-water carbonates that accumulate in arid regions, and secondly in deep-water carbonates that are well removed from a source of fresh water or water squeezed from clays (for example many chalks). Primary porosity may be lost if the sediments are deeply buried.

Secondary porosity can be created when (i) unstable minerals dissolve to leave moulds; (ii) a tensional phase causes the opening of fractures or suture seams, or (iii) there are mineralogical changes in the rock in a near-closed system so that volume changes to new denser minerals create voids (mainly dolomitization).

There are several characteristics of pore spaces and pore systems, e.g. their size, shape, time of origin, relation with permeability and so on, which help us to understand the evolution of porosity in the rock. These characteristics are used in the classification of carbonate porosity drawn up in Table 18.1 and are explained as follows.

The term 'fabric selectivity' is used for a dependent relation between porosity and fabric elements (which can have depositional and diagenetic constituents). For example, interparticle porosity is a negative of the fabric element of grains and is thus fabric-selective, whereas large caves developed along joints during a period of karst erosion bear no relation to fabric elements and are not fabric-selective. Most primary, and a large proportion of secondary, porosity is fabric-selective. Pore systems are made up of larger voids (pores) which are connected by smaller spaces or restrictions (throats). The recovery efficiency of an oil reservoir is high when the pore/throat ratio is small. Another factor which influences the recovery efficiency is the 'coordination number'—i.e. the number of throats that connect with each pore; the higher the number, the better the recovery efficiency. Recovery efficiency is further influenced by the type and degree of heterogeneity of the pore system. Porosity may show a relationship with permeability or it may not. It is not uncommon for limestones to have good porosity but low permeability; for example, voids which are within grains may not be connected to one another. Pore systems can show a tendency for fluids to flow more easily in one direction than another. Where fluids flow equally well in all directions, the permeability is isotropic, but if there is a preferred flow direction, e.g. parallel to bedding as would occur along the fenestral pores in an algal laminite, then permeability is said to be anisotropic.

18.1.2 Pore types in carbonates (Table 18.1)

(i) *Intraparticle porosity.* This is porosity *within* grains, e.g. chambers of foraminiferans, zooecia or bryozoans. This may be primary, or may occur on early diagenesis by (i) the process known as maceration where organic material rots from within the skeletal structure, or (ii) removal (probably by dissolution) of the interior

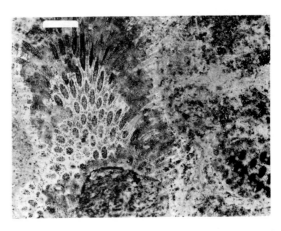

Figure 18.1 Intra-particle porosity within the chambers of colonial corals. Scale 10 mm. Pleistocene, Miami, USA

of weakly calcified grain interiors, leaving only an outer rind or cortex (e.g. *Halimeda*). This intraparticle porosity is most particularly prevalent in reef frameworks where massive and branched chambered colonial organisms abound (Figure 18.1). Permeability may be low, as pores are not necessary interconnected between grains.

(ii) *Interparticle porosity.* This is the porosity *between* grains, which is normally preserved primary porosity (Figures 5.6, 18.2). The fact that it is uncemented may be relate to a lack of water flowing through the rock, brought about by a dry climate or a protective seal of clay or evaporites, or very rapid burial, or early oil emplacement. This porosity varies with (i) sorting (better sorting gives higher porosity); grain packing— for example, spheres may have cubic packing (centre of one directly over the centre of another) giving a porosity value of about 47%, or rhombic packing (i.e. centre of one sphere directly over the junction between two beneath) where porosity is about 26%; and (iii) grain shape—with angular or irregular grain shapes, for example branched or spined skeletons, the packing may be exceedingly loose and porosity high. Even very fine carbonate grains may have a very high

initial interparticle porosity, since, unlike clay minerals, they do not all have platy shapes which with only slight mechanical compaction pack tightly together. Fine-grained carbonates such as chalks may retain their high initial porosities to burial depths of over 1 km.

Shelter porosity (Figure 7.10) is a variety of interparticle porosity where a broad platy grain has provided an umbrella for the area beneath, to protect it from filling with finer interstitial detritus as it settles. Fenestral or birdseye porosity (Figure 18.3) is also a variety of interparticle porosity where in special environments, such as supratidal levées, periodic drying-out of the sediment has produced shrinkage cracks parallel to laminations. These same environments may trap escaping gas bubbles produced by the decay of trapped vegetation.

Interparticle pore shapes are, in effect, the

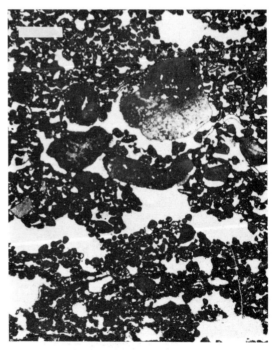

Figure 18.3 Thin section of fenestral (birdseye) porosity (white) in an oncoidal, peloidal grainstone. Ppl. Scale 2 mm. Jurassic, Paris Basin, France

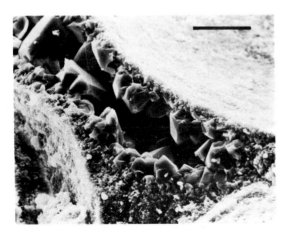

Figure 18.2 Partially lithified ooidal grainstone with some preserved primary intergranular porosity. SEM. Scale 40 μm. Jurassic, Basingstoke, England

negatives of grains (Table 18.1). Permeability may be high but depends on the throat sizes. If grains were deposited from a flowing medium, then they may be aligned, and this would imposed a degree of anisotropy to the flow of fluids through the pores. Bioturbation would mix the sediment and give a more isotropic character to the pore system.

(iii) *Enhanced primary porosity*. This is, as the name suggests, the result of the enlarging of primary (intra- and interparticle) pore spaces by dissolution. It is fabric-selective, though secondary, usually forming either during early diagenesis in the meteoric zone, or in CO_2-enriched waters.

(iv) *Intercrystalline porosity*. This is the porosity between crystals of relatively similar size that have grown in place (normally) by recrystallization or dolomitization (e.g. sucrosic) (Figure 18.4). The permeability is strongly controlled by the size of the crystals and the abundance of compromise boundaries. The smaller the crystals, the lower the permeability, because of excessive surface tension effects. The more compromise boundaries, then the smaller the throats and the lower the permeability.

(v) *Mouldic porosity*. Moulds are created by the selective removal of grains by dissolution (Figures 18.5, 18.6). This porosity is secondary, yet commonly fabric selective. A distinctive difference in solubilities between grains and framework is needed. This is usually mineralogical, e.g. aragonite *v*. calcite, calcite *v*. dolomite, or gypsum *v*. calcite. Moulds created in a monomineralic rock are related to differences in crystallinity, crystal size, organic inclusions, pri-

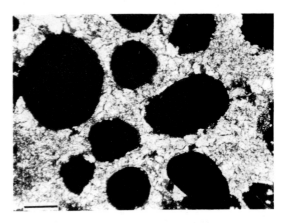

Figure 18.5 Mouldic porosity (black) generated by the dissolution of ooids in a cemented grainstone. Thin section, Xn. Scale 0.1 mm. Pleistocene, Miami, USA

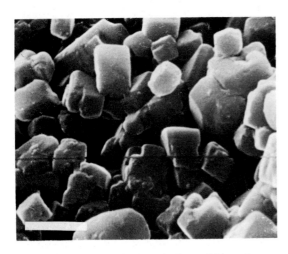

Figure 18.4 Intercrystalline porosity in a calcite mudstone. SEM. Scale 1 μm. Jurassic, Oxfordshire, England

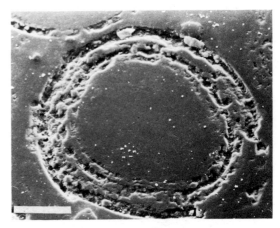

Figure 18.6 Partial dissolution of the cortices of ooids. Ooid nucleus and intergranular cement are unaffected. Polished SEM. Scale 100 μm. Jurassic, Basingstoke, England

mary porosity, etc. Some moulds may form by dissolution on burial as adjacent water-bearing clays lose their interlayer water, which is relatively fresh, or waters associated with fronts of advancing hydrocarbons are flushed through. Permeability may be low if the moulds have poor interconnection; recovery efficiency is also related to the extent of connections between moulds.

(vi) *Vuggy porosity*. Vugs are irregular secondary (dissolution) holes that cut across grains and/or cement boundaries (Figure 18.7). They are large enough to be seen with the naked eye. Vugs form by dissolution and may start from a mould, or a large intergranular (e.g. shelter) cavity. Large vugs are termed caves, or cavernous porosity, and these may be linked by channels (Figure 14.41). This type of porosity commonly relates to karst weathering in wet climates and the occurrence of a freshwater lens. Unlike moulds that form in a heterogeneous rock of mixed mineralogies, vugs usually form in homogeneous limestones (or dolomites). The size and number of vugs is crucial in determining the total porosity and permeability.

(vii) *Fracture/breccia porosity*. Fracture porosity occurs in brittle, normally homogeneous, carbonates, such as chalks or dolomites. For fracturing to create and retain a porosity it usually has to be post-burial, and may be associated with folding, faulting, salt doming, salt solution or fluid overpressuring. Fractures follow trends related to local tectonics, and where all fractures are parallel, then recovery efficiency will be low and permeability strongly anisotropic. Normally, fractures occur in interconnected conjugate sets which can allow high permeability even though porosity is commonly low. Fracturing may help greatly to create permeability pathways in a reservoir of high absolute porosity but low interconnected porosity (e.g. mouldic). Further, fracturing can allow the passage of post-burial fluids and create secondary (vuggy) porosity, perhaps via vein dolomitization.

Fractures are characterized by little relative displacement of adjacent blocks, but this type of porosity grades into *breccia porosity* where blocks are jumbled and chaotic. Breccia porosity is often associated with collapse of overlying rock due to dissolution (e.g. of limestone during karst weathering, or of evaporites during freshwater leaching), slumping, or tectonic deformation. Fracture and breccia porosities are not fabric-selective.

(viii) *Stylolitic porosity*. Porosity developed along pressure dissolution seams (stylolites) is secondary, post-burial, and may serve as a significant pathway for migration of fluids (connate waters or hydrocarbons). Secondary dissolution fabrics may develop consequent on the formation of these pathways, but normally the calcium carbonate generated by the pressure dissolution processes precipitates locally in areas of reduced stress and completes cementation. Permeability is anisotropic parallel to bedding.

18.1.3 Porosity development during burial

Figure 18.8, from Longman (1982), gives an indication of the nature and timing of porosity-forming, and porosity-destroying, processes in limestones.

Figure 18.7 Vuggy porosity in coral wackestone. Scale 20 mm. Jurassic, Oxfordshire, England

POROSITY FORMING PROCESSES

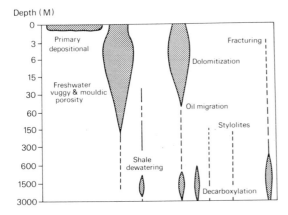

POROSITY DESTRUCTIVE PROCESSES

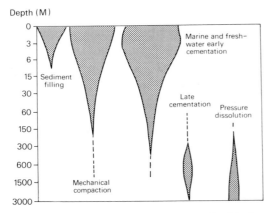

Figure 18.8 Schematic illustration of the relationship between depth and the major porosity-forming and porosity-destroying processes. After Longman (1982)

The tendency on burial of limestones is for precipitation of $CaCO_3$ rather than its dissolution. Stagnant connate waters trapped between pores at deposition are unlikely to create any significant secondary voids during burial, since the fluids would soon equilibrate with the enclosing substrates. The increase in temperature on burial will tend to bring about precipitation of

$CaCO_3$ rather than its dissolution. Also, random collision of Ca^{2+} and CO_3^{2-} with substrates favours precipitation, and these ions are hard to remove once incorporated in a crystal face. So we note that secondary mouldic porosity is created only by the introduction and percolation of undersaturated fluids which may be meteoric in origin and affect those carbonates close to an unconformity, or may be derived from neighbouring shale sequences by wholesale migration of interstitial waters.

Where undersaturated fluids do migrate into a body of carbonate rocks, they would soon become saturated unless the flow rate was relatively high. Porosity would only be created and preserved at this stage if the dissolution were selective, leaving behind stable grains to support the rock fabric. Consequently we find most secondary mouldic porosity occurs in carbonate rocks that previously had two minerals present, with one phase less stable than the other.

On burial, the increase in pressure, though it may bring about dissolution of grain contacts, does not create porosity. It normally does the reverse; by suturing grain margins the intra- and intergranular voids are contracted, and the dissolved $CaCO_3$ may precipitate locally in an area (void) of reduced stress and thus reduce porosity further. Porosity along stylolites results from a relaxation of the stress and the development of sheet cracks during a tensional phase. Alternatively, solutions may migrate better along stylolites than across them, and these solutions may promote new mineral growth or the dissolution of unstable minerals already present. During thermal maturation on burial, clays may alter (e.g. smectite to illite), giving an abundance of water and new ions, e.g. Si, Ca, Fe, Mg. This could be the source of iron which is commonly found incorporated into late, post-compaction, cements as ferroan calcite. The process of decarboxylation of organic matter within the sediments is a further method of generating fluids at depth which may be capable of dissolving carbonate. The fluids which precede the emplacement of oil into a reservoir may also be undersaturated and create a secondary porosity within the carbonate, but once the hydrocarbons are introduced no further dissolution or precipitation of carbonate will occur.

18.1.4 Porosity developed during dolomitization

Porosity can be created during the dolomitization of carbonates. The rocks must originally be fairly porous and permeable to allow the flushing of dolomitizing fluids in the first place. If the rocks are not very porous, then the dolomitization will be slow and the dolomite will fit the available space and duplicate the precursor fabric, generating no extra pore space. However, when dolomitization rates are high, as in open systems, fabric destruction occurs and large-scale dissolution of the precursor $CaCO_3$ frees the dolomite to grow into the most energetically suitable forms. Rather than mimicking the original grain or crystal size, dolomites grow irrespective of precursor fabric, forming rhombs of a sucrosic texture (Figure 18.9). In these dolomites the crystals grow with perfect shape (idiomorphic) and may cease to grow when adjacent dolomite rhombs come into contact. This is contact inhibition. As the calcite crystals that were replaced were mainly anhedral, the new idiomorphic crystals have a high intercrystalline porosity.

We note that permeability is higher in dolomites of the same porosity level as limestone; this is due to the throat geometry and the more connected system of intercrystalline pores in dolomites. Dolomitization commonly homogenizes porosity and may make permeability isotropic.

Replacement dolomite attacks unstable grains first. Consequently, it may be grains of aragonitic composition, or high surface area, or sediments of high organic content, or high porosity and permeability or with clays that have a catalytic effect, that are selectively dolomitized. If the dolomitization process does not go to completion, a rock of two or more mineral phases will result. Later percolating fluids may then selectively leach one mineral phase, creating a mouldic porosity. This commonly results from the dissolution of calcite relicts in a partially dolomitized rock (Figure 18.10).

Dolomite may show several generations of formation. The fine rhomb variety is often associated with near-surface freshwater or hypersaline settings, and a late coarse sparry dolomite is usually associated with fractures, stylolites, karst breccias, hydrothermal solutions and brines related to oil emplacement.

Figure 18.9 Fine idiomorphic rhombs of dolomite replacing micrite and developing a sucrosic texture. Thin section. Ppl. Scale 0.5 mm. Carboniferous, Isle of Man

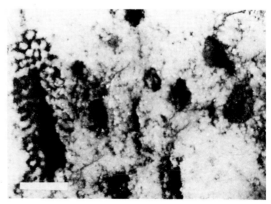

Figure 18.10 Leached coral skeletons in a dolomitized reef limestone. Scale 10 mm. Devonian, Alberta, Canada

Table 18.2 Characteristics of the common types of hydrocarbon reservoirs in carbonate rocks.

Reservoir types	I Primary intergranular porosity in platform edge grainstones (commonly oolitic)	II Isolated and platform margin reefs	III Platform slope deposits	IV Shoaling upwards cycles	V Basinal limestones	VI Diagenetic traps
% of total carbonate reservoirs	50%	20%	10%	5–10%	2%	5–10%
Porosity development	Preserved primary intergranular and intragranular porosity in well washed sorted and rounded grainstones. Enhanced primary porosity is common.	—Multi chambered colonial organisms create high intra-granular porosity. —Platy branched skeletons create shelter cavities. —Structurally high position favours exposure, karst development and secondary porosity. —Dolomitization is common (by reflux; redistribution of Mg from high Mg calcite skeletons and marine cements; mixing zone). —Massive brittle structures are prone to fracturing.	Platform derived rudites, grainstones and packstones have high inter- and intra-granular porosity at deposition. Primary porosity may escape freshwater cementation in slope setting.	—Primary intergranular porosity (birdseye vugs) in algal laminites. —Secondary intercrystalline porosity in fine grained dolomite. —Mouldic porosity after leaching of soluble evaporite minerals. —Solution breccias.	High intergranular porosity is retained if calcitic pelagic limestone do not suffer very deep burial. Primary porosity can be preserved if limestones are sealed off from neighbouring rocks. They become overpressured and interstitial water cushions compaction. —Fracturing is common in these homogeneous deposits. —Leaching of any platform derived unstable minerals in allochthonous basinal limestones may create mouldic porosity.	—Marine cementation e.g. beachrocks and hardgrounds can create permeability barriers which preserve some primary intergranular porosity in neighbouring horizons. (see text) —Leaching within the freshwater lens beneath unconformities gives mouldic and vuggy porosity. —Pervasive dolomitisation may create intercrystalline porosity.
Reservoir setting and geometry	Ooid and skeletal sand shoals develop in belts parallel and close to the break in slope on tropical platform margins. Belts may be 10–100 km long, 1–3 km wide and 5–10 m thick. Elongate bars and lobes of sands spread on to platform interior muds.	—Reefs normally are located on structural high positions so reef-building organisms escape suffocation from loose sediment. —Initial reef shape duplicates the geometry of rocky foundations, with time reef moulds to prevailing physical conditions and develops linear, crescentic, horseshoe, annular or pinnacle	Prograding wedges of platform derived debris accumulate on slope as elongate aprons parallel to the platform edge.	The thin elongate prism of tidal flat sediments parallels the coast.	Widespread sheet-like bodies.	—Diagenetic traps are prevalent in structurally high deposits which are prone to exposure and unconformity development. —Irregular to sheet-like geometry beneath unconformity.

	shapes. The three dimensional form is strongly controlled by changes in relative sea level.					
Traps	—Structural (anticlinal or fault bounded) —Stratigraphic, reservoir passing laterally into cemented sands, impervious offshore silts, lagoonal muds or tidal flat evaporites.	Stratigraphic traps. Natural mound shape may be capped by shales or evaporites. Steep reef margins create steep physical gradients which create rapid lateral facies changes.	Stratigraphic traps with an up-dip seal against cemented platform sediments	Stratigraphic traps: Sakha cycles interfinger with lagoonal muds and evaporites.	Structural traps common and may be associated with faulting, salt domes or folds.	Traps may be structural or stratigraphic. Seals are normally (or better) cemented horizons or less dolomitized facies.
Favourable aspects	—Ooids predominate in regions of relatively high salinity and arid climate. Lack of freshwater on exposure inhibits total cementation. —Platform rim is structurally high yet juxtaposed basinal potential source rocks. —Shoaling upwards sequences can develop evaporitic caps.	—Structurally high yet close to basinal potential source rocks. —High position favours leaching, dolomitization and fracturing.	Close proximity to source rocks and high preserved primary porosity are key factors in the hydrocarbon potential of these deposits.	—These deposits contain a variety of minerals—e.g. calcite, aragonite, dolomite, gypsum, anhydrite, halite which may be subjected to a range of salinities from hypersaline through to fresh. These factors promote secondary porosity. —In one depositional sequence the supratidal position is the end-of-the-line for up-dip petroleum migration.	Intimate association with source rocks.	Chemical instability of carbonates makes them especially prone to diagenetic alteration which can create a secondary porosity. Shallow water facies affected.
Examples	—Jurassic Arab C and D of Middle East —Eocene Nummulitic grainstone of offshore Tunisia —Jurassic Smackover Fm. of USA —Jurassic Great Oolite of S. England.	—Silurian pinnacle reefs. Illinois and Michigan, USA —Devonian reefs of Alberta, Canada —Permian reefs of Texas, USA —Jurassic reefs of N. Africa and Middle East —Cretaceous reefs of Mexico —Miocene reefs of Indonesia and Philippines.	—Poza Rica, Cretaceous, Mexico —Fateh Field, Cretaceous Middle East —Oligocene-Miocene Main Lst, Kirkuk, Iraq. —Scaglia Calcaire central Italy. —Scurry Reef, Texas, USA	—Up. Palaeozoic of Williston Basin, Dakota, USA —Permian; San Andreas Fm, Texas USA —Jurassic, Morocco —Liburne, Texas, USA —Zechstein, North Sea, Europe	—Danian Chalk Ekofisk, N. Sea —Wasia fm. Oman —Austin Chalk of Gulf Coast, USA —Murban, Trucial Coast, Middle East	—Edwards Fm. Texas, USA —Golden Lane, Mexico —Walker Creek Smackover Fm, Louisiana, USA —Buttasa, Arab Emirates —Bathonian, Paris Basin, France.

In summary, dolomites that replace limestones create pores by three processes: (i) dolomite is denser than calcite and so on a molecule for molecule replacement, voids will be created (an increase of $12\frac{1}{2}\%$ porosity); (ii) idiomorphic crystals develop more easily in dolomites than in calcites and this results in crystal contact inhibition, which creates a significant intercrystalline porosity; (iii) calcite relicts within a partially dolomitized limestone may later be leached to create mouldic porosity.

18.1.5 Volume changes in replacements
When calcite alters to dolomite by the reaction

$$2CaCO_3 + Mg^{2+} \rightarrow CaMg(CO_3)_2 + Ca^{2+}$$

there is a $12\frac{1}{2}\%$ decrease in mineral volume and consequently an increase in pore space. Where mineral replacements involve an increase in mineral volume, then precipitation along pores occurs, and some original grains are cut off from the solutions and can remain as relics. Such a situation occurs during the replacement of calcite by anhydrite (25% increase in mineral volume). Aragonite-to-calcite transformation involves an 8% volume increase, and anhydrite-to-gypsum, a 63% volume increase (which is why beds are so often distorted during this alteration) —Figures 14.16, 17.21.

18.2 Distribution of hydrocarbon-producing carbonate reservoir rocks
Sixty-eight percent of hydrocarbon-producing carbonate reservoirs are Mesozoic in age (USA, Central and South America, Europe, Middle East), 27% are Cainozoic (Middle East, Far East, North Africa) and 5% are Palaeozoic (North America).

In order for hydrocarbons to be trapped we need the appropriate association of nearby mature source rocks, porous and permeable reservoir rocks, an impermeable caprock, and a suitable structure on the reservoir to form a closure.

We note that in many oilfields with carbonate reservoir rocks there is a good correlation between high depositional porosity and final reservoir quality, but this is not always the case. For example, a zone that is initially more porous may be the first to cement; a neighbouring, originally less porous, zone then becomes a favoured site for dolomitization, for example, which can create secondary porosity and permeability. Also, fracture porosity may be created best in well-cemented, brittle rocks.

There are six basic carbonate reservoir types, which are summarized in Table 18.2. Types I to V are fundamentally related to the depositional environment and are facies-controlled.

Good examples of the relationship between the porosity/permeability (poro/perm) characteristics of the reservoir and the depositional and diagenetic facies are shown in the Middle and Upper Devonian reefs of Alberta, Canada. Poro/perm values relate closely to fossil and sediment zonation on these reefs (Figure 18.11) and the evolution of porosity follows a common diagenetic sequence (Figure 18.12).

However in type VI, diagenetic traps, the reservoir porosity is localized essentially by post-depositional processes and the reservoir may thus cut across depositional facies boundaries. Localization of cements or dolomitization principally by near-surface processes are the important mechanisms of porosity development or retention in diagenetic traps.

18.2.1 Diagenetic traps
Early cements in the marine environment creating hardgrounds and beachrocks are very important in porosity evolution. For, although these cements lower values of inter- and intra-particle porosity, they do not normally totally occlude primary pore spaces. However, they alter permeability sufficiently to restrict the circlation of later fluids. These fluids may be deficient in $CaCO_3$ and thus cause dissolution, or, alternatively, have an excess of $CaCO_3$ in solution and thus cause cementation. Moore *et al.* (1972) show an example of a Cretaceous beach sequence

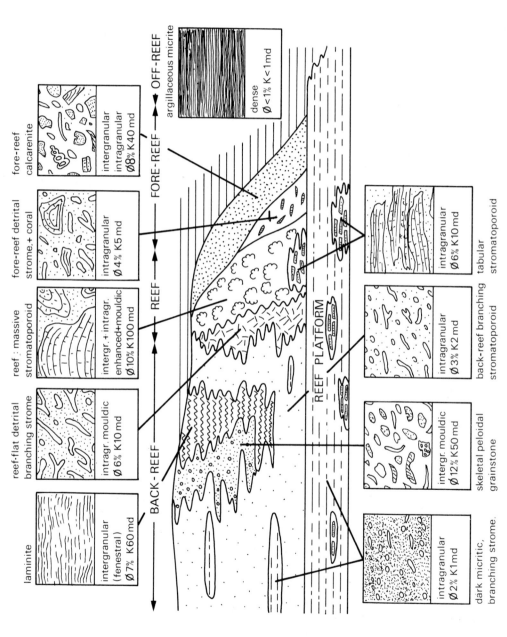

Figure 18.11 Schematic cross-section of a Devonian reef of Alberta, Canada, indicating the depositional environments, and the petrographic and poro/perm characteristics of representative rock types. After Fischbuch (1968) and Leavitt (1968)

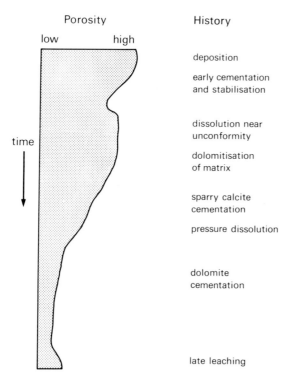

Figure 18.12 Porosity evolution in a Devonian reef carbonate of Alberta, Canada

ation. Any buried isolated horizons retaining primary porosity may later be tapped by fracturing, providing migration pathways for hydrocarbons.

Diagenesis in the freshwater phreatic zone can also bring about the retention of a lens-like porous zone in a body of limestone. As discussed in section 9.10 on freshwater diagenesis, stabilization of carbonates is much more rapid in the freshwater phreatic zone (*c.* 5000 years) than in the marine phreatic zone (*c.* 3 Ma) beneath, or the freshwater vadose zone (*c.* 200 000 years) above. Consequently, with the appropriate periodicity of sea-level movements, it is possible to form a sandwich of stabilized, grain-contact-cemented carbonates between unaltered marine lime-sands. When this packet suffers the effects of chemical compaction on burial, the two outer zones of the sandwich may become fully cemented, while the middle zone retains some primary porosity.

Dolomitization may also be localized by a freshwater lens, with replacement rhombs and dolomite cements developing at the mixing zone with salt water.

Freshwater leaching is most prevalent at unconformities which are located at the structurally high locations.

in which beachrock layers have restricted the percolation of fluids, which have caused solution of unstable grains below giving a mouldic porosity. On the other hand, Purser (1978) described Jurassic shallow-water carbonates of the Burgundy district of France, where beachrock layers restricted the percolation of fluids, which brought about the cementation of underlying horizons while the beachrocks themselves retained a portion of their primary porosity and so now act as reservoirs. The early cement fringes may also support grains during burial retarding chemical compaction (Figure 17.14). Consequently, zones which have no early cements may be better conduits for later cementing fluids, and may also be the zones that suffer compaction on burial. This reduces pore size, and supplies, by pressure dissolution, $CaCO_3$ for local cement-

Selected reading

Andrichuk, J.M. (1958) Stratigraphy and facies analysis of Upper Devonian reefs in Leduc, Settler, and Redwater areas, Alberta. *AAPG Bull.* **42** (1), 1–93.
Bebout, D.G. (1979) Secondary carbonate porosity. In *Geology of Carbonate Porosity*, AAPG Education Short Course Notes **11**, B1–B69.
Choquette, P.W. and Pray, L.C. (1970) Geologic nomenclature and classification of porosity in sedimentary carbonates. *Am. Assoc. Petrol. Geol. Bull.* **54**, 207–250.
Deffeyes, K.S., Lucia, F.J. and Weyl, P.K. (1965) Dolomitization of Recent and Plio-Pleistocene sediments by marine evaporite waters on Bonaire, Netherlands Antilles. In Pray, L.C. and Murray, R.C. (eds.), *Dolomitization and Limestone Diagenesis*, SEPM Sp. Pub. **13**, 71–88.
Fischbuch, N.R. (1968) Stratigraphy, Devonian Swan Hills Reef Complexes of Central Alberta. *Bull. Can. Petrol. Geol.* **16**, 444–550.
Harbaugh, J.W. (1967) Carbonate oil reservoir rocks. In

Chilingar, G.V., Bissell, H.J. and Fairbridge, R.W. (eds.), *Carbonate Rocks: Origin, Occurrence and Classification*, Elsevier, Amsterdam, 349–398.

Harris, P.M. (ed.) (1983) *Carbonate Buildups: a Core Workshop*. SEPM Core Workshop. **4**.

Harris, P.M. (ed.) (1984) *Carbonate Sands: a Core Workshop*. SEPM Core Workshop. **5**.

Klovan, J.E. (1964) Facies analysis of the Redwater Reef Complex, Alberta, Canada. *Bull. Can. Petrol. Geol.* **12**, 1–100.

Leavitt, E.M. (1968) Petrology and palaeontology, Carson Creek North Reef Complex, Alberta. *Bull. Can. Petrol. Geol.* **16**, 298–413.

Longman, M.W. (1982) Carbonate diagenesis as a control on stratigraphic traps. *AAPG Education Course Notes* **21**, 1–159.

McGillivray, J.G. and Mountjoy, E.W. (1975) Facies and related reservoir characteristics, Golden Spike Reef Complex, Alberta. *Bull. Can. Petrol. Geol.* **23**, 753–809.

Moore, C.H. (1979) Porosity in carbonate rock sequences. In *Geology of Carbonate Porosity*, AAPG Continuing Education Course Notes **11**, A1–A124.

Moore, C.H. (1985) Upper Jurassic subsurface cements: a case history. In Schneidermann, N. and Harris, P.M. (eds.), *Carbonate Cements*, SEPM Sp. Pub. **36**, 291–308.

Moore, C.H. and Druckman, Y. (1981) Burial diagenesis and porosity evolution, Upper Jurassic, Smackover, Arkansas and Louisiana. *Am. Assoc. Petrol. Geol. Bull.* **65**, 597–6218.

Moore, C.H. Smitherman, J.M. and Allen, S.H. (1972) Pore Cretaceous carbonate beach sequence. In *Stratigraphy and Sedimentology: Proc.*, Sec. 6, Int. Geol. Cong. **24**, 124–136.

Murray, R.C. (1960) Origin of porosity in carbonate rocks. *J. Sed. Petrol.* **39**, 59–84.

Purser, B.H. (1978) Early diagenesis and the preservation of porosity in Jurassic limestone. *J. Petrol. Geol.* **1**, 83–94.

Roehl, P.O. and Choquette, P.W. (eds.) (1986) *Carbonate Petroleum Reservoirs*. Springer-Verlag, Berlin.

Scholle, P.A. (1977) *Deposition, Diagenesis and Hydrocarbon Potential of 'Deeper-Water' Limestones*, AAPG Education Course Notes, Series 7, 1–25.

Scholle, P.A. (1977) Chalk diagenesis and its relation to petroleum exploration: Oil from chalks—a modern miracle? *Am. Ass. Petrol. Geol. Bull.* **61**, 982–1009.

Scholle, P.A. (1979) Porosity prediction in shallow versus deep water limestones—primary porosity preservation under burial conditions. In *Geology of Carbonate Porosity*, AAPG Education Short Course Notes **11**, D1–D12.

Scholle, P.A. and Halley, R.B. (1985) Burial diagenesis: out of sight out of mind. In Schneidermann, N. and Harris, P.M. (eds.), *Carbonate Cements*, SEPM Sp. Pub. **36**, 309–334.

Walls, R.A. (1983) Golden Spike Reef Complex, Alberta. In Scholle, P.A., Bebout, D.G. and Moore, C.H. (eds.) *Carbonate Depositional Environments*, Am. Ass. Petrol. Geol. Mem. **33**, 445–453.

Walls, R.A. and Burrowes, G. (1985) The role of cementation in the diagenetic history of Devonian reefs, western Canada. In Schneidermann, N. and Harris, P.M. (eds.), *Carbonate Cements*, SEPM Sp. Pub. **36**, 185–220.

Wardlaw, N.C. (1979) Pore systems in carbonate rocks and their influence on hydrocarbon recovery efficiency. In *Geology of Carbonate Porosity*, AAPG Education Short Course Notes **11**, E1–E24.

Wardlaw, N.C. (1979) The influence of pore structure in rocks on the entrapment of oil. *Can. Petrol. Geol. Soc. Memoir* **6**, 193–240.

Wardlaw, N.C. and Cassan, J.P. (1978) Estimation of recovery efficiency by visual observation of pore systems in reservoir rocks. *Bull. Can. Soc. Petrol. Geol.* **26**, 572–585.

19 Carbonates and ore deposits

Carbonates are host rocks to a large number of economic minerals. Of major importance are ore deposits of galena (PbS) and sphalerite (ZnS) which supply a large percentage of the world's total lead and zinc production. Lead and zinc minerals in shallow-water carbonates are often in ore bodies grouped in a way that has a relationship to palaeogeography, or to post-depositional structure. Several such fields occur in the midwest of the USA, and their location has given the name 'Mississippi Valley Type' to these ore deposits.

19.1 Mississippi Valley Type ore deposits

In some cases the lead and zinc have deposited with the sediments in bedded form, particularly in back-reef or lagoonal limestones. Other ore bodies are stratabound, and have accumulated in pore spaces in unbedded limestone such as reefs, fore-reef talus, mudbanks and breccias. As well as galena and sphalerite, barite ($BaCO_3$) and fluorite (CaF_2) may be present in economic quantities. Minor minerals include bornite (Cu_5FeS_4), pyrite (FeS_2) marcasite (FeS_2), chalcopyrite ($CuFeS_2$), pyrrhotite ($Fe_{1-x}S$), siderite

($FeCO_3$) and ankerite $Ca(MgFe^{+2}Mn)(CO_3)_2$. Silver and mercury are the most important trace metals, but germanium, cadmium, cobalt and nickel are also sometimes present in trace quantities. Some ore bodies show a differentiation of minerals according to facies, with copper ores dominant in lagoonal sediments and lead and zinc ores dominant in reef and fore-reef rocks.

Mississippi Valley Type ore deposits have the following characteristics:

(i) They contain simple mineral assemblages: galena, sphalerite, barite, fluorite
(ii) Their distribution is facies-controlled, with major occurrences being towards the edges of large deep sedimentary basins, especially at shale–carbonate interfaces.
(iii) They are found in coarse-grained, porous and permeable carbonates which are commonly massive, such as reefs, mud mounds, fore-reef talus, collapse breccias
(iv) They occur in passive structural regions
(v) The host rock is generally dolomitized
(vi) They are normally located in the vicinity of evaporite deposits and often found associated with hydrocarbons
(vii) The dominant ore mineralization process was precipitation into pore spaces
(viii) They form at shallow depths and low temperatures, and have not suffered any metamorphic events converting low-grade ore into higher-grade ore.

It has been suggested that these ore deposits are formed by reactions between metal-bearing brines and reduced sulphur of quite separate origins. The metal brines may originate from (i) magmatic sources and be fed into groundwater by faults from depth, or fed into the sea by volcanic springs (though the low copper content argues against this); (ii) the metals may have been adsorbed on to (basinal) clays and then released into porewaters during diagenesis and expelled on compaction; or (iii) the lead and zinc may be co-precipitated with aragonite and calcite as carbonates (cerussite $PbCO_3$ and smithsonite

$ZnCO_3$) and then later released during diagenesis into interstitial waters. The origin from clays is favoured, especially where the host carbonates are juxtaposed with basinal shales. The sulphur is most probably derived from the sulphates of the nearby evaporites. This sulphate may be reduced by bacteria or by hydrocarbons (traces of pyrobitumen occur locally in the ore deposits and reservoir rocks of equivalent age are elsewhere found to hold oil). Another possible source of sulphur is from iron sulphide precipitated by organic activity in marine muds. Sulphur isotope values are consistent with a marine origin.

Reefal ore bodies with abundant copper minerals are most common in Precambrian limestones with stromatolitic reefs (e.g. Mufulira, Zambia) or in later limestones associated with volcanic or basement source rocks.

Examples of the Mississippi Valley Type ore deposits include the Viburnum Trend, south-east Missouri, USA (host rock is an Upper Cambrian, stromatolitic reef); the Ballynoe deposit, Silver Mines, County Tipperary, Ireland (host rocks are lower Carboniferous mud mounds); and Pine Point, Northwest Territories, Canada (host rock is dolomitized barrier reef).

19.1.1 Pine Point lead zinc ore deposits

The lead zinc mineralization at Pine Point near the Great Slave Lake, Northwest Territories, Canada, is an excellent example of a Mississippi Valley Type ore deposit where mineralization in Givetian sediments has been closely associated with facies distribution, tectonic setting and diagenesis. A cross-section is shown in Figure 19.1, indicating the principal facies pattern and the location of ores. The facies pattern represents a typical platform margin suite with a barrier reef, built of stromatoporoids and corals, separating deep-water fore-reef dolomites and dark basinal bituminous limestones and shales with *Tentaculites* and pyrite from shallow restricted back-reef tidal flat sediments with stromatolites and evaporites. There are signs of exposure and karst development at the top of the

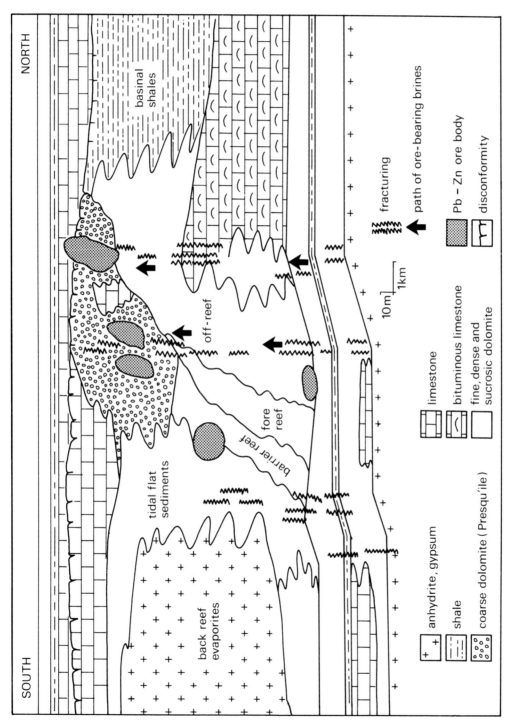

Figure 19.1 Cross-section showing the facies pattern and location of lead zinc ore deposits in Devonian sediments of Pine Point, Canada. After Skall (1975)

Pine Point Group, and the overlying limestones and shales contain stromatolites, gastropods, ostracods, calcispheres and *Charaphyta* indicative of tidal flat, lacustrine and lagoonal settings before normal open marine conditions resumed. The Presqu'ile facies is a diagenetic facies representing the alteration of platform margin reef, fore-reef and back-reef limestones to a coarsely crystalline dolomite. Most ore bodies are found within this facies and are associated with solution collapse of the strata. Many voids are centimetres in size.

The sequence of events leading to mineralization appear to have been as follows.

Gentle arching initiated a carbonate shoal, and with continued subsidence a barrier was established that separated a basin in the north from a platform in the south. Subsidence was greater in the back-reef area than in the zone where the barrier reef was developing, and parts of the back-reef area were sealed off so that they developed pools in which evaporates precipitated. It is thought that Mg-rich brines then percolated basinwards, dolomitizating lower parts of the barrier reef by reflux, to produce fine-grained dense and sucrosic dolomites. The barrier migrated basinward over its own fore-reef (10 km laterally and 200 m vertically from start to finish). Differential rates of subsidence created penecontemporaneous hinge zones parallel to the platform edge that were accompanied by slumping, fracturing and faulting. These lines of weakness were enchanced during later karst development when sea-level fell and provided conduits for later Mg-rich brines. Solution collapse breccias were created in the upper portions of the platform edge facies and it was in these zones that coarse dolomites of the Presqu'ile facies (and main ore bodies) were formed. It appears that the sediments most affected by this Presqu'ile dolomitization were limestones; the underlying sediments were already dolomitized (fine rhombs). The hinge zones were responsible for the distribution of the metal-bearing solutions. The ore bodies occur in these hinge zones

or in trends parallel to them.

There are about 40 known ore bodies in the field, which can be separated into two types: massive forms which relate most closely to collapse breccias, and tabular forms which occupy other facies. The ore contains galena, sphalerite, pyrite, marcasite and some pyrrhotite associated with dolomite and calcite gangue. The indication is that metals were carried as metal chloride complexes from adjacent basinal shales in the north in escaping chloride-rich connate brines. The sulphur originates from evaporites in the south and is reduced by bacteria to H_2S. These two solutions met in the porous Presqu'ile reef and metal sulphides precipitated.

19.2 Deep-water euxinic and sabkha-type ore deposits

Two other distinctive types of mineralization occur in carbonate rocks.

'Remac' (or Salmo) type. The carbonate host rocks appear to have formed in a deep-water, euxinic environment, as they are fine-grained, tight and dark, containing graphite and widely dispersed ribbon cherts. The stagnant setting created hydrogen-sulphide-saturated interstitial waters. Any metal-bearing solutions that entered this setting along deep faults from the basement, for example, would precipitate metal sulphides. Most ores contain pyrite, sphalerite and galena, and though they precipitated simultaneously with the host rock carbonates (syngenetic origin) they are normally found in areas where post-mineralization tectonism was intense and converted subeconomic minerals into ores.

Sabkha type. The carbonate host rocks are of supra- and intertidal origin and associated with evaporites. The deposits may be bordered on one side by lagoonal sediments and on the other by continental red beds. The metals are borne in terrestrial formation waters and carried into the hydrogen-sulphide-rich, strongly reducing, inter-tidal algal limestones. The metals (chalcocite, Cu_2S, bornite, chalcopyrite and pyrite) are deposited in an ordered sequence determined by the metals' relative solubilities. Examples of these sabkha-type ore deposits include Precambrian ores of Nonesuch, USA, and Western Australia.

19.3 Sedimentary ironstones

The main Phanerozoic ironstones are sandy, clayey and oolitic, representing deposition in shallow inland seas which were cut off from open seas by barriers of oolitic or skeletal grainstones. Ironstones do not generally have a strong association with carbonate sediments, though they do locally replace limestones, and some are chiefly siderite ($FeCO_3$) in composition, so only brief mention will be given here of the origin of these deposits. The sediments contain features indicative of deposition in very shallow agitated waters, such as broken and regrown ooids, ripped-up clasts of penecontemporaneously lithified oolites, large-scale cross-bedding, ripple marks and thick-shelled shallow-water fossils which are normally replaced by iron minerals. The main minerals forming oolitic sedimentary ironstones are goethite, haematite, limonite, siderite, chamosite and pyrite. The oxides and hydroxides formed in shallow aerated waters followed by siderite, chamosite and ultimately pyrite with increasing depth. The ironstones are chemical deposits in an environment in which clastic input was diminished because the hinterland had been reduced to a peneplain on which there was

intense chemical weathering during a hot humid climate. Rivers draining the vegetated land area carried iron minerals in colloidal suspension which coagulated on reaching salt water, where chamositic ooids developed from a gel. These estuarine sediments underwent physical agitation, creating ooid grains. The common 'spastolith' texture of chamositic ooids points to an original iron mineral precipitate on the sea bed, but sideritic and chamositic mollusc shells points to an early diagenetic replacement of calcium carbonate.

Selected reading

Callahan, W.H. (1967) Some spatial and temporal aspects of the localisation of Mississippi Valley—Appalachian type ore deposits. *Econ. Geol. Monogr.* **3**, 14–19.

Jackson, S.A. and Beales, F.W. (1967) An aspect of sedimentary basin evolution. The concentration of Mississippian Valley-type ores during late stages of diagenesis. *Bull. Can. Petrol. Geol.* **15**, 383–433.

Kesler, S.E. and Ascurrunz, R. (1973) Pb-Zn Mineralisation in carbonate rocks, Central Guatamala. *Econ. Geol.* **68**, 1263–1274.

Kimberley, M.M. (1979) Origin of oolitic iron minerals. *J. Sed. Petrol.* **49**, 110–132.

Mendelsohn, F. (1976) Mineral deposits associated with stromatolites. In Walter, M.R. (ed.), *Stromatolites*, Developments in Sedimentology **20**, Elsevier, Amsterdam, 645–662.

Sangster, D. (1976) Carbonate-hosted lead zinc deposits. In Wolff, K.H. (ed.), *Handbook of Strata-Bound and Stratiform ore Deposits*. Elsevier, Amsterdam, 447–456.

Skall, H. (1975) The paleoenvironment of the Pine Point Lead Zinc District. *Econ. Geol.* **70**(1), 22–47.

20 Quarried limestone

Limestones are quarried as a source of industrial and agricultural lime, also for aggregate and building stone. It depends upon the specific requirement as to which particular limestone type is most appropriate. When pure $CaCO_3$ is required, e.g. for agricultural lime or smelting flux in the reduction of iron ores, then the purer platform facies carbonates such as ooid or

skeletal grainstones and reefs will be most desirable. As a flux, limestone unites with the earthy constituents of the ore, such as silica and clay, to form slag which floats on the molten iron and can be drawn off. For metallurgical purposes, the limestone must be pure and especially free of sulphur (e.g. pyrite). Magnesium-rich limestones and dolomites are a source of material for use in lining the converters and open-hearth furnaces in which iron is converted to steel.

For cement manufacture, it is necessary for a quantity of aluminosilicates (clay minerals) to be present; consequently, terrigenous-rich near-shore facies are commonly exploited. Portland cement is made by heating a suitable mixture (roughly 9:1) of limestone and argillaceous materials sufficiently to cause partial fusion, creating a clinker (of tricalcium silicate (Ca_3SiO_5) with some calcium orthosilicate (Ca_2SiO_4) and aluminium silicates), which is then finely ground. This mixture of silicates possesses the property of combining with water to produce a rock-hard mass. Hard well-lithified limestones are crushed for use as concrete aggregate and as road metal. Thickly bedded and well-jointed limestones are ideal for building and facing stone purposes, since they can be relatively easily cut and polished.

Index

Numbers in **boldface** refer to Figures.